PRAISE FOR *SAFETY NET*

'Knowledge and thoughtful analysis applied to crucial policy questions. Reassuring and inspiring after the federal election.'

—ROSS GARNAUT, professorial fellow in economics at the University of Melbourne and author of *Superpower: Australia's Low-Carbon Opportunity*

'This important and timely book offers readers a deep reflection on the contemporary management of social risk in democratic systems. It is essential reading for anyone concerned with the task of ensuring our social safety net is sustainable and adapted to the modern era. Mulino's work will be critical to the development of social policies that provide dignity and security to all individuals, and protect our social cohesion and common wealth as a nation.'

—EMMA DAWSON, executive director of Per Capita

'Daniel Mulino chronicles in impressive, readable detail the global progress that societies have made in developing shock-absorbing social policies for circumstances where individuals cannot protect themselves in the course of a normal life, and proposes further development in the footsteps of Australia's greatest social and economic reformers.'

—PETER HARRIS, former chairman of the Australian Productivity Commission

'A relevant and comprehensive review of the history and future of the welfare state, and whether Australia's safety net is fit-for-purpose for the risks and challenges ahead. Daniel Mulino is to be commended on exploring ways of enhancing the safety net while recognising the importance of productivity, participation and a strong economy, along with the affordability of the welfare system.'

—PETER DAWKINS, former vice-chancellor of Victoria University and former director of the Melbourne Institute

For Sarah and Carina

SAFETY NET

The Future of Welfare in Australia

DANIEL MULINO

Foreword by Bill Kelty

IN CONJUNCTION WITH BLACK INC.

Published by La Trobe University Press in conjunction with Black Inc.
22–24 Northumberland Street
Collingwood VIC 3066, Australia
enquiries@blackincbooks.com
www.blackincbooks.com
www.latrobeuniversitypress.com.au

9781760643898 (paperback)
9781743822609 (ebook)

A catalogue record for this book is available from the National Library of Australia

Cover design by Akiko Chan
Text design and typesetting by Marilyn de Castro
Tables and figures by Alan Laver

Contents

Foreword

Safety Net is a prodigious work by an enquiring and innovative mind. It may be one of the most interesting products of the Covid-19 lockdown. It will prove to be a thorough source-book for social democrats throughout the world.

The safety net is a concept and a belief that there should be universal minimum economic and social rights for every citizen. The key safety nets are universal education, healthcare, wages and retirement benefits. The great additional safety net for the twenty-first century has been the National Disability Insurance Scheme. That right and responsibility for the environment has added another dimension to the ideal.

Tony Blair trumpeted his New Labour ideals as a 'Third Way', the free-marketeers in the US still call it socialism, and generations past talked about the 'welfare state'.

From within the system, Daniel Mulino objectively and persuasively explores the idea and ideals of how nations develop safety nets. He sets out to explore the relationship between capital and labour and the specific role of universal protections. What emerges is a textbook-like examination of the workings of an economy. In doing so, it canvasses a very wide spectrum of the political economy.

The concern for others is not new. Nomadic tribes shared food, villagers looked after the sick and the elderly, religious doctrines emerged which sanctified the responsibility for care. However, in a brutal attack on communal welfare, there was a growing and then dominating idea that poverty was a natural order, not just for the few but for the overwhelming majority.

Adam Smith railed against the acceptance of this dictum, but the Malthusians won the debate for an exceedingly long time and are influential even today. Poverty was not just the natural order for 90 per cent of the population, but was the automatic adjuster for a society where populations grew geometrically and supply of food arithmetically. To interfere with the process could only be short-sighted ineffectiveness. For the churches, it was the rod of thought that could explain the horrors of death and poverty without causing loss of faith.

It did not sit well with all people. Many in the churches and society were not ready to embrace so cruel a prescription. These were revolutionaries, poets and critics who set up to fight the dismal economists and those who were served by their analysis.

Dickens wrote brilliantly and emotionally to reject the natural order of poverty; the churches split between the charitable and the mercenary; workers sought collective support as syndicalists and unionists, and people agitated by petition and charter for a fairer society; revolts occurred throughout the world.

While it was true that most church leaders hung on to the prescriptions of poverty, and the leading media were quick to endorse the economic elites, the forces for change gathered strength.

The Left split between the revolutionaries and the constructive compromisers. The revolutionaries would forever believe safety nets were band-aids. The moderate and Fabian socialists believed that practical reformation was far more likely to succeed. Marx and Lenin were in one corner, Shaw, Wells and the Webbs in the other. Trade unions and the Labor Party tried to embrace both, but they have chiefly been organisations of democracy and far from revolutionary agents.

In a variety of countries, the safety net emerged as a counter-revolutionary tactic and the result of progressive reformists' work. The formation of the Labor Party in Australia sat between two great reforms by the ruling powers in Europe and astride one of the great concessions for democracy: the right to universal education.

One of the first great powers to legislate comprehensively for universal protections was Otto von Bismarck, the Chancellor of Germany. To counter the insurgents and to win support from the working class, there was a raft of social welfare changes. These changes, legislated between 1883 and 1887, included sickness, accident and old-age insurance. There were laws to protect women at work and prohibit the employment of children. There was a limit placed on the number of hours that could be worked.

The second great reform was the 1908/09 Budgets of Lloyd George as Chancellor of the Exchequer and a young Winston Churchill as president of the Board of Trade. As Liberals, they took a great plunge into welfarism with a budget that gradually introduced unemployment insurance, the age pension and contributory insurance for the invalid and sick.

Introduced throughout this period was one of the changes that underwrote a fairer society: the right to universal education. During this same time, the Australian political system broadly settled for the third way. In an economy that would be 'protected' from cheap overseas goods by tariffs, and from lower-priced labour from Asia by a 'White Australia' policy, we would develop our own comprehensive minimum standard pensions, factory acts, universal education and unemployment benefits, all within the nation's first decade.

As early as 1923, a royal commission on healthcare would recommend a universal national healthcare system.

The early system was so successful that it became a thorn in the side of the revolutionaries. Lenin was moved to write in 1913:

> Capitalism in Australia is still quite young. The country is only beginning to take shape as an independent state. The workers, for the most part, are migrants from England. They left England at the time when Liberal-Labor politics held almost complete sway there, when the mass of workers were Liberals … And if in England the so-called Labor Party is an alliance of the non-socialist trade unions and the extremely opportunistic 'Independent Labor Party', in Australia the Labor Party is purely representative of the non-socialist workers of the trade unions.
>
> The leaders of the Australian Labor Party are trade union officials, an element which is everywhere most moderate and 'capital serving', and in Australia is altogether peaceful and purely liberal.[1]

It is true that the ALP did not turn to Lenin or to Marx, but instead travelled along the path of the pragmatic centre – for the most part, without much direct parliamentary success at the national level. Their success lay in action by unions, state Labor governments and the political power of opposition. The Labor Party has had only one prolonged period of government in peacetime and that is the Hawke/Keating governments of 1983 to 1996.

As if to prove the non-revolutionary nature of a Labor Party, the most apt description of the philosophy of Paul Keating could be taken from Winston Churchill's speech in 1908:

> I should like to see the State embark on various novel and adventuresome experiments ... I am of opinion that the State should increasingly assume the position of the reserve employer of labour. I am very sorry we have not got the railways of this country in our hands ... and we are all agreed ... that the State must increasingly and earnestly concern itself with the care of the sick and the aged, and above all, of the children. I look forward to the universal establishment of minimum standards of life and labour, and their progressive elevation as the increasing energies of production may permit ... I do not want to see impaired the vigor of competition, but we can do much to mitigate the consequences of failure ... We want to have free competition upwards; we decline to allow free competition downwards. We do not want to pull down the structure of science and civilizations, but to spread a net over the abyss.

These universal elements all found their way into the Hawke/Keating model, which has three characteristics. The first is safety nets, the second is economic growth and the third is pluralism.

The safety nets of education, minimum wages, retirement benefits, income support and healthcare were at the forefront of the government's work. No other country in the world can claim anything like this degree of investment in the minimum rights and privileges of its citizens.

To fund that investment, it was necessary to increase economic growth – to improve the efficiency of the economy and to distribute the outcome so that wages, social welfare and profits all increased. To do all these things, while not increasing debt and inflation, it was necessary to increase productivity and competition.

The third characteristic was that it was pluralist in nature. For the most part, the ALP prefers not to extend government bureaucracy, but to operate through established groups in our society.

When all the great safety nets are considered, they have three elements: a national, a collective and an individual contribution.

The healthcare system has Medicare, private health insurance and private contributions.

There are public and private schools. Federal and state governments contribute directly. Parents pay a varying range of fees. When a person attends university, they generally pay a Higher Education Contribution.

The wages system has a national minimum wage, collective bargaining and individual contracts.

The retirement system has the pension, the Super Guarantee Contribution and personal contributions.

A socialist, pluralist and individual contribution are all part of Australia's safety net DNA. This is the nation's great compromise. The Labor Party's commitment to socialism has merged with the Conservatives' support of individual responsibility.

It is a century-old creation that has more political weight than is sometimes understood. On two occasions, Liberal parties have lost office when attacking minimum wages. The ALP has won office as the protector of national healthcare.

The Liberal government could not repeal the move to 12 per cent superannuation.

The ALP could not win government with a policy of no state aid to private schools.

The ALP lost an election because it sought to tamper with individual benefits for superannuation.

The Liberal Party of Menzies brilliantly used education to its advantage, but when it later failed to invest in education, it lost government.

Daniel Mulino makes out the case for welfare, not as an act of charity but as an investment. The most obvious is the investment in education. For a long time now, it has been evident that a society that invests in education will increase growth, productivity and the rate of adjustment to economic and technological change. The democratisation of education increases the supply of innovative and interested minds. In turn, increased education makes for a more exciting society. The Whitlam, Hawke and Keating governments invested in raising the number of young people enrolling in Year 12 and university. This in turn created a new industry for Australia, as millions of overseas students sought access to educational opportunity.

Long-term improvement in real wages coincides generally with long-term improvement in employment and living standards. The richest nations have the highest real wages.

Superannuation is a cost, but it is also a resource for investment funds. The increase in superannuation has coincided with a reduction in the risk premium Australian companies faced. As superannuation increased, so did the supply of investment funds. Australia's balance of payments improved as superannuation funds invested overseas.

However, perhaps the best example of social investment is Medicare. Australia spends about 9 per cent of its GDP on healthcare. The US spends 18 per cent but with less coverage. The difference helps Australian companies pay for superannuation and higher real minimum wages, and contributes to increased profits.

The efficiency equation of the safety net is not irrelevant. The increases in the social wage during the Hawke/Keating governments, which included age pensions, were all derived from a stringent test of government finances and included specific tax changes in respect of superannuation, asset tests for pensioners, fringe benefits and capital gains, which funded the social welfare improvements and reduced income tax levels.

Mulino's work challenges the orthodoxy of the free-marketeers but also the Left believers in the theory of the magic pudding or the call to arms for class warfare.

It is in the best tradition of the Hawke/Keating Labor model.

It is an important work for Labor in government or Labor seeking government.

Read in conjunction with Thomas Piketty's *Capital in the Twenty-First Century*, the essays of Adair Turner and the genius of John Maynard Keynes, the work will contribute to making the world a far better place.

Bill Kelty

1.
Introduction

THE WELFARE STATE EMERGED AS A RISK MANAGEMENT POLICY

Less than one month after the conclusion of the Blitz, while the UK was still reeling from the aftermath of waves of mass, indiscriminate bombing, Arthur Greenwood, the Labour Party MP and Minister without Portfolio in Winston Churchill's national coalition government, created an interdepartmental committee which would undertake a survey of social insurance programs. This seemingly minor administrative gesture would soon transform Britain and reverberate globally.

The work of this committee commenced during what was perhaps Britain's darkest hour. It was published in November 1942 and was officially (and somewhat innocuously) titled 'Social Insurance and Allied Services'. It has since become known as the Beveridge Report after its principal author, the liberal economist William Beveridge. Beveridge's report aimed for nothing less than the slaying of the 'five giants' on the road to reconstruction: 'Want ... Disease, Ignorance, Squalor and Idleness.'[1] One of the report's key planks was to recommend the expansion of social insurance so as to protect the vulnerable from the risks that we face as individuals and families.

At the same time, Australia was also envisioning widespread social reform. While Australia was still under threat of invasion, the Curtin government passed major legislation to revamp the welfare state. These reforms built upon the institutions that had been created in the aftermath of twin depressions (in the 1890s and the 1930s), including the age pension, workers' compensation schemes and a range of income-support measures. The programs created during this period would reshape Australian society. Rarely have nations had both the courage and the foresight to undertake such visionary and ambitious reforms during a period of such profound, menacing uncertainty.

The rationale for the welfare state remains compelling and relevant today. However, the institutions that compose it are in need of another burst of reform. We stand at a fork in the road. The welfare state is experiencing cost and scope pressures that threaten its continued existence as a meaningful social safety net. On top of these cost pressures, countries across the OECD, including Australia, are burdened with high debt levels thanks to the necessary spending in response to Covid-19. In the decade following World War II, Australia reimagined and expanded the welfare state while paying off the debt incurred during the war. Today, we must achieve something similar.

The welfare state is motivated by three key rationales: the universal provision of key services, redistribution and risk management. All of these are important and, typically, mutually reinforcing. But occasionally there is a tension between these rationales. Universality is critical for many essential services but can sometimes create too much of an emphasis on the delivery of services rather than a focus on the attainment of long-term outcomes. Redistribution often enhances welfare, but as its goals can be difficult to pin down, settling on agreed policy measures can be elusive in practice.

The third of these rationales, risk management, has always been key to the welfare state. Indeed, the welfare state emerged in the late nineteenth century precisely as a series of regulatory reforms in relation to pre-existing insurance schemes. In many cases, the fundamental reform was to mandate participation so as to improve the coverage and effectiveness of these schemes.

I believe that the welfare state needs to return to its roots. Of the three pillars, a greater emphasis needs to be placed on insurance and risk management (although not to the exclusion of universality and redistribution). Doing so will lead to institutions that are more outcomes-focused and capable of providing individualised, whole-of-life solutions to the most vulnerable people in our community. It will also allow us to achieve more without breaking the bank. We must embrace this opportunity. It is the only strategy that will allow us to help those in our society who need it the most, while navigating the funding pressures that are already straining some of our most important social supports.

The return to a greater emphasis on risk management could be achieved through five practical strategies in relation to risks that affect individuals and households, and three strategies that relate to risks affecting society as a whole.

The Covid-19 pandemic has exposed how much, as individuals and as a society, we depend on the welfare state. It binds our social fabric and underpins our economy. Since the emergence of Covid-19, health systems around the world have been stretched to the limit, saving countless lives. And many governments have nursed economies through the deepest downturns in almost a century with unprecedented levels of financial support. The strong performance of the welfare state during the pandemic in most advanced economies has reinforced how integral it is both in a national emergency and in our day-to-day lives.

Despite its resilience during these dark days, the welfare state is under threat from longer-term challenges. If left unchecked, these seemingly irresistible trends will increasingly undermine its effectiveness and sustainability. Since the conclusion of the World War I, the major institutions of the welfare state have grown from less than 2 per cent of GDP and a tiny fraction of government spending across the OECD to over half of all government spending and around a quarter of the entire economy. Government spending doubled or trebled as a share of the economy in most OECD countries in the space of just three decades following World War II, largely driven by the emergence or growth of social welfare. Indeed, the taxes required to fund the pillars of the welfare state continue to grow as a share of the economy, predominantly due to a combination of three factors. First, an ageing demographic which directly feeds into the two largest programs: healthcare and old-age pensions. Second, the fact that the growth rate in the costs of healthcare, aged care and many other government services exceeds economy-wide inflation and is forecast to continue to do so over coming decades. And, finally, the welfare state is expanding in areas such as disability and aged care, as well as providing support for people affected by structural economic changes arising from globalisation, technological change and the rise of insecure work.

The modern welfare state is comprised of institutions that provide assistance through a variety of means: universal service (national health services), a safety net (transfer payments to old-age pensioners and the unemployed), sector-specific schemes (for workplace and transport accidents and veterans), lifelong assistance (disability programs) and redistribution (means-tested carer payments and child support). At the heart of almost all these schemes is the provision of payments or services that are contingent on a specified and often random event, be it poor health, loss of income, disability or an accident. That is why so much of the welfare state is often referred to as 'social insurance' or a 'safety net'. At their core, many of these institutions are about protecting people when exposed to loss, in particular when the occurrence of that loss was unpredictable.

Risk management has always been central to the welfare state. In Germany, the key bills introducing welfare schemes by Chancellor Otto von Bismarck's government in the 1880s all included the word 'insurance' in the title: insurance for health, for income in retirement, for workplace accidents and for disability. And in the US, President Franklin Delano Roosevelt implemented the Old Age, Survivors, and Disability Insurance (OASDI) scheme in the midst of the Great Depression. It still exists today as probably the most effective anti-poverty measure in the United States. In the UK, the postwar 'cradle-to-grave' welfare state was built in the years following 1945 around economist William Beveridge's highly influential vision of national social insurance.

In many ways, today's welfare state has many of the characteristics of a vast insurance scheme. In that sense, social insurance is a communal venture in which we pool our resources to help those who, through no fault of their own, are left in need of assistance after fate has dealt its cards. In the words famously attributed to John Bradford, 'There but for the grace of God go I'. Framing the welfare state as an insurance scheme highlights the fact that many of us experience bad luck at some point in our lives and will therefore need support. When we think of the welfare state as redistributive, by contrast, it reinforces the 'them' and 'us' aspect, in which there is a class of people who give and a class of people who receive. When we think of the welfare state as insurance, it reinforces that most of us spend at least some time in both camps. This is partly due to the life cycle, in which we are more likely to be dependent on welfare at various stages of our life: for example, when young or old. But it is also because many of us will experience bad luck at points in our life and many individuals and households won't have the resources to self-insure.

While it is useful to invoke the underlying concepts of risk management that have been with us for centuries when thinking about the welfare state that emerged in the twentieth century, it is also important to note that there are key differences between social and private insurance schemes. The first key difference is that, while premiums are paid into a pool in both cases, unlike private insurance arrangements, government schemes often raise revenue not through risk-rated contributions but, rather, through progressive taxation. Second, participation in many elements of the welfare state is mandatory, which overcomes many of the market failures that bedevil some private insurance markets. Finally – and very importantly – government is able to manage risks across multiple generations far more effectively than private insurers. This can be critically important for those risks that affect an entire society at once, such as pandemics, climate change and an ageing society.

This book is not arguing that risk management should become the sole guiding light. A complex web of institutions cannot be reduced to a single policy mantra. Universal service delivery and redistribution should remain important features of the welfare state. For example, it will often be appropriate for schemes to provide benefits to people who haven't made a financial contribution. While insurance and risk management already play a prominent role in the welfare state, there are practical ways in which that approach could be strengthened. In some areas, such as the National Disability Insurance Scheme (NDIS), where insurance is embedded in the policy framework, the challenge is to improve risk management and service delivery. In other areas, such as aged care, healthcare for those with chronic conditions, and investment in skills, the opportunity is to explore ways in which insurance and risk management might be used as a means to improve outcomes.

The rise of government's role in the management of risk is the focus of this book: to explore the principal successes by governments to date in managing individual and society-wide risk and uncertainty – and the considerable opportunities for improvement.

I have been an elected representative at three levels of government: a deputy mayor of a local government area with a population of over 300,000; a state member of parliament (MP) and Parliamentary Secretary for the Victorian Treasury;[2] and a federal MP and member of Australia's House of Representatives Economics Committee. Many of the lessons that I have learned in these roles have arisen at all three layers of government.

I believe that we need greater productivity in government service delivery – not a significant step-up in taxes. In all three of my elected roles, I have seen government trying to do more with less. Across the OECD, government spending as a share of GDP rose significantly after World War II, more than doubling in the four decades between 1945 and 1985. Across all levels of government, the public sector now constitutes 40–50 per cent of GDP in most advanced economies, including both direct consumption of resources and transfer payments. Over the last four decades, total government expenditure as a share of GDP has remained broadly stable in most OECD nations.

A stable share of GDP for government means that tax reform has essentially become a zero-sum game in most countries, with tax cuts for some leading to higher taxes on others. This type of tax reform can still be worthwhile – for example, by shifting the burden from inefficient to efficient taxes.[3] But in such an environment, tax reform is almost always politically contentious, as the 'losers' (those paying more tax than before the reform) are generally at least as motivated and vocal as those gaining through lower taxes. In practice, this has meant that little genuine tax reform has occurred across many OECD countries in the past thirty years.

Even though the tax take has been largely stable as a share of the economy for some decades, government is being asked to do more. Our healthcare and aged-care systems are coping with rising demand and increasing costs. Other challenges also loom, such as the need to assist people to cope with structural economic change, invest in infrastructure and a growing recognition of the need for social insurance institutions to do more in areas such as aged care and disability.

I have experienced firsthand the electorate's reluctance for governments to solve emerging problems by resorting to higher taxes. As a councillor in an outer-suburban area where the population increased by more than five new families each day on average, I constantly felt the pressure to raise rates (property taxes) for the worthwhile purpose of funding better roads, new playgrounds and parks (a fundamental determinant of quality of life in new suburbs) and better maternal-health services (a core service for new families at risk of isolation). But constituents would routinely approach me to draw attention to the pressure on their household budgets arising from council rates rising faster than their wages. They would point out that, over the long term, it was not sustainable for rates to increase faster than household budgets. Of course, they were right. But I, and many other elected officials, found it all too tempting to increase rates for just one more year, particularly if population growth was booming and community demand for essential services rose with it. The same is true at state and federal levels.

People understandably want governments to figure out a way to make their already significant budgets stretch further. The only way to do this is to improve productivity at all levels of government. The key step is to look at the big-ticket items of government spending: healthcare, transfer payments, education, defence and infrastructure. We need to identify areas where expenditure can be reduced and service-delivery standards maintained – or improved. I believe that treating the welfare state primarily as a means of achieving social insurance could play an important role in achieving this. It will incentivise risk management, promote a focus on outcomes in areas of government where outcomes are currently often not even defined and lead to greater long-term sustainability in benefits programs under strain.

If, in the future, the community expresses a desire for the scope of government service delivery to expand materially, that will need to be paid for. I believe that seeking to achieve greater productivity from our existing level of investment in social insurance should be the first priority. Through a greater emphasis on a social insurance approach, it will be possible for government not just to provide existing social insurance programs to a higher standard within the current overall tax envelope but to also broaden the scope of risks the governments provides protection against. What does today's opportunity look like in the broader context of government's (relatively new) role as a risk manager?

In 1870, prior to Bismarck's reforms, and their counterparts in other countries, most people were highly exposed to risk and uncertainty. After an illness, an accident, a business failure or a harvest shortfall, individuals and households would have first turned to their own (often limited) resources. Some could have called upon their extended family or occupational associations. But these support mechanisms were typically limited in scope. Illness, accidents or unemployment beyond the control of individuals often resulted in destitution and prolonged hardship for entire families. This was the situation that had existed for most of human history.

By 1970, a mere century later, most people in advanced economies benefited from wide-ranging supports including universal healthcare, lifetime care for many serious accidents (like workplace and motor-vehicle accidents), income support following unemployment (albeit of varying generosity and length) and publicly provided income support in retirement. But there were gaps in these schemes, such as patchy support for those with a disability and limited support for those living in aged care. In the face of cost escalation and an ageing society, some publicly provided schemes were already experiencing funding pressures – a trend that has worsened in the decades since.

By 2070, a reformed welfare state should provide more effective support for our most vulnerable and drive economy-wide productivity growth. Hopefully, services are more outcomes-focused, with each individual's specific long-term needs and preferences at the centre of service provision. We already expect private-sector IT platforms on our phones to provide individualised, instantaneous, high-quality services. Even though the public sector often provides more complex services than a meal or a trip in a car, the public sector will need to move towards this model. It isn't just about individualised services. Reform should be framed around empowering beneficiaries to control what goods and services they receive and how. This will provide people with more autonomy and dignity, and ensure that scarce resources are directed towards what beneficiaries desire most. A key element in giving people meaningful control over their benefits will be access to tailored, expert advice in managing their resources and complex choices. A good example is the Service Navigation Relational Autonomy Framework (SNAF), recently developed to support the rollout of service navigation in the NDIS, but applicable far more broadly across human services.[4] This will both reduce stress and confusion for individuals and also result in better coordination across agencies, reducing the number of points of contact and wastage. Through these expert case managers and intelligent platforms/portals, individuals will input their preferences: for example, the allocation of resources by a person with a disability between equipment, therapeutic care or employment related training.

A future, higher-productivity welfare state will provide more flexibility and allow investment to be better balanced across an individual's life cycle. Some people will benefit from more up-front spending, others from more even spending over time. Individualisation should reflect this. Schemes should allocate resources according to what will deliver the best long-term outcome and not be limited by short-term budget constraints.

Behind the scenes, markets created and managed by government will connect service providers and their clients in the most efficient manner. Price signals, such as through risk-rated contributions, will create incentives to reduce underlying risks: be it by individuals changing their behaviour (switching to healthier lifestyles) or by organisations (like building safer workplaces and roads). Finally, schemes will be more robustly designed to ensure long-term sustainability. This will provide beneficiaries with greater confidence that the social contract will be honoured and will better achieve intergenerational equity by sharing the burden of costs more fairly over time.

The opportunity to reform social insurance is probably the single most important challenge for today's governments and will be the greatest future determinant of the quality of life of millions of citizens around the world.

FIVE STRATEGIES FOR DEVISING THE NEW WELFARE STATE

This book proposes five key strategies for using a risk-management approach in relation to the challenges that affect the welfare state:

1. **Long-term outcomes:** A greater emphasis on risk management is the best way to achieve better long-term outcomes for the people with the most chronic and complex needs.

One of the core reasons for placing greater emphasis on a social insurance approach is that insurance schemes seek to maximise lifetime outcomes and minimise lifetime costs. In contrast, programs funded by short-term revenue flows tend to place a greater emphasis on short-term objectives and costs. As a result, programs that are dependent on fiscal constraints tend to be subject to political and economic cycles rather than long-term policy trade-offs.

The first step is identifying outcomes. Outcomes should be the bottom line, but they are so difficult to measure in many areas of government activity that all too often they aren't the focus. Defining the desired outcome sounds obvious but it often doesn't happen in the context of social policy for three main reasons. First, social-policy programs often seek to simultaneously achieve multiple objectives. One challenge of clearly defining outcomes is to narrow the list of objectives. Is a healthcare system to be judged against average life expectancy, average quality-adjusted years of life, the capacity to live independently, mental-health outcomes, the distribution (rather than average level) of healthcare services – or all of the above? The second difficulty is that, where agencies dealing with social issues seek to achieve multiple positive outcomes simultaneously, they are faced with the challenge of how to rank and weight the many and varied outcomes that are sought, particularly where there are trade-offs. Third, it is often difficult to test what the specific net impact of a social policy is when the recipient of a benefit is typically simultaneously buffeted by many positive and adverse social interactions. This is most difficult when assessing long-term impacts, which are usually the impacts that policymakers are most interested in.

The difficulty of measuring net, long-term outcomes is a key reason why most social services are not included in the productivity measures contained within the national accounts. Over a quarter of OECD economies are described by the term 'non-market' economy (i.e. these goods and services are not offered for a price). In the market economy, price is used as a proxy for productivity as it reflects consumer preferences – that is, how much benefit a good or service provides a consumer. In the absence of prices, measuring productivity requires an estimate of net outcomes. The 'non-market' sectors of the economy are often critical to our welfare, yet they are not currently reflected in measures of national productivity since agreeing on and measuring outcomes is so difficult. Productivity growth is a core element of the economic debate in most countries, but few people realise that many of the sectors of the economy that have the most significant impact on our quality of life are effectively absent from this debate and not even captured in the official statistics.

How would a risk-management approach help? The achievement of well-defined, individualised long-term outcomes lies at the heart of an insurance contract. Indeed, an insurance premium, whether in the context of private or social insurance, will directly reflect the likelihood of harm and the expected cost of remediation. More clearly defining outcomes in the context of social insurance will not be a silver bullet. But it could materially improve the effectiveness of our major programs, particularly for those with the most complex needs, by better reflecting the precise guarantee made by the state to each individual.

2. Individual needs: An insurance approach will improve the extent to which government interventions reflect individuals' needs.

The risks that we face are idiosyncratic and so is our vulnerability to those risks. Yet many welfare schemes do not disburse payments or benefits according to need. Many schemes funded from taxes make flat payments across eligible cohorts, largely for administrative simplicity. Clearly, such payments will often not reflect individual or household need. Even where uniform benefits are means-tested, there is evidence of high rates of the most vulnerable not applying for benefits that they are eligible for due to a lack of awareness or stigma.

Other schemes provide in-kind goods and services on a universal-access basis, such as national healthcare systems. However, there is considerable evidence that even where benefits are universally accessible, they can be distributed regressively in practice. A good example is publicly funded healthcare, where people with high incomes take advantage of some specialised high-cost services at a higher rate than people on low incomes, due to a range of factors including access to information about treatment options as well as flexibility with regard to accessing services.

Many contributory social insurance schemes make payments that are positively correlated with income by design, especially where contributions are linked with employment, such as unemployment benefits in the US and Europe and many public pension schemes. In such schemes, benefits will typically not be reflective of need, by design.

In all these situations – flat benefit structures, the provision of universally accessible in-kind goods and services, and benefits linked to contributions – there is a strong case for more directly linking benefit structures with the particular needs of individuals and households. Good examples of needs-based allocation include the NDIS in Australia and aged-care packages in Japan and Germany.

Focusing on individualised outcomes could also be a catalyst for reducing the inefficiency associated with siloed service delivery to the same person. In her country-wide examination of aged care in the UK, Camilla Cavendish cited the example of an eighty-nine-year-old man who had dealt with over a hundred different carers, aides and bureaucrats over a one-year period.[5] There is no simple solution to the complexity of service delivery across multiple layers of government and by multiple agencies. A clear-eyed focus on individual outcomes could prod government to both reduce this complexity where possible and to assist individuals in navigating the systems they interact with, such as by providing professional, well-funded case managers.

3. **Individual preferences:** Governments should establish markets and other institutions that can better reflect varying preferences.

Where possible, governments should offer a range of benefit structures to reflect differing preferences. It is too infrequently acknowledged that differences in subjective preferences are distinct from differences in objective need, and that both should be reflected in scheme design. It is now possible with big data and the analysis capable of being performed by advanced IT platforms to take into account each individual's and each family's preferences. A simple example is how we help someone who loses their job in a regional area – an all-too-frequent challenge. One person might prefer assistance in the form of a lump-sum payment to help them relocate to try to use their existing skill set in another location. Another person might not want to move: they might want to stay near family and friends. A person in the latter situation might be willing to take a pay cut so as to not relocate. They might prefer assistance as a stream of payments (of the same value as the lump sum) that could support them to reskill and income support while they look for a job in another industry. Support schemes should be flexible enough to engage with each person's preferences by offering a menu of options.

Choice is often conflated with competition in service delivery. It shouldn't be. I believe that, to date, governments have focused too much on boosting supply-side efficiency through complex tendering and outsourcing arrangements. Such an approach can produce some benefits, such as efficiency through competition, innovation through a diversity of problem-solving approaches and the utilisation of expertise beyond government. But it can also come with downsides, such as the cost and uncertainty of contractual complexity, profit-skimming and cherry-picking. The most vulnerable people can be left exposed.

More attention should be paid to the demand side of the equation. Even where government is the monopoly funder and provider, it will often materially improve outcomes to offer people a range of benefit structures. Importantly, it will often be possible to deliver a range of options without adding to cost. Given varying preferences, that may be enough to significantly improve outcomes – and in ways that will be difficult to judge before it is tried. Just as global private-sector platforms have revolutionised the customer experience for many goods and services, similar technology could and should dramatically improve the experience of citizens interacting with welfare agencies.

Markets specifically designed for a particular area of social service provision will sometimes be an effective way of drawing out each participant's preferences. My proudest achievement as an MP was to help implement a market for transport services for a school for students with autism. Using auctions and optimised bus routes, it was possible to halve student travel times and totally avoid the unnecessary and highly stressful changing of buses. There are plans to extend this market to allow choice in relation to departure time (to facilitate after-school care) and mode of transport (to allow some students to use subsidised car travel to allow for more efficient bus routes). Transport markets like this could be designed to reflect each parent's and student's preferences for modes and timing of transport, as well as improving efficiency and reducing travel times. Importantly, similar markets could be adopted across many areas of service delivery, including regional and outer-suburban schools, more efficient peak-hour transport from people's homes to public transport hubs and emergency services transport such as ambulances. Many areas of social policy involve choices that are complex and involve interdependency between people in a similar way to transport. Well-designed markets, curated and managed by government, will be an important way of eliciting preferences in a way that is both efficient and safe for vulnerable people.

4. **Incentives:** A greater emphasis on risk management will create powerful incentives to reduce risk in the most cost-effective manner.

Risk-rated premiums are already used in many forms of social insurance. These can incentivise individuals or organisations paying the premium to cost-effectively reduce underlying risks, as we see premiums operate effectively in many private-sector contexts such as car insurance (lower premiums for safer driving), home and contents insurance (lower premiums for installing security measures) and private health insurance (lower premiums for embracing preventative health practices). Positive behavioural change that lowers the underlying risks managed by the welfare state could produce huge social and fiscal dividends.

Of course, risk-rated contributions won't always be appropriate. In some contexts, fully risk-rating contributions could lead to people being excluded from coverage due to affordability. The extent to which funding should reflect underlying risks was the single most important debate in relation to social insurance in Australia in the 1920s and 1930s, with the Australian Labor Party (ALP) withholding support for national social insurance unless it was funded from progressive taxation.

Pricing risk can also create powerful incentives for the organisation providing the insurance. Many workers' compensation and transport-accident schemes undertake highly creative and effective public-safety programs which both reduce the long-term risk exposure of the organisation and generate substantial social benefits. It should be no surprise that the organisations which were the original incarnation of the welfare state are responsible for some of its best public-policy practices.

Incentives could also be a powerful mechanism for better aligning the actions of agencies at different levels of government. This could involve the use of budgetary incentives. In many countries, labour-market programs at the state or local level will produce benefits that result in fiscal improvements for the national government (for example, through reduced unemployment payments). Payments from the national government to other levels of government to incentivise investment in such programs can produce better incentives than each tier of government acting alone.

5. **Sustainability:** A risk-management approach is critical to accurately measuring and appropriately responding to long-term challenges to sustainability.

One of the greatest challenges facing the welfare state is the range of cost pressures that see social programs continue to grow as a share of GDP. This includes demographic changes, such as the ageing of society and cost pressures, such as the long-term growth in medical costs relative to economy-wide inflation.

A well-designed social insurance scheme will ensure that premium levels are sufficient to cover the actuarially estimated long-term costs of the obligations assumed by the government. The first step is to calculate and report the evolving relationship between long-term revenue and the benefits promised by major schemes. New Zealand's Investment Model is an example of a social insurance scheme that rigorously and transparently reports actuarial estimates of the long-term obligations of all key benefits programs. Another good example is the OASDI scheme in the US, which regularly reports its revenue and long-term obligations. The Swedish age pension scheme is an example of a program in which actuarial estimates of long-term obligations inform both current funding and benefit levels. Sweden's pension scheme automatically adjusts both contributions and benefits levels to reflect medium-term and long-term wages growth and demographic projections to equitably distribute the burden of an ageing demographic between generations.

GUNS, GERMS AND FLOODS: THREE ADDITIONAL STRATEGIES FOR SOCIETY-WIDE RISKS

While individuals understandably focus on the risk of calamity in our own lives, society-wide risks also constantly threaten our wellbeing. The fact that this book was largely written during an extended Covid-19 lockdown is a compelling case in point! Systematic risks that affect all of society simultaneously have plagued us since time immemorial (no pun intended).[6] They include pandemics, climate change, natural disasters, structural economic change and war. By their nature, systematic risks can't be managed solely by pooling risk since they affect all of us simultaneously. They are often referred to as 'non-diversifiable' in that there are no unaffected people who can fund remediation for those who are affected. They typically require inter-temporal risk management. During a recession, societies often borrow in the present to ameliorate the severity of economic and social harm, with future generations in a better financial position left to repay the debt. In the face of an ageing demographic, some countries mandate savings by current workers so as to reduce the burden of public pension payments on future generations of (relatively less numerous) workers. And in the case of pandemics, inter-temporal risk management could take the form of investments in preparedness: in crisis-management plans and capability, in health systems able to cope with surges of illness and in the long-term investment in research and development required to develop vaccines and remedies.

The Covid-19 pandemic has highlighted the connections between systematic and individual risks. It has affected society as a whole and so required government intervention in terms of both the health and economic aspects of the crisis. These systematic risks were responded to with unprecedented levels of debt-funded income support for those losing their jobs unexpectedly, as well as to replace lost income for workers who were infected so that they would isolate rather than spread the infection. But governments were also called upon to manage idiosyncratic individual risks through existing social insurance schemes such as the intensive care capacity of public health systems. Further, the interdependency of inter and intra-generational risk-management strategies have come to light in this pandemic. Only government can walk that tightrope.

The pandemic also highlighted some of the challenges of making decisions under uncertainty. Key data in relation to the virus emerged slowly (e.g. in relation to its lethality, its transmissibility and the likelihood of variants). Decision-makers in the early months of the pandemic acted in a fog of uncertainty in relation to the emerging enemy. Moreover, even as more accurate data emerged, models struggled. Epidemiological models were about as accurate as the much-maligned models of macroeconomists. This shouldn't have come as a surprise given that both epidemiologists and economists model highly complex, chaotic systems in which human decision-making is central to determining outcomes.

Even though many countries managed aspects of the pandemic well, it is clear that we need to improve our management of systematic risks, particularly those involving uncertainty. The potential for loss and disruption arising from systematic risks is increasing due to factors such as the pace of technological change and the increasingly interconnected nature of the globe. Moreover, there is a growing realisation that existing risk-management practices are not as robust as they should be, particularly for risks that ignore national borders and require international cooperation when devising an effective response. A shift towards an insurance or risk-management approach would improve our capacity to manage systematic risks in three main ways.

1. **Better modelling and forecasting:** Investing in more accurate forecasting and modelling would involve a minuscule cost compared to the potential benefits. Improving our understanding of long-term systematic risks isn't just about improving the accuracy of our forecasts: it is also about understanding the inherent limitations of forecasting. Where more accurate forecasts are possible, society will benefit by being able to better prepare for future calamities. Where a deeper understanding of risk and uncertainty reveals the limits of what we will ever be able to achieve through forecasts and prognostication, we still gain, this time through being able to build institutions and a risk-management approach that is more nimble, more capable of responding to new information and, ultimately, more effective.

2: **Using government's balance sheet:** Systematic issues such as climate change and ageing usually involve a combination of inter- and intra-generational risk sharing. Intergenerational risk sharing is necessary where an entire community is affected by a risk at once. Intra-generational sharing is necessary where the impact at any point in time varies markedly across individuals and households. Intergenerational risks typically involve both a magnitude of resource shifting and a timespan that private insurers struggle with. The multiple pillars of the best pension systems are a good example of the need for government to play a role in intergenerational risk-sharing. The publicly funded pay-as-you-go safety net remains the core means of income support for retirees in most OECD countries. These schemes transfer resources from one generation to the next in a grand social bargain that has been one of the linchpins of the welfare state. To the extent that a declining worker base threatens the viability of such schemes, government can either mandate or subsidise savings so that generations of workers can provide for themselves in retirement, at least to a degree, reducing the burden on future, relatively less numerous taxpayers (e.g. 401(k) accounts in the US, superannuation in Australia).

The government's balance sheet can be crucial where private markets fail. Income contingent loans (ICLs) for higher education, first used in Australia but now widespread, overcome the challenge of a person not being able to use themselves as collateral for a long-term loan. It has made university more accessible for many people from socio-economically disadvantaged backgrounds. ICLs could be used in many other areas such as public housing and justice.

3. **Greater investment in preparation and mitigation:** In most countries, a vastly greater sum is spent cleaning up after disasters than on preparation, mitigation or adaptation. Many OECD countries spent more than 10 per cent of GDP in response to Covid-19. These responses are orders of magnitude greater than ongoing investment in planning and preparation for pandemics. The same is true (even if to a lesser degree) for most natural disasters. Governments should rebalance their efforts. As the late-nineteenth-century poem states: 'Better put a strong fence 'round the top of the cliff than an ambulance down in the valley.'[7]

Risk management offers guidance as to how to better fund preparedness. For example, an actuarially based biosecurity levy (for goods with a risk of introducing pests and diseases) or a small levy on inbound passengers could create a pool of resources that could be deployed to fund preparedness (e.g. medical equipment) or the capability to respond to an outbreak if (when) one occurs. Most disease outbreaks are containable, but this usually involves rapid action and considerable cost. A risk-rated contribution over time will lead to better outcomes than an ex-post reaction constrained by the budget of the day.

*

This book comprises four parts. Part I will trace the origins, rationale and history to date of the welfare state. It starts with the history of risk management and explains how this provided an important context for the development of major social insurance institutions in the twentieth century. It also shows how the development of social insurance represented a step jump in the size of government, being almost solely responsible for government expenditure more than tripling as a share of GDP over the course of the twentieth century.

Part II will describe and contrast the welfare state, predominantly in three countries: the US, the UK and Australia. The Danish sociologist Gøsta Esping-Anderson describes three main models of welfare state: the 'liberal' model (characterised by targeted benefits, private provision of income replacement where possible and relatively modest benefits); the 'conservative' model (with high benefit levels supported by contributions paid into a pool); and the 'social democratic'[8] (characterised by high benefit levels supported by progressive taxes). This characterisation is clearly a simplification, but it captures many key elements of major welfare states across the OECD.

This book will focus on three countries that all fall within Esping-Anderson's liberal category: Australia, the US and the UK. Despite the similarities in the welfare state across these three countries, Australia's institutions have distinctive characteristics. First, Australia is characterised by a high level of means-testing and targeted benefits (the highest in the OECD, with the UK close behind in fourth).[9] Second, the Australian welfare state is pluralistic. It is designed as a collaboration between the public, not-for-profit and private sectors in areas ranging from education and health to active labour market programs. Third, Australia's welfare state is funded to a greater degree than many through progressive taxes on income rather than risk-rated contributions. This is a strength (in terms of progressivity) but is also a source of long-term potential vulnerability in relation to sustainability. Finally, the Australian welfare system (and to an extent that of the UK) has evolved alongside strong regulation of wages and conditions, including a high minimum wage. This can be contrasted to that of the US. Part II explores the impact of the differences between these three main 'liberal' welfare systems.

Finally, Parts III and IV outline the opportunity for reform. This is reflected in the five strategies to improve risk management for individuals and the three strategies for society-wide risks respectively. While governments of all political stripes have made contributions to the development of Australia's welfare state, I will argue that this distinctive set of characteristics of the Australian system largely reflect the priorities and lasting policy achievements of the Australian Labor Party. I believe that the strategies that I propose in this book will build on and extend this tradition.

*

The size of social insurance programs in the modern economy, both for individual and systematic risks, reflects both the importance of the risk-management role that government plays in our lives and the massive reform opportunity it presents. This book is not an argument for small government. It is an argument for a more outcomes-focused and sustainable government. Improving the effectiveness of public-sector risk management is primarily about creating better outcomes for individuals and businesses: for those who have experienced loss, for those who are vulnerable and for those who have complex needs.

This book is also a story of marrying economic growth and fairness. Better risk management can lift economic growth since it will drive productivity growth in such a large segment of the economy – a part of the economy where productivity is too often overlooked and indeed not even measured. And it can drive that growth in a way that promotes fairness. This is not a magic pudding that can endlessly replenish itself. After all, there is no such thing as a free lunch. But there are genuine gains to be made through intelligent reform that can achieve wide-ranging social and economic benefits. We have an opportunity to build on the great successes of social insurance to date. It is an opportunity that we should grasp with both hands.

PART I

THE EMERGENCE OF THE MODERN WELFARE STATE

2.
A Brief History of Private and Public Risk Management

Before considering in detail the mechanisms by which social insurance is currently provided to help manage risk, it is important to understand the context within which both private insurance and the welfare state arose and the rationales for their widespread adoption. The following two chapters outline the history of private insurance and social risk sharing in the leadup to the twentieth century.

Managing uncertainty has been a do-or-die challenge, literally, for individuals and families and a core function of society throughout human history. We have tried to grapple with risk through self-insurance, social norms (especially the family[1]), voluntary arrangements (such as occupational guilds, friendly societies and private insurance) and, more recently, the welfare state and government intervention to prepare for and respond to society-wide catastrophes.

The arrangements that were developed in societies before the twentieth century were limited by the capacity of family, self-insurance, charitable organisations and informal networks such as guilds and professional associations to share resources and risk. Since the early twentieth century, governments in many advanced economies have developed social welfare programs that have amalgamated many of these earlier forms of risk insurance and dramatically expanded their scope. Private insurance markets have also grown significantly over the same period and often overlap with or complement social insurance. Taken together, the rise of government and private insurance over the past century has totally transformed society. In advanced economies, individuals and families now rely on the government to provide protection from many of life's gravest threats.

For most of us, insurance encapsulates everything that is boring. It is about being careful, risk-averse and cautious. It involves investing money to protect against situations that seemingly never arise. It is typified by the bureaucrat either asking us to fill in a form containing questions asking for information we have already provided on multiple occasions – or another bureaucrat telling us that we're not eligible for the benefit that the form was supposed to bestow upon us. For many, it is also indelibly linked to the insurance salesperson, prodding us to buy policies we don't understand and don't want to think about. As Woody Allen observed, 'There are worse things in life than death. Have you ever spent an evening with an insurance salesman?'[2] It represents the ultimate combination of dreariness: incomprehensibility and aggravation.

But despite our indifference, insurance is now everywhere – often without us realising it. Over half of most OECD countries' tax revenue funds social insurance programs (either through direct service provision or transfer payments) and its share continues to grow.[3] Private insurance adds a further 5–15 per cent of GDP on top of that.[4] For many individuals and households, a majority of their income is constituted by payments that are contingent on the outcome of random events and that are subject to explicit or implicit contractual or legislative arrangements of which they often have only a passing awareness.

Insurance is also critical for economic growth. No company would make mobile phones, electric cars or vaccines, investing massive amounts in risky research and development and then the manufacturing facilities required, without the many layers of commercial insurance and financial market hedging that today's modern economy offers. These firms don't rely just on private insurance. Commerce and innovation are also underpinned by social insurance. Which high-tech firms would be able to operate without healthy, well-educated workers, many of whom have directly or indirectly relied on social insurance as they have navigated life's challenges? The sexy, high-tech parts of our economy rely on insurance just as much as the public and not-for-profit institutions dedicated to poverty alleviation and providing services to the disadvantaged.

In addition to being ubiquitous and highly functional, insurance is one of humanity's great communal ventures. Insurance brings people and households together so that we can help each other in our hour of greatest need, providing succour to those whom Fortuna has cast aside. Social insurance has an even greater communal streak than actuarially neutral private-sector insurance. Social insurance encompasses redistribution alongside risk management, both within each generation and also through intergenerational transfers, which enable societies to marshal resources beneficially over the long term.

PRIVATE INSURANCE MARKETS

Managing risk lies at the heart of the modern market economy. Importantly, risk management and insurance have underpinned trade and commerce and indeed our very subsistence since the earliest societies. It is arguably one of the cornerstones of civilisation.[5]

Risk sharing in agricultural societies

The social benefits of risk sharing long precede the modern nation-state. In the most ancient human societies, agriculture or hunting dominated the economy and most households' income. The success or failure of the harvest or the hunt was a perennial risk for many households and it is unsurprising that risk-sharing mechanisms were developed in order to maximise the chances that families would be able to put food on the table. Over the millennia, risk management in agriculture has taken many forms, ranging from large-scale food storage by governments,[6] sharing risk between households[7] and risk management at the household level (e.g. holding multiple small plots as insurance against crop failure despite the potential for inefficiency).[8]

For many households, savings remain a safety net in the face of unexpected income shocks,[9] although in many contexts this form of 'self-insurance' provides limited protection. In societies in which agricultural output is a large part of most households' income, many risk-sharing arrangements have been observed. These are often informal, reflecting the fact that formal legal arrangements are either too costly to develop or in practical terms unenforceable. These arrangements are often non-anonymous, reflecting the importance of trust and (the other side of the coin) monitoring.[10]

Over time, a number of mechanisms have been developed that share risk in the context of agricultural production. These have included plot scattering (individual peasants owning multiple small plots scattered spatially to diversify productivity risk);[11] sharecropping (in which a share of the harvest is paid to the owner of the land as rent); mutual-credit organisations and other forms of group lending;[12] rotating savings and credit associations;[13] and lending and borrowing arrangements between friends and family.[14]

Detailed microeconomic studies of risk sharing in modern village economies provide insight into social mechanisms that may have existed through the ages. The economist Robert Townsend studied village economies in India, Thailand and Côte d'Ivoire. He found that, even at a highly localised level, 'evidence on actual households from a number of developing countries suggests that incomes of households in a village or region move together much less than expected'.[15] Clearly this creates opportunities for risk sharing. Townsend finds that while pooling is less than perfect, the villages display a considerable amount of risk sharing: 'The remarkable aspect of this analysis is the relatively low influence of present household income on present household consumption.'[16] In a separate study he finds that neither unemployment nor sickness had a significant impact on a household's consumption.[17]

Risk sharing in families continues to this day, even in advanced economies with large welfare states, although the evidence of its prevalence and magnitude is somewhat mixed. Several recent empirical studies find weak or no risk sharing within families in the US.[18] However, a recent Danish study using micro-level bank transfers and data from government registers finds evidence of material risk sharing within low-income households, particularly from parents and siblings to family members who have experienced negative-income shocks, expenditure shocks, family breakdowns or financial distress (but with much smaller transfers from grandparents and friends). The data showed that in the bottom decile, there was a replacement rate of 7 per cent for losses, while in the ninth decile there was a 4 per cent replacement rate.[19]

Ancient and medieval maritime risk sharing

Almost as old as risk sharing in relation to the harvest are arrangements to protect those risking resources in commercial transactions. One of the most ancient forms of insurance was used by merchants transporting their wares on the Yangtze river. As early as 3000 BCE, merchants would distribute their goods across a number of smaller vessels to protect themselves from total loss.[20] Another good example of ancient maritime risk insurance is known as bottomry, or bottomage, in which the loan used to finance a merchant voyage would not have to be repaid if the goods being transported were lost to storms or piracy. Given that the interest charged on such loans was higher than a loan without the bundled insurance, the risk associated with the voyage was effectively shared between the financier and the owner of the ship (and, indirectly, other ship owners).

In 1754 BCE, the Code of Hammurabi outlined a risk-sharing mechanism in which the repayment of a bond was contingent upon the ship successfully completing its voyage. While not strictly an insurance arrangement, this was in broad terms an ancient precursor to both the dealings in Lloyd's coffee house in seventeenth-century London and the catastrophe bonds created in the 1990s in the aftermath of Hurricane Andrew and the Northridge earthquake. Many modern social inventions are motivated and influenced by ancient antecedents – even if those responsible for rediscovering them are not necessarily aware of the connection.

Bottomry continued through Roman times as a means of facilitating the vast number of seafaring voyages required to feed the largest city of the Western world at the time. Not everyone approved, with Plutarch saying of Cato the Elder: 'He also used to lend money in what is surely the most disreputable form of speculation, that is the underwriting of ships.'[21] So did diversification, with Cato buying a small share of many ships rather than owning a smaller number directly himself.

Another major maritime risk is the need to jettison some goods when a ship runs aground. The 'Rules of Jettison' were developed around 1000 BCE and became known as the Lex Rhodia, named after the Mediterranean island of Rhodes. In essence, the rules provide that if some goods have to be jettisoned to save a ship, the value of that loss will be shared by the owners of the goods that were saved. This is the type of risk pooling that we are familiar with when we insure our houses against the risk of fire. These rules survive in the form of the York-Antwerp Rules, which were established in 1890 and which continue to apply to most maritime trade to this day.[22]

Even governments played a role in maritime risk management. A good example is the fact that contractors were able to insist that the Roman government assume all risk of loss by reason of the perils of the sea or capture in order to support a military venture in 215 BCE.[23]

Modern insurance

William Vance contends that the first explicit references to insurance are found in the records of the Chamber of Commerce of Florence from the fourteenth century. Specifically, there are records from the books of Francesco del Bene and Company from 1318 which include references to insurance costs in the trade of Flemish cloth.[24] During the fourteenth and fifteenth centuries, insurance spread throughout the other Italian city-states, as well as Spain and Holland. The first references to insurance in England relate to maritime transactions in the sixteenth century.

Insurance in the form of pooling risks among large numbers of individual policyholders coalesced in the late seventeenth and early eighteenth centuries. Modern insurance is often characterised by anonymous dealings across many thousands of individuals and firms. Given the more anonymous nature of the dealings, modern insurance relied upon formalised, standardised contractual dealings – and a high degree of confidence in contract enforcement. As will be outlined below, modern insurance also had to wait until rigorous tools of risk analysis had been developed and the collection of sufficient reliable data to undertake that analysis.

At the Fourteenth International Congress of Actuaries, reinsurance company Swiss Re contributed to a discussion of what makes a risk insurable by asserting that 'it must be possible to quantify the probability that the insured event will occur'.[25] This captures the two underpinnings of most modern insurance: the theory of probability and the data required for the quantification of risk.

Modern insurance arose in the late seventeenth century, principally in the form of life insurance and fire insurance. It is no coincidence that these emerged just decades after the development of probabilistic analysis in the mid-seventeenth century largely through the efforts of Blaise Pascal and Pierre de Fermat[26] and the subsequent creation of the first life expectancy tables.

In the 1650s, Blaise Pascal was approached by a French nobleman, the Chevalier de Mere, to solve the problem of the points. The problem of the points was defined by Luca Pacioli in 1494:[27]

> A and B are playing a fair game of *balla*. They agree to continue until one has won six rounds. The game actually stops when A has won five and B three. How should the stakes be divided?[28]

Pacioli's solution was that the stake should be divided according to the number of rounds won by each player. In the example cited above, player A would receive 5/8 (62.5 per cent) of the pot and player B 3/8 (37.5 per cent).[29]

Pascal and Fermat approached the problem differently. They assumed that each player had a 50 per cent chance of winning each subsequent game. If that were the case, player A should receive 7/8 (87.5 per cent) of the pot, not 5/8 (62.5 per cent) as Pacioli had argued. At the point that the game was interrupted, there are eight possible scenarios in terms of who wins the remaining games: AAA, AAB, ABA, ABB, BAA, BAB, BBA, BBB. In most of these scenarios, not all games would be played. For example, in all of the games in which A won the next game, the remaining two games would not be played, since A would already have won the pot. In only one of the eight scenarios, BBB, does B win the pot. Thus, B deserved 1/8 (or 12.5 per cent) of the pot.

Pascal's framework of analysis seems obvious today. Even if most of us don't visualise probability trees, it is embedded in how we see the world. Based on Pacioli's rule, a professional sports team that is down 3–1 in a seven-game finals series has a 25 per cent chance of winning the championship, if the series were interrupted at that stage. Yet if the teams were given a 50 per cent of winning each subsequent game, the team staring at a 3–1 deficit would only win one in eight series.

Most sports fans would be instinctively aware of how unlikely it is that a team would overcome a 3–1 deficit in a seven-game series, even if they don't explicitly think in terms of formal probability analysis. Of the 251

NBA playoff series in which a team has led 3–1 at some point, only 4.4 per cent (or less than one in twenty) saw the trailing team recover to win the series.[30] The Cleveland Cavaliers recovered from a 3–1 deficit in the 2016 Finals to win the NBA Championship, the only team in the history of the NBA to do so. This reflects the fact that the team that is leading is, usually, the stronger team – and therefore has a greater than 50 per cent chance of winning each remaining game. But even the simplifying assumption of a 50/50 likelihood for each remaining game is usually a decent approximation and far superior to Pacioli's approach.

The solution to the problem of the points had evaded the greatest minds of Europe for almost two centuries. Indeed, despite their vast achievements in mathematics and geometry, even the ancient Greeks struggled with even the most rudimentary concepts of probability. The earliest known form of gambling is a dice game played with an *astragalus,* or knuckle-bone. These dice were oblong with two narrow and two wide faces (and rounded ends). It is telling that in ancient times, the payoffs within this game do not take account of the different likelihoods of landing on narrow as compared to wide faces.[31]

Probability provides a quantitative basis for modern insurance, without which it would be impossible to match premiums with the underlying risks being insured. But there are limits to how accurately we can quantify risks, a challenge explored much later in the twentieth century by Frank Knight and John Maynard Keynes. This challenge suggests that there may be limits to the types of scenarios that private insurance markets can provide coverage and provides a rationale for public-sector involvement in risk management. This will be explored below.

The collection of accurate data has been central to the development of modern insurance. Less than a decade after the correspondence between Pascal and Fermat that made such great leaps forward in the field of probability, a major contribution to the statistical underpinnings of insurance was published: *Natural and Political Observations made upon the Bills of Mortality* by John Graunt, a haberdasher who, in his spare time, was arguably the first modern epidemiologist and a path-breaking demographer. This book compiled all births and deaths in London from 1604 to 1661.[32] Graunt's work provided a detailed measurement of the impact of the plague on seventeenth-century London, as well as a sobering estimate of infant mortality: 'about thirty six *per centum* of all quick conceptions[33] died before six years old'.[34]

Three decades later, Edmund Halley (of comet fame), undertook similar analysis in relation to the Silesian town of Breslau.[35] Halley took Graunt's compilation of deaths one step further and estimated the likelihood of survival at each age. Using Halley's table, it was possible to estimate the likelihood that a person of a particular age would survive for a defined period. For example, he could estimate the likelihood that a twenty-year-old person would survive until the age of fifty or eighty.

Up until Graunt's and Halley's analyses, some governments had issued annuities that made payments to the purchaser over a set period, but they didn't adjust the price of the annuity for the age of the purchaser. Mihir Desai describes annuities that were developed by Swiss bankers who bought them on behalf of five-year-old girls, then securitised them to form the basis of portfolios. 'By the time of the French Revolution,' Desai writes, 'these annuities were the dominant source of financing for government and the majority of annuitants were below the age of fifteen.'[36] It is telling that the financial precariousness of the French state in the eighteenth century, which undoubtedly contributed to the backdrop of pre-revolutionary instability, could be attributed at least in small part to something as arcane as the faulty link between life expectancy and payoffs in public-sector financial instruments.

Halley's tables were published in 1693. They inspired similar analysis across the Continent and formed the basis upon which the life insurance industry would emerge over the coming decades – even as statistically unsound practices would persist for some time.[37]

Another fascinating innovation was when the French government permitted the purchase of annuities by groups of people. These were called 'tontines'. The government paid a fixed amount to the group, which meant that as more people in the group passed away, surviving members received ever larger payments. This practice spread. Indeed, in the US, tontine policies represented 8 per cent of national wealth in the early twentieth century.[38] The size of the tontine market and concerns relating to its regulation led to regulatory scrutiny. As a result of major investigation, the state of New York banned tontines in 1906 and other states soon followed. Ransom and Sutch argue that the ban was premature:

> Considered as a financial innovation, [the tontine] was very successful. Considered as insurance, it was actuarially sound. Considered as a gamble, it was a fair bet in as much as there was no percentage for the house beyond a charge to cover administrative costs. Considered as a life-cycle asset, it proved to be an excellent investment, earning a rate of return substantially in excess of that generally available on other assets.[39]

A number of economists argue that due to their administrative simplicity and people's aversion of annuities, tontines could make a comeback in the twenty-first century.[40]

Lloyd's and risk underwriting

Insurance expanded rapidly in Europe during the eighteenth century; life, maritime, and fire and property insurance were the most prominent forms. The seventeenth-century coffee houses of London became an informal yet highly effective network for disseminating information about how the schemes worked abroad.

One of those coffee houses, opened by Edward Lloyd in 1687, would become the basis for another layer of insurance. In 1771, the Society of Lloyd's was formed. Under these new arrangements, the Members (later known as 'Names') would underwrite risks with personal unlimited liability. A *New York Times* article from 27 April 1993 highlights the significant personal risks that unlimited liability entails. The article documents many wealthy Names losing their entire personal incomes in the early 1990s – as well as a number of suicides.[41]

The type of underwriting provided by Lloyd's permitted two further developments: the insurance of more idiosyncratic risks and reinsurance. The willingness of underwriters to insure more idiosyncratic, one-off risks was important as it extended the scope of what was insurable beyond situations in which large, reliable datasets were available. Even today, Names are willing to take on risks that are difficult to quantify. John Kay and Mervyn King directly observed and documented the process by which Lloyd's Names assumed the risk of an extremely wealthy person's art collection. This is a different type of risk from, say, the average life expectancy of a 45-year-old man in London. The risk associated with the former cannot be deduced from large swathes of data collected in relation to the likelihood of billionaires having valuable art stolen from highly fortified mansions. Each billionaire's art collection is unique, and each mansion's security is differently configured from all others. Moreover, there aren't many data points to calculate this type of risk. Insuring this type of risk requires a considerable degree of judgement in addition to using what limited data might be available.[42]

The growth of Lloyd's also reflected the rise of reinsurance, or the pooling of risk among insurers. Reinsurance is important as it provides a greater degree of confidence that smaller insurers will remain solvent even in the event of extremely large losses. This has allowed the insurance sector to assume much larger risks than otherwise would have been the case. Reinsurance has become a means by which risk can be shared globally through networks such as Munich Reinsurance, Swiss Re and Berkshire Hathaway (the latter bought Lloyd's for US$7 billion in 2006[43]).

Friendly societies and mutuals

Friendly societies and mutuals (and their precursors) have been an important form of risk management for millennia. Ancient Chinese, Indian, Greek and Roman artisans formed organisations that were the precursors of medieval guilds. The ancient Greek *Eranoi* and *Thiasoi* in the third century BCE provided for the burial expenses of members.[44] These expenses were of critical importance given that the sanctity of one's burial was thought to determine the quality of one's eternal afterlife.

In the days of the Roman Empire, *collegia tenuiorum* often acted as funerary societies and were also providers of social safety nets for artisans.[45] The contributions that members made for the benefit of families of deceased members were similar to the risk sharing provided by modern life insurance. Similarly, medieval guilds often imposed dues which created pools that could support payments to the dependents of deceased members.[46]

In parallel with modern insurance, friendly societies arose in the seventeenth and eighteenth centuries which would provide risk management to members through similar mechanisms to earlier guilds, albeit often with more sophisticated risk measurement. Many friendly societies and mutuals arose during this period, some with very large memberships.

A good example is the International Order of Odd Fellows (IOOF), which, by around 1900, had nearly 2 million members and comprised 16,000 lodges. Among its social supports, the IOOF provided an early form of workers' compensation in the rapidly industrialising and increasingly dangerous American economy.[47]

Friendly societies also played a critical role in early Australian society. Between 1865 and 1900, the total membership of friendly societies grew from just over 20,000 to almost 100,000.[48] By 1913, over half the population of Victoria, South Australia and Tasmania were covered by friendly societies, and across Australia as a whole, 46 per cent of people were covered. Friendly societies and mutuals performed some functions that are analogous to modern publicly funded unemployment insurance. Indeed, Wettennhall argues that: 'Friendly societies eventually died out because government welfare legislation began providing security for workers.'[49]

In the first half of the twentieth century, the role of mutuals (and also partnerships) was very significant in most advanced economies, particularly in the development of the finance sector. These often grew out of friendly societies. A prominent example was the Halifax Building Society, which grew out of the Loyal Georgian Friendly Society, which formed in 1779 and was comprised of small businessmen who lent money to each other to build houses. Halifax was named after the small town in West Yorkshire from which it originated. After it became a building society in 1853, Halifax grew steadily over the following century and a half to ultimately become the largest building society in the UK, providing millions of people with mortgages and millions of savers with a safe place to invest.[50] One of its early areas of emphasis was financing philanthropic housing developments.[51] Oxford economists John Kay and Paul Collier (the former a board member of Halifax at the time of its demutualisation) point to the demutualisation of Halifax (facilitated by legal reforms in the UK in 1986) as an example of the many pitfalls of the transition to corporate structures for such organisations. The fate of Halifax was repeated many times over in the UK and other countries.

Scotland's financial and insurance system was built around mutuals, including household names such as the Scottish Widows' Fund and Life Assurance Society (formed in 1815), the Edinburgh Life Assurance Company (1823), Standard Life (formed in Aberdeen in 1825), the West of Scotland Insurance Company (formed in Glasgow in 1826) and Scottish Equitable (1831), among others. Demutualisation hit many of these organisations in the 1990s and 2000s as 'carpetbaggers' engineered huge one-off profits for members and finance-sector advisers arising from the corporatisation of organisations like the Nationwide Building Society, Standard Life and Scottish Mutual. During this period, some building societies, such as the Portman, the Britannia, the Coventry and the Yorkshire, resisted demutualisation (at least temporarily).

The role of cooperatives and mutuals was also prominent in the US economy. Just as in the UK, mutuals played an important role in the emerging American financial system, with Benjamin Franklin famously founding the nation's first mutual fire insurance company in 1752.[52] Cooperatives also played a pivotal role in other industries too. John Curl draws attention to the role of cooperatives across industries ranging from mining to textiles and footwear. Many of the largest cooperatives were formed between the 1860s and the 1880s. The cooperative movement peaked in the 1880s, with one study finding 334 worker cooperatives founded in that decade alone.[53] Of these, around 200 were organised by the Knights of Labor. With almost 1 million members, Curl argues that it was the largest organised labour movement in the world at the time, but they were seriously weakened following the strikes and riots of the late 1880s.[54] The actions of radicals (including anarchists) during these strikes discredited the Knights in the eyes of many and saw a number of local organisations transfer to the emerging American Federation of Labor (AFL). However, cooperatives didn't disappear, and they would continue to play a significant role during the Great Depression. As of 2015, there were over 64,000 cooperatives in the US, including almost 400 worker-owned cooperatives. In 2015, there were over 850,000 jobs in the cooperative sector and over a million families lived in cooperative housing.[55]

Australia, too, has seen the rise (and fall) of mutuals. As late as the 1920s, the Australian finance sector was comprised almost exclusively of publicly owned entities and mutuals, including a newly formed Commonwealth Bank (which undertook both retail and central banking functions), publicly owned state banks, mutuals providing pension products (such as IOOF, AMP, Colonial Mutual and National Mutual), and general insurance provided by another mutual (NRMA). Like the UK,

Australia went through a phase of demutualisations from the mid-1990s.[56] By 2020, Australia had a large, sophisticated financial sector, including the fourth- largest pool of retirement savings in the world. In addition to the change in the size of the financial services sector over the course of the century, what is striking is that mutuals now play a very limited role in Australia. Today's financial sector is dominated by private corporations (banking, insurance and funds management) and superannuation funds (a mix of for-profit funds and funds run to benefit members only).

One of the disadvantages of mutuals and other highly localised risk-sharing arrangements is that the participants often share very similar risk profiles, which makes risk diversification more difficult.[57] This contributed to the creation of modern insurance based on larger, more diversified risk pools.

Self-insurance

Self-insurance can play a role in risk management. For centuries, economists have discussed the relationship between savings and uncertainty. Milton Friedman,[58] Franco Modigliani[59] and Truman Bewley[60] all contributed to the development of the Permanent Income Hypothesis, which provides a framework for understanding life-cycle savings. Where they are able to, people will tend to save during periods of high income, predominantly for retirement, in order to smooth consumption across their lifetimes. Many empirical studies have confirmed that saving rates can, at least to a degree, be predicted by this model. Nicholas Barr emphasises the role of the welfare state in complementing individuals' attempts to smooth consumption: the 'Piggy Bank' function of the welfare state, in his words (which he contrasts with the redistributive or 'Robin Hood' function).[61] But even the 'Piggy Bank' function described by Barr involves risk management. Saving while working in order to support a decent standard of living in retirement is simple in theory, but in practice, people must contend with volatile investment returns, unexpected periods out of work and, after retirement, uncertainty in relation to sickness and life expectancy.

As will be outlined in the next chapter, the welfare state that emerged in the twentieth century built on the advances in private insurance markets and overcame some of the limitations of self-insurance and other informal arrangements.

THE EMERGENCE OF THE MODERN WELFARE STATE

The welfare state is a huge safety net based on the fundamental practices of insurance. In 1927, the great American jurist Oliver Wendell Holmes wrote that: 'Taxes are what we pay for civilised society, including the chance to insure.'[62] Even before the modern welfare state had come into existence, Holmes made the connection between taxation and risk management.

Social risk-sharing prior to the welfare state

While governments provided some assistance to the poor in pre-modern times, publicly funded programs at scale are relatively recent. In nineteenth-century Europe, publicly funded 'poor relief' had emerged in some Western European countries. These programs provided a safety net of sorts in many countries, but until the twentieth century the level of support provided was only modest. Taxpayer-funded poor relief was almost always under 2 per cent of GDP in the eighteenth and nineteenth centuries, with the exception of England and Wales in the 1820s.[63] That exception was reversed by the Poor Law Reform of 1834. Even at these new low levels, Robert Malthus complained that such practices encouraged procreation and overpopulation.[64]

During this period, public poor relief existed alongside private philanthropy, although it is likely that private charity prior to the twentieth century was minimal. Peter Lindert estimates that private charity in selected Western European countries was typically less than 1 per cent of GDP prior to 1900. Prominent examples include England and Wales at less than 0.4 per cent of GNP between 1819 and 1837, and less than 0.1 per cent of GNP between 1861 and 1876; France, where churches provided 0.17 per cent of GNP to the poor in 1790, and church and private charity constituted less than 0.5 per cent of GNP in 1880; and Italy, with charities constituting less than 0.5 per cent of GNP in 1868. In the Netherlands, private, church and government aid combined totalled between 1.46 and 1.93 per cent of GNP in 1790.[65] When the modern welfare state eventually arose, it certainly didn't crowd out a large and thriving private charitable sector, or taxpayer-funded poor relief schemes.

Bismarck and the 1880s

Otto von Bismarck's government introduced a number of social welfare programs starting in the early 1880s. Germany introduced accident insurance in 1881, sickness insurance in 1883 and old-age insurance in 1889. Bismarck at one stage referred to his program as 'practical Christianity' and saw it as a pragmatic response to ward off the excesses of socialism. When explaining the rationale for social welfare in the Reichstag, Bismarck argued:

> The real grievance of the worker is the insecurity of his existence; he is not sure that he will always have work, he is not sure that he will always be healthy, and he foresees that he will one day be old and unfit to work. If he falls into poverty, even if only through a prolonged illness, he is then completely helpless, left to his own devices, and society does not currently recognize any real obligation toward him beyond the usual help for the poor, even if he has been working all the time ever so faithfully and diligently. The usual help for the poor, however, leaves a lot to be desired, especially in large cities, where it is very much worse than in the country.[66]

Bismarck's analysis of worker discontent in the late nineteenth century would not be out of place in the current world, in which stagnant wages and growing employment insecurity for many is a key factor in driving many voters to more extreme political options at the voting booth.

It is no accident that three of the key pieces of legislation underpinning Bismarck's revolutionary social safety net included the word 'insurance' in the title: the *Health Insurance Act of 1883*; the *Accident Insurance Act of 1884* and the *Old Age and Disability Insurance Act of 1889*.[67] While pathbreaking, these schemes did not involve significant government expenditure. Unlike today, German taxpayers contributed almost nothing in the 1880s. Rather, the costs of insurance were borne by the workers themselves and by their employers.[68] In the case of workers' compensation, taxpayer subsidies were almost zero. In the case of old-age pensions, the state paid 6 per cent of insurance revenues as of 1891 and only 18 per cent as late as 1908.[69] The governments of some other countries, such as Norway and Denmark, also mandated coverage with small pension subsidies in the 1880s.[70]

The Australian welfare state

Australia was at the cutting edge of some aspects of social insurance in the first decade of the twentieth century. Its federal government was formed on 1 January 1901 in the aftermath of the bitter depression of the 1890s, which left many questioning the adequacy of existing social protections. Shortly before Federation, the colonial governments of New South Wales and Victoria had enacted non-contributory age pensions in 1900. This was a break from the contributory schemes enacted by Bismarck in the 1880s and elsewhere in Europe in the late nineteenth century. These schemes were followed by Queensland in 1907. Australia's first major national social insurance program was the *Invalid and Old Age Pensions Act 1908*, introduced by the Deakin government. These schemes were different to most social insurance arrangements of the day in that they were non-contributory[71] and means-tested. Arguably, they set a precedent that would have considerable influence in Australia for decades to come.

Additional social insurance measures at the national level were enacted by Andrew Fisher's Labor government from 1908,[72] including workers' compensation and a national maternity allowance (1912).

Marian Sawer argues that T.H. Green, the prominent proponent of social liberalism, was highly influential in both the early welfare state reforms and the progressive taxation mechanisms that financed them in both Australia and the UK.[73] Michel Freeden argues that 'there is not much doubt that the crucial financial policies were the product of liberal precepts and a liberal mind.'[74] This judgement has been echoed by Chris Bowen.[75]

Indeed, both sides of the political aisle supported the notion of social insurance. Deakin's third ministry commissioned a report into a national social-insurance scheme by the Commonwealth Statistician, G.H. Knibbs, which was received in 1910. The report supported a contributory scheme, but a political divergence was emerging in Australia that would last for decades. Many in the ALP supported social insurance, but only on the basis that it was funded out of progressive taxes.

This would play out several times over the coming decades. In 1923, the conservative coalition Bruce/Page government announced an intention to implement a national contributory social insurance scheme. A royal commission into this issue published four volumes outlining the case for national social insurance. Detailed legislation was drafted for consideration. Following the social and economic damage resulting from the Great Depression, all major party leaders ended up in support of a national social insurance scheme by the late 1930s, albeit with Labor still supporting non-contributory funding.

The conservative Lyons government made another attempt at a national contributory scheme in 1938, which included a range of elements including old-age pensions and health insurance. Conservatives – many in academia and the upper echelons of the bureaucracy – felt that the non-contributory nature of most of Australia's welfare programs was fiscally irresponsible.[76] Moreover, by this time, policymakers were increasingly concerned about the cost of pensions. In 1930, total expenditure on pensions was almost six times higher as a share of national income than in 1910, which was particularly concerning at a time when the economy was increasingly weak. These concerns have only gained traction in the intervening decades and were a major factor behind the move towards compulsory superannuation over half a century later.

In 1936, two of the three leading British experts in social insurance were 'loaned' to Australia to help devise the scheme ultimately proposed in 1938: G.H. Ince (an unemployment insurance expert) and Walter Kinnear (a health insurance expert).[77] The third leading expert, William Beveridge, did not come to Australia, but would soon thereafter write his own seminal report that underpinned the postwar British welfare state. Kinnear's report would form the basis of the subsequent debate in Australia, proposing a national, mandatory, contributory social insurance scheme covering retirement incomes, unemployment benefits and health. The Labor Party opposed the scheme on the basis that it was contributory. Ultimately, the scheme failed in the face of opposition not only from the ALP but also from the Country Party and many friendly societies and medical doctors.[78] This was such a major policy setback that Robert Menzies, who would go on to become Australia's longest serving prime minister after World War II, resigned from Cabinet in protest at the postponement of national insurance.

After the failure of the 1938 reforms, the ALP governments of Curtin and Chifley dramatically expanded the welfare state, largely during the closing stages of World War II. They did so by enacting or expanding a range of non-contributory schemes: the child endowment (1941);[79] a widow's pension (1942);[80] a wife's allowance (1943); allowances for children of pensioners (1943); and unemployment, sickness and special benefits (1945).[81] In the words of historian Manning Clark, these governments believed that:

> The task of government was to prevent the repetition of the two evils of unemployment and Japanese expansionism. Their answer to the former was the welfare state. Until 1943, lack of political strength and the grave state of the war had forced them to hold their hand. But a landslide victory in the elections of 1943 ... and a more favourable war situation gave them their opportunity. Child endowment, hospital benefits, invalid and old-age pensions, maternity allowances, unemployment and sickness benefits, and widows' pensions were either improved or begun.[82]

Each of these programs was reformed on numerous occasions over the intervening decades, including the introduction of means-testing for many benefits. National healthcare would be introduced in Australia three-quarters of a century after the first mandatory workers' compensation schemes and almost half a century after the debates surrounding national insurance of the 1920s. In 1975, Whitlam's Labor government introduced Medibank, a single-payer national healthcare system providing many services on demand and at no cost. Following the 1974 double-dissolution election, the legislation creating Medibank passed a joint sitting of the Australian houses of parliament.[83] Following the defeat of the Whitlam government in 1975, the conservative Fraser government backed only some aspects of Medibank. Following the election of the Hawke Labor government in 1983, Medicare was introduced in 1984, which returned the national health system to the model established in 1975. This system has largely been retained until the present day. Social insurance was central to the approach embraced by the Hawke/Keating governments. Many of the microeconomic reforms adopted during this period boosted overall economic growth but created economic setbacks or insecurity for some segments of society. One example was the impact of trade liberalisation on exposed industries such as car manufacturing and the textiles, clothing and footwear sector. The quid pro quo was that microeconomic reform was accompanied by a boost to the 'social wage', which included a stronger wage bargaining framework, the introduction of Medicare and other supports.

Another significant (and world-leading) expansion of Australia's social insurance system was the expansion of access to superannuation (private retirement accounts). Superannuation coverage increased from 53 per cent of employees in 1982 to 71 per cent in late 1991. The government led by Paul Keating further expanded coverage, in particular with legislation in 1992 that introduced the superannuation guarantee. These reforms created a separate pillar of support for retirees, in addition to the publicly funded age pension. This reform was reflected in the findings of the World Bank in its seminal report in 1994, which argued that retirement income systems should be built around three pillars: a public pension, mandated private savings, and voluntary private savings.[84]

The final major piece of Australia's social insurance system arrived under the Labor government led by Julia Gillard. In 2008, minister Bill Shorten established the Disability Investment Group (DIG). This group produced a major report in 2009 titled 'The Way Forward'. This report found that while Australia had a robust social security system, 'there are high levels of unmet need for disability services'. It asserted that people with disabilities and their families 'have no certainty and no guaranteed access to a system of core support'. The DIG recommended the establishment of a National Disability Insurance Scheme (NDIS), which would be based on a social-insurance approach. The government would

> assess the risk of disability in the general population; calculate the costs of meeting the essential lifetime needs arising out of these disabilities; and estimate the premium or contribution required from taxpayers to meet these needs. Instead of funding capped programs and services for people with disability to find and access, the scheme would fund on the basis of each individual's needs which would in turn drive the development of necessary care and support services.[85]

At the heart of the scheme was a model in which care would be managed to reflect lifetime needs, individualised and based on client preferences. Bill Shorten and Jenny Macklin (the lead portfolio minister for

Families, Community Services and Indigenous Affairs and the minister for Disability Reform) referred the key recommendations of the DIG report to the Australian Productivity Commission in 2011. The Productivity Commission was tasked with examining the long-term care and support for Australians with a disability. Its report echoed the DIG's call for a National Disability Insurance Scheme, which the government subsequently introduced, funded in part by an increase in personal income taxes.

The Great Depression and Roosevelt

Half a century after Bismarck, the wreckage of the Great Depression led many people to conclude that the free-market system needed to be supplemented by social supports that could provide people with protection against economic volatility.

President Franklin Delano Roosevelt's New Deal provided significant assistance for the unemployed, elderly people and the disabled in the United States. During his inaugural address on 4 March 1933, Roosevelt began by acknowledging the dire situation: 'a host of unemployed citizens face the grim problem of existence, and an equally great number toil with little return'.[86] He argued that the Depression was not due to 'a failure of substance' (he observed 'we are stricken by no plague of locusts'), but rather due to failures of the market:

> Nature still offers her bounty and human efforts have multiplied it. Plenty is at our doorstep, but a generous use of it languishes in the very sight of the supply. Primarily this is because the rulers of the exchange of mankind's goods have failed.[87]

In the face of this desperate situation, Roosevelt's address was a call to action. He laid out many policies, including the stronger regulation of the banking system, support for agricultural prices and limits on foreclosures. He also laid the groundwork for reforms that came later in his administration, by calling for 'the unifying of relief activities which today are often scattered, uneconomical, and unequal'. Roosevelt's words eerily foreshadow the findings of Australia's Productivity Commission eighty years later in relation to pre-NDIS disability supports as being: 'underfunded, unfair, fragmented and inefficient'.[88]

Roosevelt's first hundred days in office focused on emergency measures: the bank holiday; ending prohibition; establishing the Tennessee Valley Authority (a precursor to a decade-long investment in infrastructure across the nation); limiting agricultural output to boost prices; and supporting union rights.

Social insurance was introduced later, during the Second New Deal of 1935. The Second New Deal included further union reforms (the *Wagner Act* and the establishment of the National Labor Relations Board), the *Social Security Act* and the establishment of the Works Progress Administration (WPA), which provided jobs for the unemployed in building public projects such as post offices, bridges, schools and highways.

In a message to Congress in 1934, Roosevelt declared: 'These three great objectives – the security of the home, the security of livelihood, and the security of social insurance – are, it seems to me, a minimum of the promise that we can offer to the American people. They constitute a right which belongs to every individual and every family willing to work.'[89]

The *Social Security Act* of 1935 was the core of the Second New Deal and was one of the most important pieces of legislation in the history of the United States. It established the age pension, unemployment insurance and the provision of support to dependent children and people with a disability.

As in Australia, national healthcare arrived much later in the US than most other key planks of the welfare state, and even then it was far from universal. The first major step towards publicly funded healthcare was the introduction of Medicare and Medicaid in 1965 by the Johnson administration, both of which were single-payer healthcare models in which the state provided all funding. Medicare is a federal program that provides healthcare coverage for those over the age of sixty-five (and also, following an extension of the scheme under the Nixon administration, those with a disability). Medicaid is a program funded by both the federal and state governments that provides healthcare coverage for those on low incomes.

Even after the creation of Medicare and Medicaid, many Americans lacked meaningful healthcare coverage. This led to multiple attempts over the decades following 1965 to broaden it. The Clinton administration attempted to broaden single-payer coverage but failed. The Republican response was the *Health Equity and Access Reform Today Act*, which was built around an individual mandate (i.e. a requirement for individuals to insure).[90] Milton Friedman argued strongly for the individual mandate in 1991 in the *Wall Street Journal*.[91]

The individual mandate formed the basis of some states' healthcare policies, including the universal healthcare scheme adopted by Governor Mitt Romney in Massachusetts (introduced in 2006). This approach also formed the basis of Obama's *Affordable Care Act* (ACA), which was in part an attempt to bridge the gap between the competing models put forward in the 1990s. According to one estimate, 44 million Americans lacked healthcare coverage before the passage of the ACA.[92] In the increasingly partisan and polarised politics of the 2010s, the passage of the ACA didn't garner any cross-party support (notwithstanding that it was based on the approach of Senate Republicans in the 1990s and Mitt Romney's healthcare scheme while governor). It passed without a single Republican vote in either house. While the ACA significantly broadened coverage, by 2016 it was estimated that around 20–24 million people in the US remained uninsured.[93]

Beveridge and the postwar welfare state

Lloyd George was the last Liberal Party prime minister of the UK and also one of the architects of nation's earliest social welfare institutions. As Chancellor of the Exchequer, he introduced the age pension in 1908 and in 1911 he oversaw the passage of the National Insurance Act which provided workers with insurance against illness and unemployment.[94]

The post–World War II period saw an expansion of what had been, until that time, largely discrete social-insurance programs. For many, the period between 1944 and 1948 'represented the defining moment in the transition from a residual to an institutional welfare state'.[95]

While the UK was far from the only advanced economy to experience a dramatic expansion in the size of social welfare programs following the war, it did so off the back of a more comprehensive and clearly defined strategy than most countries. The 1942 Beveridge Report provided the intellectual framework for a comprehensive British welfare state. Beveridge proposed national social insurance, which he argued would provide the basis for an attack on the five giants on the road to postwar reconstruction: want, disease, ignorance, squalor and idleness.[96]

In his influential report, which set out the policy rationale for the postwar welfare state, Beveridge noted that '[t]he Plan for Social Security proposed in this Report is first and foremost a plan of how social insurance should be organised'.[97] Beveridge argued that social insurance was at the core of his conception of a welfare state:

> Under the scheme of social insurance, which forms the main feature of this plan, every citizen of working age will contribute in his appropriate class according to the security that he needs ... Each will be covered for all his needs by a single weekly contribution on one insurance document. All the principal cash payments – for unemployment, disability and retirement will continue so long as the need lasts, without means test, and will be paid from a Social Insurance Fund built up by contributions from the insured persons, from their employers, if any, and from the State.[98]

Beveridge's report built on existing work from throughout Whitehall and public-policy circles during the 1920s and 1930s and expanded the framework of national insurance first implemented by Lloyd George.[99] Beveridge had earlier advocated an 'all in' insurance scheme in 1923, which would cover sickness, unemployment, old age and workplace injuries.

Clement Atlee's landslide victory in 1945 was in large part due to the Labour Party manifesto based around the core principles of the Beveridge Report.[100] Atlee's election was remarkable in (at least) two respects. First, it was only the third Labour government in British history, following brief periods in office in 1924 and 1929–31. Second, Atlee was elected just a few months after Churchill had overseen the unconditional surrender of Nazi Germany. The result of the 1945 election demonstrated a general appetite for postwar reconstruction and social reform. Over the course of six years, the Atlee government would transform British society, with the 1948 introduction of the National Health Service (NHS) as the centrepiece.

The broader context

In pre-modern times, taxes were used almost exclusively for military conquest, roads, irrigation or building public edifices. Over the course of just the last century, the blink of an eye in the history of human civilisation, government's role has been transformed so that most taxes today are used to provide protection for those most in need – and, more specifically, to provide contingent payments for those who have suffered loss.[101]

As noted earlier, Oliver Wendell Holmes noted the civilising potential of taxation. However, it isn't quite taxes that are the civilising force; rather, it is what government does with them. The creation of the welfare state over the course of the twentieth century is perhaps the most civilising action of government in its long history.

THE PUBLIC-POLICY RATIONALES UNDERPINNING SOCIAL INSURANCE

The genesis of social insurance institutions varied considerably across countries. Imperial Germany introduced a form of social welfare in the 1880s in part to ward off radicals. In Australia, the age pension was introduced by the two largest colonies in 1900 and nationally in 1909, but other key planks of the welfare state would be implemented in a somewhat piecemeal fashion over the following decades. In some countries, such as the US, the economic and social devastation wrought by the Great Depression was the catalyst for the introduction of key social insurance measures. And in other countries, particularly in Western Europe, the need for reconstruction after World War II offered an opportunity to re-imagine society. The Beveridge Report and Atlee's ambitious response is an example of this more comprehensive approach.

In most OECD countries, the majority of the growth in the welfare state occurred between 1945 and 1985 as social-insurance programs were able to draw upon both an extended period of economic growth and a willingness on the part of many voters and governments to use higher taxation to fund more expansive programs. In most countries, the welfare state was built in a somewhat stop-start manner, with the policy rationales usually evolving as the suite of programs grew.

Multiple rationales have been offered for the development of these modern welfare programs. The most commonly cited are: (i) universal human rights; (ii) redistribution; (iii) paternalism; and (iv) insurance and risk management. These are not mutually inconsistent. In fact, I will argue that they are typically mutually reinforcing. But it is worth separately defining each in turn.

(i) Human Rights: Modern welfare programs offer a safety net that protects all. This is consistent with the many philosophical traditions that lead to the assertion of universal human rights, including many theological assertions as to the inherent value of each individual person, often tracing their way back to antiquity; the medieval natural law tradition and associated 'natural rights'; and the Enlightenment.

A number of historically important documents have encapsulated different frameworks of key individual rights and protections, with some prominent examples from the Western tradition including: the Magna Carta (1215), the English Bill of Rights (1689), the US Declaration of Independence (1776) and the French Declaration of the Rights of Man and of the Citizen (1789). For many, these universal rights directly provide a rationale for the provision of universal minimum benefits in relation to life's essentials.[102]

A more recent example of a rights framework is the UN Declaration of Human Rights,[103] which sets out a number of economic, social and cultural rights, including a number that are directly relevant to the provision by government of welfare support schemes. This framework includes the right to social security and the economic, social and cultural rights indispensable for a person's dignity.[104] Related is the right to work – and to just and favourable remuneration.[105] Finally, there is the right to a standard of living adequate for the health and wellbeing of a person and their family, including food, clothing, housing, medical care and necessary social services, and the right to security in the event of unemployment, sickness, disability, widowhood, old age or other lack of livelihood beyond one's control.[106] To apply the Declaration of Rights to the contemporary welfare state suggests providing universal access to benefits.[107]

(ii) Redistribution: Justifications for redistribution are typically underpinned by a notion of distributive justice. The two ends of the spectrum of distributive justice are *libertarianism* and *strict egalitarianism.*

Libertarians hold that people's liberties should only be constrained when absolutely necessary.[108] This is often limited to government functions such as national defence, preserving public order and the enforcement of contracts. Not surprisingly, libertarians are highly sceptical of redistribution. Robert Nozick's observation that redistribution on the basis of compulsory taxation is 'morally on par with forced labour' is illustrative.[109] In its purest form, strict egalitarianism holds that every person in society should have the same level of material income.[110]

In between these two extremes, there is a wide range of distributive justice systems relevant to assessing the merits of redistribution including those based on dessert, optimising social welfare (e.g. utilitarianism), Rawls' Difference Principle, natural law and equality of opportunity. Each of these frameworks is, to varying degrees, relevant to the design of social insurance programs.

Some of these distributive justice systems explicitly relate to notions of risk management. For example, many welfare-based distributive theories, such as utilitarianism, which seek to maximise total happiness or welfare, typically support redistributing resources from those with low marginal utility (usually the rich) to those with high marginal utility (usually the poor).[111]

Importantly, many prominent theories of distributive justice, such as Rawls'[112] as well as 'luck egalitarianism'[113] (a version of equality of opportunity), embed notions of insurance and risk management in that they allow for redistribution in order to compensate people for bad luck in the 'lottery of life'.

Many studies have focused on the negative consequences of inequality, including poorer overall public health outcomes[114] and the negative correlation between inequality and aggregate 'happiness'.[115] In addition to being inherently unfair and unethical, high levels of inequality are also socially disruptive and could lead to conflict between groups that has the potential to damage both social cohesion and material wellbeing.

(iii) Paternalism: Some social welfare programs are based on the need to assist people where decisions involve considerable complexity and uncertainty. One example is saving for one's retirement, which is difficult given the need for very long-term planning in the face of uncertainty in relation to longevity, future income, long-term average investment returns, investment volatility and future healthcare and consumption needs. In addition to the difficulty of making optimal decisions in relation to challenges involving a high degree of complexity, it is possible that some (or many) people experience cognitive biases, such as myopia (paying insufficient regard to one's future needs, particularly the distant future). As a result of these challenges, it is arguable that many individuals under-save for their retirement needs, which provides a justification for government intervention so as to avoid (or at least reduce the extent of) poverty among elderly people.

(iv) Insurance and risk management: A final rationale for social welfare programs is risk management or 'social insurance'.[116] The welfare state that arose across most advanced economies between the 1880s and World War II contained many of the risk-management practices of the private insurance industry, which by the beginning of the twentieth century already had a significant and growing presence in a number of areas, particularly life, maritime and property. As already noted, much of the welfare state legislated by Bismarck involved mandated participation in insurance pools funded largely or wholly by employers and employees.

Four rationales that are often complementary

Most social welfare programs are motivated by a combination of all four rationales. In many instances, the four rationales will be complementary. Even where a scheme is designed primarily around risk management and insurance principles, human rights, redistribution and paternalism will often be important. Human rights, which can be reflected in an aspiration of providing universal access to services, is often central to social insurance programs in that participation will often be compulsory in order to overcome adverse selection and other challenges.

Redistribution is also central to insurance (both social and private) in that, by design, an insurance scheme will redistribute resources from the pool that all contributed to, in future states of the world, in order to compensate those who have suffered loss. An additional source of redistribution for social insurance programs may arise from contributions being funded from progressive taxes rather than risk-rated premiums.

The key advantages of a greater emphasis on social insurance

While universality and redistribution are important policy rationales, a social insurance framework brings with it several advantages that are important to consider when designing programs.

The primary focus of insurance schemes is the compensation of loss. The explicit goal of many insurance arrangements is to return a person or organisation to the situation that they were in before the loss (or perhaps an even better position), as far as is practicable. Where it isn't possible to return a person or household to their former situation, a pre-agreed cash payment will sometimes be made instead. For example, an effective workers' compensation scheme will define its relationship with an insured worker such that it will provide compensation so as to enable that worker to either return to work or receive long-term income support and treatment for the injury. Structuring the relationship in terms of a well-defined outcome is advantageous both for the individual and for the overall sustainability of the scheme. Without this, there can be a tendency towards less-focused service delivery.

Outcomes-focused: Schemes designed to focus on universal access or redistribution will of course typically seek to achieve positive outcomes. But schemes primarily based on universal access or redistributive justice may end up placing a greater emphasis, in practice, on maximising the accessibility and distribution of services or benefits, potentially to the detriment of long-term outcomes.

Incentives: A key insight of economics that stands up to empirical testing in almost all settings is that individuals and organisations respond to incentives.[117] This is reflected in the design of social insurance schemes to prod individuals, firms and governments towards improved risk management and, ultimately, better outcomes. For example, an insurance program funded by risk-rated premiums will provide strong incentives for individuals and firms to demonstrate lower exposure to risk and uncertainty over time. This will tend to promote better risk management and the cost-effective mitigation of exposure.

Insurers will generally also have strong incentives to mitigate losses and provide effective compensation as both will put downward pressure on premiums. For private insurers, this improves a firm's competitive position. For public insurers, this will put downward pressure on either mandated contributions or taxes.

Targeted benefits: Public programs whose benefits are contingent on certain loss-related preconditions are often very good at targeting finite resources to those most in need. The very fact that eligibility for insurance benefits depends on loss usually means that those benefits are being provided to a household or person in need. Of course, there are instances of poor scheme design where this isn't the case (for example, where benefits are contingent on loss but are not proportionate to the loss).

Some argue that universal benefits (often justified by fundamental human rights) have advantages. Universality (or near universality) can buttress political support for a program. It can also avoid the welfare traps that are often associated with targeted schemes, such as incentives against entering the labour market and/or high effective marginal tax rates (often over 100 per cent).[118] This has been one of the key arguments in favour of a universal basic income (UBI) or negative income tax.[119] Universality can also avoid the administrative wastage of deciding who is or isn't eligible to receive welfare – which can in turn avoid the stigma attached to those in need. Neither approach is always best. With finite government resources, universality is not always an option. But where it is affordable, it should be considered.

Sustainability: A social-insurance framework is useful in forcing governments to explicitly quantify the long-term sustainability of programs. A scheme based on redistributive principles alone need not be sustainable over the longer term. For example, redistribution is typically focused on correcting the current allocation of resources, but this may need to be adjusted to account for demographic or other social change. This can be difficult in practice if beneficiaries' expectations become entrenched. In contrast, an insurance framing typically involves looking forward and ensuring that the shared pool of resources is sufficient not just to cover imminent losses, but to remedy the expected losses over the long term (as far as is practicable).

This is particularly important for schemes that make commitments to provide benefits over very long periods of time, such as old-age or disability pensions, workers' compensations schemes, mandatory transport-accident schemes and long-term care for elderly people or for those with a disability or chronic health conditions.

In 1942, Beveridge had sustainability at the front of his mind when he spoke of the key rationales for a social insurance approach:

> Whatever money is required for provision of insurance benefits, so long as they are needed, should come from a Fund to which the recipients have contributed and to which they may be required to make larger contributions if the Fund proves inadequate.[120]

Most mandatory, contributory risk-rated insurance schemes calculate and report their long-term exposure to liabilities and risk in great detail. In addition, many social insurance schemes make investments that improve their long-term sustainability even where the payoffs are indirect and difficult to measure precisely. For example, many compulsory third-party (CTP) motor vehicle accident schemes devote considerable resources to road-safety initiatives. This puts downward pressure on premiums making insurance more sustainable. Similarly, many mandatory workers' compensation schemes invest to improve economy-wide workplace safety.

This type of holistic approach to risk management is socially beneficial and can be built into a social insurance framework. Investing in preventative measures through insurance organisations can be effective as they will have rigorous methodologies for mapping the impact of such expenditure on the long-tail costs of serious injury or death.

Some governments have tried to quantify and report the long-term cost of major government programs across the public sector as a whole. Good examples include the Australian government's Intergenerational Report[121] and the US Congressional Budget Office Long-Term Budget Outlook.[122] In New Zealand, a key focus of the Investment Approach is to use rigorous actuarial modelling to identify those individuals most likely to require significant assistance over their lifetimes and to provide targeted case-management and up-front assistance to reduce those long-term costs.[123] This model will be discussed in more detail in Chapter 14.

Objective criteria: Redistribution is usually based on very high-level concepts that are often easy to define in theory but typically extremely difficult to pin down in practice. Let's take the most obvious principle underpinning redistributive justice – taking from the rich and giving to the poor to achieve equality of outcomes (or at least moving in that direction). But what does equality mean in practice? Does this mean an equal income for all people? If so, does that need to be adjusted for children – do they get the same share as adults? Even adjusting for household size and composition is fiendishly complex given economies of scale in consumption. What about adjusting for the life cycle, given that retirees generally have lower consumption needs. What about adjusting for where people live? (People in rural areas typically enjoy a much lower cost of living than people living in cities).

Is equality of income the best measure, or should it be equality of wealth? Wealth gives people a buffer to protect them against unexpected hardship. If the latter is chosen as the benchmark, how to adjust for an individual's or a household's changing stock of wealth each year, often due to shifting asset prices beyond their control. Is it realistic (or desirable) for the government to keep an up-to-date register of every individual's and household's assets?

Of course, insurance arrangements can also be tricky in practice. How does one define the loss that will trigger insurance payments? Further, how does one define what compensation or benefits are to be made to those experiencing loss (is it full or partial compensation, is it immediate compensation or assistance with long-term rehabilitation)? While not always easy to implement an effective insurance scheme, defining criteria for compensating for loss are typically more straightforward – and objective – concepts to define in practice than those underpinning many redistributive schemes.

In practice, both social insurance and redistributive approaches seek to predominantly allocate resources to those with less. Nonetheless, there are differences. A social insurance approach will direct efforts towards the achievement of clearly specified, long-term outcomes – and is committed to the explicit evaluation of whether those outcomes have been achieved. It will make use of rigorous actuarial approaches that indicate whether programs are sustainable, while using incentives, for both providers and recipients of benefits, to encourage better risk management and more effective recovery from loss.

3.
The Twentieth Century: The Era of Insurance

THE RISE IN GOVERNMENT SPENDING

The emergence of social insurance transformed government, the economy and society – for the better. For the vast majority of human history, government spending only exceeded 10 per cent of GDP during times of war. In the twentieth century, this changed and the public sector expanded dramatically as the size of government – including both direct spending and transfers – more than tripled in most advanced economies in the short space of four decades following 1945. This extraordinary shift in the scale of government largely reflects the emergence of social insurance.

Social insurance as a share of GDP

- In this book, the term 'government spending' will include both direct government consumption and transfer payments. It is important to note that when the government directly consumes factors of production, it directly contributes to GDP. Of course, it also detracts from GDP in that it takes resources from other uses. The net impact could be positive or negative.
- In contrast, when the government makes a transfer payment, it shifts resources from one person or firm to another. This is an action that does not detract from or add to GDP per se. The use of the resources by the ultimate recipient will have an impact on GDP, but not the transfer itself.

- The taxes raised for either transfers or direct spending both impose what economists refer to as a 'deadweight loss'. A deadweight loss is the economic inefficiency or distortion arising from taxation. Examples of deadweight loss include people working less hours as a result of taxes on labour, people moving house less due to stamp duty and other transaction taxes, and people saving less as a result of taxes on the income from capital. This means that taxes result in a reduction of GDP, although the uses of that taxation will offset this at least partially.
- Where taxes fund transfer payments, the transfer doesn't add to GDP. But the transfer may add to welfare, if the person being taxed values the dollar less than the person receiving the transfer payment. This will often be the case with progressive taxes.
- Where taxes fund direct consumption by government (as in defence, police and health services), that consumption of the factors of production will add to GDP. How much it adds to GDP will depend on the merits of the project. A hospital that provides much-needed services will add considerably. A bridge to nowhere will add far less.
- Broad measures of government revenue and spending capture both of these mechanisms by which assistance is provided to people. The use of broad metrics that capture overall government activity is not intended to imply that transfer payments add directly to GDP but, rather, to give the most holistic sense of the revenue burden required to fund the assistance provided.
- In some areas of social insurance, benefits are predominantly delivered through in-kind goods and services. Healthcare is probably the best example. In other areas, such as unemployment programs and the old-age pension, benefits are primarily provided through transfer payments. Since World War II, most of the increase in the size of the welfare state has occurred through higher transfer payments. This is demonstrated in Appendix 5 in relation to the US economy.

The long-run perspective: government spending in ancient societies

The relatively large size of governments in advanced economies today is a new phenomenon, less than a hundred years old. Some have estimated that government spending as a share of GDP in the times of the Roman Empire was 5 per cent of GDP.[1] In broad terms, this level of public spending continued through the Middle Ages to the early modern period, with almost all nation-states collecting no more than 10 per cent of GDP as late as World War I.[2]

Measuring taxation as a share of GDP in pre-modern societies is difficult as comprehensive public-sector account-keeping is a relatively recent phenomenon; the measuring of economic output through standardised national accounts only became widespread following World War II. In ancient societies, much taxation was in kind – either in grain, precious metals or labour. Adding to the difficulty of tracking trends is the fact that so much of the relationship between government and the private sector was informal and ad hoc. In pre-modern times, many infrastructure projects were funded by wealthy individuals, often for their own benefit or to curry favour with imperial rulers, monarchs or deities.

The labour corvée was the earliest form of taxation for which records exist.[3] A labour corvée is a requirement to provide labour, often unpaid, for a specified period of time to the state or a member of the nobility. It was sometimes used for military purposes or to raise funds for ongoing court expenses. On occasion, it could be used for large one-off projects. The pharaoh Cheops is reported to have compelled around 100,000 men to work three months a year for twenty years to build the pyramid ostentatiously housing his tomb. On an even grander scale, over 700,000 men were said to have been involved in the construction of the first Chinese Emperor's Palace, while around 800,000 were forced to build a provincial highway during the Han Dynasty (200 BCE–200 CE).[4]

Taxation rates for some could be quite high in ancient societies. Certain Egyptian peasants paid the pharaoh one-fifth of their output, while some Indian famers paid one-quarter of their output to Mauryan kings (300–100 BCE). In part, these tax rates reflected the limited tax base of agricultural societies. The scope for governments to tax was to a large extent limited by how much surplus to subsistence the agricultural workforce could produce. This also impacted on the extent to which the broader economy could support specialised, non-agricultural occupations.

Within larger empires, tax rates could vary considerably by region. For example, the Roman Empire exacted only nominal taxes in Spain and Sicily. In contrast, the fertile regions of Asia were taxed at a higher rate – generally one-tenth of perishable goods and one-fifth to one-sixth of grains. In outlying regions, such as Gaul, Britain and Spain, a corvée would often be exacted to construct roads and aqueducts.[5] Similarly, during the Chou regime (1050–250 BCE), taxes on regions near the capital were one-twentieth of total produce, while outlying provinces were obliged to contributed between a fifth and a quarter.[6]

In pre-modern China, taxation rates also varied over time. During periods of social and political upheaval or military expansion, taxes were often high, reflecting the cost of maintaining a larger military. This was the case, for example, during the period of the six dynasties from 220 to 581 CE as well as during the militarily aggressive Mongol Yan Dynasty from 1279 to 1368 CE. In contrast, during periods of stability and economic growth – as in the Song Dynasty (960–1279 CE) and the latter half of the Ming Dynasty (1368–1644 CE) – there was only minimal corvée and low rates of taxation on land and commercial activity.[7]

The limitations of taxation in ancient societies, in turn, imposed limits on what governments could spend. Governments were significantly smaller, relative to the economy, and more limited in scope than they are today. Keeping order was fundamental, and this included both keeping the peace at home and defending the borders. Hammurabi's Code enjoined Babylonian kings to ensure that 'the strong do not harm the weak'.[8] Vance argues that this core call on government extended to the code prescribing an early form of social insurance:

> We find provision that a city in which any man should be robbed of his property should be under obligation to indemnify him for his loss, while if the city and the governor permitted such disorder that a person lost his life, the family of the murdered man were entitled to be indemnified from the public treasury.[9]

In most ancient societies, military spending was the largest item of government expenditure, often by some margin. It usually constituted over half of total government expenditure during the Roman Empire.[10] This was the case up until the twentieth century, where military spending was regularly the biggest item in the budget for many states, even if it only represented a modest share of GDP.

Often, new taxes had to be introduced or existing taxes adjusted in order to fund military requirements (or adventures). In the fourth century BCE, the Roman Republic imposed a *tributum* or direct tax on property to help fund soldiers' wages. This was set at less than 1 per cent of the value of the landholder's property.

In addition to maintaining domestic order and funding the military, governments provided other, more narrowly defined functions for the broader community. Webber and Wildavsky argue that:

> in the earliest ancient governments, the first functional specialization we know about began with irrigation. In the Sumerian temple communities of southern Mesopotamia early in the third millennium BC, in predynastic Egypt, and in Shang China, temple priests organized the human energy that created the agricultural base for city civilization.[11]

This core function is also reflected in the Roman Empire's huge investment in aqueducts. During the second half of the second century BCE, an aqueduct was constructed that cost 45 million *denarii*. In a sign that project cost blowouts have always been a feature of major infrastructure ventures, aggrieved Roman taxpayers of the day could have pointed out that the entire Parthenon had cost only 2 million *denarii*.[12]

Transport was another key area of expenditure. Whether it was in ancient Mesopotamia or the expansive Roman Empire, the development of an effective road network may have been motivated by a desire to be able to more efficiently move troops and collect taxes. Once established, however, this infrastructure also facilitated commerce and improved living standards for the general population, even if as a by-product.

It's not only in ancient times that governments were small. As shown in Table 3.1, which is sourced from the work of Peter Lindert, during the period ranging from 1600 to the second half of the nineteenth century, almost all governments operated on nominal revenues of less than 15 per cent of GDP. The exception was the Mughal empire in the seventeenth century, which collected 17.7 per cent of its GDP via tax, still low by modern standards.

Table 3.1: Government expenditure as a share of GDP, 1600–1869[13]

	c. 1600	1650–1699	1700–1749	1750–1799	1800–1850	1850–1869
Japan			12.3			10.9
China			4.0–8.0		6.5	
India (Mughal)	17.7					
Ottoman Empire	2.5	2.8	3.0	3.5	4.5	6.5
Russia						12.4
Spain		10.0				
Netherlands				13.5		11.5
England/UK	2.2	4.2	7.4	9.0	7.5	

Taxation and spending in the UK from the middle ages through to modern times

The UK has one of the highest quality long-term records for government spending and revenue. The Pipe Rolls are a relatively accurate ongoing set of records for government revenue and spending covering the period between 1130 and 1833 for England and Wales. Figure 3.4 shows central government expenditure as a share of GDP for the period 1689–2018.

Government spending in England and Wales as a share of GDP hovered between 5 and 10 per cent of GDP between 1689 and 1918, rising above 15 per cent only during major wars (the War of Spanish Succession, the Seven Years' War, the War of American Independence and the Napoleonic Wars).[14] As recently as 1914, government spending as a share of GDP was under 10 per cent.

Government spending in advanced economies during the twentieth century

Public-sector revenue as a share of GDP followed a similar trajectory across most advanced economies over the course of the twentieth century. Figure 3.1 shows government spending as a share of GDP for selected advanced economies over the period 1880–2011.[15] Average public spending remained at around 10 per cent of GDP throughout the period 1880–1914. Unsurprisingly, there were sharp spikes in government spending during both world wars. During the interwar years, the average share of GDP increased (relative to the turn of the century) to around 15 per cent as some countries began to introduce social welfare programs.

Following the exertion of two world wars, the period of most sustained change occurred between 1945 and 1985, during which government revenue and spending both increased markedly. During this period, the share of government spending more than doubled from 20 per cent of GDP to around half of the economy. Since 1985, government revenue as a share of GDP has not increased, on average, across this subsection of countries from the advanced economies.

Figure 3.1: Government as a share of GDP: Selected advanced economies, 1880–2011

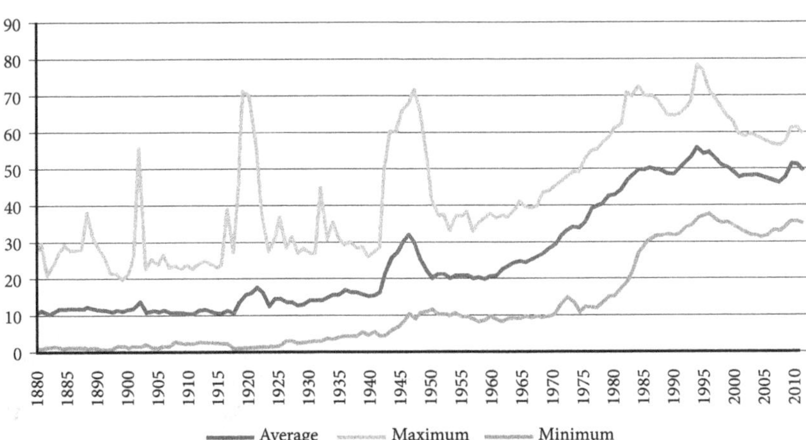

Between 1950 and 1985, government increased as a share of GDP on average across the selected economies by around 30 per cent of GDP (jumping from 20.5 to 50 per cent). In the quarter-century between 1985 and 2010, the size of government as a share of the economy stalled on average across this set of countries. Even though government as a whole didn't grow, the size of social insurance programs continued to increase by 5.3 percentage points during this period. (See Appendix 3 for a summary of changes in the size of government and social insurance spending across selected advanced economies between 1950 and 2010.)[16]

The trajectory in the role of government within the broader economy was similar across both high- and low-taxing OECD countries. Across almost all OECD countries, government spending as a share of GDP trended up, markedly, between 1900 and 1985 and has remained broadly stable since then.

Government spending in the US since 1900

As Figure 3.2 shows, government spending across all three levels of government in the US increased from 7.8 per cent in 1900 to around 40 per cent in 2020. This places the US below the mean for advanced economies. The *increase* in total government spending in the US over the past 120 years is around one third of the entire economy. This increase in the size of government occurred across all three levels of government between 1920 and 2020: local government more than doubled as a share of GDP, state government increased 10-fold and the federal government increased over seven-fold.

Figure 3.2: US government spending as a share of GDP, 1900–2020[17]

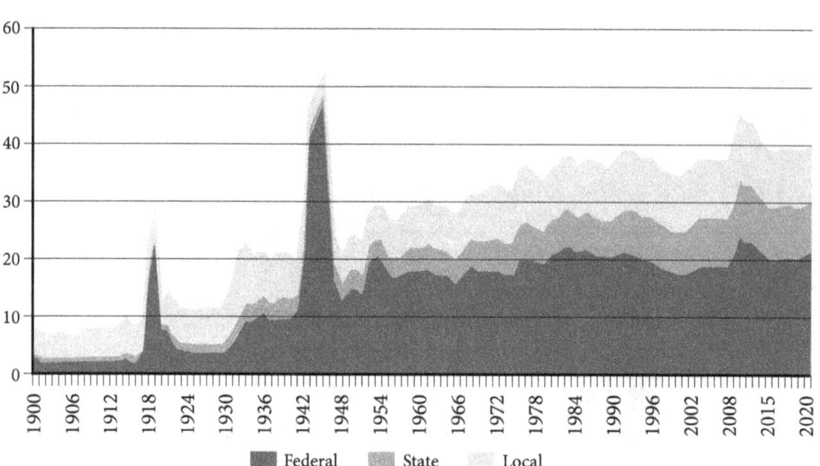

Since World War II, government spending increased across all three levels of government. Between 1950 and 2019, the federal government increased around 6 percentage points (from 14.2 to 20.7 per cent), state government increased around 5.5 percentage points (from 3.6 to 9 per cent) and local government increased around 3.5 percentage points (from

5.7 to 9.3 per cent). Between 1950 and the surge in government spending in response to Covid-19, state and local government spending increased more in proportional terms than federal spending (state more than doubled as a share of GDP).

Government spending in Australia since 1900

Since 1900, Australia has experienced a similar evolution in the size of government as other advanced economies. During the period from 1900 to 2020, spending in Australia across all levels of government increased from around 15–20 per cent of GDP to around 40 per cent. Like that of the US, Australia's level of spending sits below the average for advanced economies. Figure 3.3 shows the trajectory of total government spending as a share of GDP in Australia from 1850 to 2015.[18]

Compared to many other advanced economies, government spending in Australia was relatively high in 1900. This may reflect the high cost, in per capita terms, of providing key transport infrastructure and utilities for a small population dispersed across a large geographic area. It may also reflect the fact that, as a relatively new nation state, Australia was still investing heavily in core infrastructure and utilities. Moreover, Australia nationalised some of these functions earlier than many other advanced economies.[19]

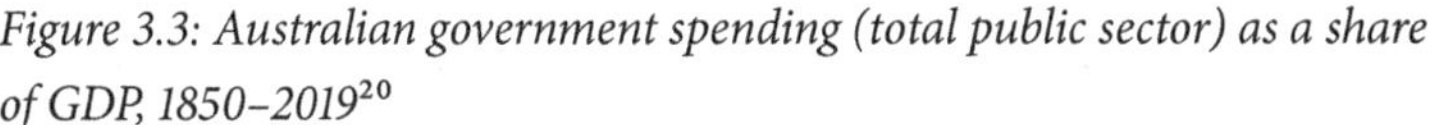

Figure 3.3: Australian government spending (total public sector) as a share of GDP, 1850–2019[20]

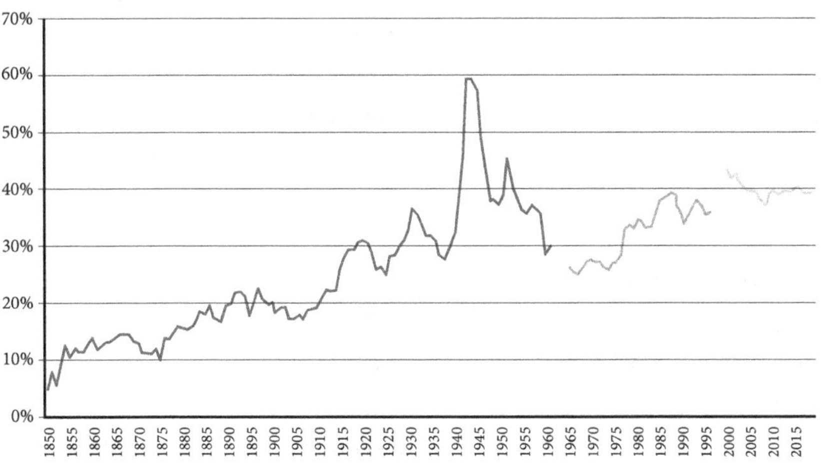

THE EXPANSION OF GOVERNMENT: A STORY OF SOCIAL INSURANCE

In broad terms, the key functions of government didn't change materially from ancient times until well into the twentieth century. Whether it was the Sumerians, the predynastic Egyptians, the Roman Empire, the great Chinese dynasties, medieval England, revolutionary America or Federation-era Australia, the core functions of government were the same: funding the the military and the palace, constructing transport infrastructure and utilities (largely water), and maintaining public order.

Before the twentieth century, the only material change in the role of government was an emerging role for the state in funding mass primary (and later secondary) education.[21] This occurred in the second half of the nineteenth century and was originally led by Germany and the US, with other advanced economies soon to follow. Lindert calculates the support per child as a share of average adult income (similar to spending/GDP), and finds that by 1880, in a number of advanced economies, the level of education support per child was between 1 and 2 per cent of average adult income: Germany (1.68); Sweden (1.47); France (1.36); Belgium (1.36); the Netherlands (1.22); the US (1.12); and Italy (1.03).[22] By 1910, some countries had increased support levels to over 2 per cent of average adult income: Germany (2.83); Sweden (2.72); the Netherlands (2.72); England/Wales (2.60); and Belgium (2.01).

Apart from this modest investment in primary education, the core functions of government in Australia, the US, the UK and Europe in 1914 were not dissimilar to those of governments dating back to antiquity. In the following graphs, I have characterised these longstanding areas of focus (the military, administration, transport infrastructure and water infrastructure) as 'Roman Empire' functions in order to reinforce how recently large-scale social insurance emerged as a major function of the public sector.

Roman Empire functions would dominate government spending in most OECD countries until the end of World War I – and for some until the end of World War II. As noted in Figure 3.4, it was then rapidly supplemented by social insurance programs that would, within a handful of decades, come to dominate government spending and positively transform both the broader economy and society. These programs focused on either transfer payments contingent on loss or the provision of in-kind services.[23]

The dramatic rise in social spending

The increase in the size of government since World War II reflected a material change in the *role* of government. In most advanced economies, spending on social services was near zero as late as 1900. By 1930, it had risen to 5 per cent of GDP in Germany – one of the first countries to introduce social welfare legislation under Bismarck – and ranged between 0.6 and 2.2 per cent of GDP in Australia, the US and the UK. This changed after 1945, and by 2016, spending on social services ranged between 18 and 30 per cent of GDP across the OECD.

Price Fishback compares the size of social welfare expenditures across OECD countries between 1900 and 2003.[24] A selection of key economies is included in Table 3.2. In addition to calculating gross public expenditure as a share of GDP, Fishback compares net public expenditure with the sum of net public and private expenditure. Net public expenditure on social welfare adjusts gross payments by government for any taxes paid on benefits, including consumption taxes and any tax concessions. Net public *and* private expenditure adds in net private expenditures, both mandatory and compulsory.

Table 3.2 shows that all advanced economies experienced rapid growth in the welfare state following World War II. Some additional features of Fishback's calculations are noteworthy. In a number of European countries, net public benefits are materially lower than gross public benefits, largely reflecting the fact that many welfare recipients pay significant consumption taxes (e.g. –6.7 per cent of GDP in Sweden, –2.9 per cent in France, –2.7 per cent in Spain, and –2.2 per cent in Italy).

In several countries, private-sector insurance adds materially to social welfare, most notably in the US. This largely reflects high levels of expenditure on private health insurance. After private insurance is added to *net* public insurance, the total size of social insurance in the US is similar to that in most Western European countries. If compulsory superannuation is added to the net public and private measure for Australia, it would be at a similar level. This would appear reasonable given that superannuation deductions are mandatory and not accessible until retirement (other than in exceptional circumstances). Annual payments out of superannuation accounts are significant and currently constitute about 5 per cent of GDP. Including this in the calculations would lift Australia in the ranking.

Table 3.2: Estimates of social welfare expenditure as a proportion of GDP, 1900–2003[25]

Country	Gross public			Net public	Net public + private
	1900	1930	2003	2003	2003
France	0.6	1.1	28.7	25.8	28.0
Germany	0.6	5.0	27.3	26.4	27.6
Sweden	0.9	2.6	31.3	24.6	26.1
United States	0.6	0.6	16.2	17.6	25.2
United Kingdom	1.0	2.6	20.6	19.9	24.6
Netherlands	0.4	1.2	20.7	18.3	23.1
Italy	0.0	0.1	24.2	22.0	22.3
Canada	0.0	0.3	17.3	17.2	21.2
Australia	0.0	2.1	17.9	18.2	20.6
Japan	0.2	0.2	17.7	18.2	20.6
Spain	0.0	0.1	20.3	17.6	17.7
New Zealand	1.1	2.4	18.0	15.1	15.5
Korea	Na	Na	5.7	7.8	8.0
Mexico	0.0	0.0	6.8	7.6	7.5

It is also interesting to contrast the size of the welfare state in Western Europe, North America and Oceania with that in Korea and Mexico. In these latter two economies, the size of the welfare state is only a third as large, as a share of GDP, as many Western European and North American economies, reflecting at least in part their stage of overall economic development.

The changing role of government in the UK

The UK has the longest continuous and reliable source of data on government spending. Figure 3.4 shows spending by major function as a share of GDP in the UK from 1689 to 2016. The data for the UK reflects how recent and how significant the shift to social insurance has been. Government spending over the past 350 years in the UK had been built around the military, largely ebbing and flowing with the demands of war. In Figure 3.4, the War of Spanish Succession (1701–14), the Seven Years' War (1756–63), the War of American Independence (1775–83) and the Napoleonic Wars (1789–15) stand out, lifting government spending to as much as 20 per cent of GDP.

In addition to the military, but imposing far less demand on the public purse, governments also built roads and performed other civil functions, such as administration and keeping the royal household well housed, clothed and fed. As with most governments through history, public spending typically constituted around 5–10 per cent of GDP, except in times of military emergency.

Like much of Western Europe, North America and Oceania, the UK started to fund mass education in the late nineteenth century, first in primary, and then in secondary and higher education. As a share of GDP, public spending on education has been largely constant since the end of World War II.

Throughout most of the postwar period, government spending patterns have expanded markedly from those of governments going back to antiquity: the military; the palace; and basic transport and utilities infrastructure. To reflect this, Figure 3.4 divides spending into three categories: 'Roman Empire' spending; education spending (which began to emerge in the late nineteenth century); and the social insurance programs of the twentieth century. What stands out in Figure 3.4 is the recent, sudden emergence of social insurance around 1914, which after just a few decades now dominates the public sector. It grew from nothing in 1900 to constituting over half of public-sector expenditure and over 20 per cent of GDP by 1980.

Figure 3.4: UK government spending by function (per cent of GDP), 1689–2016[26]

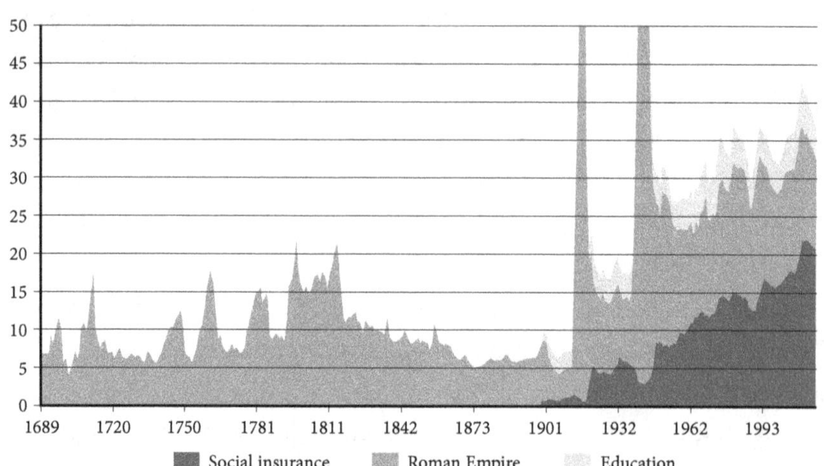

The changing role of government in the US

As it has grown as a share of the economy, the role of government in the US economy has evolved in much the same way as in the UK. As with many other advanced economies, overall spending as a share of GDP rose sharply after World War I and broadly stabilised after 1980. Appendix 7 sets out a detailed trajectory of government as a share of GDP since 1900. By 2020, social insurance constituted more than half of all federal government expenditure – a share that was continuing to grow.[27] In 2011, Ezra Klein described the US government as 'an insurance conglomerate protected by a large, standing army'. In a similar vein, Paul Krugman had earlier argued that 'loosely speaking, the post-cold-war federal government is a big pension fund that also happens to have an army'.[28]

Harvard historian David Moss takes a broader view of government and its role in risk management. He argues that there have been three phases of public-sector risk management (defined broadly) in the US since 1789.[29] The first phase, which lasted until 1900, he labels 'Security for Business'. It was during this period that the government legislated a range of measures intended to promote trade and investment, including limited liability for passive investors, banking regulation, bankruptcy laws, a fixed exchange rate and the enforcement of property rights. The second phase, running from 1900 to 1960, provided 'Security for Workers' via measures such as workers' compensation, unemployment insurance and retirement income protection. This period also included the emergence of the welfare state following the Second New Deal. Moss labels the third phase, which commenced around 1960, as 'Security for All', since government's role expanded beyond the workplace to include risk management in a much broader range of contexts: natural disaster relief; health, safety and environmental regulations; and product liability laws.

Moss's framing includes regulatory measures, such as the introduction of limited liability, that imposed little direct cost on government or taxpayers. Nonetheless, many of these measures have been fundamental in laying the platform for the United States' sustained economic growth. While this book focuses on social insurance programs, other risk-management tools deployed by government have had and will undoubtedly continue to have a significant impact on productivity and growth.

Why did the welfare state emerge?

It is beyond the scope of this book to examine the many reasons for the rise of the welfare state and how these reasons vary across countries. Peter Lindert examines this issue in great detail across most major advanced economies and persuasively argues that it is due primarily to four key factors.[30]

The first was the extension of the voting rights. This was not a straightforward, linear phenomenon. For example, as the franchise was extended to middle-class men in nineteenth-century Britain, it tended to reduce support for poor relief. In contrast, as the franchise was extended more broadly, it tended to increase support for poor relief and welfare programs more generally. Moreover, as voting rights were extended to women, political support for healthcare and childcare tended to rise.

The second key factor was the macroeconomic and social shocks of the first half of the twentieth century. Many welfare programs were created in response to economic depressions (for example, the Great Depression and the subsequent Second New Deal in the US). Two world wars also increased support for a more comprehensive social safety net in many countries.

A third factor, which affected the breadth and size of the welfare state in some countries, was the degree of ethnic fractionalisation. The more heterogeneous a population, the greater the risk that taxpayers would see the recipients of welfare as undeserving, particularly if those paying taxes and those receiving welfare were, predominantly, from different ethnic groups.

Finally, some of the more costly programs in the modern welfare state are driven by population ageing: the age pension, healthcare and long-term aged care. In many countries, support for funding these programs has been driven by the electoral power of older voters, a phenomenon that is unlikely to recede as populations age further over coming decades.

Similarities and differences across countries

Not every advanced economy implemented social welfare programs in the same way, or according to the same chronology. In the US, social insurance didn't start emerging until the Second New Deal of the mid-1930s. In the UK and many parts of Western Europe, social spending started rising two or more decades earlier.

There were also differences in the size of social insurance programs relative to the economy. In the US and the UK, social insurance rose to around 20 per cent of GDP across all levels of government by the 1980s. In many Western European nations, it had risen to around 25–30 per cent of GDP.

More than anything else, what stands out is that the similarities across Australia, the US, the UK and Europe in the arc of government spending over the past 150 years are far more striking than any differences. In all these societies, the role of government in both economic and social affairs was totally transformed, largely during the four decades following World War II. What had been a relatively unchanging core set of functions performed by government for thousands of years was turned on its head in a generation. As a result, the scope and ambition of government grew greater than ever before. Government has already done much to fulfil this ambition, but there is more to do.

A PRECISE DEFINITION OF SOCIAL INSURANCE

There is no universally agreed definition of which government programs fall within the category of 'social insurance'. For present purposes, social insurance will be defined more broadly than the definitions adopted by some economists. It will include all programs where payments or in-kind benefits are contingent on loss or harm. This is closer to the definition used by the OECD (and which is used to calculate the percentages in Table 3.2 developed by Fishback). Several points of clarification are worth making.

First, social insurance will not be limited to programs funded by 'contributory' taxes or premiums. While this can be an important distinction when designing a particular social insurance scheme, for present purposes it is not the most material dividing line. There are a number of instances of programs that provide insurance that are funded from consolidated revenue (i.e. general taxation revenue) or from sources that are not directly linked to benefits. For example, in the US, most states fund unemployment insurance through contributory taxes levied on employers. Typically, this is then directly linked to eligibility for benefits for workers who lose their jobs through no fault of their own. In contrast, in Australia and parts of Western Europe, unemployment benefits are paid out of consolidated revenue and may be distributed to people who have never paid income taxes. While this constitutes a material difference in scheme design, both types of arrangement are fundamentally about providing a measure of insurance or protection from risky and uncertain labour market outcomes.

Second, social insurance will include some means-tested programs. While eligibility for many programs is linked (at least to a degree) to contributions made, many countries either cap benefits or taper benefits above certain income thresholds. Means-testing is an extreme form of this type of structure but, where it is present, it doesn't necessarily mean that the scheme isn't, in effect, a risk-management mechanism.

Third, social insurance will include some programs that involve universal service provision. Publicly provided healthcare in Australia and the UK are examples of programs that are a combination of universal services and contingent services. Access to a general practitioner (GP) to discuss one's overall health and lifestyle is something that most people would consider to be a right. This type of service is at least partly publicly funded and universally accessible in most advanced economies.

However, much health expenditure is contingent on a certain outcome. For example:

- One's right to access the emergency department and any subsequent hospitalisation depends on having had an accident or illness that requires urgent attention.
- Eligibility to subsidised medicine and drugs depends upon a medical assessment of a condition that warrants access to the drug and, therefore, the subsidy.
- Accessing specialist services or high-cost testing usually requires a GP referral.

While in some countries, many parts of the health system provide for universal, non-means-tested access, the system as a whole tends to be categorised as a social insurance scheme in that the majority of benefits are contingent on certain events or outcomes. Moreover, those elements that are universal services, such as vaccinations or a preventative visit to one's doctor, are intimately intertwined with the effectiveness of contingent services. As will be argued, it is only through a holistic approach to funding both the preventative services and the contingent services that the system as a whole can operate more effectively. Quite often, particularly in countries with healthcare provided by multiple layers of government or by different silos within a government, the absence of a holistic approach results in worse outcomes.

Some economists use a narrower definition of social insurance, which is appropriate in many circumstances. For example, Krueger and Meyer define social insurance as 'compulsory, contributory government programs that provide benefits to individuals if certain conditions are met'.[31] By 'contributory', Kreuger and Meyer refer to taxes or premiums that are dedicated to funding the contingent benefits. Adopting a similar definition, Martin Feldstein distinguishes between social welfare programs and social insurance by arguing that the former are means-tested while the latter are 'event conditioned'.[32] Means-testing can take on a number of forms. Some programs are designed to assist those in poverty and have a similar policy rationale to targeted measures that evolved long before the modern welfare state such as poor relief in the eighteenth and nineteenth centuries. Measures such as these are largely motivated by redistributive rather than risk-management goals. In contrast, some means-testing of contingent benefits aims to balance risk-management goals with the need to ensure that finite resources go to those most in need.[33]

The reason for using a broader definition of social insurance is that the focus of this book is on improving the performance of insurance mechanisms that are either government-funded, mandated by government or heavily regulated by government. The potential for government to improve its role as a manager of risk and funder of service delivery can only be meaningfully considered using a broader conception of social insurance.

IMPACT ON ECONOMIC GROWTH AND LABOUR FORCE PARTICIPATION

Some have argued that a large welfare state may create economic inefficiencies that outweigh any benefits arising from transfer payments or services provided. Two principal sources of inefficiency are typically identified. First are the disincentives to work and save that occur as a result of the taxes that fund welfare programs. Second is the potential for social insurance to discourage work on the part of those receiving benefits.

Macroeconomic correlations

It is difficult to clearly establish causation in relation to macroeconomic phenomena. This reflects both the complexity of macroeconomic dynamics and also the lack of data points. Even where natural experiments exist, it can be difficult to estimate the impacts of macroeconomic events.[34] Correlation is a useful, even if limited, starting point. When it comes to the overarching impact of the welfare state on the macroeconomy, there is little evidence of a material negative impact of a large welfare state on either GDP performance or labour-force participation. Lindert finds that 'there has been no clearly negative correlation between social spending and GDP per capita anytime since the dawn of widespread social insurance in the 1880s'.[35] This holds true both for GDP per capita levels and growth rates.

Even if there were a positive correlation between the welfare state and GDP, this then begs the question of causation. Are countries with a large welfare state wealthy because of the existence of social insurance – that is, the investment in people via health systems and publicly funded training? Or, alternatively, do wealthy, productive societies have the luxury of investing in social welfare even if it impedes their growth? The empirical literature here is mixed. Several prominent studies have found non-negative results, but not a clear causal link between the size of the welfare state and broader economic outcomes.[36] Richard Kneller et al. find that in assessing the impact of the size of government, it is important to assess both sides of the budget – in other words, both the potentially negative impacts of taxation and the potentially positive impacts of productive investment.[37]

Economic impacts of specific programs

Identifying the economic impacts of specific welfare programs may be easier than pointing to the impact of the welfare state as a whole. While some studies have found a link between benefits and propensity to work, the statistically significant link is generally not found to be large.[38]

Gemmell, Kneller and Sanz suggest categorising welfare programs along two dimensions:

- Whether they involve investment (for example, in peoples' health or training) or transfer payments.
- Whether they are funded by efficient (less distortionary) or inefficient taxes.[39]

Not surprisingly, of the four possible permutations, they find that programs that invest in human capital and are funded by efficient taxes are the best, in economic terms. Programs that involve transfer payments and are funded from distortionary taxes have the least positive economic impact.

Even when it comes to examining the impact of specific programs, the empirical literature is mixed. One of the most intensely studied areas of relevance is the impact of taxation rates or the receipt of benefits on the supply of labour.

Principal sources of economic gain

While the potential for negative economic impacts needs to be acknowledged, social insurance also generates substantial positive economic outcomes, though they can be difficult to clearly disentangle from overall macroeconomic trends. The main sources of economic gain include the following:

- Many welfare programs achieve economies of scale, especially where services are universally provided. Despite the cliché of the 'bloated bureaucracy', administrative costs in many welfare programs are lower than private-sector equivalents (for example, in aged-care pensions, where costs for some programs are less than 1 per cent).
- Many social insurance programs invest in human capital while at the same time providing assistance to those in need.
- Social insurance can overcome problems that can arise where people with a high risk of experiencing harm dominate the risk pool, pushing up premiums and reducing the incentive for those with an average or low risk of experiencing loss participating. This is labelled 'adverse selection'. In some policy areas, the origin of the welfare state was to mandate participation, overcoming this problem. This remains a powerful force for economic gain.
- Many programs are supported by efficient taxes, including broad consumption taxes and so-called sin taxes.
- Parental leave and childcare foster productivity by increasing labour force participation by highly skilled women and reducing career interruptions.

THE RISE OF PRIVATE INSURANCE

In most advanced economies, spending on gross private-sector insurance premiums has increased over recent decades. According to the OECD, between 1983 and 2018, spending on gross premiums has increased, on average, from 5.1 per cent of GDP to 8.9 per cent of GDP per annum.[40] Howard Kunreuther and his co-authors estimate that, in 2007, annual premiums in the US totalled around US$2 trillion, relative to a total economic output of $14 trillion. This $2 trillion was comprised of $760 billion for private health insurance and managed care, $667 billion for life and health companies and $448 billion for property/casualty companies. In total, these premiums counted for 13.3 percent of GDP.[41] Swiss Re has compiled data on private insurance premiums by country since 1968, with comprehensive data available on both life and non-life insurance premiums as a share of GDP since 1980.[42] As Table 3.3 shows, in 2018, private-sector insurance constituted more than 10 per cent of GDP in six countries.

Table 3.3: Countries with the highest private-sector insurance penetration, 2018[43]

Country	Life (per cent GDP)	Non-life (per cent GDP)	Total (per cent GDP)
1. Taiwan	17.5	3.4	**20.9**
2. Hong Kong	16.8	1.3	**18.1**
3. South Africa	10.3	2.6	**12.9**
4. South Korea	6.1	5.0	**11.1**
5. United Kingdom	8.3	2.3	**10.6**
6. Denmark	7.6	2.8	**10.4**
7. Finland	8.1	1.8	**9.9**
8. Netherlands	1.7	7.5	**9.2**
9. Japan	6.7	2.1	**8.8**
10. France	5.8	3.1	**8.9**
United States	2.9	4.3	**7.2**
Australia	3.5	2.1	**5.6**

The interdependence between social and private insurance

In many areas, social insurance and private insurance complement one another. For example, many households and businesses insure property against loss for natural disasters. But governments still play a significant role in pre-disaster mitigation and post-disaster recovery and income support. Public and private insurance also coexist in relation to healthcare services in many OECD countries. Publicly funded health services provide the cornerstone of social insurance, yet private insurance also plays an important role. Indeed, in many countries it is heavily subsidised by taxpayers or mandated in certain circumstances.

SOCIAL AND PRIVATE INSURANCE IN 2020

The size of annual transfer payments through all public and private social insurance programs in Australia is staggering. By 2020, it was approaching half a trillion dollars per year – and it is still rising. The key areas of public and private expenditure are set out in Table 3.5. Together, social and private insurance total around A$500 billion in Australia per annum, which constitutes over one-quarter of Australia's total GDP of around A$2 trillion.

Philanthropy also plays a critical role in Australia, totalling around A$30 billion per annum ($12.5 billion from individuals and $17.5 billion from business).[44] This supports around 56,000 registered non-profit organisations that operate throughout the community. The impact of philanthropy is far greater than these headline figures suggest, given the impact of countless volunteers. It is worth noting that philanthropy remains similar in size relative to the economy as it did in the records of an earlier era compiled by Peter Lindert. Much as in Western Europe, social insurance has not displaced philanthropy but rather complemented it.

Table 3.4 groups social insurance programs into broad themes. This reflects the interdependency (and overlap) between major programs. For example, much of the expenditure of transport-accident schemes, workers' compensation schemes and veterans' programs will occur within the broader health system. By far the two largest components of social and private insurance identified in Table 3.4 are healthcare (worth over A$250 billion) and old-age income support (A$150 billion). This is a far larger share of GDP than those areas of expenditure that often capture the most media commentary, such as unemployment insurance at just A$16 billion. Most revenue for social insurance in Australia comes from general taxes, with the principal exceptions of workers' compensation, mandatory third-party transport-accident insurance, mandatory retirement savings accounts (superannuation) and income-contingent loans in lieu of up-front university fees. Benefits are distributed through a mixture of cash payments and in-kind services.

It should be stressed that, given the complexity of the modern welfare state, Tables 3.4 and 3.5 are not exhaustive representations of welfare spending. They do capture the major areas of expenditure, but a range of smaller programs and taxpayer subsidies are not included. This doesn't affect the overall conclusions that can be drawn.

Social and private insurance in the US in 2020

Table 3.5 sets out the key expenditures on social and private insurance in the US in 2020. It is broken down according to spending at the federal, state and local levels, as well as private insurance. The fourth column indicates transfers from the federal to state and local governments in each area of risk management. Table 3.5 demonstrates that the overall amount of funding for social and private insurance, relative to the economy, is substantial. Together, these risk-management programs total around US$7 trillion. There are substantial contributions from the federal government, from state/local governments and also from the private sector. As in Australia, the funding of the health system and related programs (US$3.9 trillion) and the old-age income system (US$2 trillion), is far larger than any other components. (Appendices 1 and 2 set out the data sources for Tables 3.4 and 3.5, respectively.)

Table 3.4: Social and private insurance in Australia in 2021 ($A billion)[45]

	Public program	Public p.a.	Private p.a.	Revenue source	Benefit distribution
Health	Cth	86.4		Consolidated revenue (CR)	In-kind benefits: combination of on-demand and rationed
	State	56.2		CR	
	Private insurance		16.7 payments (5.9 rebates)	Private	
	Out of pocket		29.8	Private	
	Other institutions		13.5	Various	
Workers' compensation	Mandatory insurance pool	8.25	4.0	Mandated employer contributions	In-kind, cash
Transport accident	Mandatory insurance pool		2.2	Mandated employer contributions	In-kind, cash
Veterans' affairs		7.7		CR	
Disability	NDIS	20.4		CR	In-kind: distributed in part by client choice
	Carers' allowance	9.4		CR	Cash
	Disability support pension	17.8			
TOTAL HEALTH AND LONG-TERM CARE (approx.)		**200**	**70**		**>> A$250 billion**

	Public program	Public p.a.	Private p.a.	Revenue source	Benefit distribution
Old-age income	Age-related payments	50.1 Pension	11.5 Life benefits	CR	Cash in-kind benefits
	Super-annuation	41.1 Tax conc.	40 >> Pensions	Mandated + vol. savings	Tax benefits for conts Investment returns
Supported living	Aged care	21.2	4.9		
TOTAL AGE (approx.)		**110**	**50 >>**		**>>$150 bn**
Unemployment	UI Active labour market	20.2 2		CR	Cash in-kind benefits
Family assistance	Family tax benefit	18.3		CR	Cash
	Child care subsidy	7.9			
	PPL	2.4			
Homelessness	Public housing	4.3		CR	In-kind, rationed
University education	HECS/ HELP ICL (repayments)	6.3 (3.8)		CR Contingent loan	Up-front cash Contingent repayment
	Income support	3.6		CR	Cash, means-tested
Property / natural disasters	NDRRA	1.0		CR	In-kind, cash
	General ins. fire + ind.		11.9 2.1		
FEG	Contribu-tions	0.16			
TOTAL (approx.)		**350**	**150**		**>>$500 bn**

Table 3.5: Social and private insurance in the US in 2020 (US$ billion)[46]

	Public program	Fed. $bn p.a.	Transfers (Fed. – S/L)	State $bn p.a.	Private $bn p.a.	Revenue source	TOTAL $bn p.a
Health	Medicare	750					
	Medicaid	447	(447)	686 597			
	Medical services	147.9		254.5	1200 376	Ins OOP	
	Workers' comp. (M)	5.8		62.3			
	Veterans' affairs	236					
	Disability – OASDI	149.5					
	Transport accident (M)						3886
Old age	OASDI	948.3			678		
	Govt employee pensions	53.8		344.1			2024
Unemploy-ment	Cont. schemes	29.9	(7)	38.4			61
Property/ casualty	Natural disasters	10–88					121 (approx.)
	Private				634		634
Family assistance		287	(114)	122			295
Housing		51.2	(8)	57.6			101
GROSS TOTAL		**3194**	**(576)**	**1564**	**888**		
NET TOTAL		**2618**		**1564**	**888**		**7071**

The relative size of social insurance programs

One thing that is striking from Tables 3.4 and 3.5 is the massive disparity between the size of social insurance programs. In Australia, the health system and old-age income supports are around fifteen and ten times larger than unemployment benefits, respectively. In the US, the health system is around sixty times larger than state and federal unemployment insurance spending combined. This is reflected across the OECD.

In the two decades leading up to Covid-19, unemployment insurance constituted 0.4 per cent of GDP in the US, 0.7 per cent of GDP in Australia and 0.8 per cent of GDP across the OECD.[47] The disparity in the size of these programs raises questions as to whether some programs are given too little emphasis. Are labour-market programs so small relative to health and retirement income programs due to benefit levels that are too low or eligibility criteria that are too tightly defined? Does this have a negative impact not just on the welfare of recipients but, more broadly, on people's willingness to take risks in the labour market? The latter may have material, negative, long-term economic consequences.

4.
How Does Insurance Work in Practice?

There are three principal risk-management mechanisms: (i) risk pooling; (ii) the allocation of risk from one party to another party in a better position to bear it, for mutually beneficial compensation; and (iii) risk reduction. Effective risk management often involves a mixture of these mechanisms.

RISK POOLING

Risk pooling is very intuitive and has underpinned risk management since the earliest human societies. To explore the benefits and limitations of risk pooling, consider for simplicity a community of a hundred households, each inhabiting a dwelling of equal value. If one out of the hundred houses will burn down over the next twelve months, and that risk is shared uniformly across all dwellings, a risk-pooling mechanism would be useful to provide protection against anyone becoming homeless from fire. This is fire insurance. If each household pays a premium of 1 per cent of the cost of rebuilding their house each year and pools those contributions, then at the end of the year there will be sufficient funds to rebuild the house that randomly burned down.[1]

In practice, the size of the pool that will be required to be maintained by the insurer will depend on both the average number of houses that burn down each year – and the variability of this number. If the insurer could somehow be certain that only one house will burn down each year, then it will be sufficient to collect actuarially fair premiums at the beginning of the year and invest them safely until the funds are required to compensate the owner of the house that suffered the loss.

Life is rarely so certain, however. While one house may be the average that burns down each year, it may be three in some years and zero in others. In order to be able to guarantee solvency, the insurer will probably keep more capital reserves than would be sufficient to rebuild one house – but not necessarily much more, if the households' risks in the pool have a low correlation. The insurer may keep reserves sufficient to cover, say, 95 per cent of contingencies and then arrange access to liquidity at short notice should it be required (although guaranteed access to liquidity will come at a cost, and will push up premiums, even if only slightly).

The pooling of risk works well in many cases, including fire and other property damage, life insurance and theft. For most people, the payment of a premium is a worthwhile expense since it provides a guarantee that certain extremely bad outcomes can be avoided, such as being left homeless due to fire damage, or being left in poverty due to the serious injury or the death of a family breadwinner. However, even with a simple mechanism such as risk pooling, complications arise.

Adverse selection

Now consider the situation in which the houses are all of equal value, though with varying risk of being destroyed by fire. If half of the houses in the community have a 1 per cent chance of burning down each year and the other half have a 2 per cent chance of burning down, then the average risk across all households will be 1.5 per cent. This could be accommodated by a higher premium of 1.5 per cent of the typical house's replacement cost. If all houses paid an annual premium of 1.5 per cent of the cost of rebuilding their house, the pool of funds would be sufficient, on average, to rebuild the fire damage incurred. Total premiums would be too low to cover the cost of rebuilding in a year when two houses burnt down and too high when one house burnt down – but, on average, the pool would be sufficient to cover the required costs.

However, a 1.5 per cent premium will not be good value for the houses that only have a 1 per cent chance of burning down. If premiums for all households are set at 1.5 per cent of house value, those households which are at lower risk are less likely to participate in the pool (presuming that they know they are at lower risk). Only the households with a 2 per cent chance of burning down will be willing to take part, but then premiums will have to rise to 2 per cent in order for there to be sufficient funds to rebuild the houses that do randomly burn down.

If it is possible for the insurer to identify which houses have a 1 per cent chance and which have a 2 per cent chance of burning down, then a solution to this problem would be to charge a different premium to each type of household. However, if only the owners of houses have accurate information in relation to their risks and it isn't possible for an external party (such as an insurer) to accurately determine the risk of each dwelling burning down, then it may not be possible to offer fair-value insurance to lower-risk households. In such a situation, the only solution may be to charge the higher premium and insure the fifty high-risk households.

This problem affects many types of insurance and is called adverse selection. It was first formally identified in 1970 by George Akerlof in an economics paper about the used car market.[2] Akerlof shows that, if there are unobservable characteristics of used cars that might make them undesirable, purchasers will assume that there is a material risk that any used car is of poor quality, or a 'lemon'. If the purchaser isn't able to determine the quality of a car, they may only be willing to offer a low price for any car. This might result in a breakdown in the market. Akerlof demonstrated how this information asymmetry could also affect insurance markets. The 'lemons paper' has become one of the most cited and influential papers of the past fifty years.[3]

Rothschild and Stiglitz built on this work to show how 'pooled' equilibriums may not be possible in insurance markets where insurers can't determine who the high-risk and low-risk customers are.[4] In such a situation, market equilibrium may require insurers to offer only partial insurance to some consumers, for example through high excesses.

Since these pathbreaking theoretical papers, a vast empirical literature has arisen testing for whether adverse selection exists in different contexts. Chetty and Finkelstein find that, while the evidence for adverse selection is mixed across different insurance markets, there is strong evidence for its presence in some of key areas of social insurance such as longevity insurance (annuities) and health insurance.[5]

David Cutler and Richard Zeckhauser undertook an extensive review of the literature in relation to health insurance markets and found a positive correlation between insurance coverage and health risks, which is consistent with adverse selection (although not conclusive).[6] A notable example of the impacts of adverse selection on real world insurance markets was the health insurance market for Harvard University staff. Cutler and Reber document how the scheme entered a 'death spiral' after lower-risk (younger) employees started to leave the scheme, which in turn prompted premium increases and further declines in enrolment.[7]

The presence of adverse selection can result in underinsurance, particularly among certain groups. Possible welfare-enhancing policy responses to adverse selection include: mandating insurance (which has occurred in many countries in relation to workers' compensation and transport accidents); tax subsidies for some or all people; and restrictions on characteristic-based pricing (such as requiring community-rating by private health insurers). These policies are present in the design of many of the key programs that constitute the modern welfare state.

Moral hazard

Another challenge for insurance markets is the possibility that people's behaviour may be affected by the protection afforded by insurance. This is often referred to by economists as moral hazard.

One possible manifestation of moral hazard is the possibility that someone who has health insurance may decide to take less care of their health or even take up riskier pursuits (such as contact sports), knowing that the medical costs associated with any injuries will be covered; there is limited evidence of this, however. A likely more material behavioural change that arises in relation to healthcare is the increased likelihood of insured people seeking additional costly treatments, as well as the increased likelihood of their doctors prescribing additional costly medical treatment.[8] As with adverse selection, the problem of moral hazard arises when there is asymmetric information and, specifically, where insurers find it difficult or impossible to tell which people will alter their behaviour once they have insurance.

Moral hazard can also refer to situations where people don't necessarily take more risk but, rather, fail to undertake sensible risk mitigation.

Let us return to the example of insuring one's home against the risk of damage by fire. It may be possible for households to reduce the fire risk of their dwelling. For example, they may be able to install fire alarms that allow fires to be put out before they engulf the entire property, thereby limiting the risk of damage. Imagine that each dwelling was worth $100,000 and therefore premiums were set at $1000 per year. If a fire alarm cost $100 to install and reduced the chance of fire damage by half, then it would be cost-effective for every household to install a fire alarm. This would enable premiums to drop to $500 per year and would mean that all households saved money ($400 in net terms in year one and $500 for each subsequent year of the life of the alarm). This measure, by reducing the underlying riskiness of dwellings, improves social welfare. Some households may not be willing to install fire alarms (for reasons that may include a suspicion that the investment may not be effective, liquidity constraints and inertia). Other practical examples include the installation of enhanced household security in order to deter theft and lifestyle improvements to reduce health risks.

In this simple example, it may be welfare-enhancing for the manager of the risk pool (either a private insurer or government) to mandate that any participant in the pool must install fire alarms. However, in many cases, households that make investments to reduce the riskiness of the asset being insured may not fully benefit from those investments if the insurer doesn't reduce their premiums accordingly. The insurer may fail to adjust premiums for a range of reasons. It may be difficult to determine the impact of the investment on the underlying riskiness of the asset, for example, or there may be a lack of competition between insurers or inertia among consumers.

In the context of social insurance, moral hazard often refers to the risk that the safety net provided by the social insurance programs may create incentives not to re-enter the labour market. This is often raised by those arguing that unemployment insurance and other welfare programs are too generous. In research undertaken for the Australian government Department of Education, Employment and Workplace Relations (DEEWR), economists from the Melbourne Institute of Applied Economic and Social Research found that:

> The single most consistent and substantive set of results obtained in the study is the negative relationship that exists between employment outcomes and the level of benefit payments. The point estimates of the reduced form analysis indicate that a $10 per week increase in net eligibility for transfer payments is associated with reduced odds of labour force participation by between 1 and 3 per cent for 4 out of 6 population subgroups (single men and women without children being the exceptions), and reduced odds of employment given labour force participation by between 2 and 6 per cent for 5 out of 6 population subgroups (single men being the exception).[9]

These findings are supported by evidence from Quebec and Austria.[10] However, this remains a contentious area. Peter Whiteford argues that countries with lower benefit replacement rates have higher unemployment rates,[11] and David Richardson from the Australia Institute questions the strength of evidence behind the claim that higher unemployment benefits reduce labour force participation.[12]

One way of managing moral hazard is for insurers to exclude coverage of certain risky behaviour. For example, standard health policies might exclude coverage for extreme sports. Insurers might only cover such activities through policies with higher premiums. One challenge with this approach is the difficulty of clearly specifying the full range of risky behaviour that insurers may worry coverage could induce.

Imperfect information on the part of consumers

Adverse selection and moral hazard are both problems that arise when insurers have limited information about the risk profile and preferences of people or firms seeking insurance (termed 'information asymmetry'). Problems can also arise when consumers of insurance have limited information about or understanding of the risks and uncertainty that they face or about the key elements of the insurance policies that they are offered.

Most consumers are sufficiently well informed about a product's characteristics when they purchase groceries or clothes for markets to function well. Their knowledge of product quality and the appropriateness of products to their circumstances will be far more limited in relation to highly complex, often technical products such as health services and the choice of educational institution for either themselves or a dependent. In addition to being highly complex, choices in relation to these services will often have long-term implications which can be difficult or impossible to meaningfully estimate. Moreover, the consequences of making a bad choice can be very serious. This is not the case when purchasing a poor-quality brand of breakfast cereal or watching a movie that doesn't live up to expectations. Imperfect information on the part of consumers can be just as important as the information asymmetry that often bedevils insurers. Imperfect information can impact insurance consumption when consumers experience difficulty assessing either the underlying risks that they face or the key characteristics of the insurance products that could manage those risks.

Externalities

An 'externality' is a technical economics term for a commonly understood situation: where an individual (or firm) acts in a way that reflects how that action will affect that individual, but not society more broadly. A negative externality exists where there are incentives for a person (or firm) to act in such a way that their actions reduce overall social welfare. The textbook example is a factory polluting a river or the air. If the factory doesn't have to pay to clean up their pollution, it will have a strong financial incentive to produce more output and pollution than is socially desirable.

There are also positive externalities, which can arise where an individual (or firm) doesn't capture all the benefits of their actions. This can create an incentive to undertake too little of the costly but beneficial activity. The textbook example is research and development, particularly where it leads to insights that are of very broad application that may benefit many others but where it is difficult for the individual or firm investing in the R&D to capture those benefits.

The concept of an externality is important for both social and private insurance. The presence of an externality may result in the underprovision of risk management. For example, consider highly contagious diseases. When an individual contracts such a disease, they experience direct harm from the disease. But they also impose a negative externality on others by increasing their exposure to infection. It will be important to design risk-management institutions so they reflect externalities.

Correlation of risks

In the simple example of 100 identical houses of which one will randomly burn down each year, the mechanics of risk pooling are straightforward. Each house pays 1 per cent of the house's rebuild cost into a pool and that pool funds the rebuild of the house that burns down. But what if the 100 homes are grouped into suburbs of varying sizes and that, instead of a single house burning down each year, an entire suburb burns down every few years. What if the suburbs vary in size (from, say, five to ten houses) and suburbs burn down every few years, with a random time period in between?

If the average number of homes that burn down each year is still one, then the annual premium required from each household for the pool will still be 1 per cent of the value of the house – over the long run. But now there is an added challenge for the insurer in knowing how much capital to have on hand in case a lot of houses burn down in a particular year.

In theory, if larger, suburb-wide blazes occurred with predictable frequency, then the insurer could simply save up households' annual premiums and use that larger pool to fund each suburb-wide rebuild. But if the timing of suburb-wide blazes was unpredictable, the insurer will need guaranteed access to capital at short notice. For example, an insurer would need to be able to cope with a situation in which two or three larger blazes occurred in consecutive years. The cost of guaranteed access to capital will be passed on to consumers and will reduce the efficiency of insurance as well as, potentially, the rate of take-up of insurance.

Two types of forecasting challenges arise in this situation. First, it is usually more difficult to estimate the timing of less frequent, more devastating events (for example, a suburb-wide blaze). Second, estimating the correlation of risks (in this example, the correlation of houses burning down within a suburb) is generally more difficult than estimating the average risk across a large population. This means that insurers and capital markets may not be very accurate when assessing how much of a capital guarantee to arrange.

Inter-temporal pooling for systematic risks

The extreme case of risk correlation arises where the risks being managed are highly correlated across an entire community. As noted earlier, the fact that many people in the same workplace or profession faced highly correlated risks limited the extent to which mutuals and friendly societies could provide protection from economic shocks. In extreme cases, an entire society may be affected by a risk such as a pandemic or an economic depression. This will make it difficult or potentially impractical to shift the burden of loss between different parts of that community.

Where 1 per cent of houses burn down each year, the pooling of risks works well. To highlight the challenges of highly correlated risks, imagine that, in addition to the annual risk of one random dwelling out of the hundred burning down, a bushfire attacks the town every 100 years that burns down all 100 dwellings. This is a very different type of risk – a systematic risk that pooling can't easily manage. When all houses burn down, the total loss will far exceed the amount that can be covered by the premium paid in each year. The only way to manage this separate systematic risk is to save up a separate pool of resources over time. There are two options.

First, the community of 100 households could pay an additional 1 per cent each year for a separate long-term fund. If that fund was able to build up over 100 years (or less if investments were made with a positive real rate of return), it would be able to fund the rebuild of the entire town after a one-in-100-year bushfire. Where the fund fell short, it might be possible to borrow part of the costs of a rebuild and pay off that debt with premiums collected in later years; unless insurance was mandated, however, there would be a strong incentive to discontinue the policy after the rebuild.

Alternatively, if the community of 100 households formed part of a larger society or nation, it might be possible for that larger society to provide assistance during times of natural disaster. For example, a national government could create a larger pool in which each component was a community rather than a household. Communities would contribute to the national government via taxes. When an individual community experienced a bushfire (or other natural disaster), the national government would be in a position to fund the rebuild.

The second type of arrangement wouldn't solve the underlying challenge of systematic risks if a natural disaster affected the entire nation. As Robert Shiller argues, risk sharing should be able to assist even in this scenario as it should be possible to create mutually beneficial risk-sharing arrangements between nation-states.[13]

To manage some systematic risks, such as an ageing demographic, society may need to shift resources across time. This will typically involve reducing consumption at times when income per capita is highest and increasing consumption during times when the loss of economic activity arising from ageing is greatest.

From the household perspective, either doubling premiums or paying a systematic risk tax to the government would involve doubling the annual cost of risk management in the example above. This would reflect the fact that, if there was a systematic one-in-a-100-year risk in addition to the annual 1 per cent random chance of each individual house burning down, the risk of a particular house burning down would have doubled.

The key point is that when risk is truly systematic and affects an entire community from beyond which assistance can't be sought, optimally managing that risk will require the inter-temporal shifting of resources. This often requires intervention by government.

Market failure and social insurance

The combination of information asymmetry (adverse selection and moral hazard), imperfect knowledge on the part of consumers, externalities and systematic risks can result in private insurance markets based on the pooling of risk either collapsing or only working in limited circumstances. Nicholas Barr argues that private markets for unemployment insurance only function in very limited circumstances and that private markets for health insurance often require many of the characteristics of social insurance (such as community rating) to function even in a limited fashion.

One rationale for the welfare state – and social insurance in particular – is the need for the state to step in where private insurance markets can't overcome the challenges outlined above. This is corroborated by the arguments that policymakers and legislators use when arguing for particular reforms. Moss finds that, in the US, policymakers and legislators advocating for social insurance programs 'proved surprisingly sophisticated in their economic treatment of risk and of the government's role as a risk manager'.[14] Part of the challenge for today's massive social security programs is developing ways in which to improve this capacity to manage risk.

ALLOCATION OF RISK

A second risk-management mechanism is the allocation of risk between parties to a transaction. In some instances, the allocation of risk between two parties to a transaction is prescribed by law. Indeed, a great deal of economic activity occurs under the umbrella of laws whose principal purpose is to regulate risk allocation.

Perhaps the best single example is limited liability, which Nicholas Murray Butler, then president of Columbia University, described as the 'greatest single discovery of modern times ... Even steam and electricity are far less important than the limited liability corporation, and they would be reduced to comparative impotence without it.'[15] Limited liability provides considerable protection to passive investors. Given that the majority of investors do not wish to devote themselves to actively running the firms they invest in – or even to monitoring their affairs all that closely in most instances – this regulatory innovation was critical for linking vast amounts of saving with productive ventures. Other examples of regulation that are primarily risk-allocation mechanisms include product liability laws, bankruptcy laws and bank deposit guarantees.

There is also a wide range of situations in which two (or more) parties to a transaction will voluntarily shift risk, usually with some compensation being given to the party assuming risk. Consider an example that often finds its way into economics textbooks: a farmer who is concerned about the uncertainty of the price that the market will offer for his or her crop at the time of harvest.

Let's assume that, at the time of planting, the farmer forecasts a 50 per cent chance of a price of $5 per bushel of wheat at the time of harvest and a 50 per cent chance of a price of $15 per bushel of wheat at the time of harvest. The farmer would prefer to reduce that level of risk. If the farmer has to make a number of financial decisions at the time of planting – such as investing in new equipment and how much to plant – the farmer will prefer to reduce the level of uncertainty surrounding his or her future finances when making those decisions.

A risk-averse farmer would clearly prefer a guarantee, at the time of planting, of $10 per bushel of wheat at harvest time to the uncertainty of waiting until harvest time for the price. But would the farmer prefer a guarantee of $9 or $8 or $7 to the risky outcome? That depends upon how risk-averse the farmer is. And who would offer such a guarantee? This is where risk allocation between parties with different levels of risk aversion can be useful.

For a risk-neutral person or entity, a 50/50 chance of $5 or $15 is worth $10. In other words, a risk-neutral person is indifferent to these two outcomes. They would therefore gladly purchase a 50/50 chance of $5/$15 for less than $10.

A win-win trade can easily be arranged between a farmer seeking greater financial certainty at the time of planting and a risk-neutral person or entity. In this example, if the farmer had a level of risk aversion that made him or her indifferent between $8 and the 50/50 chance of harvest prices of $5/$15, then a mutually profitable trade could occur at any price between $8 and $10.

At any price in this range, the farmer would gain a certain payment worth more than the gamble of the uncertain price of the crop at the time of planting. And the risk-neutral party would gain a risky asset for a lower price than its value.

Some well-resourced traders in financial markets are risk-neutral in practice. The opportunity to trade with large entities with a greater appetite for risk can be highly beneficial for individuals, small businesses – and farmers!

Lloyd's of London is also a good example of sharing risk between people with low wealth and people of high wealth. The 'Names' within Lloyd's of London were wealthy members of the British gentry (later, wealthy people across the globe) who were willing to take on risk from people who were usually of lesser means.

This type of situation constitutes a common form of risk management in society. It underpins derivatives markets and many different types of financial hedging arrangements.

Information asymmetry

As outlined above, risk allocation can be based upon differences in risk tolerance. It can also be based upon differences in assessments or forecasts of risk. For example, person A may forecast the possible outcomes of the price of wheat at harvest time as a 50 per cent chance of $5 and a

50 per cent chance of $15. Person B may forecast the likelihood of possible outcomes as 10 per cent chance of $5 and a 90 per cent chance of $15.

Even if both person A and person B had the same level of risk aversion, they will place a different value on the risky value of wheat at harvest time. If both were risk-neutral, then person A would value the risky asset at $7.50, while person B would value it at $14. Therefore, any trade of the risky asset from person A to person B at a price in the range $7.50–$14.00 would result in mutual gain.The differences in their forecasts may come down to access to different information or the use of different forecasting methodologies.

Combinations of pooling and risk allocation

In many situations, a combination of pooling and risk allocation is used. In the example of the uncertain outcome of the wheat market, we can consider both the downstream and upstream impacts of high and low prices. A high price at harvest will be good for the farmer and bad for the baker. And vice versa for a low price at harvest.

If both the farmer and the baker are risk-averse, then it would make sense for them to agree on a price of $10 at planting. No matter which price occurs at harvest time, one of them will have forgone some potential profit. But it will be worth it for both to forgo that potential gain for the guarantee of a sure price and the benefits that will provide both of them in terms of business planning.

This is analogous to the pooling arrangement discussed earlier. A low price is a bad outcome for the farmer and a high price is a bad outcome for the baker. By pooling their resources and agreeing on a compensation scheme that is contingent on the actual harvest price, the person suffering loss as a result of the bad price outcome (high or low) is protected. The beneficiary of the price outcome in effect loses that benefit via an implicit premium that is paid to the other party.

While this is simple in theory, farmers and bakers don't have time in practice to find each other and organise hedging contracts that create a risk pool. This would involve unrealistically high search and transaction costs to be worthwhile.

That's where financial markets and market-makers come into play. What is more likely is that farmers and bakers find it feasible to trade standardised derivatives on a market, such as a futures exchange. A 'market-maker', who is a professional risk taker, can provide the liquidity that allows such markets to function effectively. In addition to providing liquidity, the market-maker will generally have a higher risk tolerance than the other two parties. Even after the market-maker earns a profit from interactions with both other parties, all three will typically be better off.

Risk allocation and social insurance

While most of the larger social insurance programs are built on risk pooling, some programs use risk allocation. Two key examples of where governments have regulated the allocation of risk between private parties (i.e. without a direct impact on government spending) are limited liability and product liability. In contrast, a good example of risk allocation where the government itself has assumed some of the liability is the use of contingent loans. This mechanism is explored in more detail below. Such loans often involve governments shifting risks from individuals to the taxpayer, particularly where the likelihood of outcomes is difficult to quantify. The assumption of risks by government in such situations may make sense where the activity being promoted is socially worthwhile.

RISK REDUCTION

Reducing the extent of underlying risk is the third type of risk management. There are many instances in which governments regulate risk by proscribing certain risky activities. This includes an almost endless list of legislation and regulations: workplace safety laws; road safety rules like speed limits; building and construction standards; standards for medical equipment and drugs; food and safety standards, and the list goes on. Risk control governs how and when we work, including ubiquitous professional and occupational licensing. In some instances, governments will invest in infrastructure to directly reduce risk, including flood levees; road safety infrastructure; air traffic control infrastructure; and on the list goes.

Risk reduction often has material economic consequences. Effective regulation can increase economic output by increasing people's confidence in transacting and investing. It can also prevent substandard goods and services from being provided, thereby avoiding significant economic and social harm that could arise from the use of such goods or services. And many risk-reduction investments can limit or fully remove the risks associated with natural disasters or productive but risky activities such as transport.

Of course, regulation to reduce risk can also cause economic damage. By definition, it proscribes certain activities, limiting the range of what can be consensually contracted. It also potentially adds to the costs of providing many services, for example where professional and occupational licensing limits the supply of labour. And risk reduction can be highly costly, such as investments in infrastructure to mitigate the risk of natural disasters. Clearly, the balance of economic costs and benefits is relevant when assessing each regulatory intervention.

5.
Risk and Uncertainty

The concept of risk implies the possibility of loss, injury or other adverse circumstance. Risk connotes an unknown future. If a person is in a position where a future bad outcome is certain, that could be described as unfortunate or tragic, but it is not risky.

Quantifying risk

We are all familiar with the concept of risk. When we roll a die in a boardgame we might hope for a 3 and dread a 5 – but until it stops bouncing, we won't know the outcome of the risky situation. In a contrived game involving dice or cards, risk is usually well defined and easily quantifiable. We know that the chance of a head on a coin toss is 50 per cent, as is the chance of a tail. We also know that the chance of each number on a six-sided die is 1/6. Even this level of understanding, while embedded in our worldview, is a relatively modern phenomenon. As already discussed, in Ancient Greece, Imperial Rome and other pre-modern cultures, games were played with dice made of animal bones in which the game's payoffs did not accurately reflect the shape of the dice.

Most of the risk in our lives beyond boardgames involves problems involving high stakes and odds that are much more difficult to calculate. What are the chances of our house burning down next year? What is the chance of me losing my job through no fault of my own, either because the company I work for goes broke or the economy goes into recession? What is the chance I become very sick?

At a societal level, the future scenarios are often even more difficult to quantify. What is the likelihood of war within the next twenty years?

What will the impact of current CO_2 pollution be on mean global temperature in 100 years?

The variability of outcomes at the individual level

In many ways, managing risk for individuals and families is more difficult than for insurance companies (and, on top of that, the former do not have risk-quantification departments!). Part of the challenge in managing risk for individuals is the inherent difficulty of estimating likelihoods from small samples. In general, it is possible to be considerably more accurate in estimating risk for large groups than for individuals. If we randomly select a fifty-year-old from the population and estimate that person's life expectancy, we will be able to calculate an expectation – say, eighty-five years. Of course, that person's actual life span could fall anywhere between fifty and 120. Our confidence in using the population average (eighty-five) to estimate that person's life span will depend in part on how dispersed actual lengths of life are across the population. If, instead of a single person, we took a random sample of 1000 people, it would be possible to estimate the life expectancy of that group, on average, with far greater accuracy. Group averages are typically less variable than those of individuals. And the variability of group averages declines as the size of the group increases. This reflects the 'law of large numbers'.[1]

An example of this statistical phenomenon that we are all familiar with is opinion polling. If a television reporter randomly asks five people on the street their voting intentions, we instinctively know that this is a quite unreliable gauge of community sentiment. There is a high probability that this small group will turn out to be unrepresentative. A poll based on a large random sample provides a far more reliable estimate of voting intention. For this reason, we are accustomed to seeing samples of well over 1000 when conducting political polling. As we have seen in recent years, even polls of this size can be materially off the mark. Even those not trained in formal statistics understand that as the sample size increases, we can be more confident in the result.[2]

As individuals, trying to manage the risk associated with our longevity, our health or our long-term finances, we deal with a sample size of one. Where an individual's idiosyncratic characteristics are known, it is usually possible to estimate their risks more accurately. For example, if a person's health attributes are known (whether they smoke, drink or exercise), it will be possible to more accurately estimate their life expectancy. With the rise of big data, insurers now know far more about us than was the case ten or twenty years ago. Indeed, in some situations, large corporations, possibly ones we have never heard of, now know more about our exposure to potentially life-changing risks than we do ourselves. This has resulted in far more accurate estimation of risk at the individual level in a wide range of contexts.

Somewhat perversely, improvements in data collection and analysis have now reached the point where risk can be accurately assessed at such a granular level that the potential to pool risk is being undermined in some situations. Examples of this include the ability to determine flood risk at the household level, genomic testing that allows health insurers to more accurately assess each individual's susceptibility to a range of conditions, and the tracking of driver performance to assess each driver's risk of accident. Ironically, in the modern world, the challenges of adverse selection may have reversed. Insurers may now know more about our susceptibility to risk than we do.

A good example of the relationship between granular data and the effectiveness of risk pooling is flood risk. For many decades flood risk was estimated at a high level, often by postcode or even town. Flood insurance would often be offered to all but the very highest-risk properties, with a considerable degree of cross-subsidisation in premiums. In Australia, over 90 per cent of homes are at almost no risk of flooding. These households were (and are) provided with cover for flood nonetheless and, in the past, often subsidised the flood coverage of low- and medium-risk households. Today, many of these cross-subsidies have been unwound. This is a good thing in terms of the fairness of premiums for households who face no risk of flooding. But it can result in considerably higher premiums for households identified as having a material risk of flood damage.

The accurate identification of high-risk individuals, households and firms reduces the extent of cross-subsidisation when setting premiums. However, it also results in much higher, and sometimes unaffordable, insurance costs for some.

Computational challenges

Even if individuals could overcome the inherent difficulty of small sample estimations, there remains the computational challenge of estimating risk. This can be overcome, at least to a degree, through competitive markets. Even if individuals themselves can't accurately compute likelihoods, competitive insurance markets should see consumers offered premiums that come close to reflecting fair value. Insurers who charge premiums that are too high will lose market share (if there is sufficient competition). Insurers who charge premiums that are too low will eventually become insolvent when claims come due for payment.

CONTRASTING RISK AND UNCERTAINTY

What about situations in which even the actuaries and statisticians can't accurately estimate the likelihood of different outcomes? Frank Knight, an economist at the University of Chicago, wrote a seminal book on uncertainty: *Risk, Uncertainty and Profit*, published in 1921.[3]

Knight distinguishes between risk and uncertainty. Consider a situation in which a person randomly draws a ball from an urn containing five red balls and five black balls. In such a situation, the person is able to accurately estimate the level of risk: there is a 50 per cent chance of a red ball and a 50 per cent chance of black ball. In contrast, consider a person drawing balls from an urn containing red and black balls in unknown proportions. Knight argues that this situation entails not risk – but uncertainty. In a situation involving uncertainty, it isn't possible to meaningfully quantify the likelihood of a red or black ball.

Knight makes the point that it is more difficult to make insurance decisions in the face of uncertainty than risk. Similarly, it is more difficult to make an investment decision where there is uncertainty as opposed to where there is risk. Knight argued that entrepreneurs often act in the presence of uncertainty, of an unknowable likelihood of success or failure.

At around the same time, Keynes also explored the distinction between risk and uncertainty in a significant contribution to the theory of probability in 1921.[4] Later, Keynes argued that uncertainty was critical to the role of money in the business cycle: 'There is, however, a necessary condition failing which the existence of a liquidity-preference as a means of holding wealth could not exist. This necessary condition is the existence of uncertainty as to the future of the rate of interest.'[5]

This distinction potentially has practical implications and may determine where insurance is or is not offered by the private sector. Where does Knightian uncertainty exist, as opposed to risk? Knight argued that life insurance is an example of a quantifiable risk whereas accident and fire insurance are examples of unquantifiable uncertainty. He went on to argue that, in effect, it was impossible to quantify the risk associated with fire: 'The typical application of insurance to business hazards is in the protection against loss by fire, and the theory of fire insurance rates forms an interesting contrast with the actuarial mathematics of life insurance.'[6]

Knight's observations on insurance are interesting in several respects. First, the contrast in the varying difficulty of calculating likelihoods across two real-world scenarios: life insurance and fire insurance. Second, it demonstrates that it is arguably possible, with improved data quality and analytical capacity, to move a category of contingency from 'uncertainty' to 'risk'. It was indeed true that life insurance premiums were based upon more reliable statistical analysis in the 1920s than fire insurance. Rigorous life expectancy tables were developed in the late seventeenth century, initially in the UK and the Netherlands. These formed the basis for the life insurance industry to expand rapidly – to the point where annuities were widely used as a form of government financing in the early nineteenth century. While fire insurance had been in existence for approximately the same period (since the Great Fire of London in 1666), the quality of data did not allow an accurate assessment of the fire risk of each individual building at the time Knight wrote his analysis. Since Knight wrote his seminal book, the insurance industry has been able to price fire risk far more accurately. Fire risk is perhaps an example of where, through better data and modelling, society has gained a far better appreciation of the number of red and black balls in the urn. Similarly, accident and sickness insurance are far more accurately priced than in Knight's or Keynes' day.

Finally, and perhaps this is a challenge that governments and policymakers too often underestimate: there remain many contingencies that still do not lend themselves to quantification. Even after dramatic improvements in the volume and quality of data – and similar improvements in computational capacity – many potential losses remain stubbornly uncertain rather than risky.

UNCERTAINTY IS UBIQUITOUS

Uncertainty plays a key role in the economy. Keynes argued that uncertainty is critical to macroeconomic dynamics and business cycles. One of Knight's key conclusions was that uncertainty plays a key role in long-term growth rates thanks to the role that it plays in innovation, entrepreneurship and business formation. One of the key examples of uncertainty that Knight cited was an entrepreneur at an early stage of building an innovative business who is trying to predict the outcome of investment in R&D and estimate future economic conditions and future demand for new products and services.

More recently, Mariana Mazzucato has argued that the assessment of whether a particular startup will succeed is a form of Knightian risk:

> The real Knightian uncertainty that innovation entails, as well as the inevitable sunk costs and capital intensity that it requires, is in fact the reason that the private sector, including venture capital, often shies away from it. It is also the reason why the State is the stakeholder that so often takes the lead, not only to fix the markets but to create them.[7]

The mobile phone, the internet and cracking the puzzle of nuclear energy can all be traced back to significant early-stage participation by government. Arguably, what underpins this is government's willingness to invest in the face of uncertainty.

Clearly, this also has implications for the types of contingencies that the private sector will insure. There is a vast range of scenarios that are conceivable but that are difficult to quantify as they are one-offs or perhaps have never happened. Many such examples are easy to describe: a major terrorist attack using a weapon of mass destruction; two fully laden 747s crashing into each other over a major city; or the theft of a rare painting.[8] Yet there is a demand for insurance in many of these situations.

Reinsurance is often the mechanism by which private insurance markets are able to provide coverage for such scenarios, often by spreading the associated potential losses across a large number of insurance firms. In turn, each of these firms manages the potential for loss arising from difficult-to-quantify events by diversifying across a wide range of such risks (or uncertainties).

John Kay and Mervyn King argue that many decision-makers face situations that are, in practical terms, impossible to meaningfully quantify. They provide the example of President Obama trying to decide whether or not to approve the mission to raid the compound in Abbottabad in which the CIA suspected Osama bin Laden was hiding. Obama was faced with experts with widely varying views. According to Kay and King, '"John", the CIA team leader, was 95 per cent certain that bin Laden was in the compound. But others were less sure. Most placed their probability estimate at about 80 per cent. Some were as low as 40 per cent or even 30 per cent.'[9] What possible use are such disparate numbers to a decision-maker? Clearly taking the average of everyone's guesstimate would be of little use. And even if these various probabilities could somehow have been numerically combined, at what threshold would it have made sense for Obama to have given approval?

Arguably, notwithstanding this lack of clarity, Obama received more useful advice in relation to uncertainty than most of his predecessors. Sherman Kent left his position in the Yale department of history to join the Research and Analysis Branch of the newly formed Coordinator of Information (COI) in 1941. This would later became become the Office of Strategic Services and, later still, the Central Intelligence Agency (CIA). Kent was highly influential in establishing the US intelligence community's methodological approach to processing data when trying to understand uncertainty. In March 1951, when evaluating the likelihood that the Soviets would invade breakaway Yugoslavia, the Office of National Estimates concluded that 'an attack on Yugoslavia in 1951 should be considered a serious possibility'.[10]

Kent was later asked by a State Department official what 'serious possibility' meant in terms of mathematical odds; Kent responded with the figure of a 65 per cent chance of attack. The State Department had interpreted the memo to imply much lower odds and, when asked by Kent, his team suggested that 'serious possibility' implied anything ranging from 80 per cent to 20 per cent. Kent later argued that words should be assigned mathematical ranges, with 'certain' as 100 per cent; 'almost certain' as 87–99 per cent; 'probably' as 62–87 per cent; 'chances about even' as 40–60 per cent; 'probably not' 20–40 per cent; 'almost certainly not' 2–12 per cent; and 'impossible' as 0.[11] Kent's proposal was rejected – although as we have noted, possibly as a belated victory of sorts for Sherman Kent, President Obama was presented with quantitative estimates rather than words by his key advisers. How much of an advance that represented is debatable.

In situations that are difficult to quantify, decision-makers invariably have to exercise judgement. Philip Tetlock explored the use of judgement in the largest and most rigorous evaluation of expert opinion to date. Over a period of twenty years, he asked detailed questions of 284 experts from a range of fields, including government officials, academics and journalists. Together, this group made around 28,000 testable predictions over two decades, ranging across varying lengths of time horizons.

Unlike many of the questions that pundits are asked on television or that consultants are asked by clients, Tetlock's questions were very precise and asked for specific answers that could be evaluated as either being ultimately correct or not. Tetlock didn't ask, 'Do you think Greece will default at some point?' He asked: 'Will Greece default within the next twelve months?' He didn't ask: 'Will there be conflict in the South China Sea?' He asked: 'Will there be a clash involving fatalities in the South China Sea within the next three years?' Many of the questions involved uncertainty in that it was nearly impossible to meaningfully quantify the likelihood being tested. The forecasters had to rely on informed judgement.

Tetlock identified a sub-group of forecasters who performed particularly strongly. These weren't the best educated, the most intelligent or the most famous (indeed, there was a strong negative correlation with fame!). The best predictor of success was someone's level of confidence: the less confident they were, the better the predictions. Why? Tetlock argues that the forecasters with a low level of confidence were more likely to be foxes than hedgehogs; people open to many ideas and perspectives rather than one big idea. These people were more curious, constantly seeking more information and updating their predictions.

As difficult as Obama's choice was, Kay and King argue that the choices that most households face in planning for retirement are at least as difficult: 'The principal uncertainty President Obama faced was binary – either bin Laden was in Abbottabad, or he was not. Judging how long you will live is more difficult.' Unlike a life insurance company which is estimating the life expectancy of the *average* fifty-year-old, a household has to estimate what will happen to a particular fifty-year-old (an estimation with considerably more variance) and then make often irreversible choices with decades-long implications involving myriad complex financial products. Social insurance can play a positive role in helping people navigate this uncertainty.

Black swan events

Black swan events are a sub-category of uncertainty. Taleb defines a black swan event as one that:

- is an outlier so beyond normal expectations that even the possibility of its occurance is extremely difficult to estimate;
- has a dramatic impact when it occurs; and
- is explained in hindsight as if it were predictable.[12]

In the examples of uncertainty given by Knight, the event is well defined and at the forefront of a person or firm's thinking – but it is difficult or nearly impossible to quantify the likelihood of each potential outcome. A good example is the likelihood of a particular startup with a highly novel idea succeeding. The product or service that the startup is trying to promote is well known. The financial situation of the startup is known. The leadership team is known. What is almost impossible to meaningfully estimate is the chances of success of the product.

In the case of black swan events, there is the added challenge in that the event is so far beyond everyday experience that it does do not even occur to most (if any) people. Taleb identifies several examples of these events: the scale of World War I, the rise of Hitler, the rise of the

Internet, the ubiquitous take-up of the personal computer, the collapse of the Soviet Union, and the September 11 attacks.

It is worth examining in detail the extent to which events like this are indeed foreseeable and, if they are, whether it would be possible to quantify the likelihood of such events in advance. For example, the degree to which the September 11 attacks were foreseeable has been the subject of considerable speculation.

There were any number of indicators that could be pointed to, ex post. These include: previous terrorist attacks (including the World Trade Center bombing in 1993, attacks on US embassies in Kenya and Tanzania in 1998 and the USS *Cole* in 1999), thwarted preparations for other terrorist attacks, interceptions of communications relating to potential attacks, and a growing awareness of threats relating to specifically to the possible use of aircraft (including internal memos from the FBI and the CIA, circulars from the FAA and alerts from external entities such as flight academies). The implication of course is that, were people paying attention, the September 11 attacks could have been foiled.

The difficulty with this line of reasoning is that it would be possible to create similar list of indicators or warnings for many events that didn't occur: an attack on the New York subway; an attack on a major city by ship; a chemical or biological attack; a cyber-attack; an attack on a major European or Asian city; and the list goes on. We now know that on 11 September 2001, planes flew into the World Trade Center and the Pentagon. It is nearly impossible to meaningfully quantify the odds of all of the other myriad possible attacks that didn't occur.

In *Pearl Harbor: Warning and Decision*, Roberta Wohlstetter examines the many reasons why the US military didn't predict the attack by the Japanese Navy.[13] One such reason is the fact that they were far more preoccupied by the possibility of domestic sabotage by Japanese descendants living in Hawaii. While this seemed a plausible risk to defend against at the time, it was then proven that focusing attention in defending against sabotage was highly counter-productive as it involved all aircraft and ships being placed in close proximity to each other to make monitoring them easier. As it turned out, it also made them a much easier target for aerial bombardment. As Wohlstetter observes:

> It is much easier after the event to sort the relevant from the irrelevant signals. After the event, of course, a signal is always crystal clear; we can now see what disaster it was signalling since the disaster has occurred. But before the event it is obscure and pregnant with conflicting meanings.[14]

Black swan events are relevant to risk management by government since many of government's largest policy challenges involve both systematic risk and uncertainty. To the extent that an event creates a potential for systematic losses, the policy challenge for government will be exacerbated if the likelihood and magnitude of those losses cannot be meaningfully quantified.

Recessions, volcanoes and grey rhinos

Niall Ferguson has contrasted the arrival of Covid-19 with the outbreak of World War I. In doing so, he refers to the concept of 'grey rhinos'.[15] Wucker defines grey rhinos as being 'things that [are] dangerous, obvious, and highly probable'.[16] According to Wucker, this would include climate change, a financial crisis at the global policy level, Hurricane Katrina, the 2008 financial crisis, cyber-attacks, wildfires and water shortages.

An analogy to at least some of the situations described above is a volcano in which pressure builds up over a long period of time. While it may be obvious that the volcano will blow at some point, it is usually extremely difficult to pinpoint when. Ferguson argues that, even though tension had been building for some time in the lead-up to war, the outbreak of hostilities took most political actors and financial markets by surprise.[17]

This is confirmed by the response of financial markets, with currencies, bonds and equities all shifting materially upon the news of war, reflecting the fact that investors were as surprised as policymakers and commentators. Ex post, events often look far more 'predictable' than they do at the time.

Several systematic risks have the characteristics of grey rhinos, such as economic crises and climate change. During the years leading up to the 2008 financial crisis, there were undoubtedly pressures building in the international financial system. But most economists and market participants were taken by surprise by the precise timing and nature of the meltdown. Among economic forecasters, it has long been known that turning points and economic meltdowns are more difficult to predict than trends or changes in trends.[18]

The boundary between uncertainty and risk

Some of the greatest thinkers in science, philosophy, economics and history have grappled with the boundary between uncertainty and risk. This issue ultimately goes to the heart of the very nature of the universe in which we live. One of the deepest questions in relation to existence is how predictable it is. For some, this goes to the heart of how *knowable* it is. In 1814, Pierre-Simon Laplace, the great French polymath, argued in extreme terms for the universe as determinist:

> An intellect which at a certain moment would know all forces that set nature in motion, and all positions of all items of which nature is composed, if this intellect were also vast enough to submit these data to analysis, it would embrace in a single formula the movements of the greatest bodies of the universe and those of the tiniest atom; for such an intellect nothing would be uncertain and the future just like the past would be present before its eyes.[19]

According to Laplace, with ever greater computing power we will be able to remove all uncertainty from forecasting, predicting and modelling. We just need more data, more computing power and more sophisticated models.

Others argue that there are inherent limits to the knowability of the world. Chaos theory gained prominence in 1972 following the publication of a paper called 'Predictability: Does the Flap of a Butterfly's Wings in Brazil Set Off a Tornado in Texas?'.[20] In this paper Edward Lorenz, a professor of meteorology at MIT, did not contend that a butterfly's wings cause major events on the other side of the world in the sense that we typically use the notion of causation. Rather, he argued that in highly complex real-world systems (and the mathematical models that we use to understand them), tiny changes in starting conditions can have material and difficult to predict impacts on overall outcomes. A decade earlier, Lorenz had discovered that changing an input into a meteorological model from 0.506127 to 0.506 resulted in dramatically different long-term forecasts.[21]

Henri Poincaré was a French mathematician, physicist, and philosopher of science – a person with accomplishments so wide-ranging within mathematics that he has been referred to as the 'last universalist'.[22] He contributed to a seemingly simple problem in Newtonian physics. In a system with two bodies (for example, planets or balls on connected pieces of string), it is possible to accurately predict their motion into the indefinite future. However, the addition of a third body complicates matters greatly. Even if the third body has little impact initially, over time its impact will become explosive (as with minuscule parameter changes in Lorenz's climate models).[23] Even with just three bodies, it can become effectively impossible to model behaviour over the long run. Of course, reality is far more complicated than this highly stylised three-body scenario.

This is an issue that bedevils modellers of many phenomena, be it of the economy, climate change or pandemics. McCloskey argues that 'sensitive dependence on initial conditions' (as the core precondition of chaotic conditions is sometimes referred) arises from many situations that are non-linear. The impact on our capacity to understand the world around us and make meaningful predictions about the future is profound:

> The butterfly can take flight either in the parameters (that is, in the confidence about the model imposed) or in the initial conditions (that is, in the confidence about the observations of the world's condition).[24]

What is clear is that, regardless where one sits on the spectrum between Laplace and Poincaré, our capacity to accurately quantify uncertain situations generally diminishes: (i) the greater is the complexity of the system being studied, including the number of interactions within it; (ii) the more 'non-linear' it is; and (iii) the longer is the future time horizon we are studying. Goldin argues that the increasingly interconnected nature of the world makes extreme events more likely: this is the 'butterfly effect' of globalisation.[25]

A bridge between risk and uncertainty

Uncertainty and risk aren't binary options. Sometimes we know precisely how many red and black balls are in the urn. Sometimes we have no idea. Often, we have a rough idea.

Frank Ramsey, a genius polymath whose intellect burned brightly and briefly at Cambridge in the 1920s and who made major contributions to philosophy, mathematics, logic and economics before his untimely death at twenty-six, approached probability as a 'logic of partial belief'.[26] First, he rejected the notion that 'we can sharply divide beliefs into those which have a position in the numerical scale and those which have not'.[27] We are used to thinking about probability *objectively*, in terms of the likelihood of something occurring between 0 (impossible) and 1 (a certainty). Keynes proposed that probability could be worked out by starting with a hypothesis that could be tested using evidence based upon our intuition. Ramsey strongly disagreed and argued 'there really do not seem to be any such things as the probability relations [Keynes] describes'.[28]

What if, instead, we think about not just a person's beliefs about the likelihood of something occurring – but also how strongly they held those beliefs: 'the pretensions of some exponents of the frequency theory that partial belief means full belief in a frequency proposition cannot be sustained.'[29]

Ramsey distinguished between deductive reasoning and inductive reasoning. In the case of deductive reasoning, if we are absolutely sure of the premises, then we can be absolutely sure of what is derived from those premises. In probability this is like determining, almost as a matter of logic, what the odds are of rolling a particular number on a fair die. In the case of inductive reasoning, matters are considerably fuzzier. Based on the last century of history, how likely is a terrorist attack in New York City this year? How likely is it that a particular plane will crash before reaching its destination? If we have seen a million white swans, how likely is a black swan? Or a green one?

Ramsey creates a framework of 'partial beliefs'. It is arguable that most situations that we face in the real world involve partial rather than certain beliefs. How would you measure the strength of those beliefs quantitatively? Ramsey proposes a person's willingness to act on those beliefs. The analogy that Ramsey uses is:

> I am at a cross-roads and do not know the way; but I rather think one of the two ways is right. I propose therefore to go that way but keep my eyes open for someone to ask; if now I see someone half a mile away over the fields, whether I turn aside to ask him will depend on the relative inconvenience of going out of my way to cross the fields or of continuing on the wrong road. But it will also depend on how confident I am that I am right ... I propose therefore to use the distance I would be prepared to go to ask, as a measure of the confidence in my opinion.[30]

Ramsey's fork in the road scenario is powerful for two key reasons. First, it reinforces the limitations of deductive reasoning. Each fork in the road is unique and therefore previous experience offers only so much guidance as to the correct path to take. Second, an opinion expressed after introspection is a limited measure of belief. Seeing how far someone is willing to walk out of their way to test the correctness of the path that they have chosen is a far better gauge.

This book does not presume to wade into the battle waged by intellectual giants on the philosophical underpinnings of probability and uncertainty. Rather, it is sufficient to acknowledge that this debate reflects the broader challenge as to how we quantify future likelihoods. The real world is a combination of dice throws (accurately quantifiable) and potential plane crashes (not easily quantifiable). Deduction involving fair dice is sometimes useful, but all too often subjectivity comes into play. And once subjectivity comes into play, we need to determine the best way to aggregate competing views of future likelihoods.

Individuals, families, corporations, non-profit organisations and governments constantly make assessments of future likelihoods, even when not explicitly admitting as such. For example, when a government decides whether to invest and, if so, how much to invest in healthcare, or a flood levee or pandemic preparedness – and does so at the expense of other competing claims on finite resources – it acts *as if* guided by a subjective estimate of future likelihoods. Even if it isn't possible to meaningfully assess the likelihood of future events in mechanistic odds or percentage chances, it would be useful to be more explicit about how estimates of risk and uncertainty are guiding our decisions.

A sensible approach

The presence of any or all of the challenges arising from uncertainty shouldn't deter us from modelling and abstracting, but where they are present, we should be more cautious. First, we can behave more like Tetlock's humble but highly effective super-forecasters, being willing to search out new information and constantly update our estimates. Second, techniques such as scenario planning encourage more expansive thinking, dreaming up situations that may not initially be on our radar. This will put us in a better position to deal with black swans. Even if it is difficult to put precise numerical estimates on the likelihood of each scenario, being aware of their possibility at all is extremely useful. Third, we should think beyond a world of point estimates, such as expected value – and acknowledge how fuzzy or uncertain our understanding is in different settings.

Finally, one way of dealing with the inherent unknowability of uncertain situations is to hedge against all scenarios. Many individuals appear to use rules of thumb, such as guaranteeing a roof over their family's head by insuring their home, without relying on a detailed evaluation of the precise likelihood of each risk. In a world of uncertainty and unmeasurable risks, concepts such as maximin (guaranteeing a certain minimum outcome) can make sense. Risk-sharing strategies that provide a minimum level of protection against all scenarios can be useful where identifying and quantifying extreme outliers is difficult or impossible. This is precisely the approach that many households appear to adopt.

Table 5.1 sets out the key characteristics of different types of contingency. Understanding the nature of different types of risk and uncertainty is important in determining where private insurance markets (and sometimes social insurance programs) might struggle to provide coverage and how governments can best deal with this through program design.

Table 5.1: Types of contingency

Type of contingency	Example	Label
Inconceivable risk	Asteroid (before one had been sighted) The wheel (prior to its invention) Smartphone (in 1500, even Da Vinci didn't sketch this)	Unknown unknowns[31]
Conceivable risks that are 'off the radar' and not able to be meaningfully quantified	9/11 (was conceivable, planes had already hit Empire State Building, had been warnings of airborne threat) The internet Black swan (people had seen white swans) Green swan	Black swan
Unquantifiable risk of events that are 'on the radar' Knightian uncertainty	Pulling balls from an urn (not knowing per cent of respective balls) Two aircraft crashing above a city or at airport The eventual success of a highly innovative product or service Theft of rare art from a billionaire's house and other highly idiosyncratic situations	Knightian uncertainty
Quantifiable risk – but with large error bounds	When a war will start When a recession will start When a volcano will blow Pandemic severity (given imperfectly known starting conditions) Macroeconomic 'turning points'	Grey rhino Turning points Thick tail events
Quantifiable risk – that can be relatively accurately estimated	Pulling balls out of urn (knowing per cent of balls) Fire risk Longevity risk Workplace injury Transport accidents	Quantifiable and insurable risks

PART II

THE MODERN WELFARE STATE AND SOCIAL INSURANCE

6.
The Current State of Social Insurance

The twenty-first-century welfare state in most advanced economies constitutes between 20 and 35 per cent of the entire economy. It is critical that governments make these programs work as effectively as possible for the sake of the beneficiaries as well as for the productivity of the overall economy.

TYPES OF SOCIAL INSURANCE PROGRAM

In most advanced economies, social insurance covers risk in five key areas: old age and retirement; healthcare; labour markets; the protection of property; and poverty alleviation or income support.

Social insurance is provided through a wide range of programs, set out in Table 6.1 below, which outlines and contrasts the key characteristics of major social insurance programs:

- Funding mechanisms: The three main funding mechanisms are general taxation revenue; mandatory contributions; and voluntary contributions.
- Risk-rated: Some social insurance programs are risk-rated (such as workers' compensation and transport-accident schemes), some are partially risk-rated (such as social security and unemployment insurance in the US) and some are not risk-rated at all (such as universal healthcare).

- Personal accounts: Some social insurance mechanisms build up capital reserves in accounts that are used to provide benefits for individuals. These accounts are managed by a wide range of governance mechanisms and involve a wide range of control by the individual both in terms of the level of contributions and also how funds are invested (for example, superannuation accounts and the NDIS in Australia).
- Systematic risks: Some social insurance schemes manage systematic as well as individual risks. These include old-age income schemes, property protection and healthcare. Where systematic risks are managed, it is necessary to implement intergenerational risk-sharing mechanisms.
- Short-term costs versus long-term outcomes: There can be trade-offs between containing costs in the short term and achieving long-term outcomes. Managing long-term costs and achieving optimal long-term outcomes may require high up-front expenditure, which can be challenging if social insurance expenses are funded out of taxes.
- Transparency: Social insurance programs have different levels of transparency in the reporting of whole-of-life costs and long-term liabilities.
- Benefits: Some social insurance programs distribute benefits in cash and others as a combination of cash and in-kind goods and services. There are also distinctions between whether benefits are distributed according to a defined formula or entitlement schedule, or whether benefits are provided according to the desires of recipients, whether that be on-demand or rationed where supply is limited.

Almost all the key institutions of the welfare state either pool, transfer or mitigate risk.

Table 6.1: Principal types of social insurance

Theme	Program	Funding			Risk-rated	Personal accounts	Systematic risks	Outcomes	Reporting long-term liabilities	Allocation
		Tax	Mand. cont.	Vol. cont.						
Old age	Public pension	×					Dependency ratio	Benefits vs taxes trade-off	Partial	Defined cash/ in-kind
	P-A-Y-G		×		Partial				×	Defined cash
	Mand. accounts		×			×				Variable cash
	Vol. saving			×		×				Variable cash
	Life insurance			×	×	×			×	Defined cash
Health	Universal healthcare	×					Dependency ratio Pandemics	Upfront costs and prevention as a means of controlling whole-of-life costs and improving long-term outcomes.		On-demand or rationed in-kind
	Private ins			×	Partial				×	Defined in-kind
	NDIS	×				×			×	Choice in-kind
	NIIS	×	×		×				×	Defined cash/ in-kind
	CTP		×		×				×	Defined cash/ in-kind
	Workers' comp.		×		×				×	Defined cash/ in-kind
	Medical indem.		×		×				×	Defined cash
	Veterans' affairs	×								Defined in-kind

Theme	Program	Funding			Risk-rated	Personal accounts	Systematic risks	Outcomes	Reporting long-term liabilities	Allocation
		Tax	Mand. cont.	Vol. cont.						
Labour markets	Unemployment insurance (Australia/ Europe)	×					Business cycle			Defined cash/ in-kind
	Unemployment insurance (US)		×		Partial					
	Income protection			×	×		Business cycle		×	Defined cash
	Lifetime accounts	×	×			×	Automation			Defined in-kind
Protection of property	Home and contents			×	×				×	Defined cash/ in-kind
	NDRRA	×					Natural disasters	Mitigation vs remediation		Defined in-kind
	Mitigation	×					Natural disasters			Defined in-kind
Income support	Poor relief	×								Defined cash
	Public housing	×								Defined in-kind

RETIREMENT INCOME POLICY: AN EDIFICE WITH MULTIPLE PILLARS

The old-age pension was one of the first social insurance schemes introduced in many countries. It has proved to be highly effective at reducing poverty among retirees (albeit not eliminating it). In most advanced economies, increasing life expectancy and falling fertility rates have resulted in rising old-age dependency ratios, which have placed a strain on publicly funded pensions. This has resulted in a range of measures to supplement publicly funded pensions with personal savings accounts.

An intergenerational compact

Edmund Burke, while commenting (not altogether favourably) on Rousseau's conception of a social contract, wrote that 'society is indeed a contract', going on to describe the state as 'a partnership not only between those who are living, but between those who are living, those who are dead, and those who are to be born'.[1] Perhaps in no area of government is this multi-generational compact clearer than the provision of assistance to elderly people.

The multiple pillars of retirement income policy

The World Bank argues that old-age programs should be designed so as to help both elderly people and the economy as a whole. Retiree income programs should help elderly people by facilitating savings, providing a basic income floor and insuring against risks such as longevity, ill health, disability and inflation. The World Bank argues that retirement incomes policy should also support the overall economy by minimising hidden inefficiencies that impede growth, ensuring that benefits are sustainable and being transparent.[2] Out of these micro and macro policy objectives, the World Bank identifies three functions of a retirement system: redistribution, saving and insurance.[3] The OECD defines three key 'indicators' that broadly reflect the World Bank's policy objectives: adequacy, insurance and redistribution.[4] Similarly, in comparing pensions systems, the CFAMercer Global Pension Index assesses retirement income frameworks against three criteria: adequacy, sustainability and integrity.[5]

While the World Bank, the OECD and Mercer indicators are not identical, they capture the core challenge: to provide a decent income to people in retirement, to protect retirees from risks such as longevity and inflation and to perform these functions in a way that is sustainable.

In order to achieve these varying policy objectives, it is necessary to use more than one program. This is the genesis of the 'pillars' approach that many organisations and public-policy experts use to approach and assess retirement income support. The World Bank suggested that a retirement income system should contain three key pillars: a pay-as-you-go publicly funded pension, mandated savings and voluntary savings. Some other institutions suggest variations on this theme with additional pillars relating to workforce participation for the elderly or breaking the publicly funded pension into a basic, means-tested payment and other payments related to average income while in the workforce.

What is common across all these formulations is that a well-functioning retirement income framework should contain both a publicly funded pension and private savings, whether mandated or voluntary. The former achieves social insurance, providing individuals with insurance for longevity, inflation and investment risks that are difficult to obtain through the private sector. Private accounts complement the pension by taking pressure off the taxes necessary to support the pension, particularly with a worsening dependency ratio. In addition, private accounts generate a pool of savings with long-term macroeconomic benefits.

The interaction of public pensions and private accounts also helps to manage systematic risks that arise from a worsening dependency ratio by shifting resources across time so that generations of workers supporting a high number of retirees are not left doing so entirely through a tax-funded transfer system. In a system featuring private accounts, the (relatively) high population cohort of retirees would have shifted some resources across time to at least partially support their own retirement through a portfolio of assets that they own and derive income from.

Inter- versus intra-generational pillars

Perhaps the key distinction between the various pillars of these schemes is between those that are taxpayer-funded as compared to those that involve individuals saving for their own future retirement. Taxpayer-funded pensions are payments from today's taxpayers to today's retirees. They represent intergenerational risk-sharing that only a government can mandate. In contrast, personal accounts represent each generation providing for itself by saving. Each of these arrangements has pros and cons, and the best retirement systems are typically a combination of the two.

Pros and cons

A public pension system can achieve social insurance in ways that private markets struggle to achieve. One issue is the difficulty of achieving universal coverage in annuities markets. As discussed in Chapter 4, there is information asymmetry in private annuity markets which can result in adverse selection. Specifically, if the prices of annuities don't reflect fair value for people with low life expectancy, these people may leave annuities markets. This may then drive up the price of annuities, resulting in a spiral in which increasing numbers of people leave the market. As Feldstein notes, 'A mandatory social insurance program like traditional Social Security circumvents this asymmetry of information by providing everyone with a retirement annuity rather than a lump sum at retirement age'. But whether this is beneficial will depend in part upon people's spending preferences. Some people will want to access at least some of their retirement benefits in the form of lump sums (for example, in holiday homes). In addition, bequest motives may vary considerably.

Many retirement income schemes were initially built around universal means-tested pensions or taxpayer-funded pay-as-you-go schemes in which payments were, and sometimes continue to be, linked to lifetime average earnings. This made sense given the benefits of such schemes. They provide strong intergenerational risk-sharing arrangements that provide retirees with inflation- and longevity-protected income streams. Second, they are administratively simple.[6] Finally, such schemes usually achieve redistribution (by skewing benefits towards low income earners) while maintaining political support by providing substantial benefits to middle- and high-income earners.

But the tax rates required to fund such schemes are problematic – and are becoming increasingly so in most advanced economies as populations age. High tax rates cause direct inefficiency and deadweight loss, and may also reduce the capital stock as compared to a system in which people save for their own retirement. Further, depending on how redistributive such schemes are, they may result in increased tax evasion, particularly where someone perceives that they are receiving less than they put in. Even though publicly funded pensions are good at providing insurance, relying solely on a taxpayer-funded insurance can generate the risk of a government unexpectedly reducing real benefits while a person is in retirement.

Mandated or voluntary savings can offset this macroeconomic challenge of higher taxes being required to fund pensions. In the context of an ageing society, savings involve generations with a high population transferring capital from their working lives to their retirement years so as to reduce the burden of their pensions on future, less populous generations.

While mandated savings can strengthen the long-term viability of the retirement income system, this pillar involves some policy challenges. For example, people with gaps in their employment histories or poor investment outcomes can end up with low balances. This can be particularly problematic for women and people who experience unexpected job losses. Finally, without widespread adoption of annuities, mandated savings pillars will leave at least some people exposed to inflation, longevity and investment risks as they grapple with the complexity of managing large lump sums over retirements of uncertain length.

A multi-pillar approach

It is important to separate the saving, risk-management and redistributive functions of retirement income policy. The redistributive and risk-management functions should be publicly managed and tax-financed. This was the findings of a World Bank Policy Report that a tax-funded retirement income policy 'has the unique capacity to pay benefits to people growing old shortly after the plan is introduced, to redistribute income toward the poor, and to co-insure against long spells of low investment returns, recession, and private market failures'. The key savings pillar should be fully funded and based on mandated private savings.[7] This pillar should be supplemented by voluntary savings.

A multi-pillar approach balances the strengths and weaknesses of different mechanisms to achieve the best overall outcome for the individual retiree and the economy more broadly. Pay-as-you-go and means-tested pension schemes have strong risk-sharing characteristics – both between and within cohorts. Supplementing these schemes with a combination of mandated and voluntary savings arrangements reduces the pressure on public schemes and also builds the capital base of the economy, especially at a time when labour force growth will be decreasing or negative.

A MIX OF PUBLIC AND PRIVATE: HEALTHCARE

The provision of healthcare is the most costly and complex of all social insurance schemes. In most OECD countries, it is built on the foundation of publicly funded universal (or near universal) healthcare. Added to this are a range of public and private schemes that provide healthcare or long-term care in relation to particular contingencies such as disability, accidents in the workplace or transport accidents.

Universal publicly funded healthcare

The bedrock of the provision of health services in most advanced countries is universal (or near-universal) healthcare. These systems provide in-kind benefits on either an on-demand or a rationed basis. In Australia and the US, publicly funded healthcare services are provided by all three levels of government. Universal healthcare (in its various forms) constitutes one of the two largest social insurance programs, along with the age pension, in almost all OECD countries. In addition, publicly funded healthcare is one of the areas of government spending that is forecast to grow fastest over coming decades.

In contrast to most OECD countries, most healthcare provision in the US is supplied through private insurance, usually linked to employment. Since the passage of the *Affordable Care Act* in 2010 (often referred to as 'Obamacare'), private health insurance retains its central role in the provision of healthcare, but is now subject to considerable additional regulatory obligations. Publicly funded healthcare schemes like Medicaid and Medicare are intended to be safety nets for elderly people and those on low incomes.

Australia has adopted a mixed approach, in which private health insurance and household out-of-pocket expenditure are a relatively large share of healthcare expenditure, compared to many European countries.

Private health insurance

In most advanced economies, private insurance complements the public provision of healthcare services. In Australia, just over 40 per cent of people have some form of private health insurance. In the US, private healthcare is more extensive, being linked to most employment contracts. Among the reasons public health is so central in most countries are the information challenges discussed earlier: adverse selection, moral hazard and imperfect information.[8]

Adverse selection: Information asymmetry in relation to an individual's underlying health condition is a serious challenge in many areas of health insurance.

We are entering an era where genomic testing and the use of big data may be reducing and possibly removing this challenge. Indeed, we may soon find ourselves in a situation where insurers know more about our current and future health prospects than we do ourselves. Modern medicine is increasingly able to accurately assess someone's health quickly and at little cost. Perhaps even more importantly, genomic testing and other forms of modern medicine such as the application of big data to an individual's circumstances are enabling insurers to estimate the likelihood of illness far into the future. This is problematic for people seeking private health coverage in that these technological advances threaten to drastically increase the cost of insurance for those with certain pre-existing conditions. That is why in many countries, private health insurers are prevented from fully risk-rating their products. In Australia, community rating restrictions mean that insurers are only able to discriminate on the basis of gender. It should not be assumed that these types of restrictions on risk-rating will continue indefinitely.[9]

Moral hazard: Once a person has health insurance, there will be an incentive for at least some people to take fewer precautions with their health.[10] There is no clear empirical basis for thinking that this is a material determinant of people's behaviour, probably given the many non-financial benefits associated with good health (e.g. quality of life and longevity) and the material non-financial costs associated with serious medical conditions. Most analysis of moral hazard in relation to healthcare focuses on the consumption of services among insured individuals and the decisions made by their health practitioners. There is at least some empirical support for the contention that moral hazard leads to higher health expenditure.[11]

Imperfect information: Healthcare services are characterised by a great deal of complexity. Unlike buying groceries or clothes, consumers are often overwhelmed by the choices they are offered by health care professionals. There are numerous elements of this complexity:

- Healthcare services are highly technical and are becoming increasingly so. Many doctors struggle to convey core concepts to patients, particularly those with language difficulties or mental-health issues;
- Consumers are often poorly informed about the specific healthcare services that they are being offered, particularly in emergency situations where there is little time for patients or family to digest information and decisions need to be made quickly;
- In many situations, there is an inherent uncertainty as to the likelihood of success of different treatment strategies. This can make it difficult even for experts to understand what the prospects for the patient are;
- Quite often, doctors (or other professionals) will offer choices to patients in relation to different treatment strategies in situations that involve a great deal of uncertainty. While allowing patients input into decision-making is worthwhile and has been a positive development in patient care, some patients seek unambiguous, certain, 'expert' advice rather than multiple options with often ill-defined likelihoods of success;
- Competition can be of limited usefulness. In the case of simple or homogeneous goods or services, competition can improve quality and put downward pressure on price. In the context of healthcare services, getting a second opinion can sometimes be useful, but competition is inherently more limited given the challenges outlined above. Moreover, competition in healthcare can lead to declining quality in some

contexts, such as where the desire for higher profits results in pressure to reduce the length of stay in hospitals or take fewer expensive tests.

The consequences of decisions in relation to healthcare can be extremely serious, literally 'life or death' or, if not, still potentially irreversible.

Together, these three information challenges create considerable difficulties for private insurers in relation to covering health risks. Principally, these difficulties relate to the effectiveness of consumer choice, gaps in coverage for pre-existing conditions, gaps in coverage for elderly people and in relation to elective procedures and pregnancy, and cost containment.

Workers' compensation

Legislated workers' compensation schemes first arose in the late nineteenth century. The first scheme was enacted by Bismarck in the late 1880s. While he originally intended for it to be publicly funded, opposition to this model resulted in the adoption of a model in which employers and employees co-funded the scheme. This would become the model adopted throughout Europe and the UK. Almost all of Europe had enacted compulsory workers' compensation schemes by 1900. As noted above (in Chapter 2), these legislated schemes replaced less formal arrangements (such as 'friendly societies' in the UK and Australia, and 'Krankenkassen' in Germany) that had already arisen in response to the difficulties of winning compensation through court proceedings.[12]

It was between 1900 (in South Australia) and 1926 (NSW) that Australian states introduced workers' compensation schemes, based on the British model enshrined in the 1897 act.[13] These schemes were generally no-fault and restricted compensation to bodily injuries. With the exception of Queensland and the Commonwealth, the underwriting and administration of workers' compensation claims was undertaken by private insurers until the early 1980s. As a result of claims pressures and administrative inefficiency, there was a move towards public underwriting in some jurisdictions during the 1980s. Currently in Australia, there is a mix of publicly underwritten and administered (Commonwealth, Queensland); publicly underwritten with outsourced claims administration (NSW, Vic., SA); and privately underwritten (WA, Tas., ACT, NT).[14]

Support for veterans

Programs to support veterans often go under the radar, but they are significant programs in many countries, both in terms of funding levels and the number of vulnerable people who rely upon them. In the 2020/21 US federal budget, veterans' programs totalled US$236 billion in spending, which included US$119 billion in income support, US$93 billion in hospital and medical care and US$15 billion in education, training and rehabilitation.[15] In Australia, spending on veterans' programs totalled A$13.2 billion in 2017/18, of which $7.4 billion was spent on compensation and support, $5.3 billion on healthcare and $440 million on enabling services such as workplace training. Veterans' programs in Australia supported around 166,000 veterans and 117,000 dependents.[16]

The Productivity Commission reviewed the performance of Australia's veterans' support programs, reporting in 2019. Much like its review of pre-NDIS government support for people with a disability, the Productivity Commission found that the current system is overly complex and difficult to navigate for veterans; poorly targeted in some areas; inefficient in parts; and insufficiently focused on outcomes. One of the key recommendations arising from the review is a need to focus on the lifetime welfare of veterans, better balancing both their short-term and long-term wellbeing.[17]

Motor vehicle accident schemes

Motor vehicle usage was not widespread during the first decade of the twentieth century. Between 1903 and 1914, there were over two and a half times more deaths from electric trams in Sydney than cars.[18] Despite this, as early as 1900 there was significant concern in some quarters about the universal adoption of cars:

> The real truth is that when the motor comes into universal use life will not be worth living. … A horse does not like to run a man down if he can help it, but a machine of steel and brass will delight in killing people.[19]

After 1910, car usage increased sharply. In 1910, there were 4000 registered motor vehicles in NSW and 2735 in Victoria. By 1925, the national total was 300,000. Unsurprisingly, the number of serious accidents increased as well. In 1925, 700 people were killed as a result of motor vehicle accidents; by 1930 the figure had risen to more than 1000.

While victims had access to the common law, this was problematic for several reasons: the expense and delay of court proceedings; the onus on the defendant of proving fault; and the difficulty of extracting compensation even in the case of victory in court, given that only around half of motorists held third-party liability insurance.[20]

The limitations of common law redress resulted in consideration of mandatory third-party insurance. Legislation mandating third-party motor vehicle insurance was passed in two US jurisdictions in the 1920s (Connecticut in 1925 and Massachusetts in 1926) as well as in the UK in 1930. Similar legislation was passed in Australia in all states and territories between 1935 and 1949, starting with Tasmania.

Initially, private insurers provided underwriting and claims administration in all Australian jurisdictions. Between the late 1940s and the early 1970s, most Australian jurisdictions moved towards public underwriting as a result of the cost pressures, delays and the administrative complexity associated with the common law system.

In Australia, third-party motor vehicle insurance currently varies across jurisdictions. There is a range of approaches to entitlements and benefits, with jurisdictions ranging from pure no-fault (NT); to a mix of no-fault with common law add-ons (Vic. and Tas.) and pure common law (NSW, QLD, WA, ACT). Similarly, there is a mix of approaches to underwriting across jurisdictions, with some adopting public underwriting by a monopoly (Vic., Tas., NT, WA) and some private underwriting with competition (NSW, QLD, SA, ACT).[21]

In 2006, the NSW government established the Lifetime Care and Support Authority (NSW–LTCSA) for those who had suffered catastrophic injuries (such as spinal injury or brain trauma) in motor vehicle accidents. There were two key rationales behind the LTCSA. The first was to provide assistance to people in managing large amounts of compensation to meet complex and potentially varying requirements over the course of their lifetime. The second was to achieve consistency and equity in the provision of benefits and services across claimants. Each year, around 180 people enter the scheme on an interim basis, with approximately 120 remaining in the scheme as lifetime participants. As at 31 December 2021, there were 1728 participants in the scheme, of which 319 were interim.[22] As will be discussed below in Chapter 14, several elements of LTCSA are worth considering for broader adoption across social insurance programs involving the management of complex, long-term problems.

Disability

Support for people with a disability was one of the earliest features of the modern welfare state. It was a key plank in Bismarck's reforms and as well as Roosevelt's *Social Security Act*, which underpinned the New Deal. In Australia, the National Disability Insurance Scheme (NDIS) is one of the great social-policy reforms of the postwar era.

While not all expenditure within the NDIS is related to healthcare, it is included within the broader healthcare ecosystem as that reflects a significant proportion of expenditure within the scheme. The challenges that led to the establishment of the NSW–LTCSA – namely the difficulty of managing resources over across a person's entire lifespan and achieving equitable funding between people with different requirements – had long applied to people with a disability. This is partly what inspired the creation of the NDIS. As outlined earlier, the findings of the Disability Investment Group in 2008 resulted in a Productivity Commission report recommending the establishment of the NDIS.

In 2012, an Intergovernmental Agreement was signed by all states and territories for the launch of the NDIS, making way for its establishment in 2013.[23] In the 2020/21 budget, the NDIS was allocated A$20.4 billion.[24]

Accidental injury

In its final report in relation to the NDIS, the Productivity Commission recommended the establishment of a no-fault National Injury Insurance Scheme (NIIS) to operate in parallel with the NDIS, particularly given that the NDIS did not cover acquired injuries.[25] The recommendation to establish an NIIS echoed the findings of the Woodhouse Royal Commission in New Zealand in 1967, which argued that limitations, inconsistencies and delays in common-law remedies justified the establishment of a national injury compensation scheme which would totally replace the common law.

The New Zealand Accident Compensation Corporation (ACC), which began operating in 1974, now employs over 3500 staff, processes over 2 million registered claims and manages an investment portfolio of over NZ$50 billion. The ACC is designed to assist people in managing resources across long recovery periods, possibly their entire lives. It also sets itself clearly defined targets. Around two-thirds of clients return to work within ten weeks (slightly above the ACC's target) and, for those not in the workforce, over 87 per cent return to independence (slightly below the ACC's target).[26]

Despite many good outcomes, there are some who question the scheme's design. In a retrospective on the Woodhouse Royal Commission, Geoffrey Palmer argued that the scheme only reflects around half of the recommendations arising from the Royal Commission. He writes that:

> The major policy issues upon which the Woodhouse approach did not prevail included the administrative arrangements, the methods of financing, the compensation payments themselves, particularly opposition to lump sums and the design of the systems for determining disputes about eligibility, and the causes of, and the degree of, incapacity. Had the Report been followed, it would have been easier to integrate the scheme into the rest of the income support system.[27]

In particular, Palmer argues that it was a mistake to adopt a fully funded model rather than a pay-as-you-go approach, as recommended by Woodhouse. The former has resulted in the building up of large reserves, which resulted in a great deal of controversy in relation to premium levels. Palmer also argued that the model ultimately adopted in New Zealand doesn't place accident prevention and rehabilitation at the core of service delivery as recommended but, rather, that it focuses too much on compensation.

Those advocating for a fully funded approach argue that the benefits include actuarial rigour in setting contribution levels, transparency in relation to scheme sustainability, and limiting the impact of short-term budget constraints on benefit levels.

In Australia, making progress with the NIIS has been difficult, thanks in part to the complexity of aligning multiple jurisdictions, each with their own existing schemes. To date, there have been no material steps towards harmonisation of motor vehicle accident insurance, workers' compensation or medical indemnity insurance. Progress in relation to types of accident without clear funding streams has been even more limited.

Long-term care

Publicly funded pensions were among the first planks of the welfare state in most countries, including Germany (established in the 1880s), Australia (1900–1909), the UK (1908) and the US (1935). The previous chapter outlined the significant size of retirement income-support programs in most OECD countries. These programs now constitute the second-largest single welfare program in most countries after healthcare.

The income support provided by public pensions has made a huge difference to the standard of living of retirees. A 1913 study of 100 elderly people in Greenwich Village in New York found that only twenty-seven were able to support themselves.[28] For those unable to support themselves or rely upon family, the only option was a poorhouse or almshouse. These institutions were usually funded by local or municipal government and often involved some requirement to work. The conditions in many poorhouses were appalling, involving poor sanitation, punishment and separation of men and women. While poorhouses provided accommodation to people of all ages, by the 1920s and 1930s in the US, two-thirds of poorhouse residents were elderly.[29]

What is striking about support for retirees is that income-support programs like the age pension were far quicker (and easier) to implement than long-term, holistic support, including healthcare and accommodation. For example, in the US, according to Mabel Nassau:

> In the years following the passage of the Social Security Act of 1935, the number of elderly in poorhouses refused to drop. States moved to close them but found they could not. The reason old people wound up in poorhouses, it turned out, was not just that they didn't have money to pay for a home. They were there because they'd become too frail, sick, feeble, senile, or broken down to take care of themselves anymore, and they had nowhere else to turn for help.[30]

As many poorhouses closed in the US in the 1950s, large numbers of the elderly people that had been housed there were moved to hospitals. After lobbying from hospitals, funding was provided for new institutions to take the pressure off hospitals: 'nursing homes'. The very name of these institutions reflected the fact that responsibility for many dependent elderly people had, in effect, passed to the healthcare system.

Given the chronic health needs of many of the people that they supported, it is no wonder that nursing homes of this era had a focus on healthcare. But what has become clear over the intervening decades is that many elderly people who found themselves in these institutions have much more potential for independent living than was at first thought – and, even more importantly, much more desire for independence.

There have been many attempts around the world to provide elderly people with more autonomy and more individualised care. Providing a less institutional environment has taken many forms. In the 1960s 'co-housing' developments were pioneered in Denmark and the Netherlands, which were characterised by self-contained apartments, communal living spaces and active networks of mutual support.[31] There are now around 300 co-housing developments in the Netherlands and 160 in the US.

In the US, 'assisted living' was first developed in the 1980s with the similar goal of creating a more independent existence. Assisted living quickly grew to become a large segment of the market, although some question whether all housing so labelled provides more independence in substance.

'Retirement villages' are an additional option, typically involving large property developments limited to people above a certain age. In Australia, 11 per cent of retirees live in a retirement village, with many new developments situated near suburbs with a concentration of younger families so as to give retirees the option of living near their children and grandchildren.[32]

Even with these additional accommodation and long-term care options, many elderly people continue live on their own. Even though living alone can reflect an independent lifestyle, it can increase a person's risk of social isolation. The rate of retirees living alone isn't a problem per se, but it raises the issue of whether measures to boost social connections are worth supporting. The Beacon Hill village in Boston is an example of this approach that has inspired a number of similar programs.[33]

A number of characteristics of the long-term and interdependent nature of the health and social issues that can arise for elderly people have proved problematic for health and social-service agencies. Resource allocation over lifetimes can be difficult. The move towards NSW-LTCSA outlined above for road trauma that caused lifetime health and resource management challenges reflected the special challenges arising from long-term health conditions.

Quite often, elderly people will experience health and social issues that need to be dealt with by multiple agencies, often at different levels of government. When the agencies don't communicate with each other, the recipient of services can find the multiplicity of contacts confusing and the services that they receive can end up being disjointed. In her exploration of policies to improve service delivery for elderly people, Camilla Cavendish documents the challenges arising from the administrative and bureaucratic complexity that creeps into many systems:

> A few years ago, I met an 89-year-old gentleman who had made a note of every carer who had crossed his threshold in the previous year. He showed me the list: there were 102 names on it. Some had only come once, then vanished ...[34]

Better-quality long-term care for elderly people is an area that needs better social insurance arrangements in many countries. Given that they are at the forefront of the challenges facing ageing societies, it should not be surprising that Germany and Japan have been among the first nations to implement holistic social insurance arrangements for long-term care, particularly for elderly people.[35]

Germany introduced mandatory social insurance for long-term care in 1995. Contributions by workers are mandatory, with 90 per cent of beneficiaries covered by social insurance and 10 per cent by private insurance. Benefits are individualised, with retirees grouped into five categories of needs. Benefits can then be accessed either at home or in supported living, and are available either in cash or in kind, or a combination.

Cash benefits can be used to pay for family care. As of 2016, 80 per cent of beneficiaries chose cash benefits, which reflected 64 per cent of total scheme expenditures (€31 billion).[36] The scheme was significantly reformed in 2015–2017, by extending coverage to include people with dementia and increasing scheme funding by over 20 per cent per annum.[37]

In 2000, Japan introduced social insurance for long-term care mandating premium payments from every worker over the age of forty. Benefits are available to every person over sixty-five for all services, covering 90 per cent of needs (but with no provision for cash payments for family care).[38]

LABOUR MARKETS

Job loss is one of the greatest risks that individuals and households face. The scourge of mass unemployment has become emblematic of the economic and social harm caused by economy-wide downturns. The first image of a recession that comes to mind for many is the queues of unemployed people waiting patiently outside government offices for benefits. Before the welfare state, people queued for food and survival, often from charities, rather than cash and in-kind benefits from the government. It was the desperation and mass human misery of the Great Depression that drove many countries to introduce unemployment insurance as a key plank of the modern welfare state.

In addition to the negative impact that unemployment has on household income and short-term consumption, job loss often has profound and long-lasting impacts on self-esteem, mental health and future employability. The negative impacts of job loss can be pronounced for a range of vulnerable groups. Some older workers, particularly those with narrow skill sets, can become permanently disengaged from the labour market. Younger workers who lose a job may fail to accumulate the experience that is so critical to having more job opportunities in mid-career. And those experiencing job loss in regional areas may find themselves with few alternative options and a choice between the risk of prolonged unemployment or having to move away from family and friends.

As important as unemployment insurance has been, labour markets present several additional risks that are often less obvious than job loss, but that can be just as profound and challenging to manage:

- the risk of interruptions to one's working life, for example due to raising children or taking on a carer role. This can impact career progression and, over the long term, retirement savings;
- the risk that a particular skill or qualification will become redundant or less sought after (for example due to automation, skills-biased technological change or competition via trade);
- the risk that one's chosen career will experience lower long-term wage growth than the economy as a whole.

Some of these risks are addressed through schemes that support or complement unemployment insurance. Others remain largely unaddressed, to date.

Unemployment benefits

Unemployment benefits were introduced in the UK in 1911, in the US in 1935 as part of the Second New Deal and in Australia in 1945 following World War II. In Australia and the UK, the program is administered by the national government, while in the US it is largely administered by state governments according to rules jointly determined at the state and federal level.[39]

Australia's unemployment benefit scheme is different to those in most advanced economies in that benefits are not linked to earlier employment status. First, in Australia, unemployment benefits are generally a flat (and means-tested) cash payment that is not time-limited, along with a range of in-kind benefits and subsidies. In many other OECD countries, benefits are set as a proportion of earlier earnings. Second, entitlement to unemployment benefits in Australia does not depend upon having worked a minimum period of time, which acts as a quasi-contributory component of many other systems. These two characteristics of Australia's unemployment programs make it less like contributory insurance than many other schemes and more akin to redistributive income support.

Following the outbreak of Covid-19 in 2020, the Australian government (broadly mirroring schemes adopted in other countries) adopted a widespread wage-subsidy scheme that ultimately cost the federal government over A$100 billion. It was the largest single welfare measure in Australia's history. A wage-subsidy scheme was adopted because it was seen to have significant advantages over enhancing unemployment insurance measures alone. Importantly, wage subsidies would ensure that workers continued to be employed, even when their employer was temporarily unable to cover wages. This was seen as appropriate as the work stoppages in many sectors were expected to be temporary measures.

In the US, unemployment insurance is generally at least partially contributory, with cash support set as a proportion of previous earnings, up to a cap. Payments are generally time-limited. The replacement rate of previous wages and the time limit varies by state. In most European countries, benefits are a proportion of prior earnings, although at a higher level and for a longer period than in the US.[40]

The impacts of unemployment benefits on labour supply

The potential for unemployment benefits to create a disincentive for beneficiaries to work (described by some as 'moral hazard') is one of the most intensely studied components of the welfare state. The most commonly studied aspect of unemployment benefits is the degree to which the generosity of benefits creates a disincentive to search for or accept jobs. The generosity of unemployment benefits is typically measured in terms of the duration of benefits and the quantum of benefit payments and non-financial benefits.

Not surprisingly, empirical studies in a range of settings generally find a negative correlation between benefit duration or payment levels and the willingness of recipients to enter the labour market.[41] Having said that, it is important to note that studies have found heterogeneous impacts across different groups within society.[42] Moreover, while empirical studies generally find a negative correlation, the estimated impact on labour supply is modest in many contexts.[43]

Unemployment insurance can produce greater economic efficiency in so far as it can help encourage people to accept productive jobs with a risk of future layoffs. In addition, while unemployment benefits may discourage job search or acceptance rates at the margin, they may also allow for longer periods of job search and, consequently, higher-quality matches between jobs and skills, resulting in better long-term outcomes.

Active labour market programs

Active labour market programs aim to assist job seekers to re-enter the labour market. These programs range from brokerage and job matching through to resource-intensive training programs. They are often tailored to individual needs, with higher levels of support being provided to the most vulnerable job seekers. This is in contrast to unemployment benefits, which are typically either provided as flat payments, regardless of need (e.g. Australia) or payments that are positively correlated with past income (e.g. the US).

In some countries, labour market programs have been one of the most active areas of policy experimentation in relation to outsourcing and marketisation. The UK and Australia have been at the forefront of these developments. The evidence is mixed in relation to the extent to which this has led to either improved long-term outcomes or efficiency in service delivery.

INCOME SUPPORT

Poverty alleviation – and indeed survival itself – was the motivation for many of the earliest informal risk-sharing arrangements. In agricultural societies, sharing the harvest or the hunt was the most obvious method for minimising the threat of starvation for individuals and families.

Much later, in the eighteenth and nineteenth centuries, governments intervened in order to help some poor people survive and even, on occasion, live in dignity. But these schemes rarely exceeded 1 per cent of GDP, even as late as the nineteenth century. The English Poor Laws were a notable exception, yet even this program provided very limited relief. It wasn't until the twentieth century that income-support programs reached a significant scale.

Today, income-support schemes exist in many advanced economies for vulnerable groups, including carers and dependents. But these schemes are generally far smaller than the social insurance programs dealing with retirement incomes, healthcare and labour markets.

TAKING TURNS: MOST OF US WITHDRAW FROM THE POOL AT SOME POINT

There is a perception among some that the welfare system is relied upon by a particular group, which is funded by taxpayers. This is sometimes put into a semi-conflictual frame (more often from the conservative side of politics). In Australia, there is the language of the 'lifters' versus the 'leaners'; in the US, it's the 'makers' versus the 'takers'; and in the UK, there are 'strivers' and 'skivers'. Alliteration and rhyming are clearly important rhetorical techniques in this context.

The most insightful data about the ways in which individuals and households benefit from the welfare system comes from longitudinal studies that capture financial and social outcomes over the life cycle. Findings arising from the key longitudinal studies from the US and Australia are referenced below.

The Panel Study of Income Dynamics (PSID) has tracked more than 75,000 people in the US since the 1960s. It is described as a 'panel' as it combines cross-sectional data with data over time ('longitudinal data'). Specifically, the PSID measures characteristics of people across a cross-section of society but it also measures outcomes for individuals and families over time. The PSID data reflects how much people's (and families') incomes vary across their lifetimes. It found that, on average, a person's highest income was over double their lowest income across a ten-year period.[44]

This means that snapshots of the economy do not tend to reflect the reality of an individual's economic experience. This is especially the case with poverty rates. For example, the child poverty rate in the US was estimated to be around 20 per cent in 2013.[45] But this figure does not take reflect the churn rates of families in poverty. For example, in 2015, the proportion of children who experience at least one year in poverty before the age of eighteen is in fact around 40 per cent, and as much 75 per cent for black children.[46] On one estimate, over 60 per cent of Americans will spend at least one year in poverty between the ages of twenty-five and sixty.[47]

Data from the Bureau of Labor Statistics' (BLS) National Longitudinal Survey of Youth in 1979 (NLSY79) contains long-term longitudinal data in relation to US labour force participation and the receipt of welfare benefits for a cohort born between 1957 and 1964. Donna Rothstein shows that of the cohort of men born in this range, 22.3 per cent had at least one period of long-term unemployment (27+ weeks), 21 per cent had at least one period of intermediate unemployment (15–26 weeks) and 50.3 per cent had at least one period of short-term unemployment (2–14 weeks).[48]

Of the cohort that experienced at least one spell of short-term unemployment, the average number of periods of short-term unemployment was 2.57 across the average person's life from entry into the labour force up until 2009. While there is some overlap between these groups, what these figures reflect is the high proportion of workers who experience at least some form of unemployment during their working-age life. This means that a high proportion of people will benefit from unemployment insurance and other forms of welfare.

Similar dynamics are at play in the Australian economy. Over the long term, a significant proportion of households rely on some form of income support, even if for short periods of time. The Household Income and Labour Dynamics in Australia (HILDA) Survey is a household panel study that is the most comprehensive source of longitudinal social data in Australia.[49] In its 2017 statistical report, HILDA examined the proportion of households which had relied upon welfare support at any stage between 2001 and 2015. Among HILDA's sample, 45.6 per cent of individuals and 70.5 per cent of households received income support from the welfare system at some point during those years. Only 30.8 per cent of men and 28.3 per cent of women lived in a household where no one was in receipt of welfare at any stage between 2001 and 2015. In addition, 33.3 per cent of men received support for a period of one to three years, while only 5.6 per cent received support for the entire fifteen-year period; similarly, 29.4 per cent of women received support for between one and three years while only 8.3 per cent took benefits for the entire fifteen-year period.[50]

Australia's Productivity Commission found that, between 2000–01 and 2015–16, on average, each person spent time in five different income deciles and that close to 90 per cent of people had a difference of at least three deciles between the top and bottom deciles that they spent time in.[51] The Productivity Commission found that commonly occurring major life events – career progression, changes in living arrangements, leaving or entering the labour force, family formation and separation, retirement – often drive movements up and down the income and wealth deciles.[52] Social insurance often helps people deal with the economic disruption and loss associated with such events.

While a small minority of individuals and households have a long-term reliance on the welfare system, it is important to stress that a large majority of the population benefit from the safety net at *some point*. Most of us switch between being 'leaners' and 'lifters', not because we suddenly becoming lazy or unmotivated but, in the vast majority of cases, due to shocks that are beyond our control. Viewing the welfare state through the prism of social insurance (as opposed to redistribution) reinforces this point.

7.
Government and Systematic Risks

A wide range of systematic risks affect society as a whole and it is typically the role of government to manage these risks. These include war, pandemics, economic cycles, automation, population ageing, climate change and very significant droughts and natural disasters.

When discussing the nature of insurance in Chapter 4, a distinction was made between risks affecting an individual, a household or a firm, and risks with much wider impact. Pooling works well for individual risks which have a low correlation with each other but is less effective where risks affect a whole community or society at the same time. In the case of systematic risks, all that pooling will be able to achieve is for those that are relatively less affected to provide some compensation to those that are more affected than average.

Systematic risks require a different type of approach than risks that affect individual people or businesses. Consider the example outlined in Chapter 4 of fire risk in a community of 100 homes each of equal value. If one house randomly burns down each year on average, a premium equal to 1 per cent of each home's construction cost will be sufficient to generate a pool that can fund the rebuilding of that house.

In contrast, if that community is subject to an additional risk of a one-in-100-year bushfire that will burn down the entire community, that requires a different kind of risk management. Assuming for a moment that the community is self-contained and autarkic (that is, that it can't rely on assistance from other communities within a broader nation-state), it will only be possible to manage the systematic risk of a bushfire through intertemporal resource pooling, often involving the allocation of resources between different generations. One way of achieving this would be to build up a pool of financial resources over time that could be drawn upon, should a major bushfire occur, to rebuild the entire community. Another would be to use long-term debt to benefit a generation that is disproportionately affected by a disaster.

Two types of systematic risk

Some systematic risks involve infrequent catastrophic events: pandemics, natural disasters, major economic downturns and wars. Others, involve slowly evolving threats that emerge over decades or centuries: climate change, ageing and structural economic change (for example, arising from automation, skills-biased technological change or globalisation).

A key challenge in dealing with infrequent, catastrophic events is predicting the frequency, severity and timing of major events. We use the term 'one-in-100-year flood' – but what does this really mean? There are two issues that forecasters grapple with when it comes to infrequent events. First, is predicting the frequency of major catastrophes. In general, due to data limitations, the more infrequent an event is, the more difficult it will be to accurately estimate the underlying likelihood of the event. This is problematic as the most damaging events are generally the least frequent. A distinct challenge is that, even if it were possible to accurately estimate the frequency of a severely damaging event, it doesn't necessarily help in estimating its timing. If there is a low or zero correlation between such events, the fact that one occurred very recently or hasn't occurred for a long time may offer little or no guidance as to when the next 'big one' is due.

The second category of systematic events are what might be described as the grey rhinos. While a phenomenon that evolves over decades or longer (such as climate change) might appear to offer less of a forecasting challenge than a randomly occurring, infrequent disaster, this is not always the case. This creates profound challenges for public policy in terms of deciding when to take action to ameliorate or adapt to the impacts of such trends.

RARE, HIGHLY IMPACTFUL DISASTERS

The following section describes the difficulty of estimating the frequency of rare floods as a case study of the broader challenge that society faces in dealing with infrequent, devastating events.

Between November 2010 and January 2011, floods swept across Queensland. An area larger than Germany and France combined was declared a disaster zone. These floods resulted in the deaths of thirty-three people and economic costs that have been estimated at more than A$5 billion,[1] with some figures as high as $30 billion.[2] This wasn't the first time that Queensland had experienced extreme flooding; major floods in 1893 and 1974 have been imprinted on the collective memory of the state.

Floods are the most economically costly form of natural disaster in many countries and represent a significant risk to both human life and the broader economy. One of the most commonly used measures of risk in many countries is the one-in-100-year flood. This is often referred to as a flood with a 1 per cent Annual Exceedance Probability (AEP).[3] This is the default for setting for the 'design flood' in the US,[4] the EU[5] and Australia.[6] One-in-100-year floods are important for two reasons. First, it is very difficult to predict when one will occur. Second, when one occurs, it creates significant, widespread damage. It is the combination of these things that makes it difficult to manage the associated risks.

The difficulty of quantifying the likelihood of rare events

How confident can we be in claiming that a flood of a particular depth is a one-in-100-year event? If, in 100 years of hydrological data, one 10-metre level flood is observed, does that mean that we can say with a high degree of confidence that such a flood is a one-in-100-year event? Does it mean that we can say that the property has roughly a 1 per cent chance of serious flood damage each year and charge a premium accordingly? Unfortunately, for homeowners, insurers and governments, the answer is no. Table 7.1 shows the likelihood of a 10-metre flood being observed over a period of 100 years. The first scenario is that the true underlying probability of a flood of 10 metres is one in fifty years (or a 2 per cent AEP) and that each year there is an independent random likelihood of this event occurring. The other two scenarios are that such a flood is a 1 per cent AEP and a 0.5 per cent AEP.[7]

Table 7.1: Likelihood of a (hypothetical) 10-metre flood occurring based on different AEPs[8]

	Actual underlying frequency of 10m flood		
Observed floods at 10-metre level	**1 in 50 years** (AEP = 2 per cent)	**1 in 100 years** (AEP = 1 per cent)	**1 in 200 years** (AEP = 0.5 per cent)
Likelihood of 0 occurrences	13.3 per cent	36.6 per cent	60.6 per cent
Likelihood of 1 occurrence	27.1 per cent	37.0 per cent	30.4 per cent
Likelihood of 2 occurrences	27.3 per cent	18.5 per cent	7.6 per cent
Likelihood of 3 occurrences	18.2 per cent	6.1 per cent	1.2 per cent

The first column sets out the likelihood of a 10-metre flood occurring zero times, once, twice and three times if the underlying likelihood is that such a flood is a one-in-fifty-year event. If a 10-metre flood is a one-in-fifty-year event, there is a 27.3 per cent chance that such a flood will occur twice in 100 years of observation. This is the most likely outcome – which would seem intuitive. But there is a 72.7 per cent chance that a different number of occurrences will occur. Indeed, the second-most likely outcome (one occurrence) is almost as likely as two occurrences. Zero and three observations also have a relatively high degree of likelihood.

If the underlying true likelihood of the drought is once in 100 years, then the most likely outcome of 100 years of data is that such a flood will occur once (37 per cent). But it is almost as likely that there will be no observations (36.6 per cent). As with the one-in-fifty-year probability, if the true underlying probability is one in 100 years, then there is a substantially greater than 50 per cent likelihood that the number of observations will vary from one.

If the underlying probability is one in 200, then the most likely outcome is that there will be no such floods in 100 years of data. But there is a 30.4 per cent chance that there will be one such event and a 7.6 per cent chance of two occurrences.

If a 10-metre flood occurred once, what can we conclude? Is it a one-in-100-year event? Possibly, but not necessarily. If we observe one

10-metre flood event in 100 years, it is entirely plausible that the underlying frequency is in fact one in fifty years or one in 200 years.

As outlined earlier, if the underlying probability is one in fifty, then what we observed had a 27.1 per cent chance of occurring. And if the underlying probability is one in 200, then what we observed had a 30.4 per cent chance of occurring.

If we know how often a certain event is likely to occur, it is easy to calculate the likelihood of the event occurring a certain number of times, as in Table 7.1. In practice, our analysis works in the opposite direction. We are usually interested in, but don't know, the underlying probability. Rather, we know retrospectively how many times the event occurred over a given period of time. The difficulty is in using these observations to draw a conclusion about the underlying likelihood of a 10-metre flood.

Additional data that can be used

In estimating the risk of a rare event, we can usually deploy additional data. In the context of flooding, we can use the full distribution of rainfall data. Consider a hypothetical distribution of rainfall events as set out in Figure 7.1. The grey bars represent the number of times floods of various levels were observed over the past 100 years (hypothetically). Even though there are no 10-metre floods during this period, we can use this data to estimate an overall distribution pattern (the 'probability distribution function', or PDF). One possible PDF is the black line, which gives insight into how likely a 10-metre or 11-metre flood is.

One limitation of this approach is that the estimated likelihood of a rare event can sometimes be highly sensitive to the shape of the right 'tail' of the PDF. A very slight tweak in the calibration of the PDF for extreme events might see a 10-metre flood estimated to be a one-in-500-year or even a one-in-1000-year event.

Initial estimates of the 2011 Queensland floods, which were based on thirty-one years of rain gauge data, estimated the AEP at 0.05 per cent (which amounts to a one-in-2000-year event). After five more years of data, which included another extreme event in 2013, the AEP was reduced to 1.11 per cent (or a one-in-ninety-year event).[9]

Subsequent research has assessed the likelihood of rare flood events by supplementing rain gauge data with paleological records. The paleoflood record for the Lockyer Valley in Queensland extends back several thousand years. That time series indicates that events like the 2011 floods have occurred at least seven times over the past 1000 years, indicating that they are more common than originally estimated.[10]

Figure 7.1: Hypothetical distribution of flood observations over a 100-year period

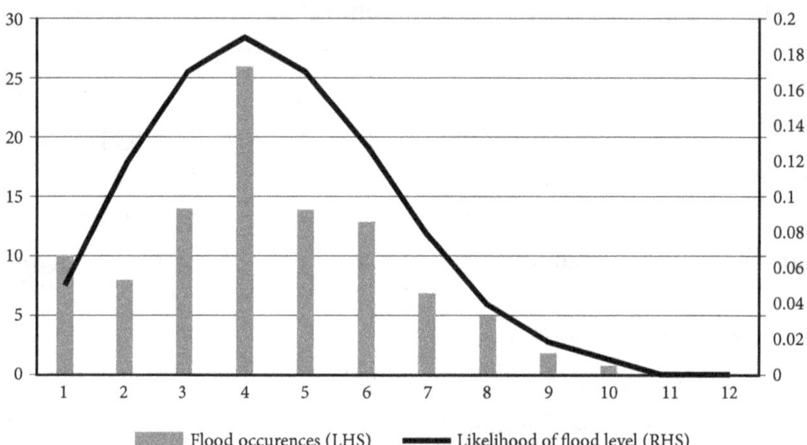

Second, we can use hydrological and engineering analysis to assess the likelihood of extreme events such as a 10-metre or 11-metre floods. This analysis could use detailed height mapping and flood mapping to estimate water flows in a range of scenarios. Detailed flood maps are now available for high-risk areas across most of Australia, the US, the UK and Europe.

In our hypothetical example, a combination of historical and hydrological data may demonstrate that an 11-metre flood is not physically possible, while a 10-metre flood is possible, but highly unlikely.

Combining all available evidence to estimate the likelihood of rare events

Thomas Bayes, an eighteenth-century preacher, philosopher and statistician, developed a powerful analytical framework for using observed data to make inferences about the underlying probability of different events. He developed one of the most powerful statistical insights in the history of the discipline. In short, Bayes' Law produces an estimate of the likelihood of a future event based on knowledge of past conditions that might be related to the potential future event.

In this case, Bayes' Law helps to describe the likelihood of a future 10-metre flood based on how often 10-metre floods – and other similar depth floods – have occurred in the past.

Bayes' Law is simple to describe:

$$P(A|B) = \frac{P(B|A) \times P(A)}{P(B)}$$

In words, this equation states that the probability of A, given that B is true, is equal to the probability of B, given that A is true, multiplied by the probability of A and divided by the probability of B.

While it is simple to state Bayes' Law, it is typically difficult to apply it to estimate likelihoods in practice.

To give a simple example with regard to estimating the likelihood of a flood, imagine that we are trying to choose between two scenarios. Scenario A is that a 10-metre flood is a one-in-fifty-year event. Scenario B is that a 10-metre flood is a one-in-100-year event. Now imagine that we consider each of these scenarios to be equally plausible – prior to assessing the rain gauge data and hydrological analysis. This is reflected in the two boxes in the top row of Figure 7.2. Each has a 50 per cent chance of being true. We can then ask, if we observe two occurrences of a 10-metre flood: what can we conclude about the underlying probability of flood?

If the rain gauge data is that a 10-metre flood occurred twice in 100 years, what can we conclude? The two dark-grey boxes in the bottom row of Figure 7.2 reflect what we have observed. If the true underlying probability is once in fifty years, then two observations will occur 27.3 per cent of the time. This was shown in the first column of Table 7.1 earlier. In contrast, if the true underlying probability is once in 100 years, then two observations in 100 years will occur 18.5 per cent of the time. This was shown in the second column of Table 7.1.

The conditional probabilities that flow in this simplified scenario are as follows:

- P(1 in 50 | 2 occurrences) = 27.3 / (18.5 + 27.3) = 60 per cent
- P(1 in 100 | 2 occurrences) = 18.5 / (18.5 + 27.3) = 40 per cent

Here, there is a 60 per cent likelihood that the underlying probability is once in fifty years and 40 per cent that it is once in 100 years. It is intuitive that observing two 10-metre floods in a 100-year period would make it more likely that the underlying probability is one in fifty rather than one in 100. However, it is telling that there is a high (40 per cent) chance in this stylised example that the underlying AEP is 1 per cent rather than the more intuitive 2 per cent.

Figure 7.2: A simplified Bayesian estimation

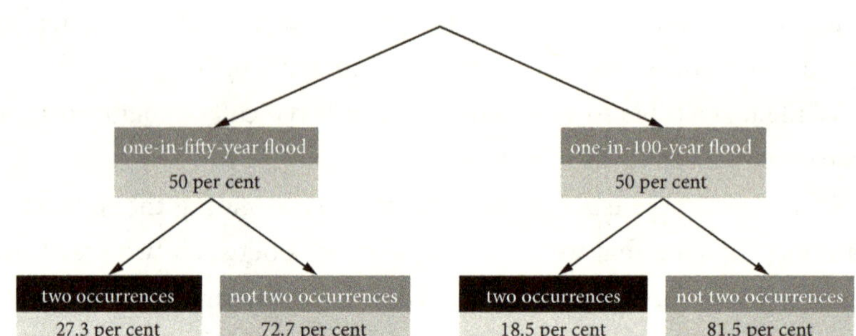

A more complete Bayesian analysis faces two significant complications. First, there are not two underlying scenarios to choose between (as in Figure 7.2 above). There are many potential underlying probabilities, ranging from very frequent through to extremely infrequent. In order to undertake a comprehensive Bayesian analysis, we would need to calculate the likelihood of a 10-metre flood in all potential scenarios.

Second, it is not obvious what *a priori* probability to attribute to each of these scenarios. In the simple example above, we assessed each of the two scenarios as equally plausible. In order to attribute a likelihood to each potential scenario, we could use a PDF, such as the one shown earlier in Figure 7.1, but the accuracy of such a distribution would be limited by the data. There is a wide range of possible PDFs, and in many situations, it is not obvious which one to choose.[11]

Using the power of modern computers, it is now possible to estimate this large set of possible scenarios. A recent paper using Bayesian techniques estimated the characteristics of a one-in-100-year flood in a region of the UK based on long-term rain gauge data and flood-peak discharge from historical records.[12]

Based on historical data, the statistical estimate of the flood discharge associated with a one-in-100-year flood is 1341 mm. Importantly, there is a high degree of uncertainty around this estimate, even using today's most powerful computational techniques. The 95 per cent confidence interval of that estimate (the most commonly used error bounds in statistics) are 1177 mm and 1631 mm. That implies a 95 per cent confidence interval with a range of 454 mm, which represents an error margin that is around a third as large as the median estimate.

For a government agency planning how much to invest in a levee, this is a high degree of uncertainty. The cost of reinforcing a levee to withstand a 1631 mm discharge may be significantly greater than the cost of withstanding a discharge of 1341 or 1177 mm.

Moreover, this level of uncertainty also provides challenges for insurers. An insurer will generally charge a premium that reflects both the likelihood of an event and the cost of remedying the damage associated with it. The damage caused by flood discharges of 1177 mm, for example, will vary across communities. A statistical model with a high degree of uncertainty around what constitutes a one-in-100-year event makes it difficult to set premiums for rare events at a level that will accurately reflect the long-term expected value of loss.

Table 7.2: Estimated flood discharge at various flood AEP levels

		Estimate of flood discharge (mm)			
AEP	**Median estimate (mm)**	**95 per cent CI lower bound (mm)**	**95 per cent CI upper bound (mm)**	**95 per cent CI range (mm)**	**Range relative to median**
one in two years	621	574	670	96	15.5 per cent
one in 70 years	1289	1144	1538	394	30.6 per cent
one in 100 years	1341	1177	1631	454	33.9 per cent
one in 1000 years	1766	1405	2588	1183	67.0 per cent

Changing underlying risk profile

An additional, and significant, complication with flood data is the fact that the underlying trend may be changing as we add to our stock of observations. In many areas, climate change is already having a material impact on rainfall levels, which, in turn, is impacting on flood frequency and severity.

It may be that, in 1990, a 10-metre flood was a one-in-100-year event but that, with climate change, it is now a one-in-eighty-year or one-in-fifty-year event. If we haven't experienced any 10-metre floods in the past three decades, it will be very difficult to estimate this. Even with a constant risk profile, it is extremely difficult to estimate the true underlying frequency of rare events. If the underlying frequency itself is changing, the task is even more difficult.

Correlation across time – are events independent?

The discussion above describes the difficulty associated with estimating the frequency of rare, devastating events. As outlined, it is typically not possible to accurately estimate the frequency of such events with a high degree of confidence.

An additional challenge is identifying whether there is a correlation between events across time. Let's imagine for a moment that we have enough high-quality data to estimate that floods of a particular depth occur roughly every 100 years. If one occurred last year, does that mean that we should expect the next such flood in around 100 years? Or could another such flood be just around the corner?

With a fair dice, if you throw a six, that tells you nothing about the next roll. The likelihood of a six is the same as it was for previous roll. Dice rolling is an example of *independent* random events. Despite many people's intuition, the same is true of roulette wheels. If the ball has landed on a particular number after recent spins of the wheel, that makes it neither more nor less likely that the same number will appear on the next spin.

In contrast, some events are cyclical. A string of poor economic outcomes will typically be followed by a recovery. There is a negative correlation in such a time series. Similarly, some macro-weather events such as El Niño and La Niña are dependent on broad cycles. Their occurrence is generally followed by several years without either event.[13]

What about floods, earthquakes or bushfires? The data is often unclear. If a once-in-a-century natural disaster occurs, that doesn't necessarily tell us much about whether another such event is around the corner. A good example of this is the floods that occurred in the UK in 2007, which were, in many regions, followed by devastating floods in 2015.

Australia's recent policy reforms

When the Queensland floods hit, I was economic adviser to the Hon. Bill Shorten, at that time the Minister for Financial Services (and also leader of the development of the NDIS). In the immediate aftermath of the floods, government's first priority was to deal with the emergency itself. But after that, the scale of the floods prompted questions as to the adequacy of private insurance markets and public-sector preparedness.

Some useful reforms were implemented over the coming years. To improve the functioning of private insurance markets, government significantly increased its funding of flood mapping. Legislation was also introduced to standardise the definition of 'flood' in private insurance policies. Up until that time, the word had meant different things in different policies: riverine flood ('water from below'), storm-induced flooding ('water from above') and other variants. Most consumers assumed that flood coverage included all water damage. There was also additional funding for mitigation, although as noted by the Productivity Commission, even after this increase, mitigation remained insignificant compared to post-recovery funding. As a package, these reforms were a significant step forward.

One of the great challenges that I am convinced needs far greater attention is the extent to which we continue to allow residential and commercial developments to be approved in areas of risk – not just risk from flooding but also storms and bushfires. Too often, local government has an incentive to allow development (for the additional property taxes over time) and can do so knowing that other levels of government will largely be responsible for post-disaster recovery. Federations can work well, enabling decision-making to be devolved where suitable, but in the case of natural disaster risks, too many of the incentives are currently misplaced.

The 2011 Queensland floods were described by many as a one-in-100-year event. Just eleven years later and at the time of writing, even worse floods are inundating south-east Queensland and northern New South Wales. They are being described by many as a one-in-100-year event (or even a one-in-1000-year event by the NSW premier). Nothing could highlight more the challenge we face as a society in predicting and preparing for extreme events.

BROADER PUBLIC-POLICY IMPLICATIONS: GUNS, GERMS AND WATER

Infrequent, systematic risks: four policy levers

Our society faces several systematic risks that affect so much of our community and economy when they eventuate (infrequently as that may be) that long-term investment is necessary. These events include war, pandemics, major natural disasters, climate change and macroeconomic shocks like a financial crisis or a material fall in our terms of trade. Because systematic risks affect all or a large part of society, short-term risk pooling isn't an effective mechanism. To effectively deal with systematic and infrequent risks, it is generally necessary to spread some of the investment over time. To leave all the response to the time of the event itself is generally inefficient and may materially limit society's options. Generally, society has four major policy levers when it comes to infrequent, systematic risks:

- **Risk mitigation:** Reducing the underlying risk of an event occurring (to the extent possible).
- **Ongoing investments in risk-management capability:** Examples of ongoing capability include a fire department or military on constant standby. Investment in this kind of capability could be thought of as an annual 'premium' that a society pays in order to shift resources across time. For systematic risks, it is generally necessary to make ongoing investments so that additional resources are available at the time of the event. Of course, some of the 'premium' could involve investment in resources that also have uses at times other than during a crisis (for example, rural firefighting appliances can also be used for suburban housefires in regional cities/communities; ICU wards that are used to deal with pandemics are also used for general medical treatment in normal times; and many defence assets can be used for non-military purposes).
- **Intergenerational resource shifting:** For some systematic risks, shifting resources across time will be a key plank of risk management. For example, in response to an economic crisis, it will often improve overall welfare to shift resources to periods of low per capita output

(for example, by borrowing for fiscal stimulus) from periods of high per capita income (by repaying the government debt later).

- **Crisis management and recovery:** The use of resources to deal with the crisis itself and then the recovery phase.

Consider national defence. The policy levers could be thought of in the following terms:

- **Risk mitigation** would include our investment in building up relations with neighbouring and other nations and also our ongoing investment in the diplomatic corps.
- **Ongoing investments in risk-management capability** would be reflected in the annual defence budget during times of peace, which builds up not only defence materiel but also human capital in the form of expertise and experience. This is analogous to an annual 'premium'.
- **Intergenerational resource shifting** can occur in relation to war when governments borrow to prosecute a war and repay that debt through taxes paid by following generations.
- **Crisis management and recovery** including ramping up expenditure on the military during times of war, as well as the cost of recovery. The latter could include the medical and long-term costs of providing aid to veterans and the cost of rebuilding any communities that suffered damage.

Table 7.3 sets out the four policy levers for the major infrequent, systematic risks.

Table 7.3: How government invests before, during and after infrequent, systematic shocks

	Long-term mitigation	Ongoing 'premium'	Intergenerational resource shifting	Post-event expenditure
War	• Ongoing efforts to build links between nations • Diplomacy	• ~2 per cent of annual GDP devoted to defence spending	• Paying off wartime debts over time	• Significant increase in military spending, depending on the scale of the conflict
Pandemics	• R&D into vaccines • Building up a health system, including both infrastructure and expertise, in anticipation of future pandemics	• Maintaining stockpiles of PPE • Investment in plans for dealing with emergencies • Health system capacity which can be repurposed (e.g. ICU wards)	• Paying off debt associated with healthcare costs and responding to the economic consequences of the pandemic	• Increase in health system capability in order to deal with surge in cases • Economic support for unemployed and businesses affected by the pandemic
Natural disasters	• Investment that protects communities from harm, such as: flood levees; land-clearing	• Investment in plans for dealing with emergencies • Investment in emergency services capability	• Paying off debt associated capital investments in mitigation, such as flood levees	• Local, state and federal programs to provide assistance for natural disaster damage and income support
Climate change	• Reducing carbon output contribution	• The annual economic cost of transitioning to low-carbon economy over the medium to long term	• Sharing both mitigation and adaptation costs fairly across generations	• Dealing with increased risk of natural disaster, rising sea levels, falling agricultural productivity etc.
Economic shocks	• Diversifying economy	• Taxes on resource extraction which are invested in the productivity of the broader economy	• Paying off debt over time that has been incurred to deal with short-term responses to the economic shock	• Economic stabilisers: unemployment insurance; local economic stimulus for communities negatively affected

An ounce of prevention is worth a pound of cure

One of the key challenges for public-policy makers is striking an appropriate balance between policy levers. Given that there are so many calls on government spending at any given time, it is all too tempting to reduce short-term funding for mitigation or for preparation, both of which may produce benefits that may not crystalise until far into the future. But short-term cost cutting of these investments can greatly magnify the costs that eventually arise when a crisis unfolds.

Consider one aspect of the recent Covid-19 pandemic: the demand for personal protective equipment (PPE). Unsurprisingly, the demand for PPE in Australia grew exponentially along with the exponential rise in the number of confirmed cases. Given that demand was also rising in other countries and that the immediate global supply of PPE was limited to a small number of sources, the price of PPE rose sharply. On 11 April 2020, *The Guardian* reported that one PPE supplier had raised the price on a box of masks from A$9.60 to $22.60; the price for a box of gowns rose from $90 to $175.[14] Later that same month, even greater price gouging was alleged, with one company charging $786 for a box of face masks that would usually cost $40.[15]

It will be far less costly to gradually build up a stockpile of PPE over time, rather than trying to access large quantities at short notice in the middle of a crisis. This will be true for the cost effectiveness of building capacity in relation to most crises. Building up capacity and expertise over the longer term will almost always be cheaper than short-term adjustments. One of the key challenges in deciding how much to invest in mitigation and ongoing preparation is estimating the likelihood of rare but very costly events.

Is an ounce too much or not enough?

The analysis of what constitutes a one-in-100-year flood has much broader public-policy applications than where and when to build flood levees. There is a range of probability distribution functions that describe the frequency of natural phenomena. It is worth examining the issue in more detail.

Most of us are familiar with what is typically referred to as the 'normal' distribution. This distribution describes many phenomena that we observe in everyday life: baby birthweights, human height, blood pressure, scores on standardised exams, daily stock-market returns, the volume of milk production from cows, the length of carrots and cucumbers, the average NFL player retirement age, the distribution of deer per acre, and average monthly temperatures.[16]

A normal distribution has a bell shape. It has two key statistical characteristics that stand out. First, the normal distribution is symmetric about the mean (or average). This means that the distribution looks the same for observations below and above the mean.

Second, most of the observations bunch around the mean. The standard deviation of any distribution is a measure of how much dispersion the observations exhibit. One shorthand way of thinking about the second characteristic of the normal distribution is the 68–95–99.7 rule. It states that approximately 68 per cent of observations will lie within one standard deviation either side of the mean, 95 per cent within two standard deviations and 99.7 per cent within three standard deviations.

Consider male height. The average height of men in in the population of twenty countries in North America, Europe, East Asia and Australia is 5'10", with a standard deviation of 3 inches. This means that 68.3 per cent of mean have a height between 5'7" and 6'1"; 95.5 per cent of men have a height between 5'4" and 6'4" and 99.7 per cent between 5'1" and 6'7". The fact that less than 0.3 per cent of men have a height either less than 5'1" or above 6'7" reflects the fact that the normal distribution has 'thin tails' – i.e. very few observations sit a long way from the mean.

Moving along the tails of the normal distribution results in an exponentially decreasing likelihood of observations. To give a sense of how thin the 'tails' of a normal distribution are, consider the likelihood of someone being seven feet tall. A height of 7'1" would be five standard deviations from the mean. As noted, only 0.3 per cent of people are more than three standard deviations from the mean. Given the symmetry of the distribution, this means that 0.15 per cent would be more than three standard deviations above the mean, or taller than 6'7". But to move up just two more standard deviations dramatically reduces the odds of an occurrence. The likelihood of someone being more than five standard deviations from the mean, if the population is distributed normally, is one in 1.74 million. Given that the distribution is symmetrical, there is therefore a one in 3.5 million chance of a man being taller than 7'1".

The normal distribution was discovered by Abraham de Moivre, an eighteenth-century statistician. It was originally referred to as the 'Gaussian distribution', after the great mathematician Carl Friedrich Gauss, who extended de Moivre's work.[17] It was later renamed the 'normal' distribution by the statistician Karl E. Pearson, who, perhaps with an inkling of regret, said that the name 'has the disadvantage of leading people to believe that all other distributions of frequency are in one sense or another abnormal'.[18]

Pearson's concern is well founded, since there are many other probability distributions that are extremely important for our understanding of the world that behave very differently to the normal distribution. In particular, there is a class of distributions that, in contrast to the normal distribution, exhibit 'fat tails'. For these distributions, events a long way from the mean are still rare – but they will usually be many times more common than with a normal distribution.

The power-law distribution is an example of a distribution function with fat tails. It describes many empirical datasets: the number of people having at least a given income; the number of cities above a certain population; the number of charges per criminal offender; many of the laws underpinning physics, astronomy and biology; word frequency; telephone calls received on a single day; the intensity of wars; bird species sightings; the number of copies of bestselling books (1895–1965); the severity of terrorist attacks; and many aspects of financial market behaviour.[19]

Figure 7.3 below shows the distribution of US city sizes based on 2019 census bureau data. This data is clearly not normally distributed. First, it is not symmetric but 'skewed'. The mean of this sample of the largest 788 cities in the US is a population of 162,618. Out of the total dataset, 631 observations fall below the mean and 157 are greater than the mean.

Second, there is a frequency of 'extreme' observations that would almost certainly not occur if the data was distributed normally. With a population of 8.34 million, New York City is over twenty-one standard deviations above the mean. The populations of Los Angeles and Chicago are also extreme, lying 9.9 and 6.6 standard deviations above the mean, respectively. In a sample that is distributed normally, an observation 6.5 standard deviations above the mean would occur only one in

12.4 billion times. A city the size of New York would be nearly impossible in a normal distribution of urban centres.

Figure 7.3: Distribution of US city sizes, 2019

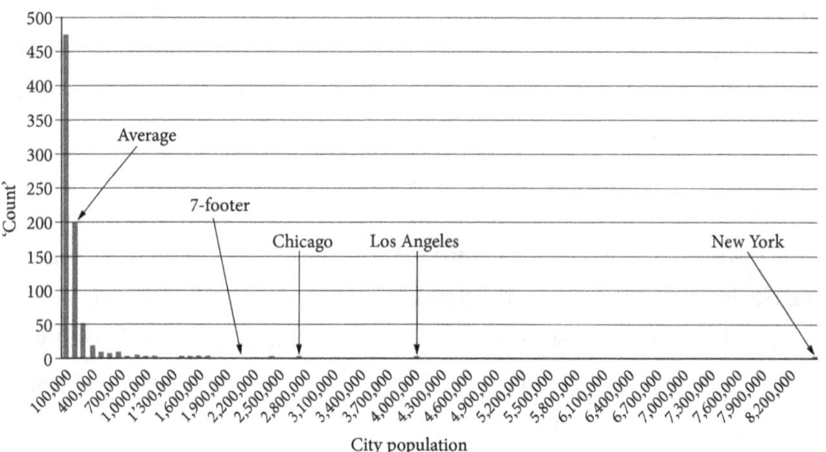

In the normally distributed population of males, the chance of someone being 7'1" is about one in 3.5 million. 'Seven-footers' are so rare in the broader population that almost one in five play in the NBA.[20] In the context of a sample of just 788 US cities, there are three cities far more 'extreme' than the likelihood of a seven-foot-tall man. The fact that such a small sample of less than 800 cities contains three outliers that are each far more extreme than a one-in-3.5 million event in a normal distribution, indicates how much thicker the tails of the power-law distribution are than the normal.

When expanding the data set of urban centres to all 19,500 'incorporated places' in the US, the comparison becomes even more stark. Incorporated places include both cities and towns and collectively cover over 200 million people. Of this larger data set, the mean size of an incorporated place in the US is 10,608 people. The standard deviation of this larger dataset is 83,873. This means that, with a population of 8.34 million, New York City is approximately 100 standard deviations above the mean. While New York is a marvel, the existence of a bustling city of 8 million people is probably less surprising to most people than would be a 31-foot-tall man.[21]

In human height, five standard deviations away from the mean is exceptionally rare. After billions of human beings have walked the Earth, twelve standard deviations above the mean is a once-in-history event.[22] In contrast, in a phenomena distributed with fat tails, an observation over 100 standard deviations from the mean is almost to be expected.[23]

Why is this so important for present purposes? Many of the systematic, infrequent events that we consider in this chapter, including war, natural disasters and economic crises, are distributed with fat tails.

There is some disputation as to which specific function is appropriate for each type of event. Arnab Chatterjee and Bikas Chakrabarti find that power-law distributions[24] are appropriate for natural disasters (including earthquakes, rainfall and fires), as well as deaths from war and human conflict.[25] In contrast, Clauset et al. find the power-law distribution is a good description for some phenomena (terrorist attacks, intensity of wars), but not for others (forest fires, earthquakes). Even in these latter cases, though, the underlying distribution most likely exhibits fat tails.[26]

Notwithstanding this debate, it is critical that public policy is designed so as to prepare for extreme wars, natural disasters and economic disruptions that are (much) more common than we might at first blush think, given that we are so used to observing the world through the prism of the thin-tailed 'normal' distribution.

Pandemics

The Covid-19 pandemic demonstrated how susceptible an interconnected world is to disruption. The virus emerged in October 2019 and within six months, it had wreaked havoc on much of the global economy and overwhelmed many national health systems. Pandemics are not black swan events. They are white swan events whose frequency is very difficult to estimate. As Ian Goldin notes, a global pandemic did not make it into the top ten material risks identified by the World Economic Forum in 2020.[27]

Given that the Spanish Influenza and Covid-19 were separated by almost exactly 100 years, this begs the question – were these two pandemics one-in-100-year events, as is so often stated?

Figure 7.4 shows the distribution of major pandemics between the year 0 CE and 2020, with the death count for each pandemic (in thousands) adjusted for world population.[28] The Black Death of 1353 has the largest estimated adjusted death count of 2.67 billion (after adjusting for today's larger global population). The Plague of Justinian in 541 has an estimated adjusted death count of 2.25 billion. And more recently, the Spanish Flu has an estimated adjusted death count of around 200 million.

Figure 7.4: Pandemics death counts, 0–2020 (adjusted for world population)

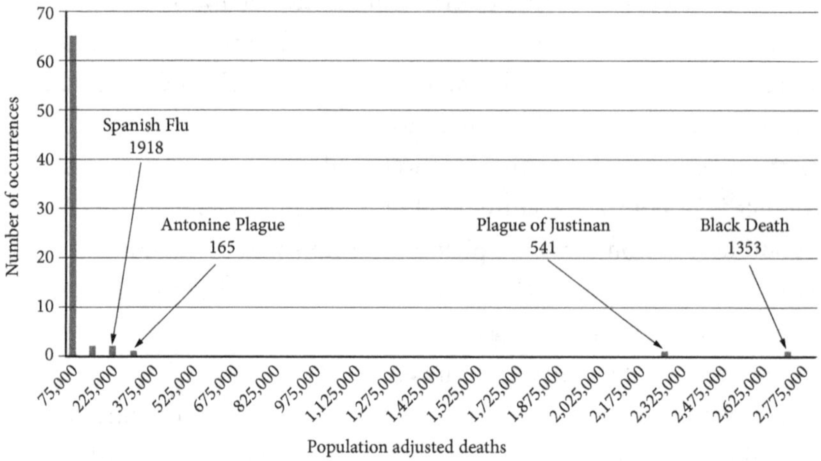

What is clear from Figure 7.5 is that the distribution of pandemics is much more similar to the distribution of city sizes in the US than it is to human height; it is non-symmetric and has several extreme outliers. It is likely that the data in Figure 7.4 is incomplete. Not all events are recorded accurately – or at all – in the historical record. However, to the extent that data is missing, it is likely to be clustered around the smaller observations since very large events are more likely to be recorded in prominent sources. Therefore, adding any missing data is likely to add to skewness of the dataset rather than reduce it.

In order to separately consider those pandemics which might be more relevant to the twenty-first century, the graphs in Figure 7.5 show the distribution over time of different types of pandemics. The panels on the left show various types of pandemics for the period 0–2020, and the panels on the right show the period 1500–2020, so as to focus on more recent trends. The panels correspond to the major categories of pandemics: plague; cholera; tropical diseases; and respiratory illnesses.

Figure 7.5: Pandemics with more than 100,000 deaths, 0–2020 (and 1500–2020)[29]

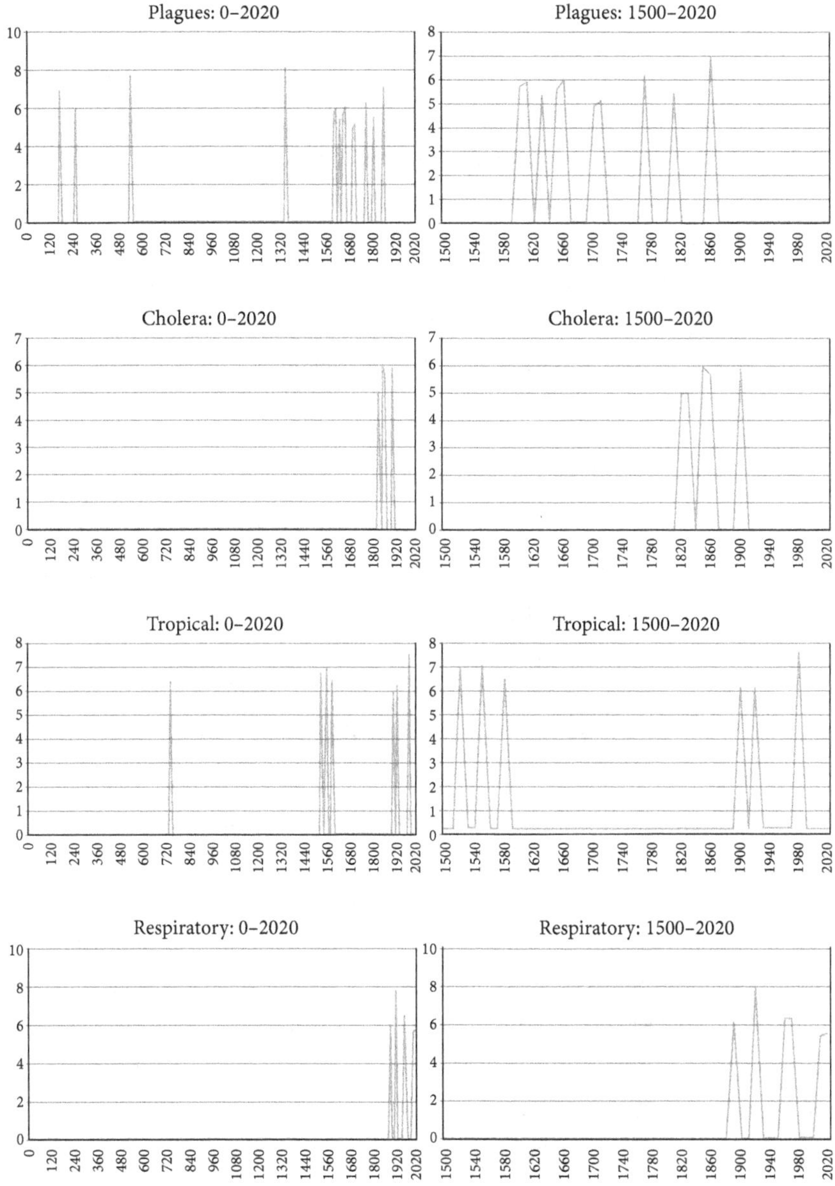

Cholera and respiratory pandemics have both appeared in clusters. There were six major cholera outbreaks in the nineteenth and early twentieth centuries (some are combined as single peaks in the graph). There hasn't been a major cholera outbreak for over a century.

Respiratory pandemics have occurred regularly over the past 150 years. This is a risk that does not appear to have receded even though vaccines have been found for Covid-19.

In estimating future risks, it would appear reasonable to assume that the risk of major plague and cholera outbreaks is minimal, albeit not zero. Outbreaks of tropical diseases or respiratory viruses appear more likely.

Another challenge is that it is unclear whether the underlying risk of pandemics is increasing. Ian Goldin argues that those tasked with risk evaluation are often backward-looking and that, in relation to pandemics, have 'failed to incorporate the fundamental changes that globalisation, technological change and increased population density have caused to the nature of future risks'.[30]

Wars and defence spending

Defence spending can be thought of as an annual 'premium' to build up resources and expertise that can then be expanded at short notice in times of crisis. If the ongoing annual expenditure in defence capability were not made, building up a military capability rapidly would be far more costly per unit of functionality. More importantly, there would be severe limitations on what capability could be developed at short notice. Experienced officers cannot be purchased at a moment's notice. Cutting-edge equipment is difficult to purchase when many other nations are actively seeking the same scarce resources.

There is a sound rationale for ongoing defence spending, but it is worth rigorously evaluating the amounts spent. At around 2 per cent of GDP, it is one of the largest items of government expenditure. Spending too much on defence means less expenditure on other government services, or increasing the burden of taxation. Not spending enough, however, is a potential risk to national security. Given the challenges of quantifying the likelihood of future conflicts, it may be that alternative approaches, such as scenario analysis, can provide a better basis for comparing different outcomes.

In his 2011 book, *The Better Angels of Our Nature*, Steven Pinker argued that we are living through the most peaceful era in human history.[31] Although deaths from war have, unsurprisingly, dramatically decreased since 1945, Pinker emphasises that war between major powers could occur again in the future:

> Of course, the numbers in a dataset cannot be interpreted as a direct readout of the underlying risk of war. The historical record is especially scanty when it comes to estimating any change in the likelihood of very rare but very destructive wars. To make sense of sparse data in a world whose history only plays out once, we need to supplement the numbers with knowledge about the generators of war.[32]

This analysis of the generators of war is somewhat analogous to using hydrological and engineering analysis to supplement rain-gauge data when trying to estimate the future likelihood of floods. Pinker goes on to argue that, for a range of reasons, war between major powers has become far less likely than it has been for most of the past five centuries. Among these reasons are an increase in trade and economic interdependence, the growing share of democratic governance, the rising destructiveness of modern armaments (and, therefore, reluctance to use them due to the risk of counterstrike) and a change in the mindset of most nations towards war. Since the writing of that book, some of these factors have shifted, at least to a degree, towards a higher risk of conflict.

Many argue that, given how rare major wars are, it is inappropriate to draw conclusions from just seventy years of peace. John Gray argues that Pinker's overarching conclusions are incorrect, noting that at least some of the reduction in direct major-power conflicts is a result of the 'balance of terror', which creates a threat of nuclear annihilation.[33] John Arquilla agrees.[34]

Adopting a more statistical approach that focuses on extreme value theory and fat-tailed distributions, Cirillo and Taleb examine the number of deaths for all major conflicts over the past 2000 years. One of their key conclusions is that, notwithstanding the fact that there hasn't been a major war for seventy years, 'no particular trend in the number of armed conflicts can be traced'.[35] Their fundamental point is that seventy years of peace between major powers doesn't change the fact that an extreme event could be just around the corner.

An added complication is that, just as with floods and climate change, there is a chance that we may be witnessing a breakpoint in the underlying trend. If this were occurring, it would only exacerbate the challenge of estimating the underlying likelihood of future war.

This debate is clearly of great importance. Unfortunately, it is highly unlikely that, even with great effort from the world's finest statisticians, it will be possible to derive a meaningful and useful estimate of when the next major conflict will occur. The likelihood of future war is probably more akin to Knightian 'uncertainty' than quantifiable risk. Notwithstanding this, the debate is useful in that it frames the key risks that public-policy makers face and the potential factors that underpin the underlying uncertainty.

In response to this uncertainty, most countries' defence budgets are (approximately) a fixed proportion of GDP per annum, except at times of war, when spending increases, or during a period in which a war is thought to be imminent. For most governments, this portion of GDP is arrived at by combining a set of policy analyses:

- A qualitative assessment of short-, medium- and long-term threats to national security;[36]
- Spending as a share of GDP by other nations, including both allies and non-allies;
- Experience gained over time in relation to what the minimum 'baseline' capacity needs to be in order to ramp up effort at short notice.

A baseline of 2 per cent of GDP is currently used by many NATO countries, including Australia, as a benchmark for defence spending. This is an example of an approach to dealing with uncertainty that has been developed over centuries. It is worth considering using a similar approach – setting a defined annual contribution in the budget – for funding mitigation and preparedness for other systematic risks involving uncertainty such as natural disasters and pandemics.

GREY RHINOS: THE CHALLENGE OF EXTRAPOLATING LONG-TERM TRENDS

The second type of systematic risk is the long-term trend which threatens significant social, environmental or social damage if left unchecked. This includes climate change, an ageing demographic and structural economic trends (such as automation and globalisation).The following section examines the challenges of forecasting the environmental and economic consequences of climate change as a case study in the difficulty in managing these grey rhinos.

The distinction between a one-in-100-year event (floods and pandemics) and slowly evolving trends like climate change is useful, but as with any categorisation, life is more complicated. Where does an event like World War I fit in? Were the decades leading up to the Great War like a volcano, in which the pressure of increasingly tense international relations was inevitably going to result in a major conflagration? Or should it be thought of as a highly infrequent event, the magnitude of which wasn't foreseeable? Both are defensible positions.

Grey rhino case study 1: Climate change

The impact of increasing concentrations of carbon dioxide (CO_2) in the atmosphere is one of the great policy challenges of our age. It is a global tragedy of the commons. Higher levels of atmospheric carbon dioxide will cause an increase in mean global temperature, which will, in turn, produce rising sea levels, more frequent and severe storms, greater variability in climate and lower mean agricultural productivity in many areas.

Most major climate models published since the 1970s have been proven largely accurate. Moreover, in their evaluation of climate modelling, Hausfather et al. find no evidence that climate models 'have systematically overestimated or underestimated warming over their projection period'.[37] This is heartening and provides confidence in the overarching methodology being used by the scientific community. However, it is important to note that these findings tend to relate to a model's performance over one or two decades. Developing climate policy requires forecasting the impact of human behaviour over much longer time horizons. Longer-term projections involving dynamic variables raise a number of challenges that go to the heart of the limitations of modelling per se.

Understanding the extent of uncertainty in climate modelling

Climate change policy is an area of policy bedevilled by uncertainty given both the long-time horizon of forecasting required and the highly complex and arguably chaotic nature of both climatic and economic systems.

Some of the key uncertainties that policymakers face include:

- The extent of future pollution and, specifically, the resultant atmospheric concentration of carbon dioxide. This will depend upon a range of factors including long-run population growth; economic growth; technological change; and the rate of adoption of new technology;
- The impact of a given future atmospheric concentration of carbon dioxide on the climate;
- The possible social adaptation to changing climate conditions;
- The broader economic consequences of climate change;
- The costs of climate abatement in the long term.

This chapter will not explore the trade-offs involved in designing an optimal policy response to human-caused climate change. What is relevant for present purposes is the uncertainty surrounding estimates of both the environmental and economic impacts of climate change in the long run (half a century or more in the future) and how policymakers should respond to this uncertainty in present-day decision-making. Designing policies to address climate change is a good example of decision-making in an environment of uncertainty. Rigorous quantification should be undertaken wherever possible, but it will also be necessary to recognise the inherent limitations of forecasts over very long periods of time.

Ross Garnaut argues that the ongoing work of the Intergovernmental Panel on Climate Change (IPCC) has 'made some contact with risk, more with uncertainty, and most of all with the wide territory in between them'.[38] The IPCC draws upon a multitude of sources and a diversity of modelling approaches and aggregates these results such that the combined estimate is hopefully a better indicator than any individual model or approach. But ultimately, it often frames its conclusions in terms of uncertainty rather than claiming to have derived a clear probability distribution (or 'risk').

Two of the key elements of uncertainty that have attracted much attention and controversy are the link between future carbon dioxide levels and changes in mean surface temperature, and the impact of different abatement strategies on economic growth, as well as the distribution of those impacts. Each of these will be briefly explored as they provide insights into how uncertainty should be approached.

The key elements of integrated climate modelling

The first step in developing a decision-making framework in relation to climate change is to estimate the impact of human activity on the climate. A key element in this step is to estimate the impact of a rising CO_2 concentration in the atmosphere on mean temperature (and other aspects of the climate). One relevant concept that is commonly used is 'climate sensitivity', which refers to the increase in mean temperature that would result from a doubling of atmospheric CO_2.

Estimating the impact of rising atmospheric CO_2 concentration on the climate is just the first step. The impact of human activity on the climate is then linked to the implications of that climate change on society through a range of measures, including the impacts of temperature changes, extreme weather events and agricultural productivity on economic activity and quality of life more broadly. This is often summarised in a single measure such as the impact of human-induced climate change on per capita consumption.

Most climate models project significant potential economic impacts over the longer term as a result of rising mean global temperatures. Nicholas Stern found that a business-as-usual approach would result in a fall in per capita consumption of 2.1 per cent by 2200 (with a loss of up to 5.9 per cent in the 95th percentile), and by 10.9 per cent when the increased likelihood of catastrophes and non-market impacts were included (up to 27.4 per cent in the 95th percentile of modelled scenarios). In the 'High Climate' scenarios, the percentage loss of consumption was even greater.[39]

William Nordhaus, who received the Nobel Prize for his trailblazing work on the economics of climate change, developed a model with a baseline scenario in which there is a mean negative impact of 4.3 per cent on output per capita by 2100.[40] The final major component in modelling an optimal response to climate change is to estimate the costs of mitigation and adaptation and then to estimate the 'optimal' mitigation and adaptation strategies.

The IPCC Fifth Assessment Report on mitigation estimated the impact of 'cost effective' mitigation strategies compared to a baseline strategy (business as usual). The fifth IPCC Assessment Report found that limiting carbon dioxide concentration to 450 parts per million would result in a 4.8 per cent reduction in consumption; limiting concentration to 580–650 parts per million would result in a 2.3 per cent reduction in consumption.[41]

Modelling our impact on the climate

It is possible to assess how well climate-change models have performed – at least in the short run – by comparing their predictions with temperature changes since they were published. Clearly it is only possible to test the long-term accuracy of a model decades after it has been published. Studies of climate models published back to 1975 have found that they generally do a good job of estimating climate change and that errors appear to be declining (albeit moderately) over time. This is confirmed in a recent meta-study of seventeen models by a research team at the University of California, Berkeley.[42] The accuracy of major models in predicting future temperature change was confirmed by a later meta-study by Hausfather et al.[43]

The sensitivity of global surface temperature to rising carbon dioxide levels is a critical element of understanding both our impact on the Earth's climate and how we should respond to that. The accuracy of climate models in relation to this measure is of particular importance. Critically, across a range of models using different approaches, estimates of climate sensitivity have been largely consistent over the past eight decades.

Column 3 of Table 7.4 shows estimates of climate sensitivity from models dating back to 1896. Three measures of climate sensitivity are typically used. The transient climate response (TCR) is the short-term response of climate to a doubling of CO_2. The equilibrium climate sensitivity (ECS) is the impact after the atmosphere has had time to adjust to the increased CO_2 concentration (for example, following the decades that it will take for the additional CO_2 to disperse into the deep oceans). And finally, the Earth system sensitivity (ESS) is the very long-run equilibrium after changes in ice sheets and vegetation cover. Typically, the TCR will be the lowest impact. Most climate models estimate the ECS. The ECS measures from key models are reported in Column 3.

Svante Arrenhius, one of the earliest winners of the Nobel Prize for Chemistry, published a paper in 1896 on the influence of atmospheric carbon on ground temperatures. He estimated that doubling the

Table 7.4: Uncertainty in relation to 'climate sensitivity'

Date	Model	Climate sensitivity to 2 × CO_2	Error bound
1896	Arrhenius	4.95–6.05	
1938 (*Qty Ryl MS*)	Callendar	3.3	
1955 (*Tellus*)	Plass	3.6	
1973 (*Science*)	Sawyer	2.4	
1975 (*Nature*)	Broecker	2.4	
1979 (Charney report)	US Ntnl Acad Sciences	3.0	1.5–4.5
1981 (*Science*)	Hansen	2.8	
1988 (*Jnl Geophys Research*)	Hansen et al.	4.2	
1990 (IPCC Assessment Report 1)	IPCC aggregation	2.5	
1995 (IPCC Assessment Report 2)	IPCC aggregation	2.5	
2001 (IPCC Assessment Report 3)	IPCC aggregation	2.8	
2007 (IPCC Assessment Report 4)	IPCC aggregation	3.26	2–4.5
2013 (IPCC Assessment Report 5)	IPCC aggregation	3.0	1.5–4.5
2020 (*Rev Geophysics*)	Sherwood et al.	3.0	2.3–4.7
2021 (IPCC Assessment Report 6)	IPCC aggregation	3.0	2–5

concentration of carbon dioxide (from the lower level at that time) would result in temperature increases ranging from 4.95 to 6.05 degrees, depending on the latitude. Between 1938 and 2013, almost all prominent models have estimated a temperature sensitivity to a doubling of CO_2 of between 2.5 and 3 degrees.

While the consistency in estimates of climate sensitivity is a good indicator that our models have a firm handle on this indicator, it is important to examine how the level of uncertainty surrounding estimates of climate sensitivity has changed over time. One of the most striking features of Table 7.4 is that even though the estimate of ECR has remained very stable over three-quarters of a century, and despite the fact that our modelling capacity and understanding of climate science has increased dramatically during that period, the level of uncertainty surrounding our best estimates of ECR has not fallen much.

The Charney report, which was published in 1979, was the first comprehensive assessment of global climate change due to increasing levels of atmospheric CO_2.[44] It provided a range of climate sensitivity of 1.5–4.5 degrees, the same as the fifth IPCC AR report in 2013, published thirty-four years later. Note that the 1.50–4.50 band in IPCC AR5 was a 66 per cent confidence band. In contrast, the IPCC AR6 band is 90 per cent band, so between AR5 and AR6, the level of uncertainty has reduced materially for a 3 degrees Celsius median estimate.

One possible explanation for the fact that uncertainty levels aren't falling, despite increased computing power and model sophistication, is that earlier models, including the Charney report, may have understated the level of uncertainty in the underlying modelling. Andrew Dressler disputes the claim that the level of uncertainty in relation to climate sensitivity has remained stable over the past four decades, contending that earlier studies materially understated uncertainty levels:

> I think that the idea that 'uncertainty has remained the same since the late 1970s' is wrong. If you look at the Charney report, it's clear that there were a lot of things they didn't know about the climate. So their estimate of uncertainty was, in my opinion, way, way too small.[45]

Dressler's claims are plausible, but even if true in relation to 1970s models, it appears that the dramatic increase in computation power in the past twenty-five years hasn't materially reduced uncertainty.

Another possible explanation might relate to the inherent complexity of estimating climate sensitivity. The short-term physics of CO_2 doubling are relatively straightforward: a doubling of carbon dioxide will result in an increase in temperature of slightly more than 1 degree.[46] Complications arise when trying to estimate feedback effects. These include the impact of atmospheric water vapour, clouds, land ice cover, sea ice cover, vegetation cover and ocean-heat transport.

Since 1995, climate models have become far more sophisticated as increased computing power has enabled both the inclusion of richer interactions between elements of the environment and more granular modelling. The first trend in model improvement is reflected in successive additions of elements to models (many relating to the feedback mechanisms described above): 1970s (CO_2 emissions; rainfall); 1980s (clouds, land surface, prescribed ice); IPCC AR1 ('swamp' ocean); IPCC AR2 (volcanic activity; sulphides; oceans); IPCC AR3 (carbon cycle, aerosols; rivers, overturning oceanic circulation); IPCC AR4 (atmospheric chemistry, interactive vegetation).[47]

The second key change is granularity. Climate models generally use grid cells, with each cell representing an area (of either land, ocean or atmosphere) and a depth. Each cell will, as much as possible, reflect the conditions of the land, ocean or atmosphere at that point in space as accurately as possible. The smaller the grid cell, the more accurately each cell (and therefore the model) can represent that space. The smaller the grid cell of a model, the higher its 'spatial resolution'. The impact of improved computing power is reflected in the size of grid cells across the first five IPCC assessment reports. Given that a doubling of a model's spatial resolution will generally involve a ten-fold increase in computing power, the change in resolution between IPCC AR1 and IPCC AR5 involves many millions of times more computations due to improved resolution alone, without including the added climatic elements noted above.

As a general rule, a model should be complicated enough to shed light on the phenomenon that is being modelled, but not so complicated that it comes to resemble the complexity of the phenomenon itself. One of the key characteristics of a model is how many aspects of the real world are incorporated into the model. In a climate model, this might include surface temperature, oceanic absorption of heat, the extent of different types of vegetation, sea levels, atmospheric conditions, feedback effects from ice coverage and so on. If a model has three elements that are interdependent, there are eight different ways in which these elements of the model can interact. If there are twenty elements to the model, there are over a million permutations. Carslaw et al. call this the 'wiggle room' of a model.

Clearly, adding more degrees of freedom adds exponentially to the complexity of a model. While dramatic improvements in computing power are enabling modellers to add more and more sophistication, increasing the complexity of models can add so many moving parts that it can be extremely difficult to disentangle how the various parts are interacting. This can make it difficult to understand with clarity what is happening. However, it may be difficult to reduce the number of elements within a model without suffering from the reverse problem of oversimplification.

Achieving the right balance is one of the perennial challenges of modelling in all fields of research.

A recent meta-study of climate sensitivity estimates over the past two decades found little if any reduction in uncertainty in relation to climate sensitivity.[48] The review compared the results of over 100 studies. It grouped the models into five types of approach and calculated the climate sensitivity ranges of each type of model: climate models (2.00–4.50); studies that select climate models based on empirical climate characteristics (2.20–4.80); studies based on global and oceanic heat changes (1.20-3.80); palaeoloclimate studies (2.0–5.20); and studies combining a range of approaches (1.70–4.50). Over the past two decades, the best estimate of climate sensitivity has remained centred on 3.0 degrees with a range of 1.5–4.5.

A recent study combining multiple lines of evidence narrowed the range of uncertainty to 2.60–3.90 (66 per cent range) and 2.30–4.70 (90 per cent range).[49] These results will be reflected in the next IPCC report. The key sources of uncertainty in estimating climate sensitivity have been: (i) difficulties in improving the accuracy of long-term estimates of temperature change; (ii) the delay in reducing the amount of 'noise' in estimating the trend in global atmospheric temperature in the late twentieth century; and (iii) better modelling of certain processes such as clouds, water vapour and aerosols.[50] The Sherwood et al. study reflects improvements along all three dimensions. Whether this narrows the uncertainty band in relation to estimates of climate sensitivity remains to be seen.

Modelling the economy

The first issue that this chapter focused on was uncertainty in modelling the link between emissions and changes in the climate. Another key area in which modelling uncertainty arises is the extent to which climate change caused by rising levels of human-caused CO_2 concentration will impact adversely on the economy.

A key benchmark of interest to economists and policymakers is how the trajectory of per capita economic output (or consumption) will be affected by the 'optimal' abatement and adaptation strategy. The optimal abatement strategy will maximise discounted social welfare based on the costs and benefits of abatement and adaptation. The type of modelling required to determine optimal abatement adds a layer of complexity to estimating climate sensitivity in that it involves the interaction of two inherently complex and dynamic systems, climate and the economy. To model this requires integrated assessment models (IAMs): in other words, models that integrate the impacts from two domains (environmental and economic) into a single framework.

IAMs rely upon estimates of long-run population growth, the rate of technological innovation and adoption, and overall rates of economic growth. While uncertainty persists in relation to some climactic phenomena, as noted above, uncertainty in relation to economic factors is probably even more problematic in deriving accurate long-run forecasts. In a recent study of the uncertainty in climate change models, Kenneth Gillingham et al. found that uncertainty in relation to economic parameters such as total factor productivity 'have a much greater influence on outcomes than the uncertainty about population or climate sensitivity'.[51]

The forecast cost of abatement through the increased use of renewables and other clean energy strategies has fallen significantly over the past decade and is projected to continue falling. But falling mean estimates of abatement costs doesn't necessarily imply that our level of *uncertainty* over the long run has changed. In estimating the future trajectory of the cost of abatement, we are dealing with the inherently uncertain space of technological innovation decades into the future. As Knight and Mazzucato have pointed out in relation to both the development and adoption of innovation, this lies within the realm of uncertainty rather than easily quantifiable risk.

Some have asserted that innovation in renewables, and specifically the cost of generating electricity via solar and wind power, will follow an arc akin to Moore's law.[52] If this were the case, it would assist in forecasting the cost of that particular type of generation. But even if that were the case, the overall cost of abatement would likely continue to be very difficult to predict.

In 2008, Nicholas Stern estimated the impact on per capita consumption in 2200 using three measures: the economic consequences measured in terms of market impacts (-2.1 per cent, with error bounds of -0.3 per cent and -5.9 per cent); market impacts plus the cost of the increased risk of catastrophes (-5.0 per cent, with error bounds of -0.6 per cent and -12.3 per cent); and market impacts plus the cost of the increased risk of catastrophes and non-market impacts (-10.9 per cent, with error bounds of -2.2 per cent and -27.4 per cent).[53] William Nordhaus finds broadly similar impacts, with economic damages to 2100 output of the baseline scenario estimated with a mean of -4.3 per cent and a standard deviation of 3.7 per cent.[54] What is striking about both sets of estimates is not just the potential for significant economic harm if climate change is not limited, but the wide error bounds of long-run forecasts.

Nordhaus tracks estimates of economic impacts arising from the DICE model (Dynamic Integrated model of Climate and the Economy) over the period 1989–2017 (published results cover the period 1992–2017). This study also compared the DICE 2016 model with the latest IPCC model at the time (IPCC 8.5). Over the course of the period covered by the review, the major revisions in estimates from the DICE model arose from the economic component of the model. The key revisions in the economic modelling included: a major revision in expected output per capita in 2100 (revised up 3.5-fold between 1990–2017), an upward revision of 60 per cent in the 'damage function' (a function estimating the economic damage arising from climate change) and a change in the estimate of the social cost of carbon from US$5 to US$31 per tonne of CO_2 (with a wide 95 per cent uncertainty band in the 2016 DICE model of US$6–US$93 per tonne).[55]

In a separate review, Nordhaus explores the level of uncertainty in IAM estimates of long-run environmental and economic variables. He finds that the level of uncertainty for economic variables such as output, damages and the social cost of carbon is far higher than for environmental variables like carbon concentrations and temperature increase.[56]

The economic benefits of reducing uncertainty are significant. One recent study estimated a net present value benefit of around US$10 trillion if the level of uncertainty surrounding the TCR (the transient climate response) could be halved.[57]

How should policymakers respond?

This chapter has assessed two specific issues that involve uncertainty: the link between increased CO_2 emissions and increased mean global temperatures, and the economic costs of abatement compared to allowing emissions to increase.

It is important to stress that the best climatic and economic models are performing well. Estimates of the trajectory of mean global surface temperature have turned out to be accurate and generally within the published confidence bounds of prominent models. But we also need to acknowledge that policymakers face a challenge of layered uncertainty and that, even as our models continue to grow exponentially more powerful and detailed, there appears to be a range of climatic, economic and social phenomena that involve unresolvable uncertainty.

I believe that there are two key lessons for policymakers. First, we need to adopt an approach that is as quantitatively complete and rigorous as possible – though we must also incorporate decision-making processes that adjust quickly as more information comes to hand. Second, in the face of uncertainty, our decision-making must account for the possibility that scenarios remain plausible outside the realms of our confidence bands.

Grey rhino case study 2: The grey wave

Long-term demographic trends are like social ocean liners: they move very slowly, they take a long time to change direction and, when they have an impact – such as the impact of an ageing society on pension costs – their impact is momentous. That is why so much effort is devoted to developing the most accurate long-term demographic forecasts.

The in-built momentum of demographic change helps in pinning down accurate forecasts. But as with most long-term forecasts, even small changes in underlying assumptions will generate significant divergences in end results. This is reflected in a debate within the demographic community surrounding the likely trajectory of birthrates over coming decades that might appear arcane and technical – but the side of this debate that is correct will ultimately have profound economic and geopolitical consequences.

The UN medium variant projection estimates that global population will grow to 9.8 billion in 2050 and 11.2 billion in 2100.[58] The medium variant projection could be considered the 'best guess', with the UN's demographic model also producing high and low variants. The UN has done a good job of estimating long-term global population growth in the past, so these projections should be taken seriously.

But it is important to note that a significant number of prominent demographers are now forecasting a faster drop-off in fertility rates than is assumed in the UN medium variant projection. Wolfgang Lutz at the International Institute for Applied Systems Analysis predicts that global population will stabilise by mid-century and decline thereafter. Jorgen Randers, author of *The Limits to Growth*, predicts that global population will peak at 8 billion in 2040 before dropping off. Hans Rosling, *The Economist*, Bricker and Ibbitson and Deutsche Bank have all held to a similar position.[59] These lower global estimates are consistent with figures released in China in early 2020 that reflect a fertility rate at its lowest point in seven decades; and a persistent and significant gender imbalance of 30 million more men than women.[60]

How different are the worlds of the UN medium projection and the alternative low-fertility projections? In economic, social and geopolitical terms, they are very different.

If global population peaks at 8 billion by mid-century, the abatement task, per capita, is materially easier than the UN is currently suggesting it will be. If the low fertility forecasters are right, a significant amount of abatement could occur through there being fewer people than we had thought there would be.

Second, the lower fertility scenarios will have significant geopolitical consequences in terms of the relative economic and military potential of the major powers. In the UN projection, the population of India, China and the US in 2100 will be 1.66 billion, 1.36 billion and 447 million, respectively. In this scenario, India's population will be around four times as large as that of the US, while China's will be about three times larger. This means that India only requires a per capita productivity rate of 25 per cent of the US level, while China will need a rate of 33 per cent in order for their aggregate economies to be larger than the US.

In contrast, according to the Vollset et al. model's 'reference scenario' (i.e. the medium variant), the 2100 population of India, China and the US would be 1.09 billion, 731 million and 335 million respectively. First, these are much lower figures. According to the Vollset model, China's population in 2100 will be not much more than half as large as the UN's best guess estimate. Second, the ratio between the China and the US is more like 2:1 than 3:1, which is a major difference in both economic and geopolitical terms.

As a further example of how much of an impact low fertility could have in terms of relative power, in the Vollset reference scenario, the population of Nigeria is forecast to be larger than China in 2100 (790 million vs 731 million) and, critically important for economic growth prospects, the number of working-age adults in Nigeria is forecast to be around 20 per cent higher in Nigeria than China (around 500 million vs 400 million).

This represents the significant variation between models. But there is also considerable variation, in the long term, *within* each model. For the UN, world population in 2100 across the low, medium and high variant projections are 7 billion, 11 billion and 17 billion – a huge range. For the Vollset et al. projection, the low, medium and high scenarios are 6.8 billion, 8.8 billion and 11.8 billion. This represents a much smaller range of uncertainty than the UN projections, but a substantial uncertainty band nonetheless.

The purpose of this book is not to adjudicate between the various expert forecasters and their models. Rather, it is to emphasise that, for policymakers, it is important to acknowledge the double-barrelled uncertainty that we face when dealing with demographic change: both *between* models and *within* models. Life would be easier if we could reduce the magnitude of both types of uncertainty. But to the extent that we can't, we will need to make sufficient allowances today in our planning and also develop institutions that are flexible enough to adjust as new information comes to hand.

The old-age dependency ratio

Many countries – and almost all high-income countries – will experience a sharp increase in the old-age dependency ratio (OADR) over coming decades. The OADR is the ratio of those over the age of sixty-five years to the working age population (fifteen to sixty-four). As already discussed, the growing proportion of retirees in the population lies at the heart of the challenge of providing dignity and security in retirement and will likely be a key driver of healthcare and long-term care costs. A key aspect of this policy challenge is forecasting the long-run OADR.

The increase in the OADR reflects a fundamentally good outcome (we're living longer, on average), but it will require higher taxes for pensions and increased investment in healthcare and long-term care. A key policy challenge is the uncertainty associated with long-term forecasts of the demographic profile.

Three things are particularly noteworthy about the data. First, there is a wide range of outcomes across countries. For example, based on the 2020 *Lancet* study, in 2050, the OADR in the US and Australia is forecast to be around 0.36, compared to 0.47 in Germany and 0.51 in China. In 2050, the OADR in China is forecast to be over 40 per cent higher than the US (0.51 vs 0.36). By 2100, the gap between China and the US will be almost 20 percentage points in the reference scenario (0.66 for China vs 0.46 for the US).[61]

Second, the situation worsens across all countries between 2050 and 2100. This is a systematic risk, as discussed in Chapters 4 and 6. Effectively managing this risk will require government action, ideally using a combination of calibrated intergenerational transfers (such as taxpayer-funded PAYG pension payments) and personal savings (both mandatory and voluntary).

Third, it is noteworthy by how much the degree of uncertainty rises between 2050 and 2100. For the 2050 scenarios, the confidence band for the OADR for each country is 2–3 percentage points (other than Germany). For the 2100 scenarios, the range between the maximum and minimum OADR estimates blows out to 28 percentage points for the US, 30 for Australia and 50 for China. While this outcome is decades away, the risk-management mechanisms required to be able to accommodate such a wide range of potential outcomes need to implemented today.

The intergenerational aspect of an ageing society requires government intervention. The very wide range of possible outcomes over the long run requires government action with in-built flexibility to adjust to changing circumstances.

PART III

REFORMING SOCIAL INSURANCE

8. Why Reform Is Important

MANY PEOPLE'S INCOMES HAVE STALLED

A growing number of workers in the US, Australia and the UK are experiencing increasing job insecurity, particularly those on lower incomes. Coupled with the fact that many workers and households on low incomes have seen little real wages growth in recent decades, there is a growing resentment at how the spoils of productivity growth and globalisation are being shared. These changes in the economic and social landscape don't just reinforce the importance of existing social insurance programs. They also raise questions as to whether additional programs are needed for new risks that have emerged over recent decades.

Wages as a share of national output are falling

Most macroeconomic models that attempt to explain long-run growth assume a constant, 'steady-state' split of national income between labour and capital. Based on twentieth-century data for the US and other advanced economies, this split was assumed to be around two-thirds labour and one-third capital.[1] Thomas Piketty finds that, when examined over the longer run, these shares are in fact not constant.[2] Over recent decades, the share of national output accruing to capital has been rising. In assessing the underlying causes for this trend in Australia, the Reserve Bank (RBA) attributes the growing capital share of income to a range of factors, but highlights an increase in the returns accruing to owners of housing, a rising share of national income going to capital in the finance sector and, in some sectors, changes in trade.[3] This long-term structural change in how the spoils of the economy are shared is having widespread consequences.

Wages have stalled for low income earners – but not for everyone

Increasing income and wealth inequality across the OECD in recent decades is well documented.[4] This follows a period of declining inequality during the period 1900–1980 – the same years of the welfare state's expansion.[5] Rising inequality has had profound implications on the distribution of not just disposable income but life expectancy, the social and financial stability to marry, quality of life, job satisfaction and overall happiness.[6] One of the key drivers of inequality is that wages for workers at or near the median in the US, the UK and Australia have stalled, in real terms, in the face of technological change, increased trade with low-wage economies, an influx of low-wage and often temporary migrant labour and, in some contexts, adverse regulatory outcomes such as laws restricting union bargaining and low minimum-wage settings. In the US, wages are currently a lower share of GDP than at any time since the Federal Reserve started collecting data in the 1940s.[7] According to Jane Gravelle:

> Over the 1979–2018 period, real wages in the US at the 10th percentile of the hourly wage distribution grew by 1.6 per cent, whereas wages at the 50th percentile grew by 6.1 per cent and wages at the 90th percentile grew by 37.6 per cent.[8]

The difference in growth rates is even starker when comparing wages growth for the average worker with the growth enjoyed by those on extremely high incomes. This is an important comparison since it is covered so frequently in the media and, for many, has become emblematic of worsening inequality and unfairness. While wages as a share of GDP have been dropping, CEO salaries have been on the rise. Over the last four decades, CEO remuneration has risen a staggering 900 per cent, while the average worker has seen an increase of just 12 per cent.[9]

The rise of trade with China has had a major impact on manufacturing jobs in the US.[10] Generally, globalisation is seen as reducing the number of low-skill jobs in sectors within high-wage advanced economies.

Several governments have implemented programs to assist individuals and communities adversely affected by trade. One example is the Trade Adjustment Assistance (TAA) program in the US. While trade generally produces aggregate gains, programs like the TAA have all too often left those worst affected by international trade deals with little assistance.[11]

In contrast to the impacts of trade with emerging economies, technological change (automation, robots, AI) tends to result in greater polarisation in wages, reducing the number of middle-skill jobs. Recent technological change has underpinned productivity growth across the US economy as a whole, but has generated relatively smaller benefits for less skilled workers.[12] Katz and Goldin argue that inequality isn't attributable to the inherent nature of technological change alone. They contend that it arises from the interaction between technology (the demand for skilled workers) and the education system (the supply of skilled workers). It is this interaction that ultimately determines the relationship between skilled and unskilled wages. During eras of high investment in education, there is a high supply of skilled graduates. This results in a lower skill premium, all other things being equal. The reverse is true where education falls behind in the 'race' with technology.[13]

This story is repeated in Australia, which has, over the past decade, experienced the lowest wages growth on record.[14] Average annual growth in real wages in the five years to November 2018 was just 0.5 per cent per annum. This was significantly lower than the average recorded in the five years to November 2013, which was 1.8 per cent per annum.[15]

Brynjolfsson and McAfee describe this as 'the Great Decoupling'. During the three to four decades following World War II, median family income grew in tandem with productivity growth in the US. Over the past two to three decades, median family income has stalled, despite the continued growth of productivity. This is reflected in Figure 8.1.

The impact of sustained income stagnation has had a profound impact on people's perception of progress. In the years following World War II, 90 per cent of people in the US earned more than their parents. Today, that figure is 50 per cent. This is reflected in the expectations of today's generation, with only 37 per cent of people in the US believing that their children will be better off financially than themselves, only 24 per cent of people in Canada and Australia and only 9 per cent in France.[16]

Figure 8.1: The decoupling of real wages and productivity growth in the US[17]

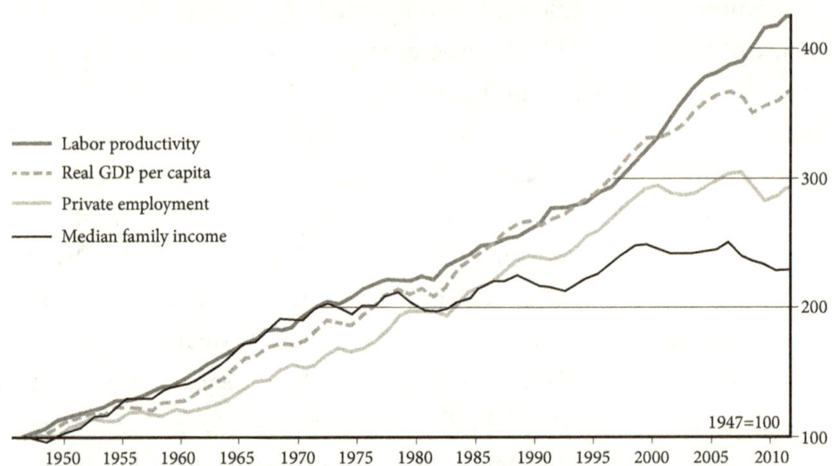

The impact of this uneven income growth could be felt for decades. In addition to negatively impacting the welfare of households, uneven wages growth across an economy, particularly when sustained over long periods of time (as has occurred in the US), will also have an impact on the distribution of retirement savings.

Not only has the level of median income stalled, but the volatility of family income in the US has increased substantially since 1972. In 2014, before-tax family income volatility was more than double what it was in the early 1970s. Concerningly, volatility was higher for less-educated people than for the well-educated, and for low-income families than for those with a high income. Increased volatility did not seem to be correlated with higher risk tolerance – suggesting that it was not voluntarily embraced.[18] If average family income in the US was a stock, investors would be most displeased with having to put up with a sharp increase in volatility for no increase in returns!

RISK IS INCREASING, INCLUDING FOR THOSE ON LOW INCOMES

In addition to stalled real wages, many workers in Australia, the US and the UK – particularly those on low incomes – face growing job insecurity.

Arne Kalleberg defines precarious work as characterised by employees bearing additional risks and receiving limited benefits (like healthcare and retirement benefits). In recent years, there has been a rise in the proportion of precarious employment across many advanced economies.[19] This is epitomised by the 'gig' economy, in which many employees work as individual contractors assuming considerable income risk with little compensation for that risk.

Guy Standing refers to this group of people as the 'precariat'. He argues that even more significant than their unreliable income is that 'the precariat has no occupational identity or narrative to give to their lives. This creates existential insecurity, and is accompanied by the fact that for the first time in history many people have education above the level of labour they can expect to obtain.'[20]

Rapid technological change, driven by advances in computing power and robotics, has made some skills and occupations partly or wholly redundant. These trends potentially threaten even more workers over coming decades. While there has been considerable debate in recent years in relation to the nature of the threat posed by automation to the economy as a whole, there is little evidence yet of a fall in the overall participation rate[21] or a material rise in inter- and intra-sector job churn rates.[22] Having said that, it is clear that many low-skill workers in advanced economies are experiencing growing job insecurity coupled with lower wages growth as a result of skills-biased technological change.

Lillian Alexander examines the Australian labour market and finds that, even when unemployment was low in 2018, this masked a number of growing areas of insecurity: less than half of Australian workers in permanent full-time work with leave entitlements; over a million Australian workers classified as 'independent contractors' with few entitlements and superannuation rights; over a million workers paid through labour-hire firms or employment agencies; and the rise of the gig economy, with few worker protections and, in many cases, many risks assumed by workers.[23] Similarly, Rebecca Cassells finds that, between 2009 and 2016, the rate of precarious work in the Australian economy increased for both genders, but to a greater degree for men.[24]

There is some pushback to this narrative, with some arguing that an increase in 'precarious' employment is often asserted without clearly defining the concept. For example, Robert Sobyra argues that, in the Australian labour market, there was no upward trend in casualisation between 2000 and 2016, that there has not been an increase in involuntary job loss between 1994 and 2017 and that the rate of self-employment declined between 1992 and 2018.[25] In part, the fact that there was no upward trend in the rate of casualisation may reflect the fact that there is an increasing number of types of insecure work. It may be that the proportion of insecure work is growing even if the rate of casual work is stable. Today, what is sometimes referred to as 'non-standard' arrangements are far more diverse and include casual workers, employment through labour-hire firms, individual contractors and 'gig' workers.

For many people, changes to risk-sharing arrangements between employers and employees are central to the story of job insecurity. Many employers claim that more 'flexibility' is needed to boost the economy-wide rate of productivity growth. This is often a euphemism for employers having more rights to change the amount and timing of work at short notice. This represents a shift in who bears the burden of risk in relation to the demand for a firm's goods, or supply-chain disruptions. Employers often seek flexibility as a way of shifting risks onto workers – and in many instances do so without paying compensation for the reallocation of risk.

In the gig economy, workers are often obliged to assume many of the burdens of running a small business, such as establishing a business entity, taking out insurance and investing in equipment. But they do so without the upside financial returns that typically accrue to those assuming risk in establishing a firm. A person delivering pizzas on a moped or a driver for a platform that allocates rides using a complex, unseen algorithm often assumes considerable demand-side and business risks – but can end up working for less than the minimum wage once all costs are netted off. In the US, the Economic Policy Institute estimated that Uber drivers earn on average US$9.21 per hour after netting off expenses, which is materially below the minimum wage in most markets.[26] Understandably, many people in these situations feel frustrated with the risk-return trade-offs they bear, although they often persist if they feel that they have limited alternative options.

Rising job insecurity raises questions as to whether labour market regulation is sufficiently balanced. A key element of this challenge will be how union and employer relations are governed. Another increasingly important aspect of regulation is how arrangements are regulated that are contrived to look one way when the relationship is, in substance, something quite different.

Covid-19 has caused deep recessions in all major economies, which have hit those in insecure work the hardest. Job losses in hospitality, retail and other service sectors have been particularly pronounced, with casuals often the first to be laid off. The Covid-19 recession has laid bare the fact that, in the modern economy, many who bear the greatest risks don't share the spoils of a growing pie.

But the combination of stalled wages for many on low incomes and growing job insecurity doesn't require a pandemic to become problematic. Unexpected household shocks such as job loss, a serious health problem or family breakdown can hit those families hardest that don't have the financial resources to build up a buffer. In the US, Pew found that in 2013 over half of households (55 per cent) did not have enough savings (or easily accessible liquid assets) to cover a single month's income. Indeed, the bottom 40 per cent of income earners have liquid savings that could cover fifteen days or fewer of a gap in income – a mere two weeks; the bottom 20 per cent of earners can cover only nine days.[27]

Disappearing opportunities for middle-skill workers

A related aspect of workplace change is the sharp reduction in well-paid middle-skill jobs in recent years. This was particularly evident in the US between 1979 and 2012, at the same time as there was a sharp increase in the share of low-skill and high-skill jobs.[28] This US trend is matched by changes in employment shares in sixteen EU countries between 1993 and 2010.[29] Lawrence Katz and Robert Margo attribute this, in part, to the way in which technology has increased the demand for cognitive and interpersonal skills and reduced the demand for routine analytical and mechanical skills. These describe many middle-income white-collar and manufacturing positions respectively.[30] This shift in the distribution of jobs has had a negative impact on the opportunities available to many people, particularly those with less education or skills.

The disappearance of many middle-skill occupations raises a question as to the adequacy of existing social programs such as unemployment insurance. Do we need to explore opportunities to provide protection not just against job loss but also against the disappearance of an occupation or a reduction in the remuneration of a skill set? According to Robert Shiller's seminal book *The New Financial Order*, we do.[31] Even without specific markets for occupational risks, additional government support in mid-career training may go some way to mitigating this type of risk.

Geographic concentrations of disadvantage

One of the most challenging aspects of current social trends is the geographic concentration of disadvantage. OECD research has found that, across high-income countries, the productivity gap between the most productive regions and the average has widened by 60 per cent over the past two decades.[32] Paul Collier shows how this has created considerable risk for the inhabitants of many regions and cities where large firms or entire industries have either grown relatively slowly (compared to the overall economy) or shut down entirely. Two examples he gives are the steel industry in Sheffield in the UK and the automotive industry in Detroit in the US. Both Sheffield and Detroit are cities that once benefited from specialisation, economies of agglomeration and comparative advantage. Where cities are heavily reliant on a particular industry, a rapid decline in that industry's competitive position can create a cycle in which quality jobs disappear and property prices fall. For those individuals and families reluctant to relocate due to longstanding roots in an area, it may be necessary to take a significant pay cut to remain employed. Those willing to relocate may have few options as falling property prices may make it difficult to move to regions with strong employment markets.

Geographic risk doesn't just take the highly visible form of an industry closing and leaving behind empty factories and warehouses. The hollowing of middle-skill jobs has a geographic dimension in the US, but one that is less obvious. David Autor's analysis of granular US labour force data shows that the fall in the proportion of middle-skill jobs in the US is reflected in a decline in well-paid jobs for middle-skill, non-college graduates in urban areas in particular: both blue-collar production jobs and white-collar administrative support jobs. Autor finds that the urban non-college wage premium has fallen dramatically since 2000.[33]

For these people, the cost of living (and housing in particular) often hasn't declined, but remuneration and job security have. While Autor's analysis of the declining urban non-college wage premium is based on US data, the decline in middle-skill jobs is a feature of many EU labour markets[34] and it would not be surprising if similar relative declines in middle-skill remuneration had occurred in at least some of these countries.

An increasing share of workers aren't working as much as they want to

For most of the twentieth century, unemployment was the characteristic of the labour market that attracted almost all policy and media attention. In recent years, it has become increasingly clear that underemployment is just as significant an issue.

In Australia, there has been a long-term inversion between the unemployment rate and the underemployment rate over recent decades. Throughout the 1970s and 1980s, unemployment was markedly higher than underemployment. Not surprisingly, the unemployment rate captured the vast bulk of attention by economists and commentators throughout this period. Since 1990, the underemployment rate has steadily tracked upwards. In the late 1990s and early 2000s, the two measures were roughly equal. Ever since 2002, the underemployment rate has been higher than the unemployment rate and the gap has steadily widened.[35] In part, this reflects the growing prevalence of part-time work. The burden of increasing underemployment in Australia has increasingly fallen on low-skill workers and women.[36] The immediate impact of the Covid-19 recession was to exacerbate these trends, at least in the short term. Much of the short-term labour market impact of Covid-19 was in reduced hours, a reflection of the shifting of demand risk onto those in insecure work. This is shown in Figure 8.2.

The labour market in the US has not seen this crossover in the underemployment and unemployment rates, but the underemployment rate appears to be trending upwards over time. Just as worryingly, over recent decades, each successive economic downturn appears to have produced a higher-rate of under-employment than the preceding one.[37]

Exposure to unemployment and underemployment risk could have serious consequences, not just for household welfare in the short run but, as with sustained periods of low wages growth, it could also have long-term savings implications that could affect income security for many households in retirement.

Figure 8.2: Unemployment and underemployment in Australia, 1990–2020

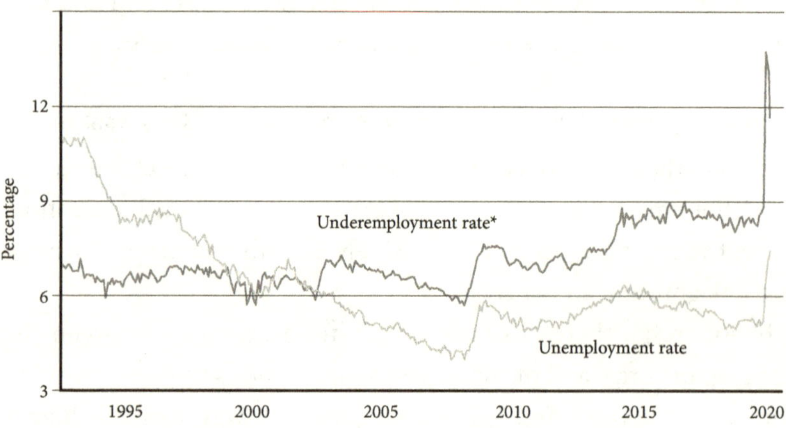

The challenge of managing many complex risk management options

Many people are aware that they face major risks like serious illness, accidents or the challenge of providing for themselves during retirement. But it is difficult for most of us to find the time to attend to dealing with all these risks.

For example, some argue that people are myopic when it comes to retirement risk and use this as a justification for public-policy intervention such as mandated savings. In addition to short-sightedness (for many), there is also a high degree of disengagement, which means that many people don't even get to the point of making a long-term savings decision at all. Studies have found that default options have a significant impact on people's choices in retirement accounts, with many people opting for and staying with an offered default level of contributions and investment risk regardless of what it is.[38]

Many people simply don't have the bandwidth to even think about the many risks that they face – and the many risk-management options that they have at their disposal. This isn't always irrational but is often the result of prioritising some issues over others.

THERE IS A GROWING PERCEPTION THAT RISK IS NOT BEING SHARED FAIRLY

Despite the significant safety net currently provided by social insurance, many vulnerable people justifiably feel that they have not shared sufficiently in the substantial growth of recent decades. For many, wages have stagnated while at the same time people have been exposed to additional risks not currently protected by social insurance.

In assessing the vote against Brexit, Matthew Goodwin and Robert Ford coined the term 'The Left Behind' to characterise voters who 'turned against a political class they saw as dominated by socially liberal university graduates with values fundamentally opposed to theirs, on identity, Europe – and particularly immigration'. These voters were typically older, white and socially conservative.[39]

Similarly, according to Victoria Bateman, a sense of resentment and a sense of feeling 'forgotten, despite having been instrumental to the beginnings of Britain's longer-term growth' was one of the driving forces behind a section of the Brexit vote.[40] Matthew Goodwin and Oliver Heath conclude:

> In this respect the vote for Brexit was delivered by social groups that are united by a general sense of insecurity, pessimism and marginalization, who do not feel as though elites, whether in Brussels or Westminster, share their values, represent their interests and genuinely empathize with their intense angst about rapid social, economic and cultural change.[41]

The election of Donald Trump in 2016 has generated a wave of similar analysis. Well before Trump considered running for president, the US was deeply polarised. One study found that the degree of impact by trade in a commuting zone or district was correlated with an increasing market share for the Fox News channel, a rise in the likelihood of electing a Republican to Congress and a stronger polarisation in campaign contributions.[42]

For some time, political scientists have grappled with the intertwined strands of economic and cultural issues. Thomas Frank found that many socially conservative blue-collar voters were more likely to have voted

Republican in recent elections because the political choice has been increasingly framed in terms of cultural issues rather than economic.[43]

Over the past several years, a significant body of analysis has emerged suggesting non-economic factors behind the Trump vote. Polarisation in the US is also closely correlated with race, class and geography. Lilliana Mason finds that:

> The American political parties are growing socially polarized. Religion and race, as well as class, geography, and culture, are dividing the parties in such a way that the effect of party identity is magnified … A single vote can now indicate a person's partisan preference as well as his or her religion, race, ethnicity, gender, neighbourhood, and favorite grocery store. There is no longer a single social identity. Partisanship can now be thought of as a mega-identity.[44]

Diana Mutz argues that, while it was less-educated voters who gravitated towards Trump between 2012 and 2016, it was not out of economic insecurity but rather a reflection of 'dominant groups that felt threatened by change and a candidate who took advantage of that trend'. She found that income and job insecurity were less important than a desire for one's group to be dominant, concerns with trade and China, a feeling that the 'American way of life is threatened' and a view that high-status groups like men, Christians and whites are discriminated against.[45]

These conclusions are consistent with Frank's finding that economic issues had been intermingled with social issues by a political positioning by the GOP that had been underway well before Trump.

Ezra Klein points to the debate following the 2016 election between those who argue that economic anxiety was the key factor versus those suggesting that it was racial resentment (or, in other contexts such as the UK and Europe, perhaps resentment towards immigrants or elites). An important question – and an extremely difficult one to test – is causation. Did growing inequality and exposure to economic risk among less-educated, working-class voters make them more open to latching onto cultural issues or was it the other way around? In the US context, Sides, Tesler and Vavreck found evidence that, between 2012 and 2016, causation ran from racial resentment to economic anxiety. It is unclear whether these conclusions can be applied to other time periods in the US or other political contexts.[46]

Another emerging material factor appears to be a generational fall in faith in democratic institutions. A World Values Survey found that 30 per cent of US millennials believe that democracy was essential to their well-being, compared to 50 per cent for those born in the 1960s and over 70 per cent for those born in the 1930s. Similarly, in both the US and Europe, the tendency to conclude that democracy is a 'bad' or 'very bad' way to run a country increased the younger the cohort.[47] Similar percentages of belief in democracy among millennials were found in Australia, the UK and Sweden.[48]

The frustration of millennials with traditional democratic institutions and parties is reflected in their drift towards non-traditional, more extreme political parties and candidates, of both the right and left. In the 2017 French presidential elections, more than half of voters aged eighteen to twenty-four voted for either far-left candidate Jean-Luc Mélenchon or far-right candidate Marine Le Pen.[49] In Austria in 2016, more than 42 per cent of voters under the age of thirty voted for far-right candidate Norbert Hofer, a prelude to Sebastian Kurz's victory the year after. Young support can also be found for ethnically majoritarian and nationalist agendas promoted by leaders such as Rodrigo Duterte in the Philippines.[50] The rise of young support for left candidates such as Bernie Sanders and Jeremy Corbyn is not driven by a rejection of democratic institutions per se, but is probably in part a reflection of despair with 'traditional' politics.

Clearly both the vote for Brexit and the vote for Donald Trump are extremely complex social phenomena that resist simple, mono-causal interpretations. But one strand that runs through much of the Brexit and Trump analysis is that many socially conservative blue-collar workers feel left behind and economically insecure and, whether they voted primarily on the basis of economic issues or on 'cultural' issues, the angst they feel as a result of current distributional arrangements, including the distribution of risk and reward, is profound and deep-seated.

In Australia, a similar phenomenon has occurred in the drift of many working-class voters to One Nation and other parties that present themselves as 'anti-establishment' (including the various well-funded iterations of the billionaire mining magnate Clive Palmer's political interventions).

These voters tend to hail from the regions and outer suburbs, reflecting many of the same economic and social concerns as those in the US and the UK.[51]

For present purposes, the fact that many socially conservative, working-class people use their resentment towards cultural elites in London, US coastal enclaves or Canberra to vote a particular way is not the key concern. What is critical is that coexisting with this culture war – and probably exacerbating it – is a feeling of resentment towards economic injustice and a growing exposure to uninsured economic risks.

Raising taxation materially would be problematic

In the six decades between 1920 and 1980, taxation as a share of GDP increased sharply in most advanced economies; most of that increase occurred in the four decades after World War II. The vast majority of this additional revenue went to funding social insurance programs. This book has argued that, in most cases, these programs have been highly beneficial, saving many vulnerable people from poverty, ill-health and homelessness. However, it is important to acknowledge that, while these programs have been beneficial, higher taxes impose distortionary costs on an economy.

On average, growth in the size of government as a share of GDP stalled across the OECD after 1985. Across a selection of major advanced economies, government increased by almost 30 percentage points between 1950 and 1985 (from 20.5 per cent to 50 per cent of GDP).[52] Over the following twenty-five years, government spending remained stable on average across this selection of countries. While overall tax levels differ across countries (for example, the US is around 10 percentage points lower than Europe), what is perhaps surprising is how similar the trend since 1980 has been across the OECD. The slowdown in the rate of increase of tax levels occurred in almost all advanced economies at roughly the same point in time. In the UK and the US, this was likely inspired by the Reagan and Thatcher revolutions, but the general trend in the size of government across the OECD suggests that each country made its own evaluation.

The cross-country trends in government spending since 1980 suggest that the population of most OECD countries is broadly happy with the size of government. In most advanced economies, the community doesn't want to see government retreat from its core functions or reduce the scope of key social programs. But it also doesn't want the burden of materially higher taxes. That may change if the community asks government to provide additional services – or services to a higher standard. This will ultimately be a question of trade-offs: improved service delivery in lieu of lower disposable income, with the distribution of people losing disposable income depending on the progressivity of the tax system.

Will there also be a trade-off over the medium and longer term between higher taxes and economic growth? The evidence in relation to the relationship between the overall tax take and long-term growth rates is contested. There is certainly not a simple and unambiguous negative correlation between taxes as a share of GDP and income per capita or long-term economic per capita growth rates.[53] As discussed earlier in Chapter 3, there is not a clear correlation or demonstrated causation between the size of the public sector and GDP per capita or productivity growth.

The relationship between taxes and growth undoubtedly depends in part on what government spends its revenue on – some government programs are more growth-promoting than others. The relationship is also complicated by the fact that macroeconomic performance is affected by many determinants in addition to taxation levels. Not surprisingly, econometric studies have produced mixed results in relation to the effect of overall taxation levels on economic growth.[54]

Another factor reducing the likelihood of a further material hike in overall tax rates is the fact that, in 2021, OECD public-sector indebtedness is far higher than in 1990. In 1990, average central government debt across the OECD was 36.4 per cent of GDP. By 2021, that figure had increased sharply to over 90 per cent of GDP.[55] In response to Covid-19, the level of central government debt across the OECD rose around 20 percentage points between 2019 and 2021.

Increased spending in response to the Covid-19 recession, while justified, increased indebtedness across the OECD in the short run and will put a strain on future budgets as interest rates inevitably rise at some point. In that environment, increasing recurrent expenditure for social purposes will be even more difficult for a given revenue base.[56]

The lack of appetite in most, if not all, OECD countries for markedly higher taxes when combined with higher public debt levels following Covid-19 stimulus measures makes it more likely that in order to expand the scope and functionality of social insurance, it will be necessary to reform the way that it operates broadly within the current funding envelope. The following chapters outline how there is considerable scope to do so. They deal, in turn, with how to improve social insurance for individuals and how to strengthen measures to manage systematic risks.

9.
How to Improve Social Insurance for Individual Losses

In order to develop a strategy for improving the effectiveness of social insurance programs to manage risk and uncertainty, it is worth revisiting the genesis and rationale of these programs. In framing future reforms, five fundamental questions need to be answered. These five questions are set out below. Each will be answered in the following chapters.

Which losses should be covered?

Social insurance emerged in most countries in response to a perceived need to strengthen responses to economic deprivation – social unrest in Germany in the 1870s and 1880s, the 1890s Depression in Australia, and the Great Depression of the 1930s in the US, the UK, Europe and Australia. Many political leaders and public-policy experts argued that existing informal and somewhat ad hoc arrangements were inadequate both in coverage and the levels of support provided. In addition, there were many areas where private insurance markets were either underdeveloped or constrained by market failure.

The principal losses against which protection was provided were poverty in old age and unemployment, ill health, disability, some forms of major accident and homelessness. The losses covered by social insurance programs are similar to many of the losses that are covered by private insurance markets in that risk pooling is often an effective risk-management tool.

There are three key categories of risk and uncertainty where the scope of coverage by social insurance programs could be expanded:

- Risk and uncertainty which are already insured against but where the potential for loss is increasing for significant numbers of people. Examples include automation, longevity and long-term care.
- Risks and uncertainty which are already insured against but for which innovation allows greater coverage through improved risk management. This includes a range of risks where income-contingent loans offer a way of providing individuals with access to up-front capital.
- Risks and uncertainty which are not currently insured but which represent major risks in people's lives, such as a decline in the value of their house or their lifetime income.

Many social insurance programs have been designed to overcome limitations or failures in private insurance markets. These limitations arise from a range of sources, including information asymmetry (adverse selection and moral hazard), affordability and externalities. Mandatory coverage, subsidies and community rating are the most common design features for social insurance programs.

Who should pay?

One of the most important features of social insurance is how it is funded. There are two key dimensions to this challenge. First, should programs be funded through risk-rated contributions or from general taxation? In essence, this boils down to whether the burden of funding programs should be borne by those most exposed to the likelihood of loss or those most able to pay. At times, there have been intense debates between advocates of risk-rated contributory funding and advocates of taxpayer funding through progressive taxation. This is an important distinction and there are pros and cons to each approach, depending upon the circumstances.

The second question is whether to fully fund programs or adopt a pay-as-you-go approach. For losses that evolve over long periods of time, these approaches will impose different burdens across generations. Fully funded schemes have the advantage of sustainability and actuarial transparency. Pay-as-you-go schemes offer greater opportunities for intergenerational risk sharing.

While these two funding issues are of great importance, the debate surrounding funding sources can take attention away from the redistributive impact of how benefits are provided. The distributional impact of funding arrangements is often quite clear. For example, highly progressive income taxes place a heavier burden on high income earners (subject to compliance!). With benefits, it can be more difficult to determine distributional impacts, partly because many schemes do not track usage rates by income level or socio-economic status. Yet a number of studies have indicated that benefit take-up can in fact be regressive in some instances. In many instances, it would be beneficial to devote more effort to achieving transparency as to who benefits from, and who pays for, these programs.

How should loss be compensated?

Social insurance provides compensation for loss through a number of mechanisms. The key aspects of the distribution of benefits that are worth examining are:

- Whether they are provided through cash payments, in-kind goods and services, or a combination;
- Whether entitlements should be means-tested or universal;
- Whether there should be a universal flat-rate entitlement or a benefit level that is set based on each individual's characteristics;
- The degree of client choice in determining the timing and characteristics of benefits

What outcomes should be achieved?

The ultimate goal of social insurance is to achieve positive outcomes for individuals who have experienced loss and, in addition, for the broader society and economy. Evaluating long-term outcomes is difficult in all areas of policy, and social insurance is no exception.

It is important that more effort is devoted to explicitly defining and evaluating outcomes rigorously – and to linking the attainment of those outcomes with the most effective mechanisms for distributing benefits. This is critical for achieving value for money and containing costs.

There are several strategies that should be explored in this regard, including a greater emphasis on preventative and early intervention opportunities, investing for the long-term, joined-up service delivery and a genuine commitment to the transparent use of rigorous evaluation methodologies.

Ensuring the attainment of long term outcomes is also necessary in order to set appropriate premiums, whether they be explicit, via risk-rated contributions, or implicit, via taxation levels. Without measuring how much it costs to compensate individuals for loss, it isn't possible to set appropriate premiums.

The following five chapters deal with each of these questions in turn and make recommendations as to which reforms should be prioritised.

10. What Potential Losses Should Be Covered?

The range of risks covered by the modern welfare state is vast by historical standards. But there is good reason to believe that more could and should be done. There are three main areas where the scope of current social insurance programs should be increased:

- Risks and uncertainty which are already insured against but where the potential for loss is increasing for significant numbers of people;
- Risks and uncertainty which are already insured against but for which innovation allows greater coverage through improved risk management;
- Risks and uncertainty which are not currently insured but which represent major risks in people's lives.

RISKS AND UNCERTAINTY WHERE THE POTENTIAL FOR LOSS IS INCREASING

Two of the key risks already covered by social insurance are the potential losses associated with labour market dislocation and the adverse health and income outcomes associated with ageing. Programs dealing with labour market risk include unemployment insurance, subsidised training and active labour market programs that intervene to help unemployed people to find work. The risks associated with ageing are also dealt with through multiple programs, including taxpayer-funded old-age pensions, tax concessions for mandatory and voluntary savings, public healthcare and aged-care subsidies. The evolving nature of each of these potential risks for individuals invites a rethink of current social insurance programs.

Technological change and its impact on labour markets

The threat to jobs posed by technological change has been with humanity ever since the invention of the earliest tools. Some tools did things that a human hand alone could not – such as a hammer breaking a rock, or a spear killing a distant animal. These tools were complements to human labour. Other tools – such as a horse-drawn plough that could do the work of many people – were substitutes in that they directly replaced human labour. Some tools were both complements and substitutes. A more effective sickle is both a complement and a substitute: it is wielded by a person who becomes more productive, but in doing so, it also makes it possible to harvest a field with fewer people.

In addition to impacts at the level of firm and farm, there are macroeconomic effects that arise from these innovations. If a particular industry becomes more efficient, that frees up people to work in other sectors, thereby increasing both the aggregate quantity and scope of economic activity across a society. This has been a key driver of economic progress for millennia. But it has also induced painful transitions for individuals as they are made redundant and are forced to retrain or relocate.

After countless waves of agricultural innovation, the early stages of the Industrial Revolution saw new sources of power and more sophisticated automation. The industries that arose absorbed many workers who had previously toiled the fields. Then waves of innovation across these new industries threatened many non-agricultural occupations. The now iconic mechanised looms that replaced the work of skilled artisans in nineteenth-century England have come to represent both the increased productivity and disruption caused by technological innovation.

The Industrial Revolution was different from earlier technological transitions in the scope and speed of adoption, but not in the fundamental nature of change. Even though total employment in textiles increased over the decades following the Luddite protests – and even though average wages in the UK rose at a historically rapid rate during the nineteenth century – that was small comfort for the individuals and families losing their livelihoods, their social standing and their sense of purpose in a world without a comprehensive social safety net. There was scant state-sponsored mid-career retraining in the nineteenth century.

Society is currently experiencing a wave of technological change in the fields of information technology, computing power, artificial intelligence and robotics. Some have argued that these changes will threaten livelihoods across an even broader swathe of industries and occupations than the Industrial Revolution. The box on p.208 summarises some aspects of the debate in relation to the scope and threat of this change. Even though there remains a high degree of uncertainty in relation to how much of the economy will be adversely affected by these developments, it appears that the underlying threats and opportunities remain broadly unchanged. First, technological change promises to generate productivity growth, although the overall trend in economy-wide productivity growth remains unclear. Second, the impact of technological change will be felt unevenly across occupations and sectors. Finally, while some skills and occupations will either be made redundant or experience lower remuneration, new jobs will emerge.

Two economic forces offsetting job destruction are worth noting. First, labour force participation is at or near record levels in most OECD countries. This reflects the economy's capacity to create new jobs, even as technological innovation displaces some work. For every job lost to a robot or an AI algorithm, a new position as a health worker or educator or personal trainer or another job in the services sector has appeared. It is the change in net jobs that matters, after accounting for additional jobs created. Of course, estimating where new jobs will be created is at least as difficult (and uncertain) as pointing to jobs at risk from automation.[1]

David Autor identifies three new categories of jobs that will emerge: 'frontier jobs' (jobs at the cutting edge of technology, such as programmers and coders); 'wealth jobs' (service jobs relying on the rising wages of others, such as baristas and sommeliers); and 'last-mile workers' (jobs that are the remainder of an occupation after much has been largely automated, such as vending-machine attendants in the 1990s and underground cable locators today).[2]

Automation and job destruction in the early twenty-first century

- Today, many argue that, unlike in earlier transitions, automation, robots and AI threaten jobs across the entire economy rather than in only one sector. There are countless studies by academics, consultants and think tanks with headlines shouting: 'X per cent of the labour force will be replaced by robots!'

- At an economy-wide level, numerous studies have estimated that between 40 and 60 per cent of jobs are under threat from automation and digitisation in the coming one to two decades.[3] When taking into account the challenge of automating non-routine tasks, others arrive at much lower estimates.[4] McKinsey, for example, has adopted a granular, ground-up approach that focuses on work activities (or tasks), rather than jobs. They find that around 45 per cent of work activities could potentially be automated by 2030 and that around 60 per cent of jobs involve a set of tasks of which more than 30 per cent are automatable – although less than 5 per cent of current jobs could be fully automated.[5] Of course the potential for automation is different to what will occur in practice once real-world challenges are confronted and companies take into account the risks associated with the up-front investment required. McKinsey estimated that 25 per cent of the total time spent in the Australian workplace will be automated by 2030, but importantly the level of uncertainty around that central forecast was considerable.

- While the threat to white-collar jobs over coming decades suggests that more people are now under threat than in earlier waves of technological innovation, we shouldn't forget the death of the typing pool in the 1980s and 1990s and the countless back-office jobs already replaced by the seemingly innocuous Excel spreadsheet. This trend may accelerate and broaden, but white-collar job redundancy has been with us for quite a while already.

Australian treasurer Jim Chalmers and Mike Quigley (formerly CEO of Australia's National Broadband Network) identify five skill groupings that will be difficult to replace:

- Non-routine manual skills applied in diverse environments;
- Non-routine interpersonal skills applied in diverse environments;
- Non-routine cognitive skills requiring creativity;
- Non-routine cognitive skills involving critical thinking and problem solving where there is no predefined rules-based procedure;
- Non-routine cognitive skills requiring the acquisition and analysis of new information.[6]

Importantly, these skill groupings cover a range of sectors (agriculture, manufacturing and services), skill levels and occupation types. A wide range of occupations will be difficult to automate, including personal care and personal services, the creative arts, sports, garden maintenance, furniture removal, car repair and some aspects of food preparation. Of course, skill groupings that are difficult to automate could support new occupations which we can't yet even conceive of. Frank Levy and Richard Murnane argue that 'the challenge of "cybernation" is not mass unemployment but the need to educate many more young people for the jobs computers cannot do'.[7]

Second, much analysis examining the potential for job losses sidesteps the fact that technological change can be a complement to labour, a substitute for labour or a combination of both. A robot arm that can weld rivets is clearly a substitute for (and a threat to the livelihood of) a production line worker. Similarly, a high-speed AI algorithm assessing vast amounts of digitised information could make many legal research jobs or routine conveyancing tasks redundant.

But many technological advances may complement jobs involving human interaction. For example, it may be necessary for a GP to interact with a patient for a minimum amount of time to establish a personal connection and build trust, no matter what technology they have at their disposal. In this situation, tools that can aid diagnostic accuracy during that interaction may not require fewer doctors, but rather may improve the productivity of GPs.

The uneven impact of technological change across occupations and sectors raises questions as to whether current risk-management practices in the labour market are sufficient. In the first decades of social insurance, income support for those experiencing unemployment constituted the bulk of government intervention in labour markets. Those programs should continue but the scope of government intervention should be extended given the heterogenous nature of people's exposure to risk and level of vulnerability.

It is likely that more people will need to engage in mid-career training in the future. AlphaBeta, an economic consulting firm, found that workers will need to increase their investment in education and training by a third by 2040, and that this additional investment will be most effective if it is focused on skills that *complement* rather than compete with AI and automation.[8] In Singapore, Denmark and France, governments have embraced lifelong learning accounts to support workers needing to access mid-career retraining. Australia should consider this approach.

Living longer

The fact that life expectancy has been rising consistently across most OECD economies over the past century and a half, and elsewhere since the end of World War II, is clearly one of the long-term social trends worth celebrating.

Typically, life expectancy at birth is reported when quantifying average length of life. While this is an important measure, it can be skewed by changes in infant mortality. Life expectancy at birth doesn't necessarily reflect, for example, how many years a sixty-five-year-old person will spend in retirement. Life expectancy at birth has increased sharply across most advanced economies since the Industrial Revolution and the Enlightenment. In 1800, life expectancy in Europe was thirty-four years, thirty-five years in the Americas and twenty-eight years in Asia. By 1950, that had almost doubled to sixty-nine years in the UK and Australia, sixty-eight in the US and to the mid to high sixties in Western Europe. Life expectancy had also increased in Asia, but not by as much. In China, average life expectancy was forty-three years old; in India, it was thirty-five.

Between 1950 and 2015, there was a further increase across the advanced economies, with most of Western Europe, Australia, Canada and Japan enjoying life expectancies in the low eighties. The US was just behind at seventy-nine. During this period, it was the developing world that enjoyed the greatest absolute and proportional increase. China jumped to seventy-six years and India to sixty-eight. In addition, most of South America, North Africa and the Middle East saw life expectancy raised to the mid-seventies, and most of sub-Saharan Africa had seen life expectancy increase by over twenty years in absolute terms.

Another important dimension of longevity is the life expectancy of people at the age of retirement. When Bismarck introduced the age pension in Germany in the 1880s, the retirement age was seventy, yet average life expectancy was just forty-five.[9] Even among those who outlived the official retirement age, many didn't retire. People who worked the land (a much larger share of the population in 1880) typically worked until they died or were no longer able to labour.[10]

Similarly, when the *Social Security Act* was passed in 1935 the official retirement age in the US was sixty-five, and life expectancy was seven years lower at fifty-eight. While such a low life expectancy is not something to be embraced, it certainly made the newly introduced age pension more affordable.

Today, most retirees across the OECD can expect to live decades in retirement. These extended 'golden years' are the gift of longer, healthier lives, and a result of better healthcare and lower accident rates. This positive development is clearly life-transforming, but it makes planning for retirement more challenging for individuals and the funding of pensions and healthcare for elderly people more costly for the state.

In 1950 in the UK, a sixty-year-old person would have been expected to live, on average, to seventy-five years old. Today, the equivalent sixty-year-old person would be expected to live to the age of eighty-four – which means almost an extra decade of retirement. Similarly, a seventy-year-old person in 1950 would have been expected to live, on average, to the age of eighty. Today, by contrast, the average seventy-year-old is expected to live to eighty-six – which is an increase of 60 per cent, or six more years of life.

A consistent underlying trend over the past century has been the steadily increasing proportion of life expectancy gains that accrue beyond the age of retirement. Across a selection of sixteen high-income countries, including the US, the share of life-expectancy gains that are realised after the age of sixty-five has increased from around 20 per cent during the period 1907–1927, compared to around 75 per cent during the period 1987–2007.[11]

For individuals, one of the key challenges of increased longevity is how to use accumulated savings, whether they be voluntary savings or mandatory. A person retiring at the age of sixty-five could live a further five or thirty years. Moreover, health complications could arise immediately or far into the future. This uncertainty means that a retiree faces difficult choices in terms of how much to consume out of savings each year and how much to leave aside for one-off expenses, such as medical expenses in the event of poor health.

For the state, the rising life expectancy of people at the age of retirement has driven many countries to limit the indexation of pensions and to map out a trajectory of a gradually increasing retirement age. The other principal complication for forecasting the state's fiscal obligations is estimating the average proportion of retirement that is spent in good health as opposed to requiring supported living, long-term care in the community or intensive healthcare.

One of the most effective ways that individuals can manage the uncertainty associated with ageing is to purchase annuities with at least part of their accumulated savings. In practice, there has been a low take-up of annuities across the OECD. This could be attributable to a range of factors including incomplete markets, the awareness of an entitlement to taxpayer-funded pensions and, for some, a bequest motive. But as many behavioural studies have shown, there also seems to be a strong aversion to the use of annuities or annuity-type products in large parts of the community.[12] While taxpayer-funded pensions achieve a degree of longevity insurance in the absence of the widespread adoption of annuities, the over-reliance on lump-sum payments remains an opportunity for policy reform.

To help individuals and households better manage life expectancy and health uncertainty, governments could make annuities more attractive by offering a basic annuity product to provide a benchmark in the market. A government-provided product would provide some consumers with greater confidence than the raft of private-sector annuities currently on offer. Offering such a product would not prevent private-sector innovation and competition – but could provide a benchmark to underpin a market that is not functioning well in most countries.[13] Taxpayer-funded pensions, which form the basis of retirement income for many people, are similar to annuities in many ways in that they provide protection against longevity risk. By offering a financial annuity, governments could provide people with the added option of transferring some of their accumulated savings directly into an additional lifetime-hedged income.

Governments could also provide social insurance for long-term care. This would allow for higher-quality and more integrated care, particularly for elderly people. Many elderly people requiring long-term care are currently provided accommodation in institutional settings that allow insufficient scope for autonomous living. Moreover, too many people with chronic, complex conditions interact with multiple government agencies and other service-delivery providers, which often generates inefficiency and poor outcomes. Social insurance schemes for long-term care in Germany and Japan point to a better way forward than current arrangements in Australia, the US and the UK. These are explored in Chapter 14.

RISKS AND UNCERTAINTY FOR WHICH INNOVATION ALLOWS GREATER COVERAGE

Recent innovations in finance markets and public-sector balance-sheet management offer opportunities for governments to manage risks that have existed for a long period of time but that were difficult to pool, share or mitigate. Income-contingent loans (ICLs) are an example of a public-policy tool that has been in use for some decades but that could be used more widely.

Income-contingent loans

The box on pp. 214–15 sets out the increasingly widespread use of ICLs in relation to providing assistance to students in funding their higher education. One of the policy rationales for ICLs in this context is the difficulty of establishing private credit markets in the face of uncertainty and a lack of collateral. Risk management lies at the heart of ICLs.

Recent research suggests that there are potential applications of ICLs beyond education worth exploring. Some examples that are relevant to the scope of social insurance coverage include:

- **Healthcare out-of-pocket expenses:** Rhema Vaithianathan argues that ICLs 'offer an opportunity for those who face potentially high returns to investing in health but are cash constrained from doing so, and where health insurance systems cannot fully overcome adverse selection and moral-hazard problems'.[14] Areas of healthcare that are characterised by high out-of-pocket costs might be suitable for ICLs.

- **Public housing:** Gans and King see ICLs as a way of overcoming short-term affordability and income variability challenges for low-income households in relation to public housing.[15] The proposed scheme would not be targeted at households with more persistent income challenges. Joshua Gans and Stephen King describe how information asymmetry can lead to market imperfections in the financing of housing. A 'housing lifeline' (or ICL) could offer assistance to those households facing short-term affordability challenges by overcoming liquidity constraints.

- **Residential solar panels:** ICLs could be used to help low-income households overcome liquidity constraints preventing them from investing in solar rooftops.[16]

- **Paid parental leave:** Most OECD countries mandate access to paid parental leave for short periods of time. Tim Higgins and Bruce Chapman[17] explore the difficulty of creating a private market for loans to support leave periods of longer duration. They argue that a government-sponsored ICL scheme could supplement the standard grants scheme and provide additional options for some families.

- **Co-investment in innovation**: Many of the innovations that are held up as examples of private-sector creativity and vigour have relied heavily on public-sector early-stage investment and government procurement programs; examples are the mobile phone, the internet and nuclear energy. Government's investment in such ventures may, in large part, be due to the private sector's lack of appetite for investing in the face of uncertainty. While the extent to which the private sector has relied upon government investment can be debated, it is clear that uncertainty is a strong disincentive for private-sector investment. In some contexts, perhaps only governments, with their massive balance sheets and their focus on the public good, will ever be able to invest in truly uncertain ventures.

Dedicated funds that co-invest in innovation and, where appropriate, take profits from the sale of any capital gains could be a low-cost way to invest in innovation. These proceeds could then be reinvested. Andrew Leigh and Joshua Gans explore barriers for investors facing Knightian uncertainty in early-stage innovation. They argue that the most productive approach is to reduce initial barriers to investment rather than making the ex-post taxation treatment of (highly unlikely) profits more favourable.[18]

Israel is one of the best examples of government co-investment. The Israel Innovation Authority (IIA) has an annual budget of around US$400 million. It is responsible for R&D grants of up to 40 per cent of R&D costs. This has been extended to joint R&D programs with foreign counterparts (including the US and China), which can apply for a grant of 50 per cent of the Israeli firm's R&D costs.[19] The Technology Incubator program was founded in the early 1990s. Since that time, more than twenty-five incubators have been founded, all of which have been privatised. Today, these incubators offer government funding of up to 85 per cent of early-stage project costs for two years. The Israeli government's participation in these reflects the role that uncertainty plays. Avi Hasson, former chief scientist at the IIA, stated: 'It's key that the government takes on the riskiest investments, paving the way for private capital to follow.'[20] Australia should adopt a similar model, including collaboration with superannuation funds seeking to make long-term investments in diversified, early-stage projects.

Income contingent loans

- Income-contigent loans (ICLs) are loans where the timing and quantum of repayments are contingent on the borrower's capacity to repay the loan and, specifically, the borrower's future income. ICLs can be an effective risk-sharing mechanism in that the borrower's obligations can be reduced if their future capacity to pay is low and the lender's receipts can be increased if the borrower enjoys a positive outcome. ICL schemes have two key advantages over typical 'mortgage-type' loan arrangements: consumption smoothing and insurance against borrower default.
- In many advanced economies, the cost of higher education is shared between the state and individuals. The state makes a contribution since education generates positive externalities. Individual students are also typically required to contribute, to reflect the considerable direct benefits they receive from their degree, both through higher lifetime income and often greater job security. Where student contributions are levied via up-front fees, this can create a significant barrier to low-income students or students facing liquidity constraints.
- The first example of a government-administered ICL scheme was the Higher Education Contribution Scheme (HECS), introduced in Australia in 1989. This scheme helped university students finance their tuition costs with the option of avoiding significant up-front fees. Under the HECS scheme, students incur debts to the government which reflect a portion of the cost of their higher education. A zero real interest rate is charged on these loans and the student is only obliged to make repayments on the principal of the loan after their income exceeds a specified threshold that reflects a reasonable capacity to repay. Since the introduction of HECS, ICL schemes have been adopted in a number of other countries, including New Zealand (1992), South Africa (1994), Hungary (2003), Thailand (2006), South Korea (2012) and the Netherlands (2012).[21]
- To the extent that ICL schemes make repayments contingent on future income, the government will typically need to play a role in managing

repayments since it will have the best access to accurate information in relation to people's income and will be in the best position to efficiently enforce agreements.[22] In the Australian context, Bruce Chapman estimates that HECS is administered and enforced with total administrative costs of less than 5 per cent.

- Students face several difficult-to-quantify types of risk (and uncertainty) when deciding whether to undertake higher education: their capacity in the field, their likelihood of success in the course of study, employment and income prospects in their field in the short, medium and long term, and job security in the field in the short, medium and long term. This uncertainty also makes it difficult for lenders to assess the likelihood of repayment. In the case of loans for study, there is no collateral, of course. Without government intervention, there would be severe limitations (arguably market failure) in the market for student loans. Milton Friedman recognised this challenge in 1955, proposing government involvement to support students through either taxes or income-contingent repayments.[23] Chapman contrasts the performance of government-backed bank loans (used in the US, Canada, the Philippines and Thailand) with ICL arrangements. He finds that the repayment burdens associated with mortgage-type loans can be very high, potentially impacting materially on consumption for low income earners with student debt.[24]

Social impact bonds

Social impact bonds (SIBs)[25] are an approach to dealing with complex social issues that, in part, aims to improve the balance between investing for short- and long-term outcomes. SIBs fall within the broader category of outcomes-based contracting (ICLs are another example). While there is no universally agreed definition, SIBs typically involve the following elements:

- **A partnership:** An SIB is a partnership between government, a service provider (sometimes a non-profit organisation) and a group of people in need (the beneficiaries). Other parties that might be involved are impact investors (who might provide the capital to the service providers) and expert program evaluators.

- **The agreement:** The service provider will generally agree to provide a service, which might involve up-front capital investment, so as to achieve a clearly specified outcome. It is called a 'bond' since the service provider (sometimes in conjunction with an impact investor) will provide an up-front investment and ongoing services on the basis of a promise that repayments will be made by government that are contingent on the achievement of certain outcomes.
- **The payment:** An SIB is structured so that repayments are contingent on the achievement of certain precisely defined outcomes. This will often involve a sliding scale of repayments. Repayments to the service provider will be higher where the demonstrated net improvement in outcomes is greater.
- **The evaluation:** In order to determine the level of repayments, it will be necessary to rigorously evaluate the *net* impact of the program funded by the SIB on the specified outcomes. This will require an evaluation that clearly identifies the counter-factual of what would most likely have occurred without the treatment.

The key benefits of SIBs are threefold. First, they enable a better balancing between up-front expenditure and long-run gains than is sometimes possible when a program relies exclusively upon funds from the government's budget. Where budgets are under pressure, it can result in expenditure being skewed towards ongoing operational expenditure that is smoothed over time as opposed to more lumpy investments, even if the latter is optimal. Second, SIBs promote the more widespread use of rigorous evaluations, such as randomised control trials (RCTs). Third, SIBs encourage the trialling of innovative techniques, particularly through partnerships between governments, expert service providers and impact investors.

The first SIB was implemented in Peterborough in the UK in 2010. In May 2011, the UK government launched a £30 million Innovation Fund which funded ten SIBs for youth unemployment and education. In 2012, the first impact bond was issued in the US, in New York City, which aimed to reduce recidivism.

Several jurisdictions in Australia have trialled impact bonds. In 2013, the NSW government launched two social benefit bonds in relation to improving service delivery for children in care. Victoria's first social impact bond was issued in 2018 and aimed to address issues relating to homelessness.

As of July 2020, 138 SIBs had been implemented in twenty-five countries across a wide range of policy areas. This had resulted in more than US$440 million in expenditure. A major Brookings study of impact bonds in 2015 found that implementation had generally been in areas where government was already outsourcing or contracting out service delivery (that is, where the impact bond model would be less of a shift in the existing delivery model) and where there were complex social problems but relatively easy-to-measure outcomes.[26]

Given that so many SIBs have only recently been implemented, it shouldn't be surprising that there is not yet much quantifiable evidence of SIB performance. Almost all evaluations of SIBs in the UK to date have been qualitative.[27] When evaluating the Innovation Fund, which saw £30 million spent on ten education and youth-unemployment SIBs, Ryan Bain found that the narrow specification of outcomes was problematic:

> the funding model was the driver of behaviour and how services evolved. In the case of the Innovation Fund pilot, this ultimately reduced the overall educational attainment of participants and made no strides in preventing them from being NEET [Not in Employment, Education or Training] once they had left school never mind preventing them from being long-term unemployed.[28]

Part of the challenge in evaluating SIBs in a consistent fashion is the wide range of mechanisms linking outcomes to payments. In its study of thirty-eight impact bond projects, the Brookings Institution found many different linkages between evaluation methodologies and payment mechanisms:

> In our examination of the 38 deals, 28 of the deals use validated administrative data, six use historical comparison data, and eight use quasi-experimental and experimental methodologies (four each).

> Many of the deals (primarily the impact bond funds in the U.K.) have outputs rather than outcomes as their payment triggers. The choice of evaluation type was dictated in part by the intervention itself and in part by the desire of the investors and outcome funders to have evidence as to the causality of the outcomes.[29]

An important qualitative conclusion that Brookings drew from its study is that they did shift the focus of governments towards outcomes: 'We find that the existing SIBs have truly transformed the conversation among participating government stakeholders about procurement of social services and the transparency and accountability that go along with that. In essence, instead of paying for services, government pays for outcomes.'[30]

Despite some early successes, SIBs (and related programs) have also encountered a number of challenges, including high transaction costs, evaluation difficulties and scalability challenges.

The challenge of scalability may be the most profound. While on some occasions this may be due to limitations in access to capital, this is probably not the key structural limitation as SIBs in aggregate are still far smaller than the broader impact-investing market.

A greater challenge to rolling out SIBs probably arises from stakeholder concerns in relation to the potential for SIBs to act as a form of quasi-privatisation and a broader undermining of the public provision of social insurance programs. This could generate concerns from a number of sources including stakeholders concerned with protecting the public character of service delivery and concerns from public-sector unions on behalf of members.

Governments could explore extending the use of outcomes-based contracting, including ICLs and SIBs. The emphasis should be on areas where it is possible to clearly define and assess the achievement of long-term outcomes. Governments should fund rigorous testing of the extent to which different incentive structures impact on performance.

The gig economy

Robert Reich has described the gig economy as 'the biggest change in the American workforce in over a century'.[31] Estimating the size of the gig economy is extremely difficult due to the lack of an agreed definition.

In 2016, Katz and Krueger estimated that around 0.5 per cent of work occurred in the gig economy.[32] While significant, this is at the low end of current estimates. Mastercard estimated that the global gig economy generated approximately US$204 billion in gross volume from customers in 2018 and that this would grow to US$455 billion by 2023.[33] Some have estimated much larger proportions of insecure work when 'precarious', casual and freelance employment are included.

Regardless as to the terminology used and where the precise line is drawn between gig work and other precarious employment without benefits, it is clear that the proportion of employees who are exposed to additional risks at work is increasing. As already noted, this can take the form of employees assuming demand-side risk without additional remuneration (such as the drivers on online platforms). Often gig workers lack sick leave entitlements or automatic payments into pension schemes. And in some contexts, workers are exposed to greater occupational health and safety risks – not just in the form of a higher rate of accidents but also in so far as they tend to have far less insurance coverage when an accident occurs. A good example is the rising number of serious accidents and even fatalities experienced by food-delivery riders.[34]

Extending social insurance measures to people in precarious work – who currently miss out – makes sense. Obvious examples include strengthening of arrangements to increase coverage for pension scheme contributions and extending the coverage of transport and workplace accident insurance to cover gig and other precarious workers in dangerous occupations. Governments should work with unions and industry to develop portable entitlements for annual leave, sick leave and long-service leave. Portable long-service leave already exists in several Australian states in industries with a high turnover of staff such as cleaning, construction and community services. The advantages of risk pooling apply in the gig economy just as in broader society and it will be possible to extend coverage in many instances without hampering the innovative aspects of firms' or platforms' operations or negatively impacting on consumers.

AREAS OF RISK AND UNCERTAINTY FOR WHICH THERE IS CURRENTLY LITTLE OR NO INSURANCE

Several material risks, such as the two discussed below, have not yet been the subject of public-policy intervention. These include:

Career income risk

The risk associated with the movement in the income of one's occupation relative to overall wages is currently difficult to insure yet often has a material impact on long-term individual and household welfare. A person's lifetime income will also be affected by the likelihood of the person experiencing gaps in labour force participation due to economic shocks, family requirements or other factors.[35] Increased funding for mid-career training could offer partial insurance against this risk.

House price risk

For most people, the family home is their largest financial asset. We are familiar with insuring our home from damage, either partial damage from a tree falling on it or the risk of destruction from fire or natural disaster. But there are few opportunities for most households to buy protection for the long-term change in the value of their home relative to either other real estate or other asset classes. Given that real estate is the most valuable asset for most families, this is arguably a large gap in insurance markets. A market of this type may assist in promoting labour mobility. Where a region experiences an economic downturn, for example due to firm closure, real estate values may fall, along with labour market opportunities. This will make it more difficult for people to move to other areas with more job opportunities, should they wish to.[36]

Insurance markets for house price risk may seem unrealistic – most innovation does until it arrives! Yet something akin to this kind of insurance is already emerging. Many elderly people are asset-rich and income-poor. Often, their largest asset is their home. Downsizing for many is not attractive for a range of reasons, including transaction costs and a reluctance to move from an area which is familiar and which may contain many long-term family and social relationships.

Reverse mortgages are one way of providing people with access to equity in their home. But these can prove problematic, particularly during times of high interest rates and for people who expect to need the funds for a long period of time (interest charges accrue exponentially over time). An increasingly popular way of accessing home equity is 'home reversion'. Under a home reversion product, a financial intermediary will purchase a share of a person's home. They provide the homeowner with an up-front payment. The financial intermediary isn't able to access their share of the home equity until the homeowner sells or passes away.

The price that the financial intermediary will be willing to pay for a share of the house will depend on many factors, but three of the principal factors will be: (i) the expected likely future sale date; (ii) the expected house price at that date; and (iii) future interest rates. The first of these will be extremely difficult to estimate for each individual client. Even the second will be volatile, as house price growth tends to vary considerably by area. The only way of effectively managing these risks is to purchase shares in many houses and to estimate the likely timing of house sales and house price growth on average across many clients. This is risk pooling and the law of large numbers in practice – as we see in other areas of risk such as fire and life expectancy. Firms offering house reversion products are, in part, offering clients insurance against expected future movements in the value of their house by compensating for house price movements in a pool.

11. What Mechanism Is Best to Manage Risk?

RISK POOLING

Risk pooling works best where the following specific conditions exist: a large population of individuals, households or firms exposed to potential loss, diversifiable risks and manageable information asymmetry.

A large population is important for pooling so that the law of large numbers can assist in the accurate pricing of risk. The larger the population, the more accurate the estimates of loss will be. Large numbers also make it possible to estimate the marginal impact on the likelihood of loss of specific characteristics. For example, using data from large populations, it is possible to estimate the marginal impact on life expectancy of gender, age and health. In order to minimise cross-subsidies within a pool, it will be necessary to estimate each individual's or household's exposure to loss as accurately as possible based on their individual characteristics.

Diversifiable risks across individuals, households and firms provide the opportunity for pooling. It is critical to note that diversifiable risk doesn't mean that risk is spread homogenously across the pool. Rather, it means that there is less-than-perfect correlation in expected outcomes – some people will be in a relatively good position while others will be in a worse position, with those in relatively bad positions receiving compensation from the pool. This works well in relation to fire risk for residential houses, where some but not all houses will burn down each year and it isn't possible to identify which ones in advance.

At the other extreme, systematic risks are non-diversifiable to the extent that all participants in the pool are simultaneously affected by an adverse event. As will be discussed in the chapters on systematic risk, this requires either the creation of larger, possibly inter-regional or international resource-sharing mechanisms – or intergenerational risk sharing.

The extent to which information asymmetry is manageable will vary considerably across different types of loss. Information asymmetry is relatively manageable in relation to residential property damage but less so in relation to health insurance for illness. The more problematic the information asymmetry, the more likely is it that government will need to be involved to achieve effective risk management either through regulation or directly managing risk pools.

The quantity of insurance purchased in private markets that pool risk can be suboptimal for a number of reasons, including information asymmetry combined with adverse selection, externalities, consumer inertia and affordability issues arising from a lack of resources on the part of some consumers.[1]

The three key public-policy responses that are most commonly used to deal with these challenges are mandating insurance, tax subsidies and restrictions on characteristic-based pricing.[2]

Mandatory insurance

One of the key public-policy rationales for social insurance is the way in which adverse selection can limit the effectiveness of private-insurance markets. One obvious way of overcoming adverse selection is to mandate insurance, a solution posited in George Akerlof's original 'lemons' paper in 1970.[3] Many of the earliest forms of modern social insurance took this form, including Bismarck's workers' compensation scheme of the 1880s and early transport-accident schemes at the state level in the US and Australia during the early decades of the twentieth century. National health schemes also involve mandatory participation, although they are funded through general taxation rather than risk-rated premiums. Mandatory insurance schemes proliferated throughout the twentieth century and remain common to this day. They have proved to be an effective means of overcoming adverse selection in many contexts.

Tax subsidies

Taxpayer funded subsidies are another possible public-policy response to the under-provision of insurance in private markets. Subsidies can increase the level of insurance purchased by reducing its price. Taxpayer-funded subsidies are used to encourage private health insurance in many countries, including the US and Australia. This can be costly and result in distortionary taxes since it is typically necessary to subsidise not just the insurance purchases of the people who don't have insurance but would buy it at a slightly lower price, but also all people who have already purchased insurance.

Restrictions on characteristic-based pricing

Restrictions on the characteristics of individual consumers that can be used to price premiums (or 'community rating') is another commonly used public-policy intervention, particularly in relation to health insurance. The impact of community rating will depend upon the extent to which individuals are aware of their idiosyncratic risk profile and, therefore, the degree to which standardised premiums represent good or bad value for money, given their circumstances.

RISK TRANSFER

The most direct way in which governments can reallocate risk is to assume the risk on its own balance sheet. As set out above, ICLs are a good example insofar as the government loans money to an individual or a firm and the repayments are contingent on clearly defined outcomes. Another approach would be for a government to prescribe the allocation of risk between parties. A good example is limited liability, which is a government-constructed regulatory arrangement clearly defining the relationship between investors and a firm's creditors. By limiting liability for investors, this arrangement shifts some risk to creditors. Bankruptcy laws are another example of government regulation allocating risk between parties.

Risk transfer can be a highly impactful and cost-effective way for governments to provide support to communities. It can complement more traditional grants programs, which are typically constrained in the level of support that they can provide. A project that I was involved in as Parliamentary Secretary to the Treasurer in the Victorian government involved the transfer of risk from community sports clubs to the state government. This enabled clubs to build new changing rooms and training facilities to support new teams for young women. This project is set out in the box below. The community bonds described in this box could be made contingent on achieving certain outcomes, be they direct (for example, women's participation in sports) or indirect (such as broader community benefit).

Risk transfer – innovative financial bonds to build female change rooms

- Local sport is the lifeblood of many communities in Australia, especially in outer-suburban and regional areas. Community sports act as a focal point of social activity: not just for those participating, but for the families of team members and many others who spend a lifetime supporting a club as a volunteer or administrator. As important as they are to many communities, so many of these clubs operate on a shoestring. With the help of countless volunteers, they manage to get teams onto the field, organise social events, raise money for charity and so much more. One of the great opportunities – and challenges – for community sporting clubs is the exponential growth in interest from young women to participate. This is being driven by several factors, not least of which is the rise of televised women's sport and the way in which these amazing athletes have become role models. Unfortunately, with a scarcity of playing fields and equipment, clubs often struggle to create space for new teams to meet this growing demand. Even when clubs manage to establish new female teams, all too often the club can't afford to build women's change rooms (female teams often end up changing into their uniforms in their cars in the carparks of playing fields). Or women's teams end up having fewer training opportunities than male teams. Female teams persist despite difficulties, but this leaves many clubs wondering: how many more female teams could we support with better facilities?

- Governments provide grants, but these programs usually fall far short of demand. The Victorian government supported a A$14 million program for female change rooms. While substantial, in practice, this supported only a fraction of clubs applying. Some lucky clubs hit the jackpot, but hundreds wait in long queues. Some clubs have the resources to borrow money to upgrade their clubhouses, build additional changing rooms and toilets, or add lights (allowing more teams to practise). But most clubs aren't a good enough risk for banks to lend substantial sums to. And even if clubs can borrow, the interest rates are usually a significant burden.

- The Victorian government tried a new concept: community bonds. I led much of the negotiations for the development of these new financial instruments – and the treasurer, the Hon. Tim Pallas (to whom I was parliamentary secretary), steered the policy through Cabinet and the budget process. The new bonds involved three parties: community clubs; local government (who typically owned the sports grounds); and the state government (who provided the funding and balance sheet guarantee). The bond was in effect a loan to the community organisation. But with the state government standing behind it, these bonds avoided bank rates (5–7 per cent), for much lower AAA rates of 1.5 per cent. In fact, in the first two tranches of applications, the State government paid half of the interest, so clubs were paying less than 1 per cent interest. Clubs could afford that. Local government was involved as the owner of the land and partner with the community club. Their involvement supported high-quality project design.

- The club submitted a business case that demonstrated both community benefit (female participation) and an income stream (e.g. from function facilities or a cafe, even if modest). The business case was jointly evaluated by the Treasury and the state Department of Health (which had responsibility for sport). Clubs gained in that they paid low interest rates – and just as importantly gained an additional avenue for funding (grants or bank loans were realistic options for a small minority of clubs). Government gained in that subsiding interest payments was a fraction of the cost of granting the full amount. For an outlay of A$7.5 million, it was possible to support $100 million in bonds (which was the cost of half of the interest payments for a decade). Just as importantly, the whole process created long-term partnerships between community organisations, local government and the state government.

- One of the most amazing aspects of the policy design process was seeing the usually staid officials responsible for arranging the state government's borrowing getting excited to see a novel financial instrument helping young women's sports teams: many of them had daughters. These were experts in the minutiae of corporate and government bonds. Every day, they dealt in issuing or rolling over billions of dollars of debt, with maturities ranging from the short term to decades. Yet here we were, with world's best practice expertise in creating and trading bonds, helping to reallocate risk between local sports clubs and government for projects involving tens of thousands of dollars to build lights or toilets to give girls' sports teams a chance to participate. Since it started, this program has supported over A$400 million in projects for a government outlay of less than $30 million. For many projects, merely shifting some of the risk onto the government's balance sheet was a game changer. This model could be extended to many other areas of activity that generate even modest income streams – including environmental projects or social enterprises.

RISK MITIGATION

Government regulation aimed at reducing risk is ubiquitous: workplace occupational health and safety regulation; road safety laws, including licensing arrangements, speed limits, and alcohol and drug restrictions; food content regulation; drug approval processes; product safety regulation; limits on the use of dangerous products such as carcinogens and dangerous industrial products like asbestos); and the list goes on.[4]

There are various rationales for safety regulation, including externalities and consumer protection. The extent of regulation has generated considerable debate in many countries as to whether there is too much red tape and green tape. Many governments now require that any additional regulation be subject to benefit-cost analysis (or regulatory impact statements). While the onus should be on those proposing new regulation to show that the costs outweigh the benefits, there are many examples of risk mitigation (e.g. natural disasters) where increased investment clearly provides value for money.

12.
Who Should Pay?

There are two key questions when it comes to funding social insurance programs. First, should the pool be funded from general taxation or risk-rated contributions? Second, should schemes be fully funded or pay-as-you-go?

WHO SHOULD BEAR THE BURDEN OF LOSS?

The two mechanisms for funding pools from which losses can be compensated are risk-rated contributory schemes and taxpayer-funded programs. There are pros and cons to each.

Contributory schemes

The first modern social insurance schemes were typically contributory: Bismarck's reforms of the 1880s were good examples. Most of the New Deal welfare reforms of the 1930s were also contributory, as was the national insurance scheme proposed by Beveridge in 1942.

One of the key advantages of this approach is that it is less of a drain on taxpayer funds and therefore requires less distortionary taxes. There's no free lunch, of course: someone has to pay. In a risk-rated scheme, contributions are made in direct proportion to each pool member's exposure to possible future loss.

In some instances, third parties with a stake in the loss pay some or all of the contributions on behalf of beneficiaries. A good example is workers' compensation. Workers' compensation contributions are sometimes payable by employers – but the actual incidence of the contributions fall on both employers and employees, with the allocation of the burden depending on the relative bargaining power of the two parties.

The degree to which contributions reflect the underlying likelihood of loss varies. In some instances, social insurance contributions are fully risk-rated, with workers' compensation and compulsory motor vehicle insurance being funded on such a basis in most jurisdictions. In other cases, there is partial risk-rating. For example, the capping of old-age benefits in the US in the Old-Age, Survivors and Disability Insurance (OASDI) scheme means that some high income earners pay more into the scheme than would occur if their contributions were directly actuarially determined by life expectancy and income.

Similarly, in most US jurisdictions, unemployment insurance is not fully risk-rated. First, contributions do not reflect the likelihood of job separation. The payroll taxes for a person with complete job security (e.g. a fully tenured professor) are the same as those for a person on the same income but with highly insecure work (e.g. a person with the same income working for a start-up). Second, the relationship between contributions and benefits is non-linear and capped, skewing the ratio of benefits to contributions differently across jurisdictions.

A second advantage of risk-rated schemes is that they send price signals to those contributing to the pool. These price signals provide an incentive to more effectively manage the likelihood of loss in order to reduce future premiums. Of course, this only works if it is possible to clearly identify the link between risk mitigating actions by participants in the pool and the likelihood of future loss. Moreover, for price signals to be effective, there will need to be sufficient competitive tension in markets for premiums to adjust.

Progressive taxes

As an alternative, non-contributory schemes – which contribute indirectly through the tax system – generally rely upon progressive taxes. The principal rationale behind progressive taxation is redistributive: for the funding to be borne by those best placed to bear that burden. Progressive taxation is a key underpinning of the modern welfare state and it is difficult to imagine how the historically broad scope of social insurance that we enjoy today in most OECD countries would have been possible without it.

In the context of social insurance, the use of progressive taxation as the funding mechanism is based on the notion that it is more appropriate that those with an ability to fund the social good arising from the program rather than those with the highest statistical likelihood of benefiting from the program. This takes us back to the redistributive notions discussed earlier in Chapter 2.

The grey area

The debate between contributory and non-contributory national social insurance in Australia in the 1930s and 1940s illustrates the complexity of funding mechanisms. In the 1930s, the conservative parties favoured the introduction of a contributory national insurance scheme. Such a scheme would have been in line with the social insurance arrangements in the US, as well as those that were soon to be recommended by Beveridge Report in the UK less than a decade later.

In contrast, while the ALP supported national social insurance in principle, it strongly opposed a contributory funding mechanism, preferring a scheme funded by progressive taxes instead. A contributory scheme developed by the conservative Lyons government was defeated in 1938 along party lines, largely on the basis of the proposed funding mechanism.

When social insurance programs were later introduced by the Curtin government in the early 1940s, they were funded by increases in company, sales and income taxes. The Joint Parliamentary Committee on Social Security examined many aspects of the social insurance programs introduced in the years following 1942. Its conclusion in relation to unemployment insurance reflects the fine line between contributory and non-contributory schemes, stating that 'it is the obligation of all the potential beneficiaries to contribute to the scheme'.[1]

The committee's observation reflects the fact that, ultimately, every scheme is contributory. The balance between the potential efficiency gains of risk-rated contributions and the redistributive benefits of funding schemes through progressive taxes is, at least to an extent, a question of values.

While the choice of funding mechanism is critically important, the next section will show that even where programs are funded by progressive taxes, the end result may not redistribute resources from rich to poor as clearly as might be imagined.

Redistributive impacts of benefits

The redistributive impacts of the allocation of benefits arising from social welfare programs are often more opaque than the redistribution arising from funding arrangements. Some social welfare schemes involve considerable tax churn, with many middle-income taxpayers contributing much of the funding and also receiving considerable benefits.

There are also instances of universal schemes that, in practice, provide greater benefits to high income earners. For example, a scheme that provides a universal, non-means-tested pension will provide greater benefits, on average, to high income earners since they have higher life expectancy. Feldstein argues that, in the case of the US Social Security program, any redistribution arising from the OASDI's falling relative ratio of benefits to average lifetime income (as income increases) is offset by 'the longer expected life of higher-income individuals, their increased use of spouse benefits, and the later age at which they begin to work and to pay taxes.'[2]

A second example cited by Feldstein is unemployment insurance in Massachusetts, which is funded by payroll tax on the first US$10,800 of earnings yet pays 50 per cent of wages up to $50,000, providing substantially greater benefits for higher income earners who lose their jobs.[3] This is also a feature of unemployment insurance in many other US states.

Finally, the higher life expectancy and greater access to and use of specialist medical services in the US by high income earners led Mark McLennan and Jonathan Skinner to conclude that Medicare produced net transfers from the poor to the wealthy for both of the cohorts born in 1925 and 1945.[4] Jonathan Skinner and Weiping Zhou found that high income earners made greater use of quality-adjusted care measures such as mammography screening, diabetic eye exams and the use of AA blockers and reperfusion following heart attacks. This can arise from a range of factors, including a greater awareness of the full range of medical services on offer and more logistical flexibility to take advantage of those services on the part of medium and high income earners.

Therefore, despite a higher rate of growth in Medicare expenditure on low-income households between 1987 and 2001, this had not translated to a relative improvement in either survival rates or effective care.[5] It would be worthwhile rigorously testing the extent to which similar patterns in accessing specialist services occur in national health systems such as those of Australia and the UK.

It is important to note that even where redistribution is not progressive in practice, schemes can generate other benefits for those on low incomes. For example, while McLennan and Skinner found that, in accounting terms, the intra-generational net benefits of some elements of Medicare tended to flow from the poor to wealthy, they concluded that there were considerable risk-management benefits for those on low incomes. Specifically, they found that the insurance value of Medicare 'may be considerably higher for lower-income beneficiaries', who would probably face greater liquidity constraints and adverse selection problems in private insurance markets.[6]

Contributory schemes are not inherently less progressive than non-contributory schemes. Importantly, when assessing how progressive or regressive any scheme is, whether contributory or non-contributory, it is critical to assess the distributional impact of benefits as well as contributions. One of the challenges of doing so is that the distribution of benefits is often less transparent than funding arrangements.

WHICH GENERATION SHOULD BEAR THE BURDEN?

The second funding challenge is whether risk pools should be pay-as-you-go or fully funded. In a pay-as-you-go scheme, benefits are funded by taxes paid by current workers. In other words, present-day workers fund benefits, including those enjoyed by current dependents, both young and old. Examples of pay-as-you-go schemes include taxpayer-funded age pensions, disability pensions and unemployment insurance funded from consolidated revenue. National public health systems are similar in that they are funded out of current taxation revenue, but they provide benefits to all generations currently alive, including young and old dependents.

In contrast, in a fully funded scheme, accumulated funds are built up from contributions that are determined according to actuarial calculations as to how much will be required to cover the expected losses of members of the pool. In the case of private insurance, premiums are determined so as to build up sufficient funds to cover actuarial estimates of losses. Fully funded social insurance programs operate on a similar basis, with contributions set aside in a separate fund and invested. Examples of fully funded schemes include compulsory motor vehicle insurance, compulsory workplace-accident insurance and New Zealand's Accident Compensation Corporation (ACC).

Australia's superannuation system is a fully funded retirement income scheme in that individuals build up reserves during their working lives which they draw upon after retiring. However, since it is a defined-contribution scheme, there is no guarantee as to the amount of income one will earn in retirement.

The key advantages of a fully funded scheme are that beneficiaries are more protected from the vagaries of annual government budgets, and premiums can be set at a level that is actuarially determined. Fully funded schemes are therefore more inherently sustainable than pay-as-you-go schemes, in which the tax base is either volatile (due to business cycles) or systematically declining (due to long-term productivity decline or demographic change).

A weakness of fully funded schemes is that they are often ill-suited to intra-cohort risk management. Retirement income systems based on savings are a good example.

To rely entirely on fully funded accounts would not achieve the substantial intra-generational longevity and inflation risk management that pay-as-you-go systems have effectively provided successive generations for almost a century. As noted above, that is why most retirement income-policy frameworks are built around a multi-pillar approach. Pay-as-you-go taxpayer-funded pensions provide substantial intra-generational risk management, while mandatory and voluntary savings assist with sustainability in the face of an ageing society.

13.
How Should Loss Be Compensated?

CASH PAYMENTS AND IN-KIND GOODS AND SERVICES

There is a wide array of mechanisms by which those who have suffered loss can be compensated, ranging from cash payments to in-kind goods and services.

For simple products (such as food and clothing), it makes sense to distribute benefits in cash. Nicholas Barr argues that there is a relationship between the types of market failures that can justify social insurance and how resources should be redistributed. Markets are generally more efficient, he argues, when: (i) the better is the consumer information; (ii) the more cheaply and effectively consumers can improve their knowledge; (iii) the easier it is for consumers to understand the available information; (iv) the lower the consequences for poor choices; and (v) the more diverse are consumer tastes.[1]

The markets for food, clothes and cars are all examples of markets that largely tick all five of those criteria and that are, mostly, quite efficient for consumers. Healthcare is not, for reasons including the complexity of the choices and the significant negative consequences of making poor choices.

Barr argues that where a benefit is provided to support expenditure on goods and services in well-functioning markets (such as food and clothing), it makes sense to distribute benefits in cash. This is typically what happens for social insurance programs such as unemployment insurance and the age pension. In contrast, where funding is for services where markets don't function as well, such as healthcare, it generally makes sense to distribute benefits in-kind.

> Thus the answer to the efficiency question also offers important guidance about how best to pursue equity objectives. It is no accident that almost all countries have some sort of national health service, but none a national food service.[2]

Of course, that observation should be tempered by the presence of cash payments with strings attached even in markets that generally function well, such as food stamps and vouchers.

UNIVERSAL VERSUS TARGETED BENEFITS

Most benefits arising from social insurance programs are contingent upon loss. That is, after all, the nature of insurance. Some programs, such as the age pension and some benefits programs for children, use means-testing, which is, in a sense, a way of not providing benefits to those who can easily bear the loss. A means-tested age pension limits tax expenditure by not providing the pension to retirees who, while they have experienced the loss of income associated with retirement, have sufficient assets to not need government support. This enables finite government resources to stretch further.

There is growing debate as to whether some benefits should be universal and provided to all citizens or residents regardless of whether they have experienced loss and regardless as to their means. The universal basic income (UBI) is probably the highest-profile such proposal, but not the only example.

There are three key arguments in favour of making at least some benefits universal. First, any constraints on benefits, whether they be means-tested or contingent on having experienced some type of adverse consequences, can create stigma. Milton Friedman supported a UBI as it would end the inefficiency and indignity of mutual obligation or other limitations on entitlement.

> The proposal for a negative income tax is a proposal to help poor people by giving them money, which is what they need, rather than as now, by requiring them to come before a government official to tally all their

> assets and liabilities and be told that you may spend X dollars on rent, Y dollars on food, etc.[3]

The UBI was also supported at the time by Nobel laureate in economics James Tobin, who sat at the other end of the political spectrum from fellow laureate Friedman.

A second argument in favour of universal benefits is that many individuals or households don't take advantage of benefits that they are entitled to, due to a range of factors, including a lack of awareness, the difficulty of navigating government bureaucracy or due to a sense of stigma. Dean Plueger estimates that only 75 per cent of eligible individuals or households claimed the earned income tax credit (EITC) in the US during tax year 2005.[4] That means around 25 per cent of eligible recipients of the EITC left a considerable amount of money sitting on the table. The situation is similar in the EU, with the European Commission examining evidence from France, Poland, Portugal, Sweden and the UK to conclude that:

> The effectiveness of benefit systems in tackling poverty also depends on whether eligible people actually claim benefits. Non-take-up of benefits appears to be widespread and microsimulation results suggest that full take up of benefits could slightly reduce the proportion of people below the at-risk-of-poverty threshold.[5]

These findings were confirmed in a study of sixteen EU countries, in which non-take-up rates of up to 80 per cent were estimated. The study found that non-take-up rates were highly heterogenous, ranging across countries and types of program.[6] In the US, millions of children received free lunches at school after eligibility to the program was made automatic for families covered by other anti-poverty programs. Before this, millions of eligible families had not claimed the benefit.[7] In the US, an experiment was undertaken to improve take-up rates for the Supplemental Nutritional Assistance Program (SNAP). A group of 30,000 people who appeared as though they might be eligible were placed into several groups: a control group, a group who received information about their possible eligibility, and a group who received assistance to enrol. After nine months, 6 per cent of the control group had signed up for SNAP, compared to 11 per cent who had received additional information and 18 per cent of those who received assistance – triple the control group rate.[8]

The third challenge that can arise from means-tested benefits is the high effective marginal tax rates (EMTRs) as benefits are withdrawn. Partly in response to the disincentive associated with high EMTRs, in 1943, Juliet Rhys-Williams proposed a universal social security transfer that would provide a subsistence income.[9] In 1962, Milton Friedman posed a universal income in the form of a negative income tax:

> We should replace the ragbag of specific welfare programs with a single comprehensive program of income supplements in cash – a negative income tax. It would provide an assured minimum to all persons in need, regardless of the reasons for their need ... A negative income tax provides comprehensive reform which would do more efficiently and humanely what our present welfare system does so inefficiently and inhumanely.[10]

Friedman's proposal, supported by James Tobin, was for the universal benefit to be included in taxable income. A tax-free threshold benefits low income earners, but only to the extent that they earn income up to the threshold. So, for example, a person earning an income of half the threshold would receive only half of the potential benefit of tax-free status. In contrast, under Friedman and Tobin's proposal, all people, regardless of income, would receive the basic benefit. Moreover, since the benefit would be taxable, higher income earners would benefit less from the universal income.

A UBI (or its equivalent) has been examined on a number of occasions over the past half-century in Australia. In 1975 the Commission of Inquiry into Poverty favoured a UBI.[11] In the same year, it was also supported by the Priorities Review. Since then, the idea has been promoted by numerous prominent economists, including 'the five economists'[12] and Ross Garnaut.[13]

High EMTRs are a problem in every economy with means-tested benefits. The Tax and Transfer Policy Institute at the Australian National University examined EMTRs in Australia in a number of scenarios, including parents with dependent children and households relying on unemployment benefits. They found a number of situations in which low- to middle-income households faced EMTRs in excess of 100 per cent.[14]

Reducing participation tax rates (PTRs – or the disincentive to enter the labour market) and EMTRs (the disincentive to earn more) arising from the complexity of the UK welfare system was a key rationale behind the Universal Credit reform. Under this scheme, a range of benefits would be bundled together for ease of access. The results of the initial scheme were mixed. A recent study found that the impact on PTRs for people out of the labour market varied and that, for workers receiving means-tested benefits, around one-half would see a reduction in their EMTR, while one-third would see an increase.[15]

The principal argument against a UBI is the cost. A UBI would represent a substantial increase in the scope of the welfare state. Clearly the precise cost of a UBI would depend on the details: (i) the level of payments; (ii) eligibility (would it include all residents, or just citizens, or just adults?); and (iii) how much of current social insurance arrangements would the UBI replace?

The scope of the challenge facing a UBI is highlighted by the proportion of people who would receive government assistance who currently don't. Figure 13.1 shows the proportion of the adult population (aged fifteen and over) receiving some kind of income support in Australia between 1901 and 2008. This proportion has increased from under 5 per cent until the 1920s to over a quarter of the population since 1990. While a significant proportion of the Australian population now receives some kind of taxpayer-financed income support, somewhere between two-thirds and three-quarters of the population do not receive income support (depending in part on the stage of the business cycle). A UBI would involve payments being made to all of the people in this cohort, many of whom are well off, either because they are a high income earner or because they live in a high-income household.

Figure 13.1: Proportion of the Australian adult population receiving income support, 1901–2008

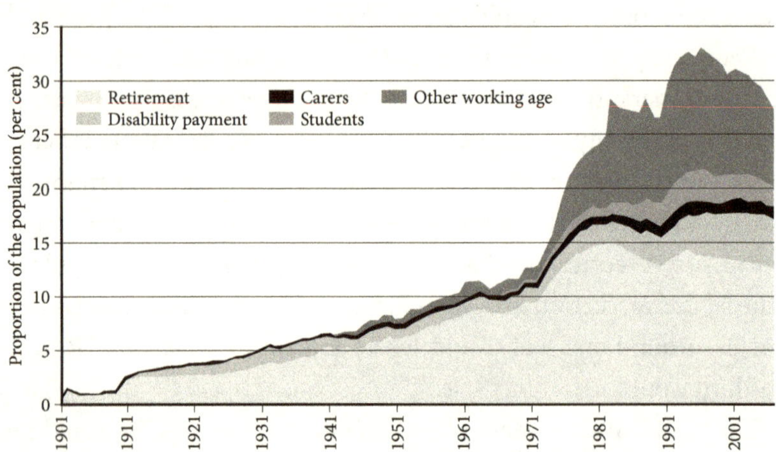

In arguing for a UBI to be implemented in Germany, Thomas Straubhaar estimates the cost of a UBI set at €1000 a month. He concludes that such a UBI is 'feasible' and could be funded by a tax on all German 'value added' (i.e. a VAT or value add tax) of around 50 per cent: a not insignificant tax impost! Similarly, a back-of-the-envelope estimate of the cost of a UBI in the US demonstrates the magnitude of the funding task. In the US, there are 265 million over the age of fifteen; 222 million people are over the age of twenty-four. A UBI for all citizens over the age of fifteen, set at US$15,000 per annum would cost $4 trillion per year; it would cost $3.3 trillion for all residents over the age of twenty-four.[16] To put this in perspective, total US federal government revenue in 2019 was $3.5 trillion. This had to cover not just welfare spending, but defence ($676 billion), net-interest payments ($375 billion) and discretionary spending on transport and other infrastructure.

These back-of-the-envelope calculations beg a further question: would it be realistic to pay a UBI at these levels and do away with all social insurance? Would people on €12,000 or US$15,000 per annum be able to pay for their own healthcare costs on a fee-for-service basis or afford private health insurance? Would vulnerable people on €12,000 or US$15,000 be able to provide for their own housing? Would people on these incomes need additional support if they experienced severe injuries or acquired a disability that imposed considerable cost?

A fundamental phallenge of a non-targeted, universal payments system is that a high proportion of the outgoings will be directed to those who don't need it, which will result in an inevitable squeeze on the resources going to those most vulnerable.

In Australia, Ross Garnaut has modelled a UBI of A$15,000 per annum indexed to CPI. Premiums would be paid to those above a certain age, for people with dependents and for the unemployed. There could be a degree of means-testing based on income and/or wealth. Garnaut argues that such a reform would involve fiscal costs but that it would increase labour force participation by 2 per cent and labour supply by 3 per cent.[17] It could also reduce administrative costs. It is worth exploring this model, or a variant of it with more detailed modelling.

A second potential issue is that it could create a disincentive to work, for some. Esther Duflo and Abhijit Banerjee review the literature in both advanced and developing economies and conclude that there is no evidence that cash transfers make people work less.[18] While some people may work less at the margin if welfare payments increase, empirical studies suggest that the overarching impact on labour supply is minimal given that most people find purpose, social connectivity and dignity in work. Importantly, in the Australian context, with its highly targeted welfare system, the reduction of effective EMTRs is likely to increase the incentive to work and more than offset any disincentives.

Some have argued that a key focus should be on dependent children.[19] Better-funded benefits for dependent children with universal or near universal eligibility, a negative income tax and slower tapering of benefits may make more sense than a UBI for all adults. Australia already has quite a robust system of benefits for children, but in other advanced economies this is an area with many gaps.

Arguably, countries like Australia already have something approaching a UBI. Payments are made to children, retirees, people who are unemployed, people with a disability, carers and others. Some of these payments are means-tested, but many of the so-called 'UBI' models proposed also involve means-testing. To some degree, the debate can get bogged down in semantics. If the modern welfare state is already close to a UBI, perhaps the issue of greatest substance isn't whether it should become totally 'universal' but rather how to manage high EMTRs and whether benefit levels are sufficient for particular cohorts.

The expense of a UBI, and the economic distortions that its cost to the public purse will create, may be greater than the problem that it is solving. Focusing on removing disincentives for those on low and medium incomes and ensuring that benefit levels are sufficient for particularly vulnerable cohorts probably makes more sense. Ultimately, whatever label we attach to such a suite of reforms is largely beside the point.

PERSONAL ACCOUNTS VERSUS ON-DEMAND SERVICES

Another important governance issue to be considered is how to allocate services and, specifically, whether services should be distributed on-demand or through an overarching entitlement that is calculated on an individualised basis.

In most national healthcare systems, individuals have a right to certain basic services, such as visits to a general practitioner. Access to more specialised (and expensive) services is generally limited by a requirement to obtain a referral. This results in scarce specialised resources being allocated on a needs basis. Typically, once an individual is able to demonstrate that the more specialised service is required, access is given, albeit that they may have to wait extended periods if supply is less than demand.

Another approach is the use of individual accounts and case managers with a funding envelope set for the particular circumstances of each individual. This approach was adopted by the NDIS in Australia. Under the NDIS, an individual receives a funding allocation based upon the severity of their disability and other factors. It is then up to the individual to allocate that funding between various competing priorities: equipment, rehabilitative services, transport and so on. The allocation of funding to different types of services will reflect that person's preferences and circumstances.

This approach can present challenges, particularly where a person has cognitive limitations or there are numerous technicalities in the equipment or services to be procured. The account-based approach can also result in challenges where a person needs to provide for themselves across their lifetime. This will present financial challenges – ensuring that the spending of a large lump sum is appropriately spread out across an uncertain lifetime. It will also present challenges in relation to balancing short- and long-term objectives – for example, the trade-off between increasing (or decreasing) the up-front investment in capital and the impact that might have on reducing ongoing operational expenses. That is why having an expert, dedicated case manager who can establish a long-term relationship will generally be critical to the success of such schemes. The potential for case managers to positively support decision-making was demonstrated by the experiment in relation to SNAP eligibility referenced above.[20]

Another potential avenue for a more individualised approach is to use big data and matching technology to top up people's payments. This would take into account irregular work patterns, hours and wages, helping to make welfare programs more responsive to people's needs and changing conditions.

14.
How Can Outcomes Best Be Achieved?

STEP 1: THE IMPORTANCE OF CLEARLY DEFINING AND FOCUSING ON OUTCOMES

The advantages of defining clear outcomes are significant. First, it provides clear benchmarks against which success can be evaluated. Second, it produces more focus in the provision of benefits since there is a clear goal. Third, clearly defined goals can improve coordination between different layers of government and across silos within a government. Many areas of social insurance are bedevilled by multiple agencies either failing to coordinate optimally or even working at cross-purposes. Finally, having clearly defined outcomes produces more transparency in reporting the effectiveness and sustainability of insurance arrangements. It is only by estimating the cost of achieving a specific outcome that program sustainability can be accurately forecast and issues of emerging cost pressure identified.

It is critical to stress that the many hundreds of thousands of people who work to deliver social-insurance programs understand all too well how important it is to focus on outcomes: the nurses, doctors and allied health professionals who work in the healthcare system; the social workers and case managers who provide assistance to people experiencing long-term unemployment; the many dedicated professionals working in aged care; and the carers and administrators in workers' compensation authorities and motor vehicle accident insurers. They already strive to achieve positive long-term outcomes every day.

The exhortation to focus on outcomes is not aimed at people who do this already with passion, expertise and dedication. Rather, it is to ask the question: are our social insurance systems helping or hindering these individuals to achieve the outcomes that they strive for? Or do systems, as currently designed, constrain what people can achieve through bureaucratic silos or buck-passing between agencies? Do our social insurance systems even measure whether outcomes are being achieved? Sometimes, the answer to these questions is that current systems, while achieving much that is positive, need to be reformed.

The orientation towards outcomes

Private-sector insurance relationships are defined by the insurance contract. The insurance contract sets out which risks are – and are not – covered. Under the terms of a typical insurance contract, the insurer seeks to return the individual or firm who has experienced loss to the situation that they were in before the loss. This might be rebuilding a house, curing an illness, providing long-term care or returning the person to work after an injury. Where full compensation isn't possible, an insurer might provide partial compensation or cash.

In considering how important clearly defined outcomes are, it is worth comparing workers' compensation with general healthcare provision.

Where a person suffers a serious workplace accident, a workers' compensation scheme funded by mandatory contributions kicks into action. The goal is clear. To provide long-term care for the person and, if possible, return the person to work. An individualised plan is developed and the person is case-managed. If greater up-front expenditure on care will reduce long-run overall costs, that is considered. That might involve purchasing equipment or paying for access to specialists. Assistance is provided either until the person returns to work or, sometimes, indefinitely if return to work is not possible. Of course, this doesn't always occur so seamlessly in practice, but individualised, case-managed care is typically a core characteristic of program design.

Contrast this with a person interacting with their health system. In Australia, the federal government funds Medicare, GP visits, subsidised medicines, aged care and a portion of hospital care. State governments largely fund hospitals (including emergency departments) and often deal with people whose healthcare issues have resulted in dire outcomes such as chronic mental-health conditions, substance-abuse issues or homelessness. Even local government authorities provide some services that support people with health or related challenges, including maternity and early childhood support, some aged-care services and community outreach. The complexity of the system makes case management and coordination far more difficult. A person with mental-health or substance-abuse issues may sporadically engage with the health system and receive care through a series of one-off interactions. A person in this situation may repeatedly present to emergency departments, which is often not just costly but also less effective than specialist services designed to address the underlying issues. There are many measures of the degree of effective integration between parts of the health system. One that is instructive – and that points to possible improvements in Australian healthcare – is that less than 20 per cent of Australian GPs were always told when a patient of theirs was seen in an emergency department (compared to 68 per cent in the Netherlands and 49 per cent in the UK).[1] The eighty-nine-year-old man interviewed by Camilla Cavendish who had engaged with over 100 healthcare and social-services workers in the space of a year is a telling example of how complex bureaucracies can be difficult to engage with for people with multiple long-term needs.[2] One difference between narrow schemes such as workers' compensation or transport-accident schemes and the wider healthcare system is that, in the former, it is generally easier for the system itself to be geared towards identifying and then achieving long-term, individualised outcomes.

There are many instances of holistic, ongoing treatment in the broader healthcare system. For example, anyone with an ongoing relationship with their GP will receive holistic care and advice. And hospitals typically do well in coordinating advice across specialisations when providing care. Nonetheless, it is difficult for any individual service provider, even a person's long-time GP, to keep track of a person's every interaction across all healthcare providers, particularly at other levels of government. One of the key opportunities for the health system is to move to more of a case-management, individualised approach, particularly for vulnerable people or for those with complex needs. At the heart of this shift would be the coordination of multiple agencies in achieving agreed, clearly defined outcomes. This won't always be the appropriate approach and it will make sense for much of the system to continue to operate on the basis of demand, as currently occurs.

We don't currently measure outcomes in the non-market economy well

One of the key challenges in moving towards a more outcomes-oriented approach is the inherent complexity of defining outcomes in most of the contexts in which social insurance operates.[3] The challenge of measuring productivity in the non-market component of the economy is rarely discussed in public-policy debates, but it underpins many of the difficulties in driving broader productivity growth.

Hidden behind the innocuous label 'the non-market economy' are some of the largest sectors of our economy with the biggest impact on our day-to-day lives. These include the key government services of health, education and training, aged care, police and emergency services, and national defence. These sectors comprise over 20 per cent of GDP and over 27 per cent of our nation's workforce.[4] Most large social insurance programs fall, at least in part, in the non-market economy.

Despite their significant contribution to most OECD countries' national accounts and GDP figures, these sectors are currently totally excluded from national productivity calculations. The key impediment to developing a more complete picture of national productivity is a lack of prices in the non-market sector.

Calculating productivity in traditional industrial activities such as manufacturing has always been a relatively straightforward task. My own electorate of Fraser was once home to Australia's largest manufacturing plant – the Sunshine Harvester Works. A century ago, if production of the firm's famous stripper-harvester could have been doubled while maintaining the same level of inputs, its productivity would have doubled.

Now consider the situation in which a modern car factory produced the same number of cars for a given set of inputs, but the quality of those cars increased. Productivity would once again have improved. But unlike a simple count of widgets (or harvesters), how are we to measure the change in quality? Measuring changes in quality is often a difficult exercise. What is the increase in a car's overall 'quality' as a result of a 50 per cent increase in its acceleration over the first ten seconds? Or the use of leather rather than vinyl chair coverings? Or the installation of higher-quality airbags?

In a market economy, price is usually a good proxy for how much quality has changed – at least in the eyes of the consumer.[5] Therefore, in a market economy, quality-adjusted output is usually calculated as a combination of price and quantity.

Things are much more difficult in the non-market economy. In the service-oriented non-market economy, we can easily calculate the value of inputs: the wages of the workforce and the cost of the equipment and infrastructure that it takes to run our hospitals, schools, emergency services and defence forces. But those services are often provided free of charge, either on-demand in the case of healthcare or as a universal 'public good' in the case of emergency services, defence and law enforcement. What is the value of the outputs when prices are not paid?

It is easy to think of many outputs produced by this non-market economy: the numbers of surgical operations performed, medicines dispensed, hours taught in the classroom and elderly people housed and cared for. Much more difficult is assessing the quality of these interventions. What is the long-term impact (either beneficial or not) of a medical treatment or an educational course? What is the impact of an investment in either equipment or training on the response times of a fire and rescue service? Moreover, where a social insurance agency simultaneously provides multiple benefits, how do we meaningfully compare and aggregate these many outputs?

The Australian Bureau of Statistics (ABS) has recently been working on this challenge,[6] building on work by the Productivity Commission in Australia, the UN, the World Bank, the OECD and a number of national statistical agencies. The goal is to calculate 'quality-adjusted' aggregate output measures, where the volume of different outputs (goods and services) are counted and aggregated using weights. With productivity at the heart of the national economic debate in most OECD countries, we must acknowledge that the largest areas of government activity and some of the most important determinants of our welfare are currently totally excluded from our productivity calculations. Producing quality-adjusted output measures for health, education, emergency services and defence will force us to be more explicit about exactly what we're trying to achieve with our large investments in these areas.

Measuring *outcomes* should be the ultimate goal. A good example of moving towards a more outcomes-based approach is the evolution from 'activities-provided' measures of healthcare to 'diseases-managed' measures. The former measures the activities provided to a patient. Using the activities-provided approach, the outputs provided by agencies are simply tallied. A high-cost activity (like hospitalisation) would add more to outputs provided than a low-cost one (like a community-based service). Yet if a low-cost activity is just as effective, then clearly any meaningful measure of productivity would reflect that a productivity gain has been achieved by treating a given disease at less cost. The disease-managed approach reflects the cost of treating the disease, as opposed to the cost of providing services.[7] While not a measure of long-term outcomes per se, the disease-managed approach is an important step in that direction.

For the purposes of policymaking and program design, the Productivity Commission argues that a more granular approach is the most useful focus:

> More granular indicators of productivity and other performance metrics (for example, outcome effectiveness, value-for-money, marginal effects of more or fewer resources) are much better suited to identify specific areas that need to be improved in the non-market sector.[8]

The difficulty of defining and measuring outcomes in the non-market economy is the elephant in the room that constrains how meaningful and complete our discussion of productivity across the economy can be. It also, in the case of social insurance programs, limits our capacity to assess how well our programs are performing and to link outcomes and premiums, a determination that lies at the heart of the effectiveness and sustainability of insurance schemes.

There is often no link between outcomes and premiums

When we think of private insurance markets, we are accustomed to thinking about the link between the insurance contract and premiums. If an insurance company promises to rebuild your house and that rebuild will cost $100,000 and the loss has a 1 per cent chance of occurring each year – it seems obvious that a fair premium is $1000 per year (with a small extra amount for the insurance company's administrative costs).

This is why the precise wording of the promise to reimburse the policyholder is so critical. The scope of the promise will directly link to the actuarially fair premium.

In the case of major social insurance programs, the desired outcome is often left unstated or is stated in very high-level, broad terms. Indeed, there are often multiple desired outcomes, which can make it difficult to set an explicit (or even an implicit) price. But this problem can't simply be avoided. We have to set a price whether we like it or not. Either we set an explicit price through a premium, or we set an implicit price through taxation rates and the overall amount that is spent. Either way, the social insurance scheme has to be funded. With or without premiums, the healthcare system will deliver complex, multi-outcome services. But those programs that are funded through premiums are forced to be more explicit about what their primary objectives are. In addition, they are forced to be more explicit in quantifying whether premiums are sufficient to achieve those outcomes. If the premiums are insufficient, but it is not possible to raise them, the outcome will need to be altered. A more explicit definition of outcomes and 'premiums' could help to achieve greater co-ordination of service provision, better outcomes for our most vulnerable and more sustainable funding streams.

Unintended consequences of narrowly specified outcomes

It will generally be easier to define outcomes the narrower they are. However, there is a risk of unintended consequences when developing overly simple KPIs for schemes dealing with complex social problems. Jerry Muller cautions against replacing 'judgment, acquired by personal experience and talent, with numerical indicators of comparative performance based upon standardized data (metrics)'.[9] Focusing on simplistic metrics and then holding service-delivery organisations to account publicly for their performance against such metrics can result in worse overall outcomes. Prominent examples include:

- Cherry picking, giving insufficient attention to those most in need, where metrics are based on average performance (for example avoiding the long-term unemployed in labour-market programs, or those with complex, chronic conditions in healthcare);

- Teaching to the test (for example, where school funding is linked to improvement in scores);
- Achieving only the outcome that is measured, when a situation involves many simultaneous problems (for example, securing a short-term job placement for a vulnerable person and ignoring their long-term health and drug issues);
- Improving reported success rates through lowering real standards (for example, suppressing wait times at hospitals by leaving injured people sitting in ambulances); and
- Fraud and misreporting, when incentive structures are poorly designed.[10]

While the problems associated with the use of overly narrow metrics and KPIs are real, the solution isn't to give up on clearly defining our objectives or seeking to achieve long-term outcomes. Rather, it is to ensure that good judgement is used. Moreover, the use of publicly reported outcomes should be informed by experts in relevant fields of practice and these measures should be constantly evaluated, updated and adjusted where appropriate.

STEP 2: PRACTICAL STRATEGIES FOR MORE OUTCOMES-FOCUSED SOCIAL INSURANCE

Reform stream 1: Individualised service and recipient choice

Providing the recipients of benefits with greater choice can produce a number of benefits. Greater choice will increase the likelihood that benefits will be better matched with each individual's preferences. Many programs achieve this by providing benefits as cash with little or no constraints on how it is spent. Where programs provide in-kind benefits, standardisation can be problematic. In the words of economists, when someone makes a choice, they 'reveal' their preferences in a way that is almost impossible to achieve when choices are being made by others. Client choice also improves engagement, which can improve the effectiveness of long-term processes like rehabilitation or training.

The Australian NDIS is an example of a scheme that is centred on the agency of the benefit recipient. One of the core principles underpinning the NDIS is that 'people with disability should be involved in decision-making processes that affect them, and where possible make decisions for themselves.'[11] It is too early to tell how effective the scheme has been at giving effect to this goal. To give effect to recipients' choices requires giving them access to detailed, accurate information in a timely way, improved literacy in relation to the meaning of that information and the range of choices; and systems that allow for active engagement with supportive and empowering professionals. The NHS Choices website is a good example of steps taken in this direction. Increased client choice has been successfully deployed in a number of health systems, including in the UK, Germany and parts of the US. In the UK's NHS, patients have been given greater choice over where they are treated, by whom and in what location. In the words of the then Secretary of State for Health and Social Care, Alan Milburn: 'This is the most fundamental change the NHS will have ever faced. It will mark an irreversible shift from the 1940s take it or leave it, top down service. Patients will be in the driving seat – and not before time.'[12]

The OECD found that: 'A deeper understanding of quality of care requires measuring what matters to people. Yet few health systems routinely ask patients about the outcomes and experiences of their care.'[13] A US physician echoed this finding:

> The larger question is: is health care a service industry? Many physicians do not believe that patient satisfaction is a legitimate pursuit. In this viewpoint, enhancing patient experience offers no value to medical care … [Yet] The ideal patient experience merges excellent medical care, high-quality outcomes, compassion, and empathy that address the emotional needs of patients.[14]

In order to deal with this deficiency, the OECD advises that patients' experience should be recorded and, in aggregate form, published through patient reported experience measures (PREMs) and patient reported outcome measures (PROMs) to assist in making the healthcare system more patient-centred.[15] PREMs and PROMs are now widely used in the US, the UK, Sweden and the Netherlands.[16] There is considerable evidence supporting the use of these measures[17] and existing pilots for PREMs and PROMs in Australia should be extended nationally once fully evaluated.

'Concurrent care' is one model that allows for increased choice among patients. In the US, a number of insurers had started to err on the side of invasive treatments after litigation which had exposed insurers to the risk of damages if they were perceived to have unduly pressured clients to avoid costly procedures.[18] The litigation itself was a reaction to the 'rationing' of expensive treatments. In the wake of this litigation, Aetna introduced 'concurrent care'. Under this approach, patients with less than one year of life expectancy could access hospice care options while not foregoing any of their rights to curative treatment options. An evaluation of this program found that the proportion of patients with less than one year of life expectancy enrolled in hospice care jumped from 26 per cent to 70 per cent. Given that patients in concurrent care had the right to both hospice and curative options, what was surprising was not the increased take-up of hospice care – but the dramatic drop-off in curative options: emergency room visits dropped by 50 per cent and the use of hospitals and ICUs dropped by two-thirds.[19]

A second study by Aetna involved patients needing to choose between hospice and curative options but the addition of phone calls from palliative nurses for all patients. That change alone resulted in increased hospice take-up, reduced ICU use and increased satisfaction.[20]

A similar study was undertaken by the Massachusetts General Hospital in 2010. One hundred and fifty-one patients with Stage IV lung cancer were allocated randomly to two groups: half received oncological care, while the other half received oncological care plus parallel visits from palliative-care specialists. These specialists would explicitly discuss with patients their goals and priorities and work with them to develop strategies aimed at maximising their quality of life based on these personalised goals. The results of the study were striking. Those who received palliative care advice in addition to oncological treatment stopped chemotherapy sooner, entered hospice considerably earlier, experienced less suffering and lived 25 per cent longer than their counterparts.[21]

Aged care is a good example of where small tweaks to reduce the institutionalisation of service delivery have delivered substantial improvements in outcomes. 'Assisted living' was designed to be an intermediate form of accommodation, between total independence and institutionalisation. It was first implemented in Oregon in the 1980s. Early evaluations showed an improvement in satisfaction, improvements in cognitive and physical functioning and a 20 per cent reduction in costs.[22] Long-term care, particularly for elderly people, is an area where many service providers are actively exploring ways to better reflect the preferences of people receiving care. This is discussed in more detail below.

Government creating a bus route auction to help students with autism

- Designing an optimal bus route seems simple, but it is in fact one of the most complex challenges in transport. The difficulty arises, in part, from the fact that each change to a route benefits some people and makes others worse off. Bus-route design is a challenge for many schools. For schools educating children with a disability, travel times can be particularly problematic, since many children with a disability find long travel times highly disruptive. In 2018, in conjunction with some of the world's top economists at Caltech and Melbourne University, the Victorian state government created a market for bus routes for a school for students with autism. Prior to the pilot, students were travelling for up to four hours every day and some students had to change buses, which many found very stressful. For some students, travel times also often interrupted learning time, with some missing their first class.
- The pilot involved designing and creating a market for bus routes. This involved separate, purpose-designed auctions for seven optimised bus routes. The results of these auctions were that travel times were reduced by over 50 per cent, with no students required to change buses. Before the pilot, more than half of the students spent longer than an hour travelling to school, with a quarter of students spending an hour and a half in transit each morning. Now, all students spend less than an hour travelling to school. And the cost to government fell![23]

- One mother said that she was a 'big fan', and stated that her son's travel times have been cut from 90 to 30 minutes each way. She reported that he is 'much, much happier and his behaviours are much more manageable both at school and at home'.

- Markets like this could be extended to include parental choice in relation to after-school care (like additional bus routes). Such markets could also give some parents the choice of alternative modes of transport (like taxis), which might allow for route optimisations that benefit all students remaining on the bus. Incorporating alternative modes of transport may create win-win situations. A parent opting for a taxi may be willing to spend a little extra for a shorter trip for their child. In turn, if that family lived a long way from other parents, their opting for a taxi (or even a subsidised family-provided car trip) may allow the bus route for others to become far more efficient. Markets like this could dovetail very effectively with the NDIS, which allows for parents to choose what proportion of a child's funding to allocate to transport.

- This is an example of using modern technology not for profit but for the public good. Markets like this should be used to benefit the students attending regional and rural schools where bus routes are extremely difficult to optimise without computers and markets. Markets like this could also improve access to train stations, shopping centres and healthcare providers for commuters in the outer suburbs of capital cities and regional centres. Government-created markets which harness the confluence of emerging technology and regulation could drive positive change that reaches every part of society. Even now, governments in Australia and overseas are developing modern markets that are dramatically improving outcomes in relation to biosecurity, environmental regeneration, educational placements and matching organ transplants and donors.

Reform stream 2: Better coordination across government silos

Integrated care is not a precisely defined term. It typically refers to the delivery of different aspects of medical care (community primary, secondary and tertiary) in a coordinated manner and in a way that is centred on each patient's whole-of-life needs. It is motivated by the potential to achieve both higher service standards and cost savings through greater coordination. Hugh Alderwick et al. examine successful integrated care approaches in the US, Germany, New Zealand and Sweden.[24] The box on the following pages offers some examples of successful implementation of this approach.

In many situations, it will make sense for agencies providing benefits to provide case management. This includes where (i) there is likely to be a long-term relationship between the agency and the recipient of benefits; (ii) there is considerable complexity in the provision of services; and (iii) the recipient faces considerable disadvantage, possibly arising from multiple, long-term and possibly intergenerational sources. Case management can be part of a more integrated approach to service delivery.

The Investment Approach was adopted in New Zealand in 2012. It is designed to identify those recipients of government assistance with the greatest lifetime needs and to provide those people with targeted, individualised and appropriately resourced services. Given that many of the most disadvantaged people access support from multiple arms of government, improving coordination across different providers of assistance is critically important to improving outcomes. Bill English, who was the Minister for Finance when the Investment Approach was introduced (and later became prime minister), stated:

> With that group of teen sole parents, for example, we no longer just give them a fortnightly benefit and wish them luck. They are now enrolled in a scheme that, among other things, ensures they are in school or training, gives them each a supervising adult, and manages their money for them. That programme is showing promising results.[25]

(See the box on the following page for a discussion of the potential for service navigation to assist with more complex needs.)

Service navigation

- Service navigation (another term for, or a similar concept to, case management) offers an opportunity for empowerment for people with complex and chronic needs, who often deal with dozens of different agencies and experts. The concept of service navigation emerged across a range of areas of human service delivery. Service navigation was seen as a way of overcoming barriers to accessing services for people who were socioeconomically disadvantaged and/or culturally and linguistically diverse. More recently, service navigation has expanded into areas such as primary healthcare, geriatric chronic illness, family decision-making in ICU care and family violence interventions.[26]
- The Service Navigation Relational Autonomy Framework (SNAF), developed in Australia, is an example of a framework for how service navigators can build relationships with and provide assistance to individuals with long-term or lifetime needs within the person's relational and social context. This can be particularly important for people who rely on others, such as people with a disability that impacts decision-making or young people. The advantages of this frame reflect a number of rationales: (i) the inherent value of individuals being able to make choices in relation to their care; (ii) the benefits of individualising service delivery; (iii) the complexity of current service delivery arrangements; (iv) the risk of manipulation or poorly directed service delivery where choice is embedded in schemes.
- The four key domains of the SNAF are for the service navigator to: (i) reinforce ethical practices; (ii) foster self-determination in the client (or capacity building); (iii) understand each person's life trajectory and support transitions across the client's life cycle; and (iv) mobilise service systems in response to each user's needs. Importantly, the SNAF is based on the notion that autonomy is not synonymous with individualism. 'People are rarely totally independent; rather, we are relational beings whose identities and interests are shaped by our connections to others.' This is particularly relevant to areas of service delivery such as aged care, disability support and the provision of services to young people.

Successful examples of integrated healthcare

- **Intermountain Healthcare** is a not-for-profit vertically integrated healthcare provider for primary, secondary and tertiary healthcare services to around 2 million people in Utah, Idaho and bordering states. Intermountain has operated fifteen hospitals since 1975, provided primary care delivery since 1982 (it now employs 1350 physicians) and, since 1983, has operated a health insurance arm. Part of the rationale for branching into insurance was to be able to capture some of the benefits arising from its integrated care model (which were previously captured by insurers cutting payments based on fee-for-service). Intermountain has been consistently ranked as the leading integrated health system in a survey of regional non-speciality healthcare systems in the US.[27] Its procedures for the prescription of medicines for cardiac patients at discharge saw the proportion of accurately treated patients rise from 57 per cent to 98 per cent.[28] Intermountain also lowered the rates of unplanned Caesarean sections (from 29 per cent to 5 per cent) and reduced costs by US$400 per birth or $10 million overall.[29]

- **Kaiser Permanente** is widely regarded as one of best providers of integrated care in the US. It is a vertically integrated not-for-profit provider that services over 9.5 million people.[30] Specialists and GPs work together in multi-speciality clinics.[31] Medical groups receive capitation payments rather than fee-for-service. The strategies adopted by Kaiser Permanente include: population risk stratification; prevention; the encouragement of self-management; care pathways; improved data management; case management; and the adoption of a target of zero unplanned hospital admissions. Kaiser Permanente's use of preventative strategies lowered the prevalence of smoking by 25 per cent.[32] Surveys support the contention that Kaiser Permanente has used case management and prevention strategies more successfully than other providers in California.[33] An example of the positive outcomes arising from this is the 89 per cent reduction in the risk of death within ninety days of a cardiac event for those enrolled in the cardiac rehabilitation program. Kaiser Permanente also performs well in international comparisons. For example, its clients over sixty-five years of age spend less than a third as many days in hospital compared to the UK's NHS.

- **Greater Autonomy in Aged-care** programs in a number of countries have tried to improve outcomes for residents adopting strategies that treat residents in a more individualised and holistic manner. Something as simple as 'having the conversation' with elderly people to understand their personal preferences is straightforward to aspire to but requires great sensitivity and experience in practice. But the payoffs are huge. In addition, many low-cost programs that reduce passivity and the feeling of being institutionalised have generated significant health and quality-of-life improvements while at the same time reducing acute health problems, interactions with hospitals and reliance on pharmaceuticals. At the heart of many of these programs is the principle of giving each individual as much autonomy as possible.

Reform stream 3: Long-term investments

Many social insurance programs devote a considerable proportion of resources to managing long-term, chronic problems. In the late 1990s, the Roberts Enterprise Development Fund (REDF) and Harvard Business School developed a methodology for evaluating the long-term social return on investment (SROI) of non-profit organisations and social-policy interventions. The fundamental premise of their project was that 'to date, the [non-profit] sector has been unable to present a cogent, well-structured framework for *ongoing* measurement of the value created by the non-profit sector ... This inability to define and understand social and economic value has made for a serious information gap and a lack of objective-performance assessments.'[34] In addition to helping the non-profit sector more clearly evaluate its performance, the REDF's work laid the groundwork for a framework to improve government's delivery of social services. In the intervening two decades, the SROI methodology first elucidated by REDF has been refined and applied in many contexts.[35]

The New Zealand Investment Approach to welfare contained a range of elements reflective of a more long-term approach, including: (i) the identification of people most likely to incur the most socially costly long-term problems; (ii) increased spending on case management, particularly for the most vulnerable, at-risk young people; (iii) the simplification of a number of benefits; and (iv) the introduction of a new actuarial model of the welfare system that would report annually and provide estimates of overall long-term welfare costs.[36] The scheme aimed to be preventative in approach and cross-disciplinary in execution. The Investment Approach satisfies a number of the scheme characteristics outlined in this chapter. This set of reforms was motivated, in part by the long-term, intergenerational aspects of welfare. It aimed to shift the delivery of services to an evidence-based, outcomes-oriented approach by using 'integrated data, information sharing, risk profiling, actuarial analyses, outcomes-based contracting and joined-up services', a willingness to work with non-government providers and a stronger emphasis on prevention and accountability.[37]

In 2017, Taylor Fry estimated the long-term welfare costs of different cohorts, particularly those that had entered the welfare system early in life. The total estimate of future payments for the 540,000 people receiving benefits in 2016/17 was NZ$72.2 billion.[38] In a 2018 submission to an Australian parliamentary inquiry, Taylor Fry referred to 'long-term benefit receipt among people entering the benefit system at an early age.' They estimated that around 75 per cent of future welfare spending for current clients was expected to relate to clients who first received benefits under the age of twenty.[39] For example, sole parents who entered the welfare system before they were twenty years old were estimated to stay on a benefit for around seventeen and a half years. This is not to suggest fault on the part of sole parents, who are juggling childcare and often highly challenging life circumstances. Rather, it is a reflection of a system that isn't doing enough to give sole parents high-quality, individualised, effective assistance. This analysis underscores that risk factors arise for many very early in their lives (for example, interaction with the child welfare system and, in particular, out-of-home care).

The long-term costs of different cohorts are often opaque under current arrangements. According to Bill English, 'That information is nearly invisible in a point-in-time view.'[40] When aggregated, these long-term costs were staggering. In 2018, Taylor Fry contended that these reforms had been successful in reducing aggregate long-term welfare costs. 'Overall, New Zealand has seen a significant reduction in future working-age welfare costs, with most of this attributable to government reform.'[41] The Investment Approach is one example of a long-run approach to investing in people to help achieve outcomes rather than providing them with services, which are considered as costs.

There is still considerable debate as to whether the Investment Approach is a big idea, a little idea 'masquerading as a big one', or an approach that isn't wholly new but that incorporates some usefully innovative elements – 'new wine in old bottles'.[42] Michael Cullen points to the need to be cautious when assessing outcomes and the costing impacts of new policies. A number of commentators who have cautiously embraced aspects of the Investment Approach have expressed concerns that focusing exclusively on actuarial models in measuring the impact of interventions on the long-run fiscal bottom line of governments might miss important social benefits that are captured by more traditional benefit-cost evaluations.[43] The patchy quality of data and the degree to which the results of the actuarial model changed based on small tweaks of the model's assumptions (e.g. long-term interest rates) should temper any conclusions as to the overall impact of the Investment Approach.

The need to embrace a longer-term perspective on the lifetime wellbeing of veterans was central to the recommendations of the Australian Productivity Commission's review into the performance of Australia's veterans' support programs. The Productivity Commission concluded: 'Well-designed workers' compensation schemes safeguard both the short- and long-term wellbeing of employees.'[44]

Reform stream 4: Early Intervention and prevention

The notion of prevention being more effective than cure is not new. The phrase *venienti occurrite morbo* – 'confront disease at onset' – was penned by the Roman poet Persius (34–64 CE) and demonstrates that the wisdom of prevention has ancient roots. It is the motto of the Royal Veterinary College, founded in 1791 and appears in the seal of the London Epidemiological Society.

Prevention occurs in many social insurance programs: vaccination programs, universal or targeted screening for cancer and diabetes, early-learning programs, and workplace safety programs funded by some workplace-accident schemes. Numerous studies have demonstrated the long-term benefits of early intervention. This includes actuarial assessments of workplace accident and transport accident programs and evaluations of early childhood programs, diversion programs for young offenders and healthcare prevention programs.

Social investment could be thought of as a form of prevention (or early intervention). My parliamentary colleagues Clare O'Neil and Tim Watts explore in detail the economic and social benefits generated by early learning.[45] Greater access to early learning (through publicly funded, universal programs) promotes greater opportunity for children from disadvantaged backgrounds, reduces intergenerational inequality, provides women with more opportunity to participate in the workforce and contributes to long-run economic growth. It also stands out as one of the best examples of the long-term, society-wide benefits of early intervention.

To what extent is early intervention an opportunity to both improve long-term outcomes and reduce fiscal pressures? Healthcare is an obvious candidate. Across the OECD, healthcare is the largest single social insurance program, averaging 8.8 per cent of GDP. Moreover, healthcare expenditure is forecast to grow faster than inflation over coming decades.

Currently, less than 3 per cent of health budgets are devoted to prevention across the OECD, with medical check-ups and dental examinations accounting for almost half of all spending on preventative care. Increased funding for preventative programs has been a focus of recent policy deliberation in many OECD countries. For example, Australia's Productivity Commission recommends the creation of funding pools for Local Hospital Networks and Primary Health Networks, equivalent to around 2–3 per cent of total funding, to be devoted to preventative care and the management of chronic conditions. These networks would be given autonomy in how these funds are expended – and the long-term impacts on patient outcomes and productivity would be evaluated.

While worthy of greater attention, the longer-term impacts of programs designed around prevention can be complicated, particularly in healthcare. First, there is the fact that many preventative measures involve considerable cost. Even though preventative measures are usually low-cost per person, large aggregate costs can accumulate when measures are applied to very large populations. Second, *some* preventative measures produce little or no benefit for the vast majority of recipients. For example, a 2012 meta-study (of fourteen studies) found that annual medical check-ups produced little or no benefit for healthy adults.[46] The combination of these characteristics means that it is important that business cases be applied to preventative measures, as with anything else.

There is no doubt that in some cases, preventative measures can achieve savings – but whether such programs can result in a material reduction in healthcare spending remains questionable. A recent US study of twenty preventative services found that total savings of US$3.7 billion could be achieved if take-up rates were increased to 90 per cent across all of the services. What is telling is that this figure (based on very high take-up rates) represents a mere 0.2 per cent of the US health budget.[47]

Perhaps even more important is the inherent relationship between prevention and key healthcare cost drivers. Clearly, to vaccinate a child against measles is orders of magnitude less expensive than curing measles after it has been contracted. Moreover, the cost of vaccinating an entire population will generally be less than curing the minority who would have been infected if no one had been vaccinated. Of course, even more important than the cost reduction is the fact that vaccination programs reduce suffering. But the potential for prevention to materially reduce costs is more ambiguous when viewed from a broader perspective. This needs to be taken into account when considering the potential for an increased emphasis on prevention to put downward pressure on overall healthcare budgets.

To reduce a person's risk of a particular malady by 50 per cent – or even 100 per cent – will likely mean a longer life, lived at a higher quality. But that extension of life will expose the person to other health risks. Each cure of a particular disease or condition leaves us exposed to other conditions.

It is well known that healthcare spending is heavily concentrated among those with particularly debilitating conditions. Some have estimated that 25 per cent of the health budget is spent on those in the last year of their life.[48] Elsewhere, it was found that in the US, 22 per cent of health expenditure was spent on the 1 per cent of the population requiring the most care (many of whom would be in the last year of life) and that 50 per cent of health expenditure was spent on just 5 per cent of the population. In that year, the half of the population requiring the least care received just 3 per cent of health expenditure.[49]

It is likely that prevention measures won't change this fundamental pattern of healthcare expenditure but, rather, for individuals benefiting from specific treatments, will delay their need for intensive care at some point. This is worthwhile of course; increased life expectancy is a core goal of the healthcare system. But to help a person avoid a particular disease or condition through early intervention probably won't mean that they won't require considerable healthcare later on.

The Congressional Budget Office studied the long-term impacts of hundreds of preventative measures and found that 'approximately 20 per cent of those services reduced health care costs while also improving health; the remaining 80 per cent increased costs and had mixed effects on health'.[50]

Some prevention will improve life expectancy and quality of life and also reduce healthcare costs. Consider many of the low-cost interventions in aged care that can improve morale, provide people with a purpose and engage with people's individual preferences. Rigorous evaluations have found that many interventions of this type improve happiness and quality of life while also materially reducing the risk of serious health complications, hospital visits and reliance on prescription drugs. Sometimes, reducing the degree of institutionalisation of a person's final years can improve quality of life and reduce cost.

In contrast, some other preventative programs will not reduce overall healthcare costs if the cost of administering the program is high relative to its benefits. Moreover, some preventative programs, such as the early diagnosis of disease among people with multiple comorbidities, may delay rather than reduce overall medical costs. These preventative programs will often be highly worthwhile but should be undertaken with a clear view as to the benefits, which may be life extension and the improvement of the quality of remaining life rather than long-term cost reduction.

Overarching summary

Rigorous evaluation is a precondition for determining whether or not outcomes are being achieved. The ideal model would involve rigorous, periodic reviews, followed by mechanisms to update program design. When outlining the rationale for the Investment Approach, Bill English noted that 'the traditional public finance structure is designed to track where every dollar goes, but was never designed to find out whether it made any difference'.[51] More rigorous program evaluation will benefit from a range of approaches, including randomised control trials and the use of statistical and actuarial analysis to quantify system-wide impacts of different approaches over the long term. Table 14.1 summarises a range of social insurance programs in relation to some of the key design features explored in this section.

Table 14.1: Programs that have already become more outcomes-focused

Program	Explicit definition	Early intervention	Long-term perspective	Client choice	Contribution risk rating	Benefit risk rating	Case management	Evidence-based evaluation
Investment Approach (NZ)		×	×			×	×	×
NDIS (Aust.)		×	×	×		×	×	
Job Network (Aust.)						×	×	×
Workers' comp. (all)	×	Some	×		×	×	×	
CTP (all)	×	Some	×		×	×	×	
LTC (NSW)	×		×	×	×	×	×	×
LTCI (Germany)			×	×	×	×	×	
LTCI (Japan)			×	×	×	×	×	
Aged care (all)	×	×	×	×			×	×

STEP 3: LONG-TERM SUSTAINABILITY

The sustainability of major social insurance schemes is one of the great challenges facing the modern welfare state. As outlined in Tables 3.4 and 3.5 in Chapter 3, healthcare and the age pension dominate social insurance payments in Australia and the US. This is the case across the OECD.

Not only are these two programs very large – they both also face the prospect of growing pressures as our population continues to age and due to cost pressures in relation to particular products and services like pharmaceuticals.

The first step in dealing with sustainability is to be aware of the size of the threat. While we are all aware that society is ageing and that this will place pressure on our healthcare, aged-care and age-pension systems, it is another matter to quantify that threat. The NZ Investment Approach is built around a rigorous actuarial measurement of the long-term cost of the promises made by the welfare system across the lives of current recipients (and of future generations). Changes in this total cost over time are an important barometer of whether the sustainability of the system is under threat or not.

The first overarching response to sustainability issues should be to attempt to improve the long-term cost effectiveness of specific government-funded interventions. While it may be necessary to increase the overall cost of social insurance as a share of GDP over time, the first step should be to get more value for money from existing (substantial) investments.

A second approach is intergenerational risk sharing. This will be discussed in detail below.

Possible policy responses

Step 1: Clearly define outcomes

- Clearly define measurable outcomes. Where possible, rigorously evaluate programs against those outcomes.

Step 2: Achieve better long-term outcomes

- Explore opportunities to give individuals more agency over the resources that suit their particular needs and preferences. Support individuals with service navigators and other expert advice where appropriate.

- Where suitable, calibrate benefits to each individual's needs – both in terms of the level of benefits provided and in the form of benefits.
- Improve links between related programs so as to achieve more holistic approaches. One model is the 'multi-pillar' approach in retirement income schemes. Explore whether similar approaches are worthwhile in areas such as healthcare and labour-market interventions.
- Adopt a long-term perspective, particularly for complex, chronic cases. Where a long-term approach is adopted, assess both the investments made and benefits using actuarial approaches that inform both sustainability and effectiveness.
- Explore opportunities for early intervention, particularly for issues that pose a risk of long-term impacts and escalating negative outcomes (and cost).
- Allow care providers the flexibility to experiment with more individualised and less 'institutional' arrangements. There are many examples of this producing significant improvements in outcomes, particularly in long-term care for elderly people.

Step 3: Long-term sustainability

- Rigorously measure the long-term liabilities of the social-welfare system based on current service levels and commitments.
- Where suitable, incorporate mechanisms that share the burden of risk management across generations.

PART IV

BETTER MANAGING SYSTEMATIC RISKS

15. Systematic Risks

Systematic risks require solutions that are suitable for managing highly correlated individual risks. Where an entire community is affected by a loss, there are generally three options:

- **Separate diversifiable losses.** To the extent that the loss impacts individuals, households or firms unevenly, it will be possible to separately identify the diversifiable and non-diversifiable elements of the losses. The diversifiable aspects will typically be amenable to risk pooling or risk sharing.

- **Risk sharing between communities, regions or nations.** If the community affected by a systematic loss is part of a larger political entity, it should seek to share risk with other communities. For example, while natural disasters will often have wide-ranging impacts, they generally won't affect whole nations. There will usually be at least some scope for less affected regions to provide assistance to more affected regions. This would, in effect, be risk pooling between regions. For some systematic risks, such as pandemics and major economic downturns, a large element of overall losses will not be diversifiable.

- **Intergenerational risk sharing.** Sharing risk between generations will be an option where the impacts of a systematic risk are spread over long periods of time. Many systematic risks create losses – or the potential for losses – over decades or longer. The profile of these losses will often unfold over a trajectory that is difficult to forecast. This characterises a number of issues currently central to public-policy

> debates including climate change, population ageing and pandemics. The sharing of losses (and gains) across generations provides major opportunities to enhance welfare. However, this strategy is often highly complex to implement. It usually requires long-range forecasting, which is inherently difficult, and therefore optimal strategies will require a degree of flexibility.

A framework for implementing intergenerational risk management could be thought of in terms of a three-stage approach. The first stage is to identify the scope and nature of the problem, including the likelihood of and extent of potential losses. The difficulty of this should not be underestimated. Many systematic risks evolve over very long periods of time (such as climate change or an ageing population) or occur randomly and infrequently, causing great devastation (such as pandemics or natural disasters).

The second stage would be to identify the desired outcome. This is the destination: how much overall loss should be accepted and how should the burden of preparation and mitigation be shared across generations. In the case of climate change, this would be the total amount of abatement sought over the long-term.

The third stage is to craft an immediate response and a trajectory to the destination based upon the best available information. In the case of climate change, this would be the desired path, over time, to reduce emissions. It is only possible to do this after having clearly defined the end goal. Given the inherent difficulty of long-range planning, it will be necessary to periodically iterate stages two and three. As the actual trajectory of losses (or the inherent frequency of random events) becomes clearer, it will be important to update the initial policy settings. In the words of John Maynard Keynes: 'When the facts change, I change my opinion.'

IDENTIFYING THE PROBLEM

The potential for social and economic loss arising from systematic risk is immense. These events can cause massive short-term harm, including loss of life. Just as much of a concern is the potential for longer-term harm, often over trajectories that are very difficult to forecast. The two key challenges when developing strategies for managing the potential for loss arising from systematic risk and uncertainty are:

- Identifying potential losses and the cost of mitigation;
- Understanding the degree of uncertainty.

In what follows, this is discussed in the context of the Covid-19 pandemic. Some of the challenges arising from uncertainty in relation to climate change and an ageing society were discussed earlier in Chapter 7.

CASE STUDY: COVID-19 AND FUTURE PANDEMICS

Covid-19 has highlighted the potential for rapidly escalating health and economic crises as a result of pandemics in a highly interconnected world. At time of writing, Covid-19 has caused the death of over 6 million people and the worst economic downturn since the Great Depression. But this pandemic was far from unprecedented. There have been no less than ten highly contagious respiratory pandemics over the past 300 years.[1] The 'Spanish Flu' garners almost all of the media attention as a point of comparison with Covid-19, but in 1957–58, the 'Asian Flu' pandemic caused over 100,000 deaths and wreaked havoc on the US economy, causing a 10 per cent quarterly drop in GDP. As recently as 2003, the SARS epidemic resulted in a collapse in Asia-Pacific air travel, despite the fact that it killed fewer than 1000 people globally.

Calls from prominent epidemiologists and public health experts to increase preparedness for a major respiratory pandemic had been widely reported in recent decades, as had prescient forecasts of widespread health and economic harm. In the aftermath of Covid-19, these experts almost unanimously insist that another pandemic remains almost inevitable.

Understanding the degree of uncertainty

One of the public-policy challenges thrown into stark relief by Covid-19 is the degree of lack of preparedness of many governments and public health authorities in matters as basic as PPE stockpiles and contingency planning. Of course, there will always be a degree of chaos and inefficiency in the response to an unexpected and highly complex event such as Covid-19. However, what shouldn't have been a surprise is that a pandemic would arrive at some point. While this unpreparedness may appear inexcusable in light of the numerous warnings and precedents over recent decades, it is critical to acknowledge the inherent uncertainty surrounding the frequency and timing of pandemics. The core policy challenge is how best to prepare, given this uncertainty.

Table 15.1 outlines the principal respiratory outbreaks of the past 150 years. It does not include the many other types of pandemics that have occurred during this period, including cholera, the plague and tropical diseases. If anything, this table under-reports the frequency of respiratory pandemics, ignoring the localised, minor outbreaks that probably occurred prior to World War II but were not closely monitored by the global media of the day.

In the 150 years prior to Covid-19 the world has seen one pandemic involving tens of millions of deaths (the Spanish Flu), four pandemics causing at least 1 million deaths and seven pandemics involving at least tens of thousands of deaths. As the title of Table 15.1 suggests, coronavirus pandemics are white (not black) swans, even if it isn't possible to predict the precise date of the next swan's arrival.

Arguably, Covid-19 should be included in the same category as the Spanish Flu, given how transmissible and lethal it is. Without highly restrictive economic shutdowns and travel restrictions, the global death count could easily have been in the tens of millions, as it was in 1919–20.

If Covid-19 is considered in the same category as the Spanish Flu, that means that over the course of the last 150 years: a Spanish Flu/Covid-19 severity event occurs every seventy-five years; a pandemic that kills at least a million occurs once every thirty years; and a pandemic that kills at least tens of thousands of people occurs once every ten to twenty years. There are many more events of lower severity. For example, in the below table, four additional pandemics killing between 450 and 2000 people are cited in just the period 2000–20. The low severity of these events does not mean that these pandemics were unimportant, since each of these events could have been much more severe with a virus strain that was slightly more transmissible and/or lethal. The fact that pandemic outbreaks of mild severity are very frequent reinforces the near inevitability of more severe pandemics at some future point in time.

As discussed in Chapter 7, coronavirus pandemics are not normally distributed. There is a clustering of low-severity events. Most tellingly, there is a much higher frequency of extremely high-impact events than would occur in a normally distributed phenomenon. Even though events such as the Spanish Flu seem rare, they are in fact much more frequent than would be the case were pandemics distributed normally, as are so many phenomena in our daily experiences. This reflects the discussion in Chapter 7, which confirmed that pandemics have a distribution which is skewed (not symmetric) and also has a fat tail (many extreme events). It is therefore challenging to use a small dataset to estimate the frequency of rare, very severe events. Yet this is precisely what governments must do in order to be sufficiently prepared for future outbreaks.

Some aspects of the Covid-19 pandemic that appeared unprecedented to many at the time, such as the cessation of much international travel, were in fact not dissimilar to events that had transpired less than twenty years earlier with the 2003 SARS outbreak. After SARS spread from China to five other countries within the space of just twenty-four hours, and to thirty countries on six continents within several months, global aviation suffered a dramatic decline. Across the Asia-Pacific, air traffic volume declined by 45 per cent and the number of flights between the US and Hong Kong declined by almost 70 per cent. Writing in 2005, Michael Osterholm presciently predicted that 'this impact would pale in comparison to that of a 12- to 36-month worldwide influenza pandemic'.[2]

This raises the question as to whether the balance between mitigation and post-event spending is appropriate. One should always be cautious in interpreting such ex-post warnings. As was the case with World War I, Pearl Harbor and 9/11, it is possible to construct timelines of warnings in relation to almost any event after the fact, but much more difficult to do beforehand.

World War I, Pearl Harbor and 9/11, however, are very different in nature from the risk of a pandemic. Each of these events had unique and arguably unprecedented characteristics that were difficult (albeit not impossible) to predict. In the case of pandemics, by contrast, there are multiple precedents which should help form the basis of a society's preparedness regime. The balance between preparedness and spending on post-pandemic recovery will be discussed below.

Table 15.1: Pandemics are white swans

Respiratory Pandemics During the Past 150 Years			
Year	**Pandemic**	**Death toll**	**Economic impacts**
1889–90	Flu	1 million	
1918–20	Spanish flu	50 million (est. 17 million–100 million)	World Bank (WB) est. 4.8 per cent of global GDP
1957–58	Asian flu	1–4 million	WB est. 2.0 per cent of global GDP
1968–69	Hong Kong flu	1–4 million	WB est. 0.7 per cent global GDP
1977–78	Soviet flu	30–40,000	
2002–04	SARS	774	• China, WB est. $15bn GDP • Canada, WHO est. $5bn • Asia-Pacific $40bn
2003	Avian flu	455	
2009	Swine flu	284,000 (estimated 151K–575K)	
2012	Middle East RS	935	
2013–19	Avian flu (China)	616	
2015	Swine flu (India)	2,035	
2017–18	US flu season	61,000 (estimated 46K–95K)	
2019	Covid-19	6 million +	Largest recession since the Great Depression

16.
The Short-Term Response: Mitigation, Risk Sharing and Preparation

SYSTEMATIC RISK MITIGATION

For some systematic risks, it is possible to reduce the underlying likelihood of loss or the damage caused by loss when it arises. A matter of considerable public-policy debate in many countries is the balance between risk mitigation and post-disaster remediation. Many countries underinvest in mitigation relative to the cost of supporting communities and rebuilding infrastructure after disasters.

For example, over recent decades, Australia's response to natural disasters has been characterised by low levels of investment in mitigation and preparedness and high (and increasing) levels of spending on post-disaster recovery. In 2014, the Productivity Commission undertook a review into Australia's funding arrangement for natural disasters.[1] It found that, during the period 2010–2016, the Australian government spent around A$13 billion on post-disaster recovery, averaging just under $2 billion per year. That figure may have increased in the years following the Productivity Commission report, particularly given the scale of the 2019/20 bushfires. At the national level, this expenditure is primarily administered through the NDRRA (Natural Disaster Relief and Recovery Arrangements) and the AGDRP (Australian Government Disaster Recovery Payment) schemes. Significant additional post-disaster recovery payments are also made at the state and local level. In addition to this expenditure by government, natural disasters result in significant losses that are insured by the private sector. Over the period 1970–2013, more than $29 billion in losses arising from natural disasters were covered by private insurance. The broader economic costs, including uninsured costs, are difficult to quantify, but are likely to be considerably higher than even that figure.

Most of the losses arising from natural disasters are attributable to a small number of events, leading the Productivity Commission to conclude that 'policy settings and natural disaster funding arrangements need to be designed well to deal with these infrequent but costly natural disasters'.[2] This returns us to the difficulty of predicting the one-in-100-year flood.

What is most telling, for present purposes, about natural disaster funding arrangements is the imbalance between ongoing resilience and mitigation payments, as well as post-disaster remediation and recovery payments. In the period 2009/10–2012/13, the Australian government made payments of A$7 billion through the NDRRA and AGDRP. State and local governments made recovery payments of approximately $4 billion. In contrast, over the same period, payments for resilience and mitigation amounted to just $115 million from the Australian government and $110 million from state and local governments. Around fifty times more was spent during this period on cleaning up after natural disasters than on preventing them or preparing for them. This calls into question the current balance between investment levels in mitigation and preparedness as compared to post-disaster relief.

A levee reduces the likelihood that a flood will impact the protected area. It will often be possible to quite accurately quantify the height of flood that the levee will provide protection against. A key element of the business case for mitigation projects will be the extent to which they lower the premiums on existing policies and expand insurance coverage to those at particularly high risk.

As outlined in Chapter 7, it is difficult to estimate the frequency and severity of rare events, such as major natural disasters. This makes it difficult to determine how much should be invested each year in mitigation and ongoing preparedness. While it is difficult to ascertain with precision the optimal level of mitigation expenditure, the Productivity Commission concluded that not enough was being spent on mitigation relative to remediation and income support. The uncertainty in determining the appropriate overall level of spending on mitigation is reflected in recommendations 3.5 and 3.6 of the Productivity Commission report into natural disaster funding arrangements. Recommendation 3.5 deals with mitigation and argues that the Australian government should gradually increase the amount of annual mitigation funding it provides to state and territory governments to $200 million.[3] In setting this figure, it acknowledged the difficulty in making precise estimates. It settled on $200 million as almost a lower bound, a figure that government could be confident it could invest without regrets.

Recommendation 3.6 states that the Australian government should publish estimates (and their confidence ranges) of the future costs of natural disasters in the Statement of Risks in the budget papers.[4] This analysis will allow mitigation projects to be evaluated with greater precision in the future. The rationale for this, the report went on to state, is that 'where governments make no explicit budget provision for the costs of recovery from future natural disasters, there is a systematic bias in risk management against mitigation and insurance'.

SYSTEMATIC RISK SHARING

Intergenerational risk sharing

Effectively managing systematic risk and uncertainty often involves shifting resources between generations. Generally, this will involve seeking to spread investment evenly over time at the macroeconomic level, much as individuals and households seek to achieve consumption smoothing over time at the individual and household level.

Where a society is ageing and each individual's pattern of work and retirement is stable, this will result in a worsening society-wide dependency ratio. In other words, the number of retirees per worker will increase. For a given capital stock, that will mean that the amount of economic output per person will fall, reducing living standards on average, no matter how that output is shared. Output per worker may rise if there is more capital per worker. This could occur if the increasing number of retirees accumulate large stocks of savings over their working lives. This is referred to by economists as 'capital deepening'. But output per person is a better gauge of welfare across society than output per worker.

With pay-as-you-go pension systems, a worsening dependency ratio is reflected in ever higher taxes on a shrinking workforce, downward pressure on pensions – or a combination of both.

Another option is to try to boost the output of the economy in the future when there will be more retirees per worker. The only way to do this, at a macroeconomic level, is to consume less today and shift resources into productive assets in the future state. Clearly there remains the issue of who owns those assets in the future and who benefits from the income they produce. But the first step is to acknowledge that the societal budget constraint is such that smoothing income for society as a whole requires a policy that increases the total productive stock of inputs (the combination of capital and labour) in the future high-dependency society. This can be done by boosting savings in the earlier period of time and using that saving to accumulate productive capital for use in a later period of time.

This aspect of consumption smoothing across time applies in relation to all systematic risks: natural disasters, ageing, business cycles, pandemics and wars. What is critical from a public-policy perspective is that typically only government can achieve this kind of consumption smoothing in a coordinated way.

Inter-regional risk sharing

Some risks are systematic in that they affect an entire community but are diversifiable to the extent that that community forms part of a larger entity, such as a nation-state. A good example of this is a natural disaster that devastates a city or region but where a national government can support recovery from the natural disaster through investment and income support.

In the same way, where an international macroeconomic shock affects countries differentially, risk sharing will be possible between nations. Many events – war, pandemics, economic downturns – can affect multiple countries simultaneously but often the impact will be uneven. Bonds with payouts that are linked to differences in impacts are one example of a risk-management mechanism that could produce significant mutual gains. The box on the following pages sets out how GDP-linked bonds could be used to better manage international macroeconomic risks.

An example of risk transfer: GDP-linked bonds

- The idea behind GDP-linked bonds is that the risk of sovereign and corporate default could be better managed if macroeconomic risks are shared between borrowers and lenders. Nobel laureate Robert Shiller proposed this idea (and has since patented a GDP-linked security).[5] What if, instead of a fixed interest rate, the repayments owed under a loan were based in part on general economic conditions? Borrowers and lenders would both share the upsides and downsides of the economic cycle. Sovereign debt in which repayments are linked to macroeconomic indicators such as GDP growth or terms of trade are one example of such loans. A key rationale for GDP-linked bonds is to provide borrowing governments (or other entities) with some protection from economic downturns. This could enable governments to implement debt-financed strategies that might currently be inhibited not by economic policy but rather by creditor concerns in relation to default.[6] With GDP-linked bonds, repayments would be reduced when governments are less able to pay. Bonds could be (but needn't be) symmetric and increase repayment obligations if GDP or other macroeconomic outcomes are unexpectedly favourable. GDP-linked debt would shift risk to large investors in a better position to withstand (or perhaps predict) future shocks– for a fee, of course. Debt of this type could potentially increase the borrowing capacity and policy options of countries with sub-AAA credit rating and also provide a more stable environment for creditors by reducing the likelihood of default crises.
- Some GDP-linked debt instruments have already been issued as part of debt-restructuring arrangements, including in Costa Rica, Bulgaria, Bosnia and Herzegovina, Argentina, Greece and Ukraine. More recently, Uruguay issued a US$1 billion bond in 2014 with principal and coupon payments indexed to nominal wages. In addition, Portugal recently issued small-denomination bonds to domestic savers with payout levels tied to GDP.[7] To date, there are no GDP-linked instruments which involve the private sector taking on both upside and downside risks.

- The potential gains from this type of debt instrument could be substantial, for countries at all levels of income. Kim and Ostry estimate that a combination of GDP-linked debt and the issuance of debt with longer maturities[8] could lower borrowing costs (since the risk of default would be lowered) and increase the 'fiscal space' (the range of borrowing outcomes) by 5–40 per cent of GDP (or 10–60 per cent of GDP if investors are risk-neutral).[9] Would GDP-linked debt be appealing to investors? Part of the appeal of GDP-linked debt would be the correlation between the underlying risk of a country's bond and other major asset classes, such as US equities. Shiller et al. argue that 'the price would be determined by the amount of systematic risk embedded in the security's returns: the more that domestic GDP co-moves with, say, US stock returns, the higher the price'.[10] The same authors find that, for G20 countries, the premium would be fairly modest, around 30 basis points, and for some countries could even be negative.[11]

PREPARATION: COVID-19 AS A CASE STUDY

The Covid-19 pandemic produced the most dramatic global health and economic crisis since World War II. It has highlighted the need for greater investment in preparedness for rare, highly impactful events. This applies to pandemics, natural disasters, major macroeconomic shocks and wars.

Preparation for the inevitable next pandemic

In May 2005, shortly before being appointed to the newly established National Science Advisory Board on Biosecurity, Michael Osterholm wrote an article in the *New England Journal of Medicine* titled 'Preparing for the Next Pandemic'. Fifteen years before Covid-19, Osterholm prophetically concluded his article with the following words:

> We need bold and timely leadership at the highest levels of the governments in the developed world; these governments must recognize the economic, security, and health threats posed by the next influenza pandemic and invest accordingly. The resources needed must be

> considered in the light of the eventual costs of failing to invest in such an effort. The loss of human life even in a mild pandemic will be devastating, and the cost of a world economy in shambles for several years can only be imagined.[12]

In 2020, Osterholm concluded that, even though 'the disease caused by the new coronavirus that emerged in late 2019 is far from gone, it is not too soon to reach a verdict on the world's collective preparation. That verdict is a damning one.'[13]

Osterholm argues that there are two levels of preparation: short-term and long-term. He draws an analogy between preparing for a storm surge. Long-term preparedness is akin to knowing that a city is at risk of being battered by a hurricane and taking advantage of the present calm to strengthen levees, construct water-diversion systems and develop and implement an emergency and evacuation plan. For a pandemic, the equivalent is building up a national medical equipment stockpile, investing in vaccine research and developing emergency plans.

Short-term preparedness is what occurs when an actual storm is approaching the city. In the days and hours when the storm approaches, the test of preparedness is whether an emergency plan is effectively implemented and stocks of food and supplies are deployed to shelters. In the case of a pandemic, this is equivalent to how authorities deploy scarce healthcare services, how the spread of the disease is recorded and traced, and, if necessary, how lockdowns are implemented.

It is worth examining how successfully governments and agencies performed at each of these levels of preparedness as a lesson for best practice for extreme events more generally.

Underinvestment in long-term preparedness

What can we do to prepare for pandemics? There are numerous aspects of preparedness for future pandemics worth considering, many of which are currently chronically underfunded in most countries.

It is important to develop detailed operational blueprints. Michael Osterholm argues that plans and blueprints should 'involve everyone from private-sector food producers, medical suppliers, and health-care providers to public-sector health, law enforcement, and emergency-management officials.' These blueprints should anticipate 'the pandemic-related collapse of world-wide trade'.[14] Given the exponential nature of caseload growth in the early stages of a pandemic, developing detailed plans for short-term deployment is critical. This should have included rapid ramping up of PPE equipment and ventilator production, the rapid manufacturing of tests and the deployment of testing and contact tracing before numbers grew beyond the capacity of systems to monitor.

Just as the military regularly engages in war games, pandemic simulations could provide much-needed practice and valuable insights. War games and tabletop exercise hosted by the John Hopkins Center for Health Security have demonstrated the importance of pre-planning and also the key risks that can arise from poor coordination and decision-making. Such exercises would be even more useful at an international level in a world in which geographic sequestration is increasingly difficult, particularly with ubiquitous air travel that can transport people to all corners of the globe well before many diseases exhibit any symptoms.

The response to a specific scenario is not the key output of such exercises but, rather, the development of operational capacity and coordination across key agencies. US general (and later president) Dwight Eisenhower stated: 'Peace-time plans are of no particular value, but peace-time planning is indispensable.'[15]

Public health infrastructure is clearly a key element in the response to a pandemic. This will include many core elements of a health system such as ICU beds, specialist practitioners, nursing staff ratios and community-health services. The capacity of the health system to provide **surge capacity** – like additional beds and ICU ward capacity, emergency and personal protective equipment – will also be critical. This surge capacity will partly be provided by a national stockpile in each country and partly by each country or region's capacity to quickly produce or access supplies and equipment at short notice.

Investment in **vaccine research** is a critical long-term plank of global preparedness. One of the fundamental limitations of market solutions in relation to the development of antibiotics and vaccines is that the time at which a need will arise for such drugs is so difficult to predict. Given this, governments will need to provide some or all of the funding for research where the timing of potential payoffs is inherently uncertain. In 2006, the US government established the Biomedical Advanced Research and Development Authority (BARDA). It is responsible for the coordinated development and purchase of vaccines, drugs and diagnostic tools. Since 2006, funding limitations have undermined BARDA's capacity to invest in long-term projects, such as a universal coronavirus vaccine.

Given the limitations of funding by many national governments, the Coalition for Epidemic Preparedness Innovations (CEPI) was launched in 2017. CEPI receives support from numerous public, private and philanthropic sources, including US$460 million from the Bill and Melinda Gates Foundation, the Wellcome Trust and a consortium of nations including Germany, Japan and Norway.

Influenza viruses are a moving target. Laurie Garrett argues that in the postwar era, the eradication of viral, bacterial and parasitic diseases was an international public health priority that created considerable optimism following successes such as the complete elimination of smallpox. That spirit 'culminated in 1978 when the members states of the United Nations signed the "Health for All, 2000" accord. The agreement set ambitious targets for the eradication of disease.'[16] Considerable progress in public health and life expectancies was made in the decades following that accord, but the mutability of microbes, viruses and parasites – both through random mutations and evolutionary natural selection – was underestimated by some. Following the supply of penicillin by the US military, Nobel laureate Joshua Lederberg found that natural selection in the bacterial world resulted in ever more resistant strains of staphylococcus and streptococcus. This natural evolutionary process continues, as Garrett writes: 'Microbes have appeared that can grow on a bar of soap, swim unabashed in bleach, and ignore doses of penicillin logarithmically larger than those effective in 1950.'[17]

Given the ever-changing nature of the biological target that we are aiming at, a universal influenza vaccine should be one of the targets for future research. Such a vaccine would provide protection, even against mutations in the flu across or even within seasons. Research into smallpox and HIV/AIDS involved coordinated efforts across multiple countries. A similar commitment would be required to find a universal flu vaccine.

Robustness of international supply chains to disruptions in world trade is critical, particularly where large economies need to be shut down for extended periods. One of the key areas of vulnerability at present is the highly concentrated production of generic drugs and reagents in China and India.

As noted earlier, less than 10 per cent of government expenditure in relation to natural disasters is spent on mitigation. The lack of funding for preparedness and mitigation is even starker in relation to pandemics. In 1995, Dustin Hoffman earned more money playing a disease-control scientist in the film *Outbreak* than the combined annual budgets for the US National Center for Infectious Diseases and the UN Programme on HIV/AIDS.[18] Hollywood's funding reflects a (perhaps surprising) influence, with the UK health secretary indicating that the film *Contagion* and its depiction of a global scramble for vaccines partly shaped his strategy in relation to the UK's vaccination rollout.[19]

Perhaps the most scrutinised area of underfunding by governments in the lead-up to Covid-19 was **national medical stockpiles**. The US Strategic National Stockpile houses approximately US$8 billion worth of medical equipment.[20] At the start of the Covid-19 pandemic, the stockpile contained 16,600 breathing machines and 12 million N95 masks. For context, California and New York combined requested 25,000 ventilators and 23 million N95 masks during the pandemic's first wave of infections.

The investment in Australia's national stockpile totalled around $750 million over the decade to 2012/13. This can be contrasted with spending on the Covid-19 induced recession of over $250 billion, as well as the additional long-term economic and social damage far exceeding that amount.

In evidence to the Senate Select Committee into Covid-19, Australia's Chief Medical Officer clarified that Australia had 15.6 million P2/N95 respirators and 9 million surgical masks in the national medical stockpile at the time of the outbreak, but no medical gowns.[21] It appears as though Australia, like many other nations, needs to re-examine how large its national stockpile should be in light of the potential for pandemics to be more frequent than earlier suspected.

A good example of the short-sightedness that beset many governments around the world was the defunding of mobile hospitals in California. In 2006, citing the Avian Flu as part of his rationale, Governor Arnold Schwarzenegger invested over $400 million in three 200-bed mobile hospitals that could be deployed within seventy-two hours. Each of these hospitals would be the size of a football field and would include a surgery ward, an intensive care unit and X-ray equipment. The initiative also included a stockpile of 50 million N95 masks, 2400 portable ventilators and the kits for setting up an additional 21,000 beds.[22] When announcing the initiative, Schwarzenegger said: 'In light of the pandemic flu risk, it is absolutely a critical investment. I'm not willing to gamble with the people's safety.'[23] Following the announcement, more than $200 million was invested in the mobile hospitals and a Health Surge Capacity Initiative. California later faced fiscal pressures following the 2009/10 recession. In 2011, facing a budget deficit of $26 billion, the program was defunded.

The California mobile hospital and surge capacity program is emblematic of the type of investment that should be part of recurrent budget funding, and not subject to business cycle risks. We know that future pandemics will occur, but since their precise timing is uncertain, it is critical that ongoing funding be made a core budget priority.

The challenge of short-term preparedness: uncertainty during the early stages

The Covid-19 outbreak was a good example of how uncertainty can impact on decision-making even after a virus has spread widely. In a *New York Times* article on 13 February 2020, at a time when over 1000 people had died from Covid, little was known about its lethality:

> There remains deep uncertainty about the new coronavirus' mortality rate, with the high-end estimate that it is up to 20 times that of the flu, but some estimates go as low as 0.16 percent for those affected outside of China's overwhelmed Hubei province. About on par with the flu.[24]

A similar level of uncertainty surrounded the virus' transmissibility. This uncertainty placed policymakers in a difficult position. While an approach based on the precautionary principle is defensible in such a situation, it eventually came with enormous costs – not just economic but also in terms of human welfare. The economic hardship caused by the lockdowns imposed by many countries around the world resulted in trillions of dollars in lost output, tens of millions added to unemployment queues and, just as importantly, reductions in living standards and life expectancy as well as an increase in death caused by substance abuse, reduced access to medical treatment for non-Covid ailments, increased family violence, gambling and heightened suicide rates.

The imposition of lockdowns – while justifiable on balance in most situations – wasn't a simple trade-off between lives and dollars. While lockdowns reduced the number of deaths from Covid-19, they undoubtedly caused increased deaths from other causes and resulted in long-term economic harm that was unevenly borne across the community.

Adaptation

A house built on stilts is a powerful image of learning to live with risk and uncertainty. Sometimes, adaptation will be the most sensible response (or partial response) to the potential for loss. In many situations, it will not be optimal or indeed possible to totally remove the underlying potential for loss.

Adaptation lies at the heart of developing sound climate-change policy. To completely halt all carbon emissions tomorrow would be unrealistic. At the other end of the spectrum, imposing no constraints on emissions would result in significant environmental costs – and ultimately economic costs, as sectors like agriculture are negatively impacted.

Between these extremes lies a middle ground, but what is the 'optimal' trajectory for reducing emissions from their current levels? Is there an optimal amount of carbon emissions? And if there is, how do we determine this level?

Table 16.1 outlines results from William Nordhaus's DICE model.[25] Each row outlines the model's estimate of environmental damages and abatement costs for a particular policy scenario. All damages and costs are estimates in trillions of US dollars (2005) in present discounted value terms (PDV).

As discussed in Chapter 7, there is considerable uncertainty surrounding the output of integrated assessment models (IAMs, in this context, are models containing both economic and environmental components.) The long-term economic impacts of different abatement scenarios are a considerable source of uncertainty. Given this, it is not the specific estimates that are of interest in Table 16.1 but, rather, the clear trade-offs that the DICE model (and other IAMs) makes transparent.

The baseline scenario, which involves very little abatement, results in high environmental damages and almost zero abatement costs. The final three scenarios involve significant abatement. Not surprisingly, these scenarios involve considerably lower environmental costs but much higher abatement costs. The second and third scenarios (optimal tax and CO_2 emissions capped at 560 parts per million) are the scenarios with the lowest total environmental and abatement costs. But these two scenarios involve higher environmental damages than the final three scenarios.

The fourth scenario involves a lower discounting of future generations' welfare (i.e. the approach adopted in the Stern Review) than Nordhaus adopts. This results in higher overall costs as a result of taking more ambitious abatement activity quickly. The higher cost of 'up-fronting' abatement benefits later generations. As will be discussed below, the choice of discount rate has a material impact on the policy response to very long-term problems, and remains an area of active debate among economists, political scientists and philosophers.

The purpose of setting out the results in Table 16.1 is not to point to a specific strategy. The PDV of economic and environmental costs in Table 16.1 will have changed markedly since 2005. Rather, the key point of Table 16.1 is to highlight that there is often a trade-off between mitigating risk and harm on the one hand and living with some degree of ongoing harm.

Table 16.1: Outcomes of the DICE model[26]

Climate policy	PDV difference with baseline	PDV of environmental damages	PDV of abatement costs	Sum of environmental damages and abatement costs
		DICE 2005 (trillions US$, 2005 prices)		
No controls baseline	0.00	22.55	0.04	22.59
Optimal tax	+3.07	17.31	2.20	19.52
Limit CO_2 to 560 ppm	+2.67	15.97	3.95	19.92
Stern Review discount rate	-14.18	9.02	27.74	36.77
Limit temperature rise to 1.5 degrees	-14.44	9.95	27.08	37.03
Limit CO_2 to 420 ppm	-14.60	9.95	27.24	37.19
90 per cent emissions cut	-21.36	10.05	33.90	43.96
		DICE 2016R2 (trillions US$, 2010 prices)		
BAU	0.0	134.2	0.4	134.6
Optimal controls	29.9	84.6	20.1	104.7
2.5 degree maximum	-43.2	43.1	134.6	177.8
Stern Review	-67.3	46.2	155.7	201.9

17. The Long-Term Solution: Balancing the Interests of Generations

THE TRAJECTORY OF NEGATIVE IMPACT AND MITIGATION COSTS

One of the most profound challenges in managing long-term public-policy issues such as climate change and an ageing demographic is how to weight the interests of different generations. Many people's first reaction would be that public policy should weight the value of generations equally. In broad terms, this could be described as a utilitarian approach. In fact, if you asked some people, their first reaction might be to say that the interests of the today's newborns and the generations yet to come should be weighted more heavily than those of today's middle-aged and elderly. But public policy usually does the opposite: it 'discounts' the welfare of people the further into the future they are, placing greater weight on the interests and preferences of those currently alive.

In our personal lives, most of us value an immediate benefit more than a guarantee to provide that very same benefit in the future. We are impatient. Satisfying the wants and desires of our present selves is usually far more compelling than satisfaction of the desires we anticipate we will have in the future.

In 1972, in the famous 'Stanford marshmallow experiment', psychologist Walter Mischel offered children a marshmallow (or for those without sweet tooths a pretzel), which they were permitted to consume immediately. The catch was that Mischel would then announce that he was about to leave the room for fifteen minutes. If, upon his return, the marshmallow was still there, the child would be rewarded for their patience with a second treat.[1] One of the most famous (and unexpected) findings of the study was that the ability to delay gratification was correlated with higher SAT scores later in life. But at the time of the initial study, the focus was on how the children managed to suppress their immediate desires:

> They made up quiet songs ... hid their head in their arms, pounded the floor with their feet, fiddled playfully and teasingly with the signal bell, verbalized the contingency ... prayed to the ceiling, and so on. In one dramatically effective self-distraction technique, after obviously experiencing much agitation, a little girl rested her head, sat limply, relaxed herself, and proceeded to fall sound asleep.[2]

For many if not most of us, delaying gratification remains a challenge for our entire lives.

To spread one's consumption over time is a very complex task and depends upon sometimes offsetting psychological tendencies. Impatience prods us towards wanting more of our consumption now, or at least as soon as possible. This desire can arise from the fact that we are hardwired to want marshmallows (or pretzels) immediately. It also arises from the very rational notion that a bird in the hand is worth two in the bush. A dollar today may be worth more than a promise of a sum greater than a dollar in the future. We could be dead at the future date. The promise to pay in the future may not be honoured. And so on.

In contrast, diminishing marginal utility prods us towards seeking to equalise how much we consume in each time period, as much as is possible. The concept of diminishing marginal utility lies at the heart of modern economies. It is a technical term for a very basic and commonsense notion: that the additional benefit from consuming more diminishes as one's overall consumption increases. In the words of George Szpiro: 'People prefer more of a good, but the more they already have, the less they value each additional unit. That's the whole of economics; all the rest is commentary.'[3]

We can think about diminishing marginal utility in terms of our favourite food. Eating a chocolate bar is enjoyable for sugar-addicted people (such as this author). Eating a second chocolate bar provides additional pleasure, but less than the first. And the third would add to welfare a little less again – and so on. The same applies to consumption more broadly. The first few dollars that we spend is generally devoted to essentials: food, clothing and shelter. The value of these essentials is almost incalculably high. As we earn and spend more, we start to branch out into more discretionary items: more fancy food, clothing and shelter; entertainment; holidays; and luxury items. For most people, the additional value of each extra dollar of income (and what it is spent on) diminishes as we start spending on discretionary items and luxuries.

The concept of diminishing marginal utility was observed in ancient Greece by Aristotle.[4] Its ancient provenance shouldn't be surprising, given how intuitive and foundational it is. In the fourteenth century, Johannes Buridanus expanded Aristotle's exposition of value and also distinguished between value (subjectively determined) and price (determined in the market).[5] However, it wasn't until much later that it was formalised.

In 1738, Daniel Bernoulli distinguished between expected value and subjective utility in his groundbreaking work on decision-making and utility, *Exposition of a New Theory of Measurement of Risk*. Even though Buridanus had earlier distinguished between price and value, Bernoulli was the first person to clearly and explicitly separate the objective and subjective elements of risk:

> Ever since mathematicians first began to study the measurement of risk, there has been general agreement on the following proposition: Expected values are computed by multiplying each possible gain by the number of ways in which it can occur, and then dividing the sum of these products by the total number of cases. The utility ... is dependent on the particular circumstances of the person making the estimate ... There is no reason to assume that ... the risks anticipated by each [individual] must be deemed equal in value.[6]

Later, in 1844, Jules Dupuit, a French civil engineer, observed that people were willing to pay more for their first unit of water consumption (used for drinking) than for the second (used for bathing) and even less for the third (used to water the garden) and so on. This diminishing willingness to pay as the quantity used increased reflected a diminishing addition to utility at the margin. This result was published in a French engineering journal and was to remain undiscovered by mainstream economics for decades. At around the same time, Hermann Heinrich Gossen, a Prussian tax collector, formalised the concept of diminishing marginal utility in 1854,[7] although his publication attracted little attention at the time.[8] The work of Dupuit and Gossen (and others) was the precursor to the 'marginalist revolution' in economics which was led by Stanley Jevons, Leon Walras and Carl Menger, three theorists working independently in different countries and in different languages in the late nineteenth century.[9] Together, they would transform economics.

While many of the underpinnings of rational decision-making commonly assumed in modern economic modelling are rightly being challenged, some core elements of this framework are present most of the time and provide valuable insights. The diminishing marginal utility of consumption is not always true for all people – but it is sensible to use it as a benchmark since it is true for most people, most of the time.[10] This is reflected in a utility function such as the one in the left hand panel of Figure 17.1. This graph shows a relationship between 'utility' or 'welfare' and how much is consumed. For present purposes, the specific units on the vertical axis don't matter as this is a basic and not realistically calibrated representation of the underlying principle. The curvature of the line means that each additional dollar of spending adds a bit less to our welfare than the dollar before it. What would it look like if utility or welfare was constant instead of diminishing? If increasing levels of consumption had a constant impact on utility, the relationship would look like the right-hand panel of Figure 17.1.

Of course, a simple line or mathematical equation won't ever capture the complexity and nuances of a person's wants and desires. Moreover, each individual will have unique preferences and risk aversion will vary across individuals.

One of the key rationales for insurance is that it redistributes future resources from people with low marginal utility (those who didn't experience loss) to people with high marginal utility (those who did experience loss). This future allocation, based on who actually experiences loss, tends to increase aggregate welfare.

Figure 17.1: Risk-averse and risk-neutral relationship between income and welfare

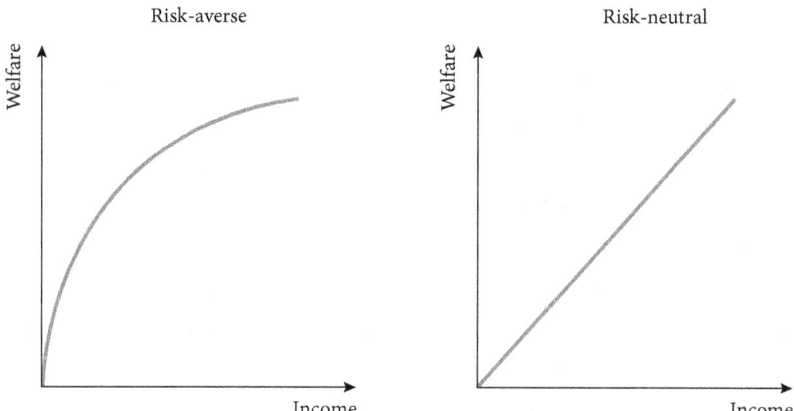

What if we use a similar concept for allocating consumption across different time periods in a person's life? Diminishing marginal utility suggests that a person will maximise their welfare if they roughly equalise consumption over time.

Economists think about human decision-making when we plan our consumption across a number of successive measures of time in light of both impatience and diminishing marginal utility. Impatience makes people want to bring forward as much consumption towards the present as possible. If you think of each period of time as having its own utility curve for consumption, then diminishing marginal utility makes us want to spread our consumption evenly across our lives. Our choices are ultimately a compromise between these two impulses.

If every person in a society has the same utility function (a big and unrealistic 'if' in practice!), total utility would be maximised by equalising consumption across all people.

If people had different utility functions, but each of their utility functions exhibited diminishing marginal utility (a reasonable assumption most of the time), maximising total utility would be achieved by distributing consumption so as to equalise *marginal* utility across all people. If people exhibited diminishing marginal utility and marginal utility was not equal for all, it would be possible to increase total utility by transferring resources from someone with low marginal utility (high consumption) to someone with high marginal utility (low consumption).

The point at which such welfare-enhancing transfers are no longer possible is where all people have the same marginal utility. While (almost) no economists believe that a person's preferences can be completely captured by a simple line or equation, the relationship between diminishing marginal utility and welfare-enhancing transfers would appear to accord with common sense and, for most of us, our lived experience. Indeed, this kind of reallocation provides the key rationale for progressive income taxation.

The same principle could be applied to a person's life. If a person's utility function (or preferences) were stable over time, maximising utility for a person across a lifetime would involve equalising consumption across each time period – or 'consumption smoothing' in the parlance of economists.[11] Of course, that isn't always possible in practice. But consumption smoothing describes most people's behaviour, albeit in broad terms: we typically save during periods of above-average income and either borrow or consume from our savings during periods of low income (for example, as students or in retirement).

But our impatience fights against consumption smoothing – and not only as children with marshmallows. Most of us are impatient our whole lives. That is why, in addition to diminishing marginal utility, most economists also imagine that we 'discount' the future, or in other words, that we weight present consumption more heavily than potential future consumption. The question remains: by how much should we discount the future? And should that discounting vary by individual based upon how impatient we are?

The real challenge for present purposes is whether public-policy makers should discount the interests of future generations and, if so, by how much. As noted above, the paradox is that most of us are impatient with our own consumption but wouldn't want to place lesser weight on the interests of our children or their children. This matters greatly for very long-term problems like climate change.

In the seminal Stern Review on climate change, a discount rate of 0.1 per cent was used to reflect the fundamental preference for the immediate that most of us have: what is often called 'inherent discounting'.[12] That rate discounted the future, but only very marginally. In essence, it treated each generation's interests equally. Stern's choice of discount rate was polarising, even among very senior economists.[13]

A discount rate of 2 per cent (which is common in much public-policy benefit-cost analysis, if not more) would imply a significantly different long-term weighting across generations. Brad de Long's observations reflect the views of those who prefer a lower discount rate for assessing long-term intergenerational welfare choices:

> 2 percent per year is unconscionable – it means that somebody born in 1960 'counts' for twice as much as somebody born in 1995, who in turn 'counts' for twice as much as somebody born in 2020; somebody born in 1960 'counts' for 256 times as much as somebody born in 2160.[14]

How much weight to place on future generations becomes more contentious the longer the time horizon. Issues such as climate change are a philosophical and public-policy challenge that we need to grapple with if we are to arrive at sensible investment and mitigation trajectories.

A second reason why public-policy makers place greater weight on the interests of current generations is that the incomes of future generations are likely to be far higher than today. Redistribution between people of different income levels today can be justified on the basis that an extra dollar is worth a lot more to a poor person than a wealthy person – so a net gain can be achieved by taxing a dollar from a wealthy person and transferring it to a very poor person. If the same argument is applied to generations, some conclude that the cost of mitigating climate change should be borne more heavily by future, more wealthy generations. Others counter that this reallocation isn't feasible since delaying mitigation will mean allowing irreversible damage to the environment (including the risk of unpredictable feedback loops).

A final reason why the future is treated differently from the present is uncertainty. We are familiar with this in the context of assets. The riskier an asset, the more we 'discount' its expected future income stream. For example, if you were offered a US government bond promising to pay a 1 per cent return in a year, you would be highly confident of receiving that payment. Not 100 per cent confident, but close. In contrast, if you invested in stock in a newly formed internet venture offering to pay 1 per cent in a year, you would be far less confident of receiving the payment.

The company could easily go bankrupt. You would 'discount' the promise to pay 1 per cent from the internet startup more than the US bond. If both a US bond and an internet startup were offering the same payment in one year, you would generally opt to invest in the bond. Generally, in order to place your money in the risky venture, you would need to be offered a higher average rate of return, compared to the bond, knowing that the likelihood of getting zero is far higher than compared to the bond.

In the case of long-term policy challenges such as climate change, uncertainty arises in multiple ways. As noted in Table 7.4, even though the vast majority of scientists are highly confident that human activity is causing an increase in mean temperatures, estimates of the impact in a century or more come with a high degree of uncertainty. This leads some to argue that we should incur less mitigation costs now just in case the future environmental damage turns out to be not as bad as expected. We should focus on 'no regrets' costs. Others counter that the irreversibility of much of the potential damage means that we should err on the side of caution and redouble our efforts. These people argue that we should focus on the possibility of outcomes at the upper end of the error bounds, not the best possible outcomes.

A related issue is the possibility that technology will save the day. Some argue that, while technological progress moves forwards in fits and starts, significant progress in our capacity to achieve low-cost carbon abatement is almost certain. We just don't know precisely when the breakthroughs will occur. According to this line of reasoning, we shouldn't overinvest to the detriment of today's generation in technology that will almost certainly be overtaken by innovations, some possibly just around the corner.[15] Again, this is countered by those who argue that we should focus on the potential for outcomes worse than our median forecast and that waiting for innovation that may not arrive in time risks allowing massive damage to the environment and our economy.

After taking all of the various elements of discounting into effect, Stern used an average discount rate of 1.4 per cent, lower than that used in most previous models of climate change, and also lower than that used in many public-policy benefit-cost analyses.[16]

DEALING WITH UNCERTAINTY

Designing an optimal long-term response to systematic risk will have to deal with the uncertainty associated with either predicting the long-term evolution of a worsening trend (ageing, climate change) or the arrival of an extreme event (pandemics, natural disasters). As is set out in Chapter 15, even if forecasting techniques improve, it is highly likely that a degree of uncertainty will remain for most long-term systematic risks.

This means that it will be necessary to incorporate flexibility into the approach. Australia's Intergenerational Report is published by the Treasury every five years and 'assesses the long-term sustainability of current Government policies and how changes to Australia's population size and age profile may impact on economic growth, workforce and public finances over the next 40 years'.[17] The report assesses the impact of demographic change on all aspects of government spending, not just the pension system. To date, five Intergenerational reports have been published.

Table 17.1 sets out why it is critical to have policy mechanisms that adjust to constantly updating expectations. This table outlines projections for the year 2042, by drawing on data from the first five Integenerational Reports for four key demographic variables: female life expectancy, male life expectancy, total population and the old-age to worker dependency ratio. Given that each report makes forecasts to different time horizons, it was necessary to interpolate between time periods so as to estimate forecasts for the year 2042 from each report for the purposes of comparability.

In the space of just thirteen years, the projections for 2042 have changed markedly for total population and the dependency ratio. The estimate for female and male life expectancy for 2042 increased across the first five Intergenerational Reports by 1.5 and 2.5 years respectively. The significant increase in life expectancy in the 2015 report was due to using the 'cohort method'. This method was only used for the 2015 report.

The median estimate of Australia's total population in 2042 was almost 40 per cent higher in 2015 and 2021 compared to the 2002 estimate. And the old-age dependency ratio projected for 2042 was around seven percentage points higher in the 2015 and 2021 reports than in the first two.

The degree of change tends to be even greater over longer time horizons. Governments need to adjust policy settings as new information comes to hand.

Table 17.1: Key demographic projections from the first five Intergenerational Reports

	2002	2007	2010	2015	2021
Female life expectancy (2042)	87.5	89.2	89.5	95.8	89
Male life expectancy (2042)	82.5	85.3	86.4	94.2	85
Population (2042)	25.3	27.8	33.3	34.7	32.5
Old-age/working dependency ratio(2042)	41	41	35	34	34

LIVING WITH CHANGE: CLIMATE CHANGE AS A CASE STUDY

The optimal long-term solution is usually not to totally eradicate the potential for loss. A good example is climate change. The Paris Agreement set a target of limiting emissions to the point where temperatures would rise by less than two degrees Celsius, and with a goal of undertaking further work to cap temperature rises at 1.5 degrees. This was broadly seen as optimal in the sense that it balanced the costs of reducing emissions against the need to avoid catastrophic climate change.

A rise of even two degrees would result in significant negative consequences for the environment and for the quality of life of many communities. By limiting the temperature increase to two degrees, which was substantially below the 'business as usual' scenario, the Paris Agreement reflects a combination of mitigation and adaptation.

Adaptation to climate change could take many forms. At the local level, adaptation could involve changed practices by households, firms and governments (local, state and national) in relation to land use, public health and infrastructure investment. Such measures could include:

- Strategies for coping with higher temperatures, such as air conditioning in schools, reducing paved areas and planting more heat-resistant trees;
- Strategies to cope with more frequent heavy rain, storms and other weather occurrences, including improved drainage, greater rainwater

storage, building standards that require more flood-resistant buildings and not approving new residential buildings in flood-prone areas;

- Dealing with rising sea levels through greater investment in sea walls, building standards that require higher and stronger foundations for buildings exposed to risk, and restricting new buildings in high-risk coastal areas.

Agriculture will need to adapt to climate change in many regions. Some areas will become more productive as a result of increasing mean temperatures and changes in the distribution of rainfall, even though average agricultural productivity at a global level will probably fall. A range of local initiatives will need to be implemented but these could be supplemented by inter-regional and international strategies that include more efficient transport of output from areas of high production to low production and R&D into higher-yield, more drought-resistant crops.

Larger projects that may require international cooperation include weather control, damming glacial lakes and geoengineering.

18. Conclusion

Social insurance has grown to become a very significant and productive part of many modern economies. It has supported untold millions to live with dignity and security in the face of the slings and arrows of outrageous fortune. From a small base of around 2 per cent of most advanced economies as late as 1914, social insurance has now grown to represent between a quarter and a third of most OECD countries' GDP and the majority of government spending. The bulk of this growth occurred during the four decades following World War II.

In only a century, social insurance has established an enviable track record in helping countless people avoid poverty, unemployment, homelessness, ill health and a lack of autonomy. However, after three decades in which the size of government as a share of the economy has been relatively stable, it is timely to ask whether we can achieve more through social insurance programs without materially adding to their cost. As I have demonstrated in this book, we have the opportunity to significantly improve the performance of most of our social insurance schemes. Our reforms should be driven not by cost-cutting but rather by the desire to achieve better long-term outcomes for our fellow citizens.

In addition to managing the risks that we face as individuals and households, social insurance also underpins the ways in which we manage economy-wide risks like pandemics, natural disasters, climate change and economic disruptions. Indeed, the intergenerational nature of many risk-management schemes means that governments are essential if loss is to be shared and managed well. The threat posed by some systematic risks is increasing, which raises the question of whether governments need to invest even more.

Australia is not unique in having developed a large, complex welfare state that acts as a vital safety net. But Australia's safety net is unique in its overall mix of funding and benefit structures. A great deal of the funding of Australia's welfare state is derived from progressive taxation, rather than from contributions. This enhances fairness but is already putting a strain on income taxes. Australia's superannuation system is one response to that pressure, but with an ageing demographic, the broader issue remains.

Australia's welfare state is also highly targeted, on some measures the most targeted in the OECD. This means that scarce resources are well directed. But it also creates high effective marginal tax rates (EMTRs), often greater than 100 per cent. And most importantly for labour force participation, these high EMTRs can impact people on low and middle incomes.

Australia's welfare state has already shown great innovation with its income-contingent loans (such as HECS), superannuation accounts, social-impact bonds, designed markets and the NDIS. Of course, there are many worthwhile innovations in other countries that we have yet to fully embrace. Australia will need to build on existing successes in the decades ahead if it is to contain costs.

Australia's welfare state is also highly pluralistic, with a significant role for non-profit organisations and the private sector in service provision. In some policy areas, as much as one-third of government funding is delivered by non-government entities, often via competitive tender. In other areas, government encourages non-government service delivery through subsidies. This pluralism has brought additional expertise and innovation. In some areas, it has generated competitive tension; in others, the presence of non-government service providers probably takes pressure off taxpayers.

While both sides of politics in Australia have contributed to this long legacy, I believe that the Australian Labor Party has been principally responsible for the core, distinctive aspects of our successful welfare state. I also believe that the approach outlined in this book based on risk management and insurance will build on these distinctive characteristics (progressivity, targeted benefits, pluralism and innovation) and that it is the best way forward.

Building on the existing strengths of the system is critical at this juncture, given the pressure that the system will come under in future decades. Existing cost pressures – like an ageing demographic and the growing costs of delivering healthcare – will only become more extreme with time, especially as Australia deals with paying off the debt it is accruing during Covid-19.

GETTING BETTER OUTCOMES FOR VULNERABLE INDIVIDUALS

All too often, the goal of achieving positive long-term outcomes is not at the centre of social-policy program design and delivery. This is typically due to two factors. First is the challenge of defining specific outcomes when most social-policy interventions seek to have multiple impacts. In some areas of risk management, it is relatively easy to pin down the desired outcome. For example, when insuring a house against fire, the outcome is usually the remediation of the house to its earlier state. In the case of an intervention to help a child from a disadvantaged family, a program may be directed towards multiple outcomes including health, education and labour force participation – and potentially ranging from short-term outcomes to dealing with intergenerational disadvantage.

Second is the challenge of rigorously identifying the net impact of a social-policy program. This is particularly challenging when a program seeks to achieve long-term benefits when an individual, household or firm will be impacted by many external forces during the period over which the social program has an affect (positive or otherwise). There is great value in being more explicit in defining the desired outcomes of each program. It not only provides greater focus and clarity, but also provides a benchmark against which evaluations can more easily be made.

Integrate social-policy programs to reflect their interdependency

When social insurance programs were first developed, each program was developed in isolation, typically in response to a particular social problem or a gap in private insurance markets. As social programs proliferated, the interdependence between programs became increasingly important and, on occasion, wasteful. A good example is retirement incomes policy. The first major efforts in providing income security and dignity in retirement were the taxpayer-funded age pensions of the later nineteenth and early twentieth centuries. Following World War II, retirement income policy has evolved into the 'multi-pillar' approach that most countries now use as the benchmark of best practice. This involves a public age pension supported by mandatory savings accounts, voluntary savings, health programs and measures to support labour market participation. The multi-pillar approach reflects the fact that each type of program has different strengths and limitations; together, however, they can produce the synergies that we see in the best retirement income systems.

Other areas of policy could benefit from a similar approach, including labour market and health programs. Labour market interventions originally evolved from unemployment insurance and accident insurance schemes. Today, governments have developed a range of programs including unemployment insurance, mid-career training, job-creation schemes (such as apprenticeships and requirements to hire from disadvantaged groups) and income-contingent loans. Some are arguing for a jobs guarantee in the face of automation, precarious work and persistent business cycles. This could take any number of forms – but any programs aiming to put a floor under unemployment and/or underemployment rates would need to dovetail with the myriad of existing programs.

Similarly, health policy has broadened dramatically over recent decades to become the largest single area of government expenditure. In many OECD countries, the core of health service provision is on-demand services provided through a taxpayer-funded national health scheme. This is often supported by taxpayer-funded subsidies for private health insurance. Many countries have significant schemes that overlap (or at least interact with) these national schemes, including mandatory workplace-accident schemes, mandatory transport-accident schemes, medical indemnity insurance, voluntary private-accident insurance, disability insurance schemes and aged-care funding (often a combination of public and private programs).

Other areas of policy involve similar creeping complexity. This complexity is not a bad thing per se. The design of programs for specific purposes or cohorts can assist in better defining and evaluating outcomes.

But the growing number of social insurance programs means that the operation of these schemes should not be undertaken in isolation. Just as retirement incomes policy has benefited from the development of the pillars approach, other areas of social insurance would gain from both designing and operating social insurance programs in a way that reflects the other programs with which they interact.

Table 18.1: Reforms to improve long-term outcomes

Goal	Policy/strategy	Existing scheme (if any)
Explicitly define long-term outcomes sought	For each individual, clearly define the long-term objective(s) The objectives may not be exhaustive	Workers' compensation Compulsory transport-accident schemes Long-term care schemes
Early intervention	Develop a business case for each early intervention (preventative) scheme Identify schemes likely to generate benefits in terms of quality of care/life vs those that also reduce overall costs	Healthcare (vaccination, screening etc.) Education (early childhood) NZ Investment Approach
Long-term perspective	Set up mechanisms to provide continuity of care over the long-term Manage trade-offs, e.g. investing up-front to achieve long-term savings Where appropriate, case management	Workers' compensation Compulsory transport-accident schemes Long-term care schemes NZ Investment Approach NDIS
Client choice	Reflect each person's individual preferences in relation to trade-offs in care options Promote engagement by the client in the design of programs	NDIS Healthcare systems with relatively high choice, e.g. Sweden, Italy, NZ, Norway and the UK
Individualised care	Packages and support levels that reflect each beneficiary's needs. Where appropriate, case management	Long-term care in Japan and Germany NDIS
De-institutionalising care	To effectiveness and reduce cost	Aged care examples in Europe and North America

Goal	Policy/strategy	Existing scheme (if any)
Integration of care across different service providers	Integrated care will be facilitated by some strategies above (e.g. defining long-term outcomes) Communication across agencies Creating incentives (e.g. that depend on long-term outcomes)	Retirement incomes: Multiple pillar approach Healthcare: Intermountain, Kaiser Aged care: Beacon Hill, Netherlands, Japan

An insurance mindset

The welfare state has always been motivated (and inspired) by a combination of redistribution, universalism and social insurance. All three of these rationales should remain key factors in the design of our major social welfare programs, but a greater emphasis on insurance will produce a number of benefits that will improve long-term outcomes.

First, it will assist in moving towards a greater emphasis on explicitly defined outcomes – and rigorously evaluating the achievement of those outcomes. Second, it will create stronger incentives to mitigate risk and uncertainty, both for individuals and for governments and insurers. Finally, it will promote greater transparency and sustainability, which will become increasingly important as our society ages and the cost of complex interventions rises.

Table 18.2: Reforms to enhance insurance practices

Goal	Policy/strategy	Existing scheme (if any)
Explicitly define long-term outcomes	Clearly define long-term objective(s) Define macro objectives for each scheme. For example, in the case of transport-accident schemes, this could include overall road safety. For mandatory workers' compensation schemes, this could include workplace safety	Workers' compensation schemes Compulsory transport-accident schemes Long-term care schemes
Sustainability	Accurately measure long-term cost forecasts Assess whether current and projected revenue streams are sufficient Develop suitable reporting arrangements	Medium-term budget modelling, e.g. CBO (US), Intergenerational Report (Aust.) NZ Investment Approach

Goal	Policy/strategy	Existing scheme (if any)
Incentives to manage underlying risks	Risk-rated contributions will create incentives for participants to demonstrate that they are managing risks Schemes (and the legislation governing them) can set out explicit responsibilities for broader risk management	Workers' compensation Compulsory transport-accident schemes
Feedback mechanisms	Premium levels will reflect the effectiveness of managing long-term risks In taxpayer-funded schemes, taxation levels will reflect the sustainability of schemes. If it is necessary to increase the tax rate, this will generate a burden for taxpayers and economic distortions	Workers' compensation Compulsory transport-accident schemes
Introducing risk-rated contributions in some contexts	Introducing risk-rated contributions could lead to: (i) better risk-reduction strategies; and (ii) building up pools of resources to deal with problems that arise	Biosecurity, where a risk-rated import charge is being considered to fund border control and quarantine costs

Cost containment

Between 1950 and 1985, the size of government spending expanded dramatically across the OECD, more than doubling on average (and more than tripling in some countries). Across the OECD, the size of government spending across all levels of government then stabilised between 1985 and 2010 to, on average, just under 50 per cent of GDP. During that time, social insurance programs grew by over 5 percentage points of GDP. This reflects social insurance expanding at the expense of other government spending (such as defence or infrastructure) in many countries.

For social insurance programs to continue effectively into the future, it will be necessary to make existing spending stretch further – without compromising quality of care. As the bus auction pilot discussed in Chapter 14 shows, policy innovation can deliver improved services at a reduced cost. This will also allow for an expansion in the scope of social insurance programs, which will be important given the need to provide more coordinated services in long-term care and for government to play a more active role in managing risk in areas such as structural economic change, automation and globalisation.

When it comes to cost containment, there are two elephants in the room: the pension income system and healthcare. These are already the two largest components of the welfare state and are expected to continue to grow, given the ageing demographic.

Across the OECD, healthcare constituted 8.8 per cent of GDP in 2015, a figure forecast to increase to 10.2 per cent by 2030. This figure would be higher if it included related programs like aged care, disability and mandatory accident insurance schemes. Public expenditure on pensions constituted 8.8 per cent of GDP and was forecast to grow to 9.4 per cent. In other words, healthcare and public expenditure on pensions constituted almost 18 per cent of GDP across the OECD in 2015; that figure is expected to rise to almost 20 per cent by 2030. Beyond 2030, it is reasonable to expect further growth, given demographic projections.

Australia is slightly above the OECD in relation to healthcare expenditure as a share of GDP (9 per cent in 2015 and a projected 13.2 per cent in 2030) and well below average in relation to public pension payments (4 per cent in 2015 and a projected 4.4 per cent in 2030). The latter is in part due to the highly targeted nature of Australia's welfare system, as well as the emerging role of superannuation in supporting retirement incomes for a growing number of older Australians. Superannuation payments totalled around 5 per cent of GDP in 2020.

The following two sections outline four ways in which cost containment can be achieved without reducing the quality of services or care provided to beneficiaries.

Strategies for containing costs associated with pensions

The first thing to note is that there is a range of policies that could be implemented that would reduce the 'costs' associated with supporting retirees at a particular benefit level while not reducing their benefits. The most obvious is to remove unnecessary barriers that impede older people participating in the workforce. Older people can find it difficult to participate in the workforce due to the nature of their career (e.g. if it involves physical work) or due to ageism by some employers. But there are many older Australians who want to work more and who face barriers created by poorly designed benefits that punish those who earn above a certain (low) threshold.

There are numerous ways in which to manage individual risk better.

One is to maintain a strong public pension, which is very effective at managing longevity, inflation and investment risks for people, particularly those on low incomes. As outlined above, policies that provide people greater access to annuities could also be explored.

Society-wide risks could be managed by strengthening the second pillar – mandatory savings. This is already strong in Australia, and annual outflows from superannuation accounts to retirees are around the same size as public pension payments as a share of GDP. A strong second pillar will help to take pressure off the public pension as society ages.

Strategies for containing costs associated with healthcare

As with public pensions, there is a range of policies that would reduce the underlying risks and costs arising from ill health. As outlined above, some of these include preventative programs, investment in outpatient care and price controls in some circumstances (like single purchaser arrangements through national health). Reducing the overlap and confusion in the administration of healthcare by federal, state and local governments will also put downward pressure on underlying costs.

Individual risks can be managed better too. More opportunities could be created for people to exercise personal choice. In the UK, the NHS is trialling more client choice and in Australia, the NDIS already allocates personal packages according to a client's preferences. There are many other countries with choice models worth examining.[1]

Another example would be the use of technology to share, retain and analyse information about patients across disparate service providers. Technology can also be used to elicit client choices, for example by creating markets as in the bus pilot trial, which enabled the parents of disabled children to express preferences in relation to transport options.

It is also worth exploring ways in which to better manage systematic risks. One example receiving attention in a number of countries is aged care and long-term care. Some countries, such as Germany and Japan, are moving towards a model based more on risk-rated contributions and individualised, needs-based packages.

Extend social insurance

Social insurance already helps individuals, families and firms to manage many of the risks that they face. But many risks are not covered. In addition, a number of risks are emerging and the potential losses caused by some existing and insured risks are becoming more extreme.

Table 18.3: Reforms for extending social insurance

Extend the Coverage of Social Insurance Using Existing Risk Pooling		
Area of risk or uncertainty	**Strategy**	**Existing scheme (if any)**
Long-term care	Building up a pool based upon risk-rated contributions	Japan and Germany
Career disruption from structural economic change (e.g. from automation, AI, globalisation)	Mid-career training accounts The use of live, granular data to provide post-school training authorities with the capability to change course structures quickly to match skills requirements of emerging jobs	Accounts in Singapore, Denmark, France
House price risk	Facilitate home reversion markets as a way of sharing house price risk	Home reversion schemes for providing access to home equity

Use Government's Balance Sheet to Manage Risk		
Area of risk or uncertainty	**Strategy**	**Existing scheme (if any)**
Community sports and social clubs	'Community bonds' with low (or subsidised) interest rates, using government balance sheet and project QA	Victorian government community sports infrastructure loans
Accessing up-front capital where collateral is problematic and outcomes are uncertain.	Income-contingent loans for public housing, health, business innovation, access to legal aid	HECS in Australia (and higher education in many other countries)
Longevity risk	Government-offered annuities to provide liquidity/consumer confidence	OASDI and other public pension pillars offer this (even if not explicitly priced for individuals)
Market failure: Thin markets, e.g. access to specialists in regional areas Coordination externalities in transport	Market design using advanced optimisation and auctions that elicit consumer preferences and promote competition among service providers	Bus pilot for school with children with autism in Victoria

SYSTEMATIC RISKS

Our society faces a number of systematic risks: pandemics, natural disasters, climate change, ageing and major economic downturns. Currently, governments tend to adopt a reactive approach to many of these risks. Adopting a more rigorous insurance framework to managing these risks will strengthen our capacity to understand the uncertainty that we face and to mitigate and manage the potential for loss.

Preparation for natural disasters and pandemics

Systematic risks would benefit from a greater emphasis on prevention, mitigation and preparation. The Covid-19 pandemic has highlighted the imbalance between investment in preparedness on the one hand and massive remediation costs on the other. In most countries, investment in preparation for systematic risks is miniscule, compared to the cost of dealing with the consequences of these events.

Quantify risk where possible – but respect uncertainty

There are many potential losses whose likelihood can be quantified with a high degree of accuracy, including the average life expectancy of different cohorts and property damage from fire for different types of building. Where this is the case, well-functioning private insurance markets often emerge. Access to masses of data and growing computing power is expanding the capacity to accurately quantify potential losses.

But even in the face of exponentially increasing computational power and ever more sophisticated models, it is becoming clear that accurately quantifying the likelihood of some potential losses remains elusive. 'Uncertainty' is a riddle that may never be solved in some contexts. In developing social insurance programs that share the burden of potential loss, we need to acknowledge the limitations of how much we can quantify the future world – and indeed, our own individual destinies. This challenge only grows the longer the time horizon, a major problem for managing systematic challenges such as climate change and ageing.

In light of this, we need to embrace three strategies. First, we need to invest more in our modelling and forecasting capability. We spend a minuscule fraction on this capability compared with the amount spent on dealing with disasters after the fact.

Second, when quantification doesn't provide sensible answers, we must be willing to use judgement. When we arrive at our defence budget each year, it isn't the solution to an equation. It is based on a benchmark that is developed by drawing upon accrued experience and judgement as to the baseline spending that makes sense given a range of factors, including: how imminent threats are; the challenges of ramping up capacity at short notice; and the spending of other nations (both competitors and allies). A similar approach should be adopted when developing an annual benchmark for investment in mitigation and preparation for natural disasters and pandemics.

Third, we must be flexible to update as new information comes to hand. We know that some of the problems that we face – such as climate change and the ageing of society – will evolve over decades, and possibly longer. In calibrating our immediate response to these challenges we should use our best possible estimates of long-term trajectories. But we must do so knowing that there is a good chance that we will be wrong and that, in all likelihood, we will need to adjust. Risks are a fact of life for both individuals and societies. Some risks are relatively easy to manage – some are a matter of life and death. Some risks can be meaningfully quantified and some cannot. Regardless of the precise nature of the unknown future, we are almost always better off facing that future collectively rather than alone. At its heart, the welfare state is built around the concept of social insurance. Our key welfare institutions work best when they are focused on long-term outcomes, individualised service delivery and sustainable sources of funding. Honing the risk-management practices of our key social insurance institutions will go a long way to improving the achievement of these overarching goals, delivering more effective and resilient protection for those who need it the most.

Acknowledgements

I wrote much of this book while in COVID-19 lockdown. This gave me occasion to reflect on the welfare state both in terms of the short-term support that it provided individuals and the challenges at a society-wide level of predicting and managing major calamities. I hope that this book points to ways in which we can strengthen our already successful welfare-state institutions.

I have been extremely fortunate that so many people have taken the time to either discuss the ideas underpinning this book and/or to closely review (often lengthy) drafts. For this I am immensely grateful.

First, to the academics who generously took the time to carefully read the draft manuscript and pass on detailed comments: Professors Peter Lindert, Kevin Davis, John Quiggin, Peter Dawkins, Richard Holden, Ross Garnaut and Mark Considine. This is not an academic book, but I hope that it benefits from and appropriately incorporates rigorous academic thinking and empirical research. And of course, as they say in the classics, all errors are my own.

Thanks also to the policy experts and thought leaders who reviewed the entire text or sections for accuracy and completeness as well as stress-tested policy ideas for their real-world applicability: Thomas Hogg, Emma Dawson, Peter Harris, Gordon Noble, Paul O'Connor, Paul Tilley, Glen McCrae, Tom Cameron, Andrea Forbes, Liam Houlihan, Alex Sanchez, Vanessa Beenders, John Trowbridge, Rod Glover, Nathan Lambert, Bruce Bonyhady, Hassan Noura, Gary Stoneham, George Karagiannakis, John Donovan, Nick Dyrenfurth and Bill Scales. The collective experience and wisdom of this group is vast. If I am ever in a position to develop or implement policy, I am sure I will once again call upon their advice. Thanks in particular to Peter Lindert and Thomas Hogg for extremely detailed comments and for ongoing correspondence in relation to matters in which they took particular interest (or issue with!).

The publishing industry is not easy to penetrate, and I greatly appreciate the insights from Richard McGregor, George Williams and Kath Cummins in relation to navigating this complex world. In addition, so many of my colleagues read drafts or discussed the underpinning policy ideas, despite the highly congested state of their diaries. Particular thanks to Andrew Leigh, who generously read the entire manuscript very carefully and made many perceptive suggestions. Thanks also to Jim Chalmers, Linda Burney, Dave Smith, Michelle Rowland and Julian Hill.

I was fortunate be working for Bill Shorten as a policy adviser when he was conceiving and then helping to implement the NDIS and NIIS. Since then, I have greatly enjoyed discussing the potential for social insurance with him. Many of those ideas are reflected in this book.

Many family members and high school and university friends supported me throughout the research, writing and editing processes. Thanks in particular to John van Beurden and Brian Dineen for such careful, thoughtful and thorough revisions. Thanks also to Julian, Adrian, Paul, Declan, Declan and Damien.

To my incredible office, thanks firstly for the stimulating and collegiate atmosphere in which we work. So many of you contributed deep insights and rigorous research without which the book would have been far poorer (or, more likely, unfinished). Thanks to Iwan for reading multiple drafts and for always going above and beyond – and to Chris Campbell, Liam O'Brien, Hasan Erdogan, Luke Parnis and Louisa Russell. Thanks also to the parliamentary library staff who pointed me to and sourced so much material – and who also researched a number of specific empirical points.

I am very grateful to Bill Kelty for writing the foreword and for many conversations in relation to the big canvas on which, at its best, Labor paints.

Thanks to Emma Fajgenbaum, Jo Rosenberg and Chris Feik from Black Inc. Thanks to Chris for taking a punt on me. Thanks to Jo for resolving so many seemingly impossible typesetting and structural challenges. And thanks to Emma for her insightful and expert editing, which went far beyond improving the structure and readability of my arguments.

Finally, and most importantly, thanks to Sarah and Carina for allowing me to leave early for work and occasionally come home late to devote endless hours poring over my (in Carina's view, 'boring') material. I am eternally grateful to Sarah for encouraging me to pursue my policy passions, and for her unwavering support. And thanks to Carina for vetoing another book for the foreseeable future.

Appendices

APPENDIX 1: SOURCES FOR TABLE 3.4

Row 1: Total health funding by source of funds from Table 3.1a, Australian Institute of Health and Welfare, 'Health Expenditure Australia 2018 19', AIHW Health and Welfare Expenditure Series No. 66, AIHW, Canberra, 2020, p. 20.

Row 3: Private health insurance pays for some or all costs of treatment in a public or private hospital as a private patient, and health services not covered under the MBS, such as dental, physiotherapy.

The Australian Institute of Health and Welfare (AIHW) explains (p. 48): 'The funds used by private health insurance providers are indirectly sourced from individuals who pay premiums to these providers. These premiums are not treated as health spending and are not reflected in health spending estimates … To avoid double counting, health insurance provider spending estimates do not include subsidies from the Australian Government through health insurance premium rebates.' Australian Institute of Health and Welfare, 'Health Expenditure Australia 2018-19', AIHW Health and Welfare Expenditure Series No. 66, 2020, p. 48.

Row 6: Relating to the figure of A$8.25 billion for public expenditure on workers' compensation. This value represents total payments made by Australian schemes in 2016–17 (Safe Work Australia, 'Comparative Performance Monitoring Report, Part 3: Premiums, Entitlements and Scheme Performance', 20th Edition, 2019). Schemes in NSW, VIC, QLD, SA and the Commonwealth are mostly public, whereas the WA, SA, TAS, NT and ACT schemes are mostly private. For schemes, see, for example, Safe Work Australia, 'Comparison of Workers' Compensation Arrangements in Australia and New Zealand', 27th Edition, 2019.

Row 6: Relating to the figure of A$4.0 billion of private insurance expenditure on workers' compensation. The sum of general insurers' underwriting performance, specifically 'Gross earned premiums' and 'Net incurred claims' for 'Public and Product Liability', 'Professional Indemnity' and 'Employers' Liability' insurances (APRA, 'Quarterly General Insurance Performance Statistics: June 2021', 26 August 2021).

Row 7: 'General insurers' underwriting performance, specifically 'Gross earned premiums' and 'Net incurred claims' for CTP Motor Vehicle' insurances (APRA), 'Quarterly General Insurance Performance Statistics: June 2021', 26 August 2021).

Rows 8–11, 13: Australian Government, 'Budget Strategy and Outlook: Budget Paper No. 1: 2020–21', 2020, pp. 6–26.

Row 12: AIHW gave a total figure of A$195.7 billion. The figure cited in this column is larger and includes some broader programs in the 'health ecosystem', some of which are broader than just healthcare per se (e.g. carer's allowance for those with disability and disability support pension). The higher figure is intended to give a sense of the large and growing size of the broader healthcare/caring sector (Australian Institute of Health and Welfare, 'Health Expenditure Australia 2018-19', AIHW Health and Welfare Expenditure Series No. 66, 2020, p. 11, Table 2.1). Note: It can be difficult to disentangle public and private spending in health. For example, a specialist is a private practitioner who can determine their own fees; Medicare may pay a specified rebate for the service with the patient paying the remainder as an out-of-pocket cost.

Row 13: A$17.3 billion life insurance direct premiums ($14.9 billion net policy revenue) (2019–20). $11.5 billion in death and disability claims ($17.2 billion gross policy expenses) (2019–20). Australian Prudential Regulatory Authority (APRA), 'Quarterly General Insurance Performance Statistics: June 2021', 26 August 2021, Table 1a. No direct income protection sources located but life insurance data includes disability premiums and payouts.

There is also 'tax expenditure' of $2.0 billion in terms of forgone tax revenue from tax deductibility of life and TPD premiums inside of superannuation. Average of the forgone revenue from the deductibility of life and total permanent disability insurance premiums provided inside of superannuation. The Treasury, 'Tax Benchmarks and Variations Statement 2020', January 2021, pp. 80–87.

Row 14: Relating to the figure of A$41.1 billion. This is an average of the forgone revenues from the sum of concessional taxation of capital gains for superannuation funds, employer superannuation contributions, personal superannuation contributions, superannuation entity earnings, unfunded superannuation, superannuation measures for low income earners, and exemption for small business assets held for more than fifteen years; less tax on excess non-concessional superannuation contributions, tax on funded superannuation income streams and tax on funded superannuation lump sums (The Treasury, Tax Benchmarks and Variations Statement 2020, January 2021, pp. 80–87).

There were A$102.1 billion employer contributions and $34.6 billion member contributions: Association of Superannuation Funds of Australia, 'Superannuation Statistics', September 2021. Especially table 'aggregate contributions'. In Australian Taxation Office, 'Taxation statistics 2018-19', 2021, it is reported that APRA regulated and SMSF super funds claimed $10.45 billion in 'Death or disability premiums/ Insurance premiums'.

Row 14: Relating to payments out of funds. Quarterly superannuation performance statistics, September 2021. APRA, 'Quarterly Superannuation Performance Statistics', September 2021, pp. 1–7. This figure reflects benefits payments for pensions from entities with more than four members. This was A$40.053 billion for the year ending September 2020 and $39.380 billion for the year ending September 2021. This does not include the component of lump sum payments used for living expenses (as opposed to being reinvested and does not include payments from entities with four members or less.

Row 15: Relating to public expenditure of A$21.2 billion. Government aged-care expenditure is sourced from Australian Institute of Health and Welfare, 'Aged Care Data Snapshot 2020 – third release', October 2020, 'expenditure summary' tab. This excludes aged-care revenue such as recoveries and cross-billing, and additional Commonwealth Government expenditure not listed separately above, such as expenditure through the Australian Aged Care Quality and Safety Commission.

Row 15: Relating to private expenditure. Individual contributions to aged care are only available for three programs. This information has been sourced from the Aged Care Financing Authority's annual report on the funding and financing of the aged-care industry (Aged Care Financing Authority, 'Ninth Report on the Funding and Financing of the Aged Care Industry – July 2021', 2021, p. 10).

Row 17: 2019–20 expenditure was much higher than normal due to impact of COVID-19 March–June 2020. Expenditure estimated to return to A$15 billion annually from 2022–23 (Australian Government, 'Budget Strategy and Outlook: Budget Paper No. 1: 2020–21', 2020, pp. 6–26).

Row 17: Australian Government, 'Budget Strategy and Outlook: Budget Paper No. 1: 2020–21', 2020, pp. 6–39.

Row 21: Social housing is housing that is made available at below market rates to low-income households who are unable to access suitable accommodation in the private rental market. It comprises public housing, community housing, state-owned and managed Indigenous housing (SOMIH) and Indigenous community housing. The term 'social housing' was coined to account for the fact that in recent years Australian governments have placed an increased emphasis on promoting private- and community-sector provision of affordable housing. The term 'public housing' refers specifically to state and territory owned and managed housing.

The figure A$4.3 billion includes Australian government funding for services provided under the National Housing and Homelessness Agreement (NHHA). It does not include non-recurrent, capital expenditure. In 2019–20 state and territory government capital expenditure for social housing was $1.4 billion. See Table 4, below for a breakdown of expenditure by state and territory. Source: Productivity Commission, 'Report on Government Services 2021: Part G: Housing and Homelessness', Canberra, 2021, Table 18A.1, Table GA.1.

Row 22: Australian Taxation Office, 'HELP Statistics 2020–21', 1 November 2021, Table 1.

Row 22: Australian Government, 'Portfolio Budget Statements 2020–21: Budget Related Paper No. 1.12', Social Services Portfolio, 2020, p. 35.

Row 23: To smooth the volatility of payments, this is a ten-year average of the NDRRA payment to the states plus ad-hoc payments in disaster-related programs. See Table 5 for annual values and calculations used.

Row 24: The A$24b figure includes the sum of general insurers' underwriting performance, specifically 'Gross earned premiums' and 'Net incurred claims' for 'Houseowners/householders', 'Domestic motor vehicle' and 'Commercial motor vehicle' insurances in APRA, 'Quarterly General Insurance Performance Statistics: June 2021', 26 August 2021. This is an overestimate for 'natural disasters' as it includes all insured activities.

Row 24: 'General insurers' underwriting performance', specifically 'Gross earned premiums' and 'Net incurred claims' for 'Fire and ISR' insurances. APRA, 'Quarterly General Insurance Performance Statistics: June 2021', 26 August 2021.

Row 25: Value of special appropriation to the attorney-general's department. Excludes recoveries. Attorney-general's department, 'Annual Report 2019–20', 2020, p. 196. In addition, there was A$107.6 million in recovered amounts added to consolidated revenue. Part 5 of the Fair Entitlements Guarantee Act 2012 allows for 'Recovery of advance' through winding up or bankruptcy or from 'eligible persons'. According to attorney-general's department, the FEG Recovery Program recovered $92.63 million of FEG Advances and associated costs, which are returned to consolidated revenue. In addition, the program recovered $14.94 million of employee entitlements that were not covered by the FEG scheme. Attorney-general's department, 'Annual Report 2019–20', 2020, p. 90.

APPENDIX 2: SOURCES FOR TABLE 3.5

Most of the figures in columns 1, 2 and 3 are from Christopher Chantrill, 'US Welfare Spending', US Government Spending, 2021. These figures have been cross-checked with official US Government data, e.g. from the St Louis Federal Reserve.

The figures relating to Medicaid and Medical Services in Rows 2 and 3 are from Centers for Medicare & Medicaid Services, 'National Health Expenditures 2020 Highlights', 2020.

The figure of US$62.3 billion relating to workers' compensation in row 4 is from David Powell & Seth Seabury, 'Medical Care Spending and Labor Market Outcomes: Evidence from Workers' Compensation Reforms', *American Economic Review*, vol. 108, no. 10, 2018, pp. 2995–3027.

The estimate for natural disaster funding in row 11 is from Jeff Stein and Andrew Van Dam, 'Taxpayer Spending on U.S. Disaster Fund Explodes Amid Climate Change, Population Trends', *Washington Post*, 22 April 2019.

The figure in row 12 is from Insurance Information Institute, 'Facts + Statistics: Industry Overview', New York, 2020.

APPENDIX 3: TOTAL GOVERNMENT SPENDING TO GDP IN 1950, 1980 AND 2010

Country	Govt/GDP 1950	Govt/GDP 1985	Govt/GDP 2010	Change 1950–1985	Change 1985–2010	Change social ins. 1985–2010
Significant increase in government share between 1985 and 2010						
Spain	11.8	30.2	47.3	18.3	17.1	8.7
Greece	26.2	41.9	57.3	15.7	15.4	8.5
Portugal	9.9	43.6	53.2	33.6	9.7	14.7
Japan	17.3	35.7	42.1	18.4	6.4	11.0
France	25.3	53.9	58.9	28.6	5.0	5.4
US	15.6	39.7	44.7	24.1	4.9	6.5
Moderate increase or decrease in government share between 1985 and 2010						
Switzerland	10.3	31.7	34.7	21.4	3.0	5.0
Germany	29.5	49.4	49.4	19.9	0.0	3.7
UK	35.6	52.9	51.7	17.2	-1.2	4.6
Sweden	19.3	55.2	53.3	35.8	-1.8	-0.7
Norway	18.0	48.9	47.1	30.9	-1.8	4.7
Austria	32.4	56.8	54.5	24.4	-2.3	4.3
Italy	18.8	58.3	55.1	39.5	-3.2	7.5
Denmark	10.4	63.7	59.3	53.3	-4.5	9.6
Significant decrease in government share between 1985 and 2010						
Ireland	24.7	62.1	57.0	37.4	-5.1	2.0
Australia	13.8	43.6	37.9	29.9	-5.7	4.6
New Zealand	23.2	42.3	35.9	19.2	-6.4	3.1
Canada	17.8	56.0	46.2	38.2	-9.8	1.1
Netherlands	26.5	63.6	52.8	37.1	-10.8	-1.7
Belgium	23.1	68.6	56.8	45.5	-11.8	2.8
AVERAGE	**20.5**	**49.9**	**49.8**	**29.4**	**-0.1**	**5.3**

APPENDIX 4: CHANGING PATTERNS OF GOVERNMENT SPENDING IN WESTERN EUROPE, 1870–2015

The changing role of government in the UK and the US is broadly matched in Europe. Figure Ap. 1 shows spending by function in Europe from 1870 to 2020.[1] As in the US and the UK, total government spending in Europe was less than 10 per cent of GDP prior to the twentieth century. Moreover, before World War I, government spending was almost entirely comprised of defence spending, justice, general administration; and basic infrastructure. As in other advanced economies, social insurance spending rose sharply across Europe during the twentieth century, increasing from almost nothing during the inter-war years to a quarter or more of the entire economy by 1980.

Figure Ap.1: Government spending in selected European countries, 1870–2015[2]

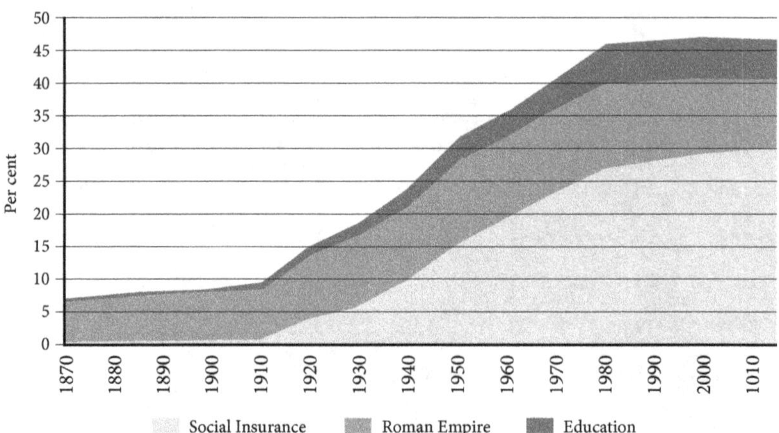

APPENDIX 5: THE CHANGING MIX OF DIRECT CONSUMPTION BY GOVERNMENT AND TRANSFER PAYMENTS

Figure Ap. 2 shows the changing role of government in the economy by looking at US GDP by value-add across major industries over the past seventy years. 'Value-add' reflects how much an industry adds to total GDP after netting off the inputs that it uses.

The industries at the bottom of each bar have grown significantly as a share of GDP since World War II: finance, professional and business services; education and health; and information. Together, these sectors have growth by 29 per cent of GDP, over a quarter of the economy. This reflects the rise of services and IT.

The industries towards the middle of the bars have stayed about the same size over the past seventy years: mining; wholesale distribution; utilities; construction; and the arts. These sectors represented just under 20 per cent of the economy at the conclusion of World War II and today.

Finally, the industries towards the top of the bars are those that have materially shrunk, as a share of value-add to GDP: manufacturing; agriculture; retail; and transport. Together, these four sectors have shrunk around 28 per cent of GDP – the mirror image of the four growth sectors. Over the periods, the share of manufacturing in GDP by value-add has more than halved, and agriculture fallen by around 90 per cent.

What is particularly telling is that the top section is largely unchanged throughout a long period of dramatic economic change. This is government. In 1947, government represented 13.4 per cent of the economy, by value-add. By 2018, the share of government was 12.4 per cent. Government's share of 'value-add' reflects areas of the economy in which it directly purchases and adds value by using or consuming goods and services – sectors such as defence; public order; transport infrastructure; some utilities; health; and education.

As can be seen in Figure Ap. 2, the period since World War II saw a sharp rise in the size of US government as a share of the economy. But this was not reflected in government's role as a direct consumer and producer of goods and services. Rather, it reflects a ballooning in the role of government in transfer payments, usually contingent on loss.

Figure Ap. 2: US GDP by industry value add, 1947–2018

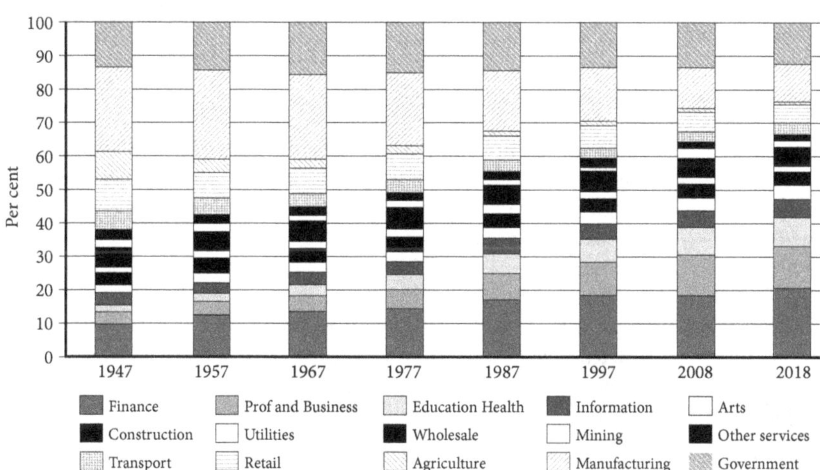

APPENDIX 6: LONG-TERM GDP AND GOVERNMENT SPENDING TIME SERIES AUSTRALIA

A number of data sources were combined:

- For GDP:
  - Barnard, ANU source papers
  - Other economic historians
  - ABS
  - RBA
  - Treasury
- For government spending by purpose:
  - ABS (both published and unpublished)
  - RBA
  - Treasury, multiple
  - Lindert, 2004, 2016, 2021
  - Fishback, 2020
  - *Our World in Data* (Oxford), which in turn relies on various sources
  - OECD, multiple

These data sources were combined to develop continues time series, to the extent possible. Deflators were used to create real variables. Where there are time series breaks, this is reflected by different shading on graphs.

Reconciling data:

- Total government/GDP:
  - Time series based on national statistical agencies vs *Our World in Data*
- Government spending by purpose
  - Time series based on national statistical agencies vs Lindert/Fishback but also vs OECD

APPENDIX 7: LONG-TERM GDP AND GOVERNMENT SPENDING TIME SERIES US

Figure Ap. 3 shows the size of US government across the same three functional groupings from 1900–2050: Roman Empire spending; education; and social insurance. Unlike the graph for the UK in Chapter 3, Figure Ap. 3 also includes projected government spending shares for next thirty years, based on Congressional Budget Office (CBO) projections.[3] This figure reflects both the increase in the overall size of government and the changing composition of spending.

Figure Ap. 3 shows government spending increasing between 2020 and 2050 based on CBO analysis. This doesn't reflect what is most likely to happen but, rather, what would have to happen to government spending as a share of GDP to maintain current policy settings. It is largely driven by public healthcare costs and social security. If the public doesn't have an appetite to increase future taxation levels (as would be required by the CBO's projections based on current policy settings), social welfare benefits could only be maintained at current levels by reducing other areas of government expenditure such as defence, education or infrastructure. One of the key issues that this book examines is how to maintain, and hopefully improve, the effectiveness of major social insurance programs while containing overall costs.

A number of data sources were combined:

- For GDP:
  - BEA
  - St Louis Fed
- For government spending by purpose:
  - BEA
  - St Louis Fed
  - Budgets
  - CBO
  - Lindert, 2004, 2016, 2021
  - Fishback, 2020
  - *Our World in Data* (Oxford), which in turn relies on various sources
  - OECD

These data sources were combined to develop continues time series, to the extent possible. Deflators were used to create real variables. Where there are time series breaks, this is reflected by different shading on graphs.

Reconciling data:

- Total government / GDP:
  - Time series based on national statistical agencies vs *Our World in Data*
- Governmentt spending by purpose
  - Time series based on national statistical agencies vs Lindert/Fishback but also vs OECD

Figure Ap. 3: US government spending by function (per cent of GDP), 1900–2050[4]

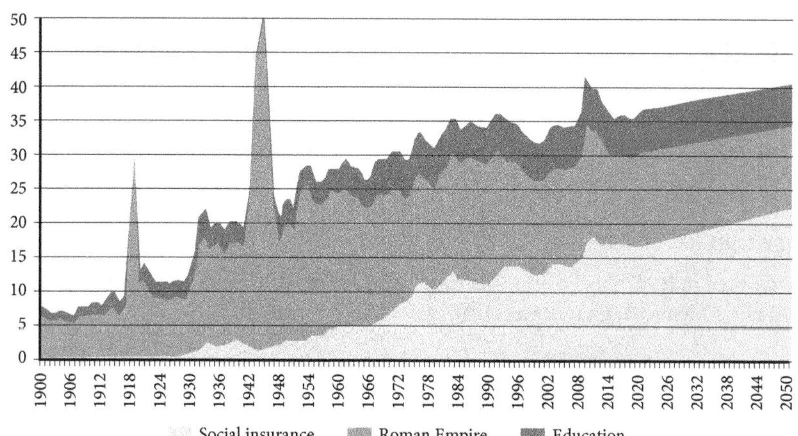

APPENDIX 8: LONG-TERM GDP AND GOVERNMENT SPENDING TIME SERIES UK

A number of data sources were combined:

- For GDP:
  - Pipe rolls
  - UK Parliamentary Library
  - UK Treasury
- For government spending by purpose:
  - Pipe rolls
  - UK Parliamentary Library
  - Historical sources (e.g. summarising budget papers 1900–1980)
  - Lindert, 2004, 2016, 2021
  - Fishback, 2020
  - *Our World in Data* (Oxford), which in turn relies on various sources
  - OECD

These data sources were combined to develop continues time series, to the extent possible. Deflators were used to create real variables. Where there are time series breaks, this is reflected by different shading on graphs.

Reconciling data:

- Total government / GDP:
  - Time series based on national statistical agencies vs *Our World in Data*
- Government spending by purpose
  - Time series based on national statistical agencies vs Lindert/Fishback but also vs OECD

Endnotes

FOREWORD

1 Quoted in R.N. Ebbels (ed.), *The Australian Labor Movement, 1850–1907*, Noel Ebbels Memorial Committee, 1960, p. 244.

1. INTRODUCTION

1 William Beveridge, 'Social Insurance and Allied Services', Cmd. (Command Paper) 6404, November 1942, p. 6.

2 The state of Victoria has a population of 6.5 million people and a budget of around A$80 billion.

3 Economists use 'efficiency' as a measure of how distortionary a tax is. The more distortionary a tax is, the more that it will negatively impact on economic output and overall welfare per dollar raised.

4 Jennifer Davidson, Ralph Hampson and Marie Connolly (eds), *Service Navigation: Research and Practice in Health and Human Services*, Macmillan Education Limited, London, 2020.

5 Camilla Cavendish, *Extra Time: 10 Lessons for Living Longer Better*, HarperCollins, New York, 2020, pp. 172–73.

6 Given the confusion that can arise in relation to the use of the terms 'systemic' and 'systematic', it is worth revisiting the way in which this book will define each term. In this book, the word 'systematic' is used to refer to risks that affect an entire society or population. In some contexts, the word 'systemic' is used for this purpose. Importantly, 'systematic' and 'systemic' are terms that do not have universally agreed definitions. They are sometimes used interchangeably. Some sources attribute 'systemic' with something that affects an entire system (such as a pandemic or economic collapse) and 'systematic' with something that involves a 'method or plan'. See 'Systematic vs Systemic: There's a System to the Difference', *Dictionary.com*, 16 June 2020.

In the specific context of risk, 'systemic risk' sometimes denotes a risk associated with a company or industry that could trigger a significant broader collapse and 'systematic risk' denotes the risk inherent to the entire market, attributable to a mix of factors including economic, socio-political, and market-related events (or 'non-diversifiable' risk). 'Systemic Risk vs Systematic Risk: What's the Difference?', *Investopedia,* 29 September 2021. For present purposes, the term 'systematic' will be used to denote risks that affect the whole of society and that are non-diversifiable.

7 Joseph Malins, *A Fence or an Ambulance*, 1895.

8 Gøsta Esping-Anderson, *The Three Worlds of Welfare Capitalism*, Polity Press, Cambridge, 1990. According to Esping-Anderson, the 'liberal' model is typified by Australia, the US, UK, Canada, New Zealand and Ireland, the 'conservative'

exists in Austria, France, Germany and Italy, and the social democratic model exists in Denmark, the Netherlands, Norway and Sweden.

9 Peter Whiteford, 'The Welfare Expenditure Debate: "Economic Myths of the Left and Right" revisited', *Economic and Labour Relations Review*, vol. 17, no. 1, 2006, pp. 35–77; Peter Whiteford, 'Targeting, Redistribution and Poverty Reduction in OECD Countries', *Welfare State Feedbacks: From Outputs to Inputs*, Conference Paper, Aalborg, 31 January – 2 February 2007.

2. A BRIEF HISTORY OF PRIVATE AND PUBLIC RISK MANAGEMENT

1 Extensive explorations of the centrality of the family in risk management can be found in many sources. Some recent examples include: Jared Diamond, *The World Until Yesterday: What Can We Learn From Traditional Societies?*, Penguin Books, London, 2012; Larry Siedentop, *Inventing the Individual: The Origins of Western Liberalism*, Harvard University Press, Cambridge, 2017; Yuval Harari, *Sapiens: A Brief History of Humankind*, Harper, New York, 2011.

2 Woody Allen, *Love and Death*, Jack Rollins & Charles H. Joffe Productions, 1975.

3 *Government at a Glance 2021*, OECD Publishing, Paris, 2021, p. 87.

4 See Chapters 2 and 3 for data and sources for these estimates.

5 For a useful discussion of the overarching role of risk and risk management in society, see: Peter Bernstein, *Against the Gods: The Remarkable Story of Risk*, John Wiley & Sons, New York, 1996.

6 This can be traced back thousands of years societies to the earlier societies, including highly sophisticated facilities in Ancient Egypt and China. See Bas Leeuwen, Peter, Földvári & Reinhard Pirngruber, 'Markets in Pre-Industrial Societies: Storage in Hellenistic Babylonia in the Medieval English Mirror', *Journal of Global History*, vol 6. no. 2, 2011, pp. 169–93.

7 Miles Kimball, 'Farmers' Cooperatives as Behavior toward Risk', *American Economic Review*, vol. 78, no. 1, 1998, pp. 224–32; Gary Richardson, 'The Prudent Village: Risk Pooling Institutions in Medieval English Agriculture', *Journal of Economic History*, vol. 65, no. 2, 2005, pp. 386–413; Marco Van Leeuwen, 'Guilds and Middle Class Welfare 1550-1800: Provisions for Burial, Sickness, Old Age and Widowhood', *Economic History Review*, vol. 65, no. 1, 2012, pp. 61–90.

8 Joseph Stiglitz, 'Incentives and Risk Sharing in Share Cropping', *Review of Economic Studies*, vol. 41, no. 2, 1974, pp. 219–56; Deidre McCloskey, 'English Open Fields as Behavior towards Risk', *Research in Economic History*, vol. 1, 1976, pp. 124–70; Deidre McCloskey, 'The Prudent Peasant: New Findings on Open Fields', *Journal of Economic History*, vol. 51, 1991, pp. 343–55.

9 Paxson finds high rates of saving out of transitory income when examining the impact of variable rainfall on farm household incomes. See Christina Paxson, 'Using Weather Variability to Estimate the Response of Savings to Transitory Income in Thailand', *American Economic Review*, vol. 82, no. 1, 1992, pp. 15–33.

10 Joseph Stiglitz, 'Peer Monitoring and Credit Markets', *Work Bank Economic Review*, vol. 4, no. 3, 1990, pp. 351–66.

11 McCloskey, 1976, pp. 124–30; McCloskey, 1991, pp. 343–55.

12 See also the German credit cooperative of the nineteenth century, which formed a model that was adopted in many other countries. See Timothy Besley, 'Nonmarket Institutions for Credit and Risk Sharing in Low-Income Countries,' *Journal of Economic Perspectives*, vol. 9, no. 3, 1995, pp. 119–20.

13 A group of individuals periodically allocates funds to one member, either randomly or by bidding, which can enhance both capital accumulation and risk-sharing if households face shocks to their health or incomes. Besley argues that his form of risk sharing is found worldwide, including Chit funds in India, Hui in Taiwan, Tontines in Senegal and Kye in Korea. See Besley, pp. 115–20.
14 Christopher Udry, 'Risk and Insurance in a Rural Credit Market: An Empirical Investigation in Northern Nigeria', *Review of Economic Studies*, vol. 61, no. 3, 1994, pp. 495–526.
15 Robert Townsend, 'Consumption Insurance: An Evaluation of Risk Bearing Systems in Low-Income Economies', *Journal of Economic Perspectives*, vol. 9, no. 3, 1995, p. 85.
16 Townsend, 1995, p. 92.
17 Robert Townsend, 'Risk and Insurance in Village India', *Econometrica*, vol. 62, no. 3, 1994, pp. 539–91.
18 Fumio Hayashi, Joseph Altonji & Laurence Kotlikoff, 'Risk-Sharing Between and Within Families', *Econometrica*, vol. 64, no. 2, 1996, pp. 261–94; Orazio Attanasio, Costas Meghir & Corina Mommaerts, 'Insurance in Extended Family Networks', NBER Working Papers No. 21059, Massachusetts, 2015; Joseph Altonji, Fumio Hayashi & Laurence Kotlikoff, 'Is the Extended Family Altruistically Linked? Direct Tests Using Micro Data', *American Economic Review*, vol. 82, no. 5, 1992, pp. 1177–98.
19 Asger Lau Andersen, Niels Johannesen, & Adam Sheridan, 'Bailing out the Kids: New Evidence on Informal Insurance from One Billion Bank Transfers', CEBI Working Papers No. 19/20, CEBI, Copenhagen, 2020.
20 Jean-François Outreville, *Theory and Practice of Insurance*, Springer, New York, 1998, p. 15. See also 'The history of insurance', *Fortius Inter Parties,* 2022.
21 Peter Temin, 'A Market Economy in the Early Roman Empire', *The Journal of Roman Studies*, vol. 91, 2001, p. 175.
22 Mihir Desai, *The Wisdom of Finance: Discovering Humanity in the World of Risk and Return,* Houghton Mifflin Harcourt, Boston, 2017, pp. 22–23.
23 W.R. Vance, 'The Early History of Insurance Law', *Columbia Law Review*, vol. 8, no. 1, January 1908, p. 1; David Moss, *When All Else Fails: Government as the Ultimate Risk Manager*, Harvard University Press, London, 2002, p. 27.
24 Vance, 1908, pp. 6–7.
25 'Back Matter', *Transactions of the Faculty of Actuaries*, vol. 22, no. 185, Cambridge University Press, Institute and Faculty of Actuaries, 1953, pp. 441–45.
26 A century before Pascal and Fermat, an Italian mathematician, Girolamo Cardano, made a significant contribution through his text *Liber de Ludo Aleae* (Book on Games of Chance), which was written around 1564 but not published until 1663.
27 Luca Pacioli, *Summa de arithmetic, geometrica et proportionalita,* Paganinus de Paganinis, Venice, 1494. Luca Pacioli was an Italian mathematician, Franciscan friar, collaborator with Leonardo da Vinci and is often referred to as 'The Father of Accounting and Bookkeeping' due his contribution to the double-entry system of bookkeeping.
28 Peter Bernstein, *Against the Gods: The Remarkable Story of Risk,* John Wiley & Sons, New York, 1996, p. 43; Florence Nightingale David, *Games, Gods and Gambling,* Hafner Publishing Company, New York, 1962, p. 37.
29 Victor Katz, *A History of Mathematics*, HarperCollins College Publishers, 1993, Section 11.3.1.

30 'NBA teams that recovered from a 1-3 deficit in playoffs', *Land of Basketball*, 2020.
31 Bernstein, 1996, p. 43; David, 1962, p. 44.
32 John Graunt, *Natural and Political Observations Mentioned in a Following Index, and Made Upon the Bills of Mortality*, In David Smith & Nathan Keyfitz (eds), *Mathematical Demography: Selected Papers*, Springer, New York, 1977, pp. 11–20. See also: Bernstein, 1996, pp. 74–75.
33 Here Graunt is probably referring to the 'quickening' of the fetus – i.e. when it first moves in the womb. 'Quicken' is taken from the Old Norse *kviker*, which is derived from the Latin *vivus*, meaning alive. See: Kenneth Wachter, *Essential Demographic Methods*, Harvard University Press, Cambridge, 2014, p. 162.
34 Bernstein, p. 80.
35 Since World War II, the analysis has focused on the city of Wrocław in Poland.
36 Desai, 2017, p. 27.
37 The English government would continue issuing annuities that did not take account of the purchaser's age until 1789. David Weir, 'Tontines, Public Finance, and Revolution in France and England, 1688–1789', *Journal of Economic History*, vol. 49, no. 1, 1989, pp. 95–124.
38 Desai, 2017, p. 28; Roger Ransom & Richard Sutch. 'Tontine Insurance and the Armstrong Investigation: A Case of Stifled Innovation, 1868–1905', *Journal of Economic History*, vol. 47, no. 2, 1987, pp. 379–90.
39 Ransom & Sutch, 1987, pp. 379–90.
40 'It's Sleazy, It's Totally Illegal, and Yet it Could Become the Future of Retirement', *Washington Post*, 28 September 2015.
41 'Many Lloyd's Investors Facing Loss of Fortunes', *New York Times*, 27 April 1993.
42 John Kay & Mervyn King, *Radical Uncertainty: Decision-Making Beyond the Numbers*, W. W. Norton & Company, New York, 2020, p. 340.
43 'Warren Buffett Rescues Lloyd's Names', *The Guardian*, 21 October 2006.
44 Vance, 1908, pp. 3–4.
45 Jonathan Scott Perry, *The Roman Collegia: The Modern Evolution of an Ancient Concept* Brill, Leiden, 2006, pp. 64–65.
46 Shashidharan Kutty, *Managing Life Insurance*, Prentice Hall of India, New Delhi, 2008, p. 156.
47 Desai, 2017, p. 24.
48 Arthur Downing, 'Social Capital in Decline: Friendly Societies in Australia, 1850–1914', Discussion Papers in Economic and Social History, no. 105, October 2012, p. 8.
49 Roland Wettenhall, 'Australia's Friendly History', *Pursuit, The University of Melbourne*. 31 August 2018.
50 Paul Collier, *The Future of Capitalism: Facing the New Anxieties*, Penguin, London, 2019, p. 83.
51 Mark Stephens, 'Building Society Demutualisation in the UK', *Housing Studies*, vol. 16, no. 3, 2001, pp. 335–52.
52 'The Dream of the 1890s: Why Old Mutualism Is Making a New Comeback', *The Atlantic*, 13 March 2012.
53 C.D. Horner, *Producers' Co-Operatives in the United States, 1865–1890*, University of Pittsburgh Press, Pittsburgh, 1978, pp. 40–41.
54 John Curl, *For All the People: Uncovering the Hidden History of Cooperation, Cooperative Movements and Communalism in America*, PM Press, Oakland, 2009, p. 4.

55 Democracy Collaborative, 'Cooperatives', Community-Wealth, accessed February 2022.
56 'Demutualised companies 1996-2019', *Delisted*, 31 December 2019.
57 Eric Grant, 'The Social and Economic Value of Insurance', Geneva Association Research Report, September 2012, p. 9.
58 Milton Friedman, *A Theory of the Consumption Function*, Princeton University Press, Princeton, 1957.
59 Albert Ando & Franco Modigliani, 'The Life Cycle Hypothesis of Saving: Aggregate Implications and Tests', *American Economic Review*, vol. 53, no. 1, 1963, pp. 55–84.
60 Truman Bewley, 'The Permanent Income Hypothesis: A Theoretical Formulation', *Journal of Economic Theory*, vol. 16, no. 2, 1977, pp. 252–92.
61 Nicholas Barr, *The Welfare State as Piggy Bank: Information, Risk, Uncertainty, and the Role of the State*, Oxford University Press, Oxford, 2001.
62 Compañía General de Tabacos de Filipinas v. Collector of Internal Revenue [1927] USSC 178; 275 U.S. 87; 48 S.Ct. 100; 72 L.Ed. 177; No. 42, 21 November 1927.
63 See Table 1.1 in Peter Lindert, *Growing Public: Volume 1*, Cambridge University Press, Cambridge, 2004, p. 8.
64 Thomas Malthus, *First Essay on Population 1798*, Palgrave Macmillan, London, 1966, pp. 53–70.
65 Lindert, 2004, p. 42. Linert uses GNP, or Gross National Product, meaning the value of goods and services produced that are owned by individuals or organisations based in the nation.
66 Frölich, Markus; Kaplan, David; Pages, Carmen; Rigolini, Jamele; Robalino, David A., eds., *Social Insurance, Informality, and Labour Markets: How to Protect Workers While Creating Good Jobs*, Oxford University Press, Oxford, 2014, p. 36.
67 Beatrice Scheubel, *Bismarck's Pension System*, in *Bismarck's Institutions*, Mohr Siebeck GmbH and Co. KG, Tübingen, 2013, pp. 77–104.
68 Lindert, 2004, pp. 172–75.
69 US Department of Commerce and Labor, 'Twenty-Fourth Annual Report of the Commissioner of Labor: Workmen's Insurance and Compensation Systems in Europe, 1909', vol. 1, Washington D.C., 1910, pp. 5, 94, 1150.
70 Lindert, 2004, p. 172.
71 Other non-contributory old-age pensions included Denmark (1891), New Zealand (1898), NSW (1900), Victoria (1900) and the UK (1908). The German scheme introduced in 1889 was contributory, as would be the US scheme introduced in the Second New Deal. The UK switched to a contributory base in 1911. See Marian Sawer, 'Andrew Fisher and the Era of Liberal Reform', *Labour History*, vol. 102, no. 1, 2012, p. 74.
72 Andrew Fisher was the leader of the Labor Party from 1907 to 1915. He served three terms as Prime Minister: 1908–1909 (minority); 1910–1913 (majority); and 1914–1915 (majority). Fisher's 1910 government was the first majority labour government in the world.
73 Sawer, 2012, pp. 72–73.
74 Michael Freeden, *The New Liberalism: An Ideology of Social Reform*, Oxford University Press, Oxford, 1978, p. 145.
75 Chris Bowen, 'Reclaiming Liberalism for the Left: Social Justice in the 21st Century', *Sydney Papers*, vol. 20, no. 4, 2008, p. 151.
76 See, for example, the views of the Auditor-General, C.J. Cerutty, who, along with Treasury, advocated strongly that the arrangements in the early 1930s were

unsustainable. See also Rob Watts, 'The Origins of the Australian Welfare State', *Historical Studies*, vol. 19, no. 75, 1980, p. 181.

77 The *Sydney Morning Herald* of Wednesday, 29 July 1936 reported that Sir Walter Kinnear (Controller of the Insurance Department of the British Ministry of Health) and Mr G.H. Ince (Assistant Secretary to the British Ministry of Labour) had arrived in Australia. Sir Walter said: 'We have come to Australia at the invitation of the Commonwealth Government, but we are not going to instruct and advise the Government on national insurance. We will give to the Commonwealth the benefit of the knowledge and experience of this matter which Great Britain has amassed during the past 25 years'. See 'Unemployment and health', *Sydney Morning Herald*, 29 July 1936.

78 Watts, 1980, p. 188.

79 This superseded the pre-existing NSW scheme which was introduced in 1927.

80 This superseded the pre-existing NSW scheme which was introduced in 1926.

81 This superseded the pre-existing Queensland scheme which was introduced in 1923.

82 Manning Clark, *A Short History of Australia*, Heinemann, London, 1964, p. 242.

83 The original Medibank legislation was rejected by the Australian Senate. This legislation was one of the bills leading to the 1974 'double dissolution' election.

84 World Bank, 'Averting the Old Age Crisis: Policies to Protect the Old and Promote Growth', World Bank Policy Research Report, Oxford University Press, New York, 1994.

85 Disability Investment Group, 'The Way Forward: A New Disability Policy Framework for Australia', Report of the Disability Investment Group, 2009, pp. 2, 6.

86 Franklin Delano Roosevelt, *Franklin D. Roosevelt's Inaugural Address of 1933*. Washington DC, National Archives and Records Administration, 1988.

87 Ibid.

88 Productivity Commission, 'Disability Support and Care: Productivity Commission Inquiry Report', vol. 1, no. 54, 2011, p. 2.

89 Quoted in Moss, 2002, p. 297. See also Franklin Delano Roosevelt, 'Message to Congress Reviewing the Broad Objectives and Accomplishments of the Administration', 8 June 1934, in the Public Papers and Addresses of Franklin D. Roosevelt, vol. 3, *The Advance of Recovery and Reform*, Random House, New York, 1938, pp. 287–93.

90 Ezra Klein, *Why We're Polarized*, Avid Reader Press, New York, 2020, pp. 80–83.

91 Milton Friedman, 'Gammon's Law Points to Health-Care Solution', *Wall Street Journal*, 12 November 1991.

92 Rachel Garfield, Orgera Kendal & Anthony Damico, 'The Uninsured and the ACA: A Primer – Key Facts About Health Insurance and the Uninsured Amidst Changes to the Affordable Care Act', Henry J Kaiser Family Foundation, 2019.

93 Congressional Budget Office, 'Federal Subsidies for Health Insurance Coverage for People Under 65: 2020 to 2030', Congressional Budget Office, Washington DC, 2020.

94 Lloyd George was Chancellor in the Asquith Government from May 1908 (replacing Asquith, who had held the role under Henry Campbell-Bannerman). While Asquith had announced the introduction of the pension scheme in his 1908 budget, the enabling legislation was formally introduced to parliament at the end of May 1908 by Lloyd George, who had by then become Chancellor). While the *Old-Age Pensions Act* received assent on 1 August 1908, it came into effect in 1909 (the year of Lloyd George's 'People's Budget'). While Lloyd George was the last Liberal

prime minister and always considered himself a Liberal, from the 1918 election onwards, he was the PM of a Conservative-dominated Coalition government.

95 This included the passage of the *Education Act 1944*, the *National Health Service Act 1946*, the *National Insurance Act 1946* and the *National Assistance Act 1948*. David Gladstone, 'Before Beveridge: Welfare Before the Welfare State', *Civitas*, Choice in Welfare, no. 47, 1999, p. 3.

96 Beveridge, 1942, p. 6.

97 Beveridge, 1942, p. 103.

98 Beveridge, 1942, p. 11.

99 See David Gladstone, *The Twentieth-Century Welfare State*, Macmillan International Higher Education, London, 1999, p. 3. 'Almost all of the ideas and proposals for reform in social security and education, for example, had been long discussed in the 1920s and 1930s. The new structures built on or simplified many of the systems that preceded them. In many cases they extended to a national-scale experiments which had been introduced by some local authorities.'

100 '1945–51: Labour and the creation of the welfare state', *The Guardian*, 14 March 2001; Dennis Kavanagh & Iain Dale, *Labour Party General Election Manifestos 1900–1997, Vol. 2*, Routledge, London, 2015.

101 Jonathan Gruber, *Public Finance and Public Policy*, Worth Publishers, New York, 2011.

102 Of course, what is 'essential' is usually very context-dependent.

103 The United Nations Declaration of Human Rights was adopted by the UN General Assembly on 10 December 1948 as resolution 217. Forty-eight member countries voted in favour, none against, eight abstained and two did not vote. Other important documents that contain similar (even if not identical) sentiments are the US Declaration of Independence, issued on 4 July 1776 and the Declaration of the Rights of the Man and of the Citizen, issued by the French National Constituent Assembly on 26 August 1789. See UN General Assembly, 'Universal Declaration of Human Rights (217 A [III])', 1948.

104 UN Declaration of Human Rights, Article 22.

105 UN Declaration of Human Rights, Article 23.

106 UN Declaration of Human Rights, Article 25(1).

107 Of course, in practice, even 'universal' schemes are often subject to some eligibility conditions or contingency requirements – e.g. that someone have a disability in order to be eligible for a disability pension. A universal basic income (UBI) or negative income tax, without any eligibility requirements or means-testing, is probably the only truly universal scheme.

108 Some key relevant references include: Friedrich Hayek, *The Constitution of Liberty*, Routledge, London, 1960, p. 11; and Robert Nozick, *Anarchy, State, and Utopia*, Basic Books, New York, 2013, p. 9.

109 Nozick, 2013, p. 169.

110 Some key relevant references include: Joseph Carens, *Equality, Moral Incentives, and the Market: An Essay in Utopian Politico-Economic Theory*, University of Chicago Press, Chicago, 1981, p. 4; Kai Nielsen, 'Radical Egalitarian Justice: Justice as Equality', *Social Theory and Practice*, vol. 5, no. 2, 1979, p. 210.

111 Diminishing marginal utility is one of the foundations of modern economics. While it can't be assumed all of the time (e.g. risk-loving behaviour such as gambling and Prospect Theory), it seems to be a reasonable description of human welfare most of the time. See Jeremy Bentham, *An Introduction to the Principles of Morals and Legislation*, Clarendon Press, Oxford, 1907 (original 1789).

112 Rawlsian distributive justice rests on the idea that if people were shrouded by a 'veil of ignorance' that prevented them from knowing their social position or personal circumstances, then their choices would result in resources being distributed more fairly across society. Choosing behind this veil would make someone more cautious and, Rawls argued, more likely to want to ensure that even the worst-off in society were not too disadvantaged. For example, not many people would support a society with slavery if there was even a small chance of becoming a slave themselves. Rawls' notion of distributive justice is closely linked with insurance and risk aversion (discussed in detail below) in that insurance is largely designed to improve people's welfare in potential future states of the world (e.g. future states in which their house burns down or they become sick). By pooling and sharing risk in relation to the unknowable future, insurance, in effect, involves people making choices behind a veil of ignorance to ensure that no one is left homeless or destitute or without basic healthcare. This mechanism closely approximates key aspects of Rawls' hypothetical environment in which people choose future distributions. See John Rawls, *A Theory of Justice*, Harvard University Press, Cambridge, 1971, p. 24; John Rawls, *Justice as Fairness: A Restatement*, Harvard University Press, Cambridge, 2001, p. 15.

113 Some advocating equality of opportunity argue that true equality of opportunity must reflect the different starting positions we all experience in the lottery of life, including different physical and mental endowments, family contexts, social standing and material resources. One response to this challenge is *luck egalitarianism*, which posits that distributional justice requires compensation for each person depending upon their starting position. Dworkins suggests a hypothetical auction in which each person, not knowing their own natural endowments, buys insurance against different outcomes in the 'natural lottery'. In many ways, this is a similar mechanism to Rawls' veil of ignorance. See Ronald Dworkin, 'What is Equality? Part 2: Equality of Resources', in *The Notion of Equality*, Routledge, London, 2001, p. 284. Since Dworkins' work, others have developed more practical methods for implementing his core ideas.

114 Robert Sapolsky, 'How Economic Inequality Inflicts Real Biological Harm', *Scientific American*, vol. 30, no. 2, 2018.

115 Andrew Clark, Paul Frijters & Michael Shields, 'Relative Income, Happiness and Utility: An Explanation for the Easterlin Paradox and Other Puzzles', *Journal of Economic Literature*, vol. 46, no. 1, 2008, pp. 95–144. This includes studies across a wide range of settings that link happiness with the distribution of income or wealth including: Germany (Ferrer-i-Carbonell 2005), the US (Blanchflower and Oswald 2004), China (Knight and Song 2006), the UK (Clark and Oswald 1996) and Latin America (Graham and Felton 2006).

116 See John Quiggin, 'The Risk Society: Social Democracy in an Uncertain World', Centre for Policy Development, Occasional Paper No. 2, July 2007.

117 This statement doesn't imply that people comply with a simple formulation of 'rational' or 'utility-maximising' behaviour – but rather that they generally respond to price signals and other incentives, and typically in ways that are purposeful and at least somewhat predictable.

118 For the Australian case, see analysis by the Tax and Transfer Policy Institute at the ANU: David Ingles & David Plunkett, 'Effective Marginal Tax Rates', Tax and Transfer Policy Institute, ANU, TTPI Policy Brief, 1/2016, August 2016.

119 As is discussed below, a UBI was supported by Milton Friedman and James Tobin, both Nobel laureates, occupying different ends of the political spectrum.

120 Beveridge, 1942, p. 11.
121 The Treasury, *2021 Intergenerational Report*, Canberra, 2021.
122 Congressional Budget Office, 'The 2019 Long-Term Budget Outlook', Washington DC, 2019.
123 Ministry of Social Development, 'Employment and Social Outcomes Investment Strategy', Wellington, 2018.

3. THE TWENTIETH CENTURY: THE ERA OF INSURANCE

1 Walter Scheidel & Steven Friesen, 'The Size of the Economy and the Distribution of Income in the Roman Empire', Princeton/Stanford Working Papers in Classics No. 010901, January 2009, p. 6.
2 Eryn Brown, 'Taxes through the Ages', *Knowable Magazine*, 25 October 2017.
3 Carolyn Webber & Aaron Wildavsky, *A History of Taxation and Expenditure in the Western World*, Simon & Schuster, New York, 1986, p. 68.
4 Webber & Wildavsky, 1986, pp. 68–69.
5 Webber & Wildavsky, 1986, p. 109.
6 Webber & Wildavsky, 1986, p. 171.
7 Denis Twitchett & John Fairbank, *The Cambridge History of China*, Cambridge University Press, Cambridge, 1978; Gang Deng, *The Premodern Chinese Economy: Structural Equilibrium and Capitalist Sterility*, Routledge, London, 1999.
8 J.D. Prince, 'The Code of Hammurabi', *American Journal of Theology*, vol. 8, no. 3, 1904, pp. 601–09.
9 Vance, 1908, pp. 5–6.
10 Jari Eloranta, 'Military Spending Patterns in History', *EH.net*, 16 September 2005.
11 Webber & Wildavsky, 1986, p. 52.
12 Webber & Wildavsky, 1986, p. 123.
13 Peter Lindert, *Making Social Spending Work*, Cambridge University Press, Cambridge, 2021, p. 33.
14 Peter Brien & Matthew Keep, 'The Public Finances: A Historical Overview', House of Commons Library, Briefing Paper No. 8625, 22 March 2018.
15 This graph represents a selection of twenty major advanced economies for which high-quality data is available: Australia; Austria; Belgium; Canada; Denmark; Finland; France; Germany; Greece; Italy; Japan; Netherlands; New Zealand; Netherlands; Portugal; Spain; Sweden; Switzerland; the UK; and the US. See Esteban Ortiz-Ospina & Max Roser, 'Government Spending', *Our World in Data*, 2016.
16 Ortiz-Ospina & Max Roser, 2016.
17 For federal government statistics, see: Office of Management and Budget and Federal Reserve Bank of St. Louis, 'Federal Net Outlays as Percent of Gross Domestic Product', 30 January 2022; Christopher Chantrill, 'US Government Spending History from 1900', *US Government Spending*, 23 November 2019. The historical statistics are largely drawn from the St Louis Federal Reserve, which is an official Census bureau publication.
18 Multiple data sources have been used to construct this time series. Details are outlined in Appendix [].
19 Robert Vincent Jackson, 'Australian Economic Development in the Nineteenth Century', Australian National University Press, Canberra, 1977.

20 The different shadings reflect that this time series is based on a range of data sources. The different lines reflect different data sources and the discontinuities in the lines reflect slight changes in how government spending is measured. The data also incorporates a GDP deflator, which is based on analysis by Julie Novak. For 1850–1962, see Alan Barnard, 'Government Financial Data, 1850–1982', Source Papers in Economic History, Paper series No. 13, ANU Research School of Economics, ANU College of Business and Economics. For 1962–1999, see Reserve Bank of Australia, 'Australian Government Budget - Annual', Discontinued Statistics, Sydney and Australian Bureau of Statistics, 'Government Finance Statistics', Canberra. For 1999–2019, see Australian Bureau of Statistics, 'Government Finance Statistics', Canberra.

21 Lindert, 2004, p. 98.

22 This is similar, but not the same as spending as a share of GDP. The support ratio for a targeted age group is a generosity measure, which is recipient-focused. In contrast, the share of GDP is an implicit tax-effort measure.

23 See Figure 13.1 of Thomas Piketty, *Capital in the Twenty-First Century*, Harvard University Press, Cambridge, 2014, p. 475. This graph shows tax revenues between 1870–2010 for the US, Britain, France and Sweden. For all four countries, tax revenues were less than 10per cent of GDP at 1900 but had risen to 30 per cent (US), 40 per cent (Britain), 50 per cent (France) and 55 per cent (Sweden) by 2010. During the period 1870–2010, a significant majority of in the increase in tax revenues as a share of GDP in all four countries occurred after 1930.

24 Fishback's definition of 'social welfare' expenditure closely matches the definition of social insurance used by the OECD and in this paper. The reasons for adopting a broad definition of social insurance will be set out in more detail in the following section. Fishback uses the OECD measures of government social welfare expenditures, which include: old-age pensions, survivor benefits (not from private life insurance), incapacity-related aid, health expenditures, aid to families, unemployment benefits, income maintenance, government job training, and housing subsidies. See Price Fishback, 'Social Insurance and Public Assistance in the Twentieth-Century United States: 2019 Presidential Address for the Economic History Association', NBER Working Paper No. 26938, April 2020, p. 30.

25 For the 1900 and 1930 estimates, see Peter Lindert, 'The Rise of Social Spending, 1880–1930', *Explorations in Economic History*, vol. 31, no. 1, 1994, pp. 1–37. For the three 2003 estimates, Fishback, 2020, Table 1, p. 30.

26 Christopher Chantrill, 'Major Spending Programs in 20th Century', *UK Public Spending*, 2020. See also Bank of England, 'A Millennium of Macroeconomic Data', Bank of England Research Datasets, 2016.

27 Gruber, 2011.

28 Ezra Klein, 'The U.S. Government: An Insurance Conglomerate Protected by a Large, Standing Army', *Washington Post*, 14 February 2011; Paul Krugman, 'Reckonings; Outside the Box', *New York Times*, 11 July 2001.

29 Moss, 2002, pp. 4–9.

30 See Lindert, 2021, pp. 40–45, 108–15. See also Lindert, 2004.

31 Alan Krueger & Bruce Meyer, 'Labor Supply Effects of Social Insurance', in Alan Auerbach and Martin Feldstein (eds) *Handbook of Public Economics*, vol. 4, 2002, Chapter 33.

32 Martin Feldstein, 'Rethinking Social Insurance', *American Economic Review*, vol. 95, no. 1, 2005, p. 3.

33 For example, unlike in the United States, there have been many periods during which the age pension has been means-tested in Australia. Despite this, I argue that it remains a key element of Australia's social insurance program.

34 A natural experiment exists where members of a population are exposed to both experimental and control conditions beyond the control of the investigators undertaking the empirical investigation. This can resemble a randomised experiment and make it easier to establish the impact of a particular event or treatment.

35 Lindert, 2021, p. 154.

36 William Easterly and Sergio Rebello, 'Fiscal Policy and Economic Growth: An Empirical investigation', *Journal of Monetary Economics*, vol. 32, no. 3, 1993, pp. 417–58; Gayle Allard & Peter Lindert, 'Euro-Productivity and Euro-Jobs since the 1960s: Which Institutions Really Mattered?' in Timothy Hatton, Kevin O'Rourke & Alan Taylor (eds), 'The New Comparative History: Essays in Honour of Jeffrey G Williamson', MIT Press, Massachusetts, 2007, pp. 365–94. For global data, see Fiseha Haile & Miguel Niño-Zarazúa, 'Does Social Spending Improve Welfare in Low-income and Middle-income Countries?', *Journal of International Development*, vol. 30, no. 3, 2018, pp. 367–98; Daron Acemoglu, Suresh Naidu, Pascual Restrepo & James Robinson, 'Does Democracy Cause Growth?', *Journal of Political Economy*, vol. 127, no. 1, 2019, pp. 47–100.

37 Richard Kneller, Michael Bleaney & Norman Gemmell, 'Fiscal Policy and Growth: Evidence from OECD Countries', *Journal of Public Economics*, vol. 74, no. 2, 1999, pp. 171–90.

38 Negative incentives from some family assistance, see Nathaniel Hendren & Ben Sprung-Keyser, 'A Unified Welfare Analysis of Government Policies', NBER Working Paper No. 26144, 2019, pp. 53–36. Negative income tax field studies in the US in the early 1970s: poor households receiving subsidies without work requirements did indeed work less during the experiment. Secondary workers in particular. Robert Levine et al., 'A Retrospective on the Negative Income Tax Experiments: Looking Back at the Most Innovative Field Studies in Social Policy', in Karl Wilderquist, Michael Lewis & Steven Pressman, *The Ethics and Economics of the Basic Income Guarantee,* Routledge, London, 2005, pp. 95–108; Robert Moffitt & Matthew Zahn, 'The Marginal Labor Supply Disincentives of Welfare Reforms', NBER Working Paper No. 26028, 2022, found that work disincentives were not strong overall, but that the size of the effect varied across cohorts.

39 Norman Gemmell, Bichará Kneller and Ismael Sanz, 'The Timing and Persistence of Fiscal Policy Impacts on Growth: Evidence from OECD Countries', *Economic Journal*, vol. 21, no. 550, 2011, pp. F33–F58.

40 Organisation for Economic Co-operation and Development, 'Insurance Spending', *OECD Data*, 2022.

41 Howard Kunreuther, Mark Pauly & Stacey McMorrow, *Insurance and Behavioral Economics: Improving Decisions in the Most Misunderstood Industry*, Cambridge University Press, Cambridge, 2013, pp. 14–16.

42 Swiss Re Institute, 'World Insurance: The Great Pivot East Continues', *Sigma*, No. 3, 2019, p. 43.

43 Ibid.

44 Glyn Davis, *On Life's Lottery*, Hachette, Sydney, 2021, p. 24.

45 See Appendix [] for a full list of sources derived for this table.

46 Christopher Chantrill, 'US Welfare Spending', US Government Spending, 2021.

47 OECD, 'Unemployment Rate', OECD Data, 2022.

4. HOW DOES INSURANCE WORK IN PRACTICE?

1 In practice, houses have much less than a 1 per cent chance of being destroyed by fire each year. Therefore, annual home insurance premiums are far less than 1 per cent of the cost of rebuilding a home. This value is used to construct a straightforward example.

2 George Akerlof, 'The Market for "Lemons": Quality Uncertainty and the Market Mechanism', *Quarterly Journal of Economics*, vol. 84, no. 3, 1970, pp. 488–500.

3 It is also a lesson in the importance of persistence. It took three rejections from prominent economics journals and four years of resubmitting for the paper to be published at all. Two of the flagship journals of economics rejected the article on the basis that it was 'trivial', while a third rejected it as the conclusions of the paper were so general that it would render any market with quality differences dysfunctional.

4 Michael Rothschild & Joseph Stiglitz, 'Equilibrium in Competitive Insurance Markets: An Essay on the Economics of Imperfect Information', *Quarterly Journal of Economics*, vol. 90, no. 4, 1976, pp. 630–49.

5 Raj Chetty & Amy Finkelstein, 'Social Insurance: Connecting Theory to Data', NBER Working Paper No. 18433, October 2012, pp. 16–18.

It should be noted that the evidence in relation to the impact of adverse selection on annuities is somewhat mixed. One study found that the actuarial outcomes for someone with an average life expectancy across the population were 4–10 per cent worse than for the average person who actually buys annuities. See: Olivia Mitchell, James Poterba, Mark Warshawsky and Jeffrey Brown 'New Evidence on the Money's Worth of Individual Annuities', *American Economic Review*, vol. 89, no. 5, 1999, pp. 1299–318. A subsequent study has suggested the impact may be around half that: Anthony Webb, 'Is Adverse Selection in the Annuity Market a Big Problem?', *Issue Brief Centre for Retirement Research*, Boston College, January 2006.

6 David Cutler & Richard Zeckhauser, 'The Anatomy of Health Insurance', in Anthony Culyer & Joseph Newhouse (Eds.), Handbook of Health Economics vol. 1, 1st edition, Elsevier, Amsterdam, 2000, pp. 563–643. One potential problem with this test (among several), is that the 'positive correlation' test can show a relationship between insurance purchases and risk aversion, rather than the insured's underlying risk profile.

7 David Cutler & Sarah Reber, 'Paying for Health Insurance: The Trade-Off Between Competition and Adverse Selection', *Quarterly Journal of Economics*, vol. 113, no. 2, 1998, pp. 433–66.

8 This could be described as 'ex post moral hazard'. This issue of whether moral hazard exists in relation to health insurance is not a totally settled question, but there is persuasive evidence that health insurance increases healthcare spending, including from two randomised experiments: Liran Einav and Amy Finkelstein, 'Moral Hazard in Health Insurance: What We Know and How We Know It', *Journal of the European Economic Association*, vol. 16, no. 4, August 2018.

9 Nicolas Hérault, Guyonne Kalb & Justin van de Ven, 'The Effects of Income Support Settings on Incentives to Work', Melbourne Institute of Applied Economic and Social Research, December 2013, p. 95.

10 Thomas Lemieux & Kevin Milligan, 'Incentive Effects of Social Assistance: A Regression Discontinuity Approach', *Journal of Econometrics*, vol. 142, no. 2, 2008, pp. 807–28; Michael Christl & Silvia De Poli, 'Trapped in Inactivity? Social Assistance and Labour Supply in Austria', *Empirica*, no. 48, 2021, pp. 661–96.

11 'Will a Newstart Boost Actually Deter Jobseekers?', *The Conversation*, 28 August 2012.
12 David Richardson, 'Inquiry into the Allowance Payment System for Jobseekers and Others', The Australia Institute, August 2012, pp. 9–10.
13 Robert Shiller, *Macro Markets: Creating Institutions for Managing Society's Largest Economic Risks*, Oxford University Press, Oxford, 1993.
14 Moss, 2002, p. 295. See also the discussion on pp. 302–11 for specific examples of how policymakers and legislators often utilised sophisticated economic concepts in support of their reform – even if they didn't use economic jargon in doing so.
15 Nicholas Murray Butler, *Why Should We Change Our Form of Government? Studies in Practical Politics*, Charles Scribner's Sons, New York, 1912, p. 82.

5. RISK AND UNCERTAINTY

1 The Law of Large Numbers was arrived at via a sequence of statistical and mathematical discoveries that included work by Gerolamo Cardano, Jacob Bernoulli and S.D. Poisson from the sixteenth to the nineteenth centuries.
2 If the population being polled is 'normally' distributed (i.e. the bell curve), the standard deviation of the distribution of the average of the group declines in proportion to the square root of the sample size.
3 Frank Knight, *Risk, Uncertainty and Profit*, Houghton Mifflin Company, New York, 1921.
4 John Maynard Keynes, *The Collected Writings of John Maynard Keynes. Vol. VIII, A Treatise on Probability*, Macmillan, London, 1921.
5 John Maynard Keynes, *The General Theory of Employment, Interest and Money*, Macmillan, London, 1936, p. 102. See also the discussion of uncertainty in chapters 14 and 15.
6 Knight, 1921, p. 249.
7 Mariana Mazzucato, *The Entrepreneurial State: Debunking Public vs Private Sector Myths*, Public Affairs, New York, 2018, p. 167.
8 Kay and King describe how the theft of a rare painting has many idiosyncratic and difficult to quantify characteristics, including the desirability of the painting and the difficult of stealing it given the way it is protected (Kay & King, 2020, Chapter 18).
9 Kay & King, 2020, Chapter 1.
10 The Office of National Estimates was responsible for synthesising all available information and using that to produce forecasts for top US officials. See Philip Tetlock & Dan Gardner, *Superforecasting: The Art and Science of Prediction*, Broadway Books, New York, 2015, pp. 52–56.
11 Jack Davis, *Sherman Kent and the Profession of Intelligence Analysis*, Defense Technical Information Center, Central Intelligence Agency, Washington DC, November 2002, p. 55.
12 Nassim Nicholas Taleb, *The Black Swan: The Impact of the Highly Improbable*, Random House, New York, 2007, pp. xvii–xviii.
13 Roberta Wohlstetter, *Pearl Harbor: Warning and Decision*, Stanford University Press, Redwood City, 1962. See also Nate Silver, *The Signal and the Noise: The Art and Science of Prediction*, Penguin Press, New York, 2012, pp. 412–18.
14 Wohlstetter, 1962, p. 387.

15 Niall Ferguson, 'Black Swans, Dragon Kings and Gray Rhinos: The World War of 1914–1918 And the Pandemic of 2020–?', *Hoover History Working Group, History Working Paper*, 2020–1, May 2020.

16 Michele Wucker, *The Gray Rhino: How to Recognize and Act on the Obvious Dangers We Ignore*, St. Martin's Press, New York, 2016.

17 Ferguson, 2010, p. 10. See also a detailed discussion of how financial markets were taken by surprise at pp. 10–23.

18 Note the difficulty of forecasting a turning point in Australia's terms of trade. There is a relatively predictable long-term trend upwards between 1998–99 and 2005–06. After 2005–06, there was an expectation that the upward trend would turn, but this was incorrectly modelled in a succession of budget forecasts. See Figure 1.1 of The Treasury, *Review of Treasury Macroeconomic and Revenue Forecasting*, December 2012, p. 3. See also the inherent difficulty of forecasting the arrival of recession even after the build-up of perceived macroeconomic imbalance.

19 Pierre-Simon Laplace, *A Philosophical Essay on Probabilities*, translated by Frederick Wilson Truscott & Frederick Lincoln Emery, Dover Publications, New York, 1951, p. 4. See also the discussion in Tetlock & Gardner, pp. 8–10.

20 Edward Lorenz, 'Predictability: Does the Flap of a Butterfly's Wings in Brazil Set Off a Tornado in Texas?', *American Association for the Advancement of Science*, 139th meeting, MIT, 29 December 1972.

21 Tetlock & Gardener, 2015, p. 8.

22 Jean-Marc Ginoux & Christian Gerini, *Henri Poincaré: A Biography through the Daily Papers*, World Scientific Publishing Company, Singapore, 2013.

23 See a useful discussion of this in Taleb, 2007, pp. 176–79.

24 Donald McCloskey, 'History, Differential Equations and the Problem of Narration', *History and Theory*, vol. 30, no. 1, February 1991, p. 33.

25 Ian Goldin, *Rescue: From Global Crisis to a Better World*, Sceptre Books, London, 2021, p. 226.

26 Cheryl Misak, *Frank Ramsey: A Sheer Excess of Powers*, Oxford University Press, Oxford, 2020.

27 Frank Ramsey, 'Truth and Probability', in Richard Braithwaite (ed.), *Foundations of Mathematics and Other Logical Essays*, Harcourt, Brace and Company, New York, 1926, p. 167.

28 Ramsey, 1926, p. 161.

29 Ramsey, 1926, p. 187.

30 Ramsey, 1926, p. 175. In his seminal book *The Foundations of Statistics*, Leonard Savage builds on Ramsey and cites an example (drawing on de Finetti) of a person with two identical eggs who is asked to guess which is rotten and is offered a financial reward for a correct answer (Leonard Savage, *The Foundations of Statistics*, Wiley, New York, 1954, p. 50).

31 This was a phrase used famously by Secretary of Defense Donald Rumsfeld at a news briefing on 12 February 2002. Nate Silver describes this scenario as 'a contingency that *we have not even considered*. We have some kind of mental block against it, or our experience is inadequate to imagine it; it's as though it doesn't even exist' (Silver, 2012, p. 421).

6. THE CURRENT STATE OF SOCIAL INSURANCE

1 Edmund Burke, *Reflections on the Revolution in France: A Critical Edition*, Stanford University Press, Stanford, 2002, p. 261.
2 World Bank, 1994, p. 233.
3 World Bank, 1994, p. xiii.
4 OECD, 'Pensions at a Glance: Public Policies across OECD Countries – 2007 Edition', OECD, 2007.
5 Mercer, *Melbourne Mercer Global Pension Index 2019*, Melbourne, 2019, pp. 15–16.
6 See Feldstein, 2005; Diamond, 2012; Moss, 2002 re the low administrative costs of government-run pay-as-you-go social security systems.
7 World Bank, 1994, p. 238.
8 For a useful discussion of the various information challenges for both private insurers and consumers of private insurance, see Barr, 2001, pp. 52–58.
9 Nicholas Barr and David Moss explore the difficulties that could arise from the use of genomic and other data to accurately price individualised risks.
10 Mark Pauly, 'Overinsurance and Public Provision of Insurance: The Roles of Moral Hazard and Adverse Selection', *Quarterly Journal of Economics*, vol. 88, no. 1, 1974, pp. 44–62.
11 Einav and Finkelstein, 2018.
12 The difficulty of winning workers' compensation cases has been described as the 'unholy trinity', given the three defences available to employers: (i) that the injury was due to the contributory negligence of the employee; (ii) that the injury was caused by the negligence of a fellow employee; and (iii) that the risk of injury was understood and assumed by the employee as part of their employment. See Andrew Fronsko & Alan Woodroffe, 'Public vs Private Underwriting and Administration of Personal Injury Statutory Insurance Schemes', Actuaries Institute Injury and Disability Seminar, 12–14 November 2017, p. 10; John Haller, 'Industrial Accidents – Worker Compensation Laws and the Medical Response', *Western Journal of Medicine*, vol. 148, no. 3, 1988, pp. 341–48. See also the discussion in Sir Geoffrey Palmer, 'A Retrospective on the Woodhouse Report: The Vision, the Performance and the Future', second Woodhouse Memorial Lecture, Victoria University of Wellington Law Review, vol. 50, 2019.
13 The ACT was the last jurisdiction, in 1951.
14 Fronsko & Woodroffe, 2017, pp. 13–14.
15 Christopher Chantrill, 'Government Spending Details for 2021', *US Government Spending*, 2021.
16 Productivity Commission, 'A Better Way to Support Veterans', No. 93, 27 June 2019.
17 Ibid. See recommendations and findings on pp. 45–79.
18 Kieran Tranter, 'The History of the Haste-Wagons': The Motor Car Act 1909 (Vic), Emergent Technology and the Call for Law', *Melbourne University Law Review*, vol. 29, no. 3, 2005, p. 846.
19 'Horse v. Motor', *The Argus*, 12 December 1900.
20 Fronsko & Woodroffe, 2017, p. 3.
21 Fronsko & Woodroffe, 2017, pp. 9–10.
22 NSW Legislative Council, Standing Committee on Law and Justice, *2020 Review of the Lifetime Care and Support Scheme*, Report 78, Sydney, July 2021.
23 Australian Government, 'National Disability Insurance Scheme Act 2013', No. 20, 2013.

24 Australian Government, 'Budget Strategy and Outlook: Budget Paper No. 1: 2020–21', 2020, pp. 6–26.
25 Productivity Commission, *Disability Care and Support*, No. 54, Canberra, 31 July 2011.
26 Accident Compensation Corporation, *2021 Annual Report*, Wellington, 2021, pp. 40, 56.
27 Palmer, 2019, p. 406.
28 Atul Gawande, *Being Mortal: Medicine and What Matters in the End*, Metropolitan Books, New York, 2014, p. 62.
29 Gawande, 2014, p. 63.
30 Gawande, 2014, p. 70.
31 Cavendish, 2020, pp. 156–58. The first such development in the UK, 'New Ground' opened in 2016.
32 Australian Institute of Health and Welfare, *Older Australia at a Glance*, AIHW AGE Report No. 83, 2018, p. 69.
33 See Gawande, 2014.
34 Cavendish, pp. 172–73.
35 Other examples include the Netherlands, Luxembourg and (through the health insurance system), Belgium. In contrast, some countries have adopted a single-payer system approach, including Sweden, Denmark, Austria and the Czech Republic.
36 Federal Ministry of Health, Germany, 'Peer Review on "Germany's Latest Reforms of the Long-term Care System"', *European Commission Host Country Discussion Paper*, Germany, 11–12 January 2018, p. 1.
37 The increase of funding of over €5 billion per year required to give effect to these reforms was supported by an increase in the contribution rate on wage incomes from 2.05 per cent to 2.55 per cent.
38 John Campbell & Ikegami Naoki, 'Long-Term Health Insurance Comes to Japan', *Health Affairs*, vol. 19, no. 3, May 2000, pp. 26–39.
39 Saul Blaustein, Christopher O'Leary & Stephen Wandner, 'Policy Issues', in Christopher O'Leary & Stephen Wandner (eds), *Unemployment Insurance in the United States: Analysis of Policy Issues*, Upjohn Institute for Employment Research, Kalamazoo, 1997, pp. 38–40.
40 *OECD Employment Outlook: Tackling the Jobs Crisis*, OECD Publishing, Paris, 2009, p. 76; as well as this briefing on US unemployment benefit duration: Center on Budget and Policy Priorities, 'Policy Basics: How Many Weeks of Unemployment Compensation Are Available?', updated February 2022.
41 In the Australian context, see Hérault, Kalb & van de Ven, 2013. For a broader examination, see Chetty & Finkelstein, 2012; Krueger & Meyer, 2002.
42 In the Australian context, see Hérault, Kalb & van de Ven, 2013.
43 For example, Hérault et al. found in the Australian context that a $10 per week increase in net eligibility for transfer payments is associated with reduced odds of labour force participation by between 1 and 3 per cent for four out of six population subgroups. The study also found evidence of a negative relationship between the level of benefit payments and hours of work. The relationship tended to be largest for those with the lowest hourly wage rates. The point estimates were that $10 per week increase in net eligibility for transfer payments is correlated with a fall in the time spent working for people in the bottom wage decile of between three minutes per week (single women without children) and fifteen minutes per week (single parents).

Studies in other countries have also found modest impacts. A German study found that one additional month of eligibility for unemployment benefits increased the period of unemployment by a tenth of a month (three days). An Austrian study found that a 4.6 per cent increase in the replacement rate of unemployment benefits (i.e. the degree to which they replace earlier wages) led to a half a week increase in the time unemployed. See Robert Moffitt, 'Unemployment Benefits and Unemployment', *IZA World of Labor*, No. 13, May 2014.

44 Jacob Hacker, *The Great Risk Shift: The New Economic Insecurity and the Decline in the American Dream*, Oxford University Press, Oxford, 2019, p. 11.

45 *Child Well-Being in Rich Countries: A Comparative Overview*, UNICEF Office of Research, Florence, 2013, p. 8.

46 Caroline Ratcliffe, 'Child Poverty and Adult Success', Urban Institute, September 2015.

47 Mark Rank & Thomas Hirschl, 'The Likelihood of Experiencing Relative Poverty Over the Life Course', *PLOS One*, vol. 10, no. 7, 2015.

48 Donna Rothstein, 'An Analysis of Long-term Unemployment,' *Monthly Labor Review*, U.S. Bureau of Labor Statistics, July 2016. See Table 1.

49 HILDA contains information on 17,000 people each year, collecting information on relationships, household income, labour force data and wellbeing data (including health and education). Participants are followed over the course of their lifetime.

50 Roger Wilkins, 'The Household, Income and Labour Dynamics in Australia Survey: Selected Findings from Waves 1 to 15', 12th Annual Statistical Report of the HILDA Survey, Melbourne Institute Applied Economic and Social Research, 2017, pp. 40–41.

51 Productivity Commission, 'Risking Inequality? A Stocktake of the Evidence', Productivity Commission Research Paper, August 2018, p. 95.

52 Productivity Commission, 2018, pp. 100–03.

7. GOVERNMENT AND SYSTEMATIC RISKS

1 Queensland Floods Commission of Inquiry, 'Final Report', March 2012, p. 32.

2 'Flood Costs Tipped to Top $30b', *ABC News*, 18 Jan 2011.

3 The 1 per cent refers to the fact that such an event has a 1 per cent likelihood of occurring each year.

4 United States Geological Survey, 'Floods and Recurrence Intervals', June 2018.

5 The European Commission, 'The EU Floods Directive', Directive 2007/60/EC.

6 Each Australian jurisdiction has its own guidance material. As an example, see the following: Office of the Queensland Chief Scientist, 'How Do We Estimate the Chance of a Flood Occurring?', 12 June 2018.

7 The table below assumes that each year's rainfall is an 'independent' event, i.e. that the outcome in that year is not dependent on what occurred in the years preceding it. This may not be a realistic assumption in many instances. For example, in some areas, high or low rainfall years may come in groups or clusters if associated with a broader climatic event such as an El Niño or La Niña. For the purposes of this discussion, the possible interdependence between observations can be avoided as it does not affect the fundamental risk assessment challenge being described.

8 The probability of observing a particular number of occurrences (n) over a period of y years of data given an underlying annual exceedance probability (AEP) of x per cent is the multiplication of two elements: the likelihood of n occurrences multiplied by the number of ways in which n occurrences could occur over y years.

First, the likelihood of n occurrences arising during y years, which is ([x/100]^n).([(1-x)/100]^(y-n))

Second is the number of different ways in which this could occur, which is (y choose n), or the binomial coefficient y!/[n! (y-n)!)].

9 Jacky Croke, 'Old Floods Show Brisbane's Next Big Wet Might Be Closer Than We Think', *The Conversation,* 11 January 2017. See also The Big Flood, 'Extending the flood record'.

10 *The Conversation,* 11 January 2017.

11 See Muhammad Rizwan, Shenglian Guo, Feng Xiong & Jiabo Yin, 'Evaluation of Various Probability Distributions for Deriving Design Flood Featuring Right-Tail Events in Pakistan', *Water*, vol. 10, no. 11, 2018, for a discussion of the pros and cons of various PDF in a particular context.

12 Brandon Parkes & David Demeritt, 'Defining the Hundred Year Flood: A Bayesian Approach for Using Historic Data to Reduce Uncertainty in Flood Frequency Estimates', *Journal of Hydrology*, vol. 540, September 2016, pp. 1189–208.

13 El Niño and La Niña are based on the El Niño Southern Oscillation (ENSO). While a La Niña doesn't always follow an El Niño, the occurrence of either an El Niño or a La Niña is generally followed by at least two to three years without either an El Niño or a La Niña year.

14 'Corporate Suppliers of Masks and Gowns Price-gouging Not-for-Profit Aged Care Providers', *The Guardian,* 11 April 2020.

15 'Medical Supply Company Charging $786 for a Box of 20 Face Masks Accused of Exploiting Coronavirus Crisis', *ABC News,* 22 April 2020.

16 See the Galton Board for references for each of these empirical regularities.

17 Casper Albers, 'De Moivre-Gauss-Laplace: Extraordinarily Normal', *Nieuw Archief voor Wiskunde*, vol. 5/19, no. 1, 2018, pp. 37–38.

18 Desai makes reference to Charles Sanders Peirce as having been credited with naming the distribution as the 'normal'. See Desai, 2017, p. 21.

19 Ulrich Muller et al., 'Statistical Study of Foreign Exchange Rates, Empirical Evidence of a Price Change Scaling Law, and Intraday Analysis', *Journal of Banking and Finance*, vol. 14, no. 6, December 1990, pp. 1189–208.

20 '7-footers: 17-percent chance of playing in NBA', *Boston Globe,* 9 March 2014.

21 New York City is 102.5 standard deviations above the mean in this dataset. A person who is 102.5 standard deviations above the mean in a normally distributed population would be over 31 feet tall.

22 Robert Wadlow is the tallest recorded human being at 8'11'.

23 Taleb contrasts 'Mediocristan' (normally distributed populations such as human weight and height) with 'Extremistan' (such as wealth, book sales and academic citations). In Mediocristan, black swans are almost impossible. See Taleb, 2007, pp. 32–37.

24 In statistics, a power-law distribution is one in which the relative change in one quantity results in a proportional change in the other quantity, regardless of the initial size of the two quantities. What does this mean in practical terms? Unlike a 'normal' distribution, a power-law distribution will not be symmetrical – there will be many observations of a small quantity and a 'long tail', i.e., a much higher

frequency of extremely high value observations than in a normal distribution. This can be seen in Figures 7.3 and 7.4. Even though extremely high values are still rare in a power-law distribution, they are far more common than in the normal distribution. This can make their relative frequency seem deceptively low to both non-experts and expert modellers alike when in fact their likelihood can be far higher than we would expect (or estimate) if we presume a framework of the normal distribution.

25 Arnab Chatterjee & Bikas Chakrabarti, 'Fat Tailed Distributions for Deaths in Conflicts and Disasters', *Reports in Advances in Physical Sciences*, vol. 1, no. 1, 2017.

26 Aaron Clauset, Cosma Rohilla Shalizi & M.E.J. Newman, 'Power-Law Distributions in Empirical Data', *SIAM Review*, vol. 51, no. 4, December 2009, pp. 661–703. Clauset, Shalizi & Newman consider a range of fat-tailed distributions including the power-law, the exponential, the stretched exponential, the log-normal, the Yule and the Poisson.

27 Goldin, 2012, p. 224.

28 Pasquale Cirillo & Nassim Nicholas Taleb, 'Tail Risk of Contagious Diseases', *Nature Physics*, vol. 16, 2020, pp. 606–13. There is considerable uncertainty for many of the death counts, so a simple average of the upper and lower estimates is used.

29 Each panel shows the log of deaths (unadjusted). This reflects the distribution of pandemics over time rather than the relative severity of various pandemics.

30 Goldin, 2012, p. 225.

31 Steven Pinker, *The Better Angels of Our Nature: Why Violence Has Declined*, Viking Press, New York, 2011.

32 Steven Pinker, *Enlightenment Now: The Case for Reason, Science, Humanism and Progress*, Viking Press, New York, 2018, p. 162.

33 'Steven Pinker is Wrong about Violence and War', *The Guardian*, 14 March 2015.

34 John Arquilla, 'The Big Kill: Sorry, Steven Pinker, the World Isn't Getting Less Violent', *Foreign Policy*, 3 December 2012.

35 Pasquale Cirillo & Nassim Nicholas Taleb, 'On the Statistical Properties and Tail Risk of Violent Conflicts', Tail Risk Working Papers, October 2015, p. 12.

36 Even though our security intelligence makes constant assessment of national security threats, it is worth noting that military expenditure as a share of GDP did not increase materially in the lead-up to either World War I or II. There has been considerable debate among historians as to the extent to which either of these conflicts was 'expected'.

37 Zeke Hausfather, Henri Drake, Tristan Abbott & Gavin Schmidt, 'Evaluating the Performance of Past Climate Model Projections', *Geophysical Research Letters*, vol. 47, no. 1, 2020, p.47.

38 Ross Garnaut, 'A Decision-Making Framework' in *The Garnaut Climate Change Review*, Cambridge University Press, Cambridge, 2008, pp. 7–9.

39 Nicholas Stern, *The Economics of Climate Change: The Stern Review*, Cambridge University Press, Cambridge, 2007, pp. 162-63.

40 William Nordhaus, 'Evolution of Assessments of the Economics of Global Warming: Changes in the DICE Model, 1992-2017' NBER Working Paper No. 23319, April 2017, p. 12.

41 Ottmar Edenhofer, Ramon Pichs-Madruga & Youba Sokona, 'Climate Change 2014: Mitigation of Climate Change', Working Group III Contribution to the Fifth Assessment Report of the Intergovernmental Panel on Climate Change, IPCC, Cambridge University Press, Cambridge, 2014, p. 15.

42 'Study Confirms Climate Models are Getting Future Warming Projections Right', *NASA Climate*, 9 January 2020.
43 Hausfather, Drake, Abbott & Schmidt, 2020, p. 47.
44 The climate scientists who contributed to the Charney Report described their gathering as an 'Ad Hoc Group on Carbon Dioxide and Climate'. Jule Charney et al., 'Carbon Dioxide and Climate: A Scientific Assessment: Report of an Ad Hoc Study Group on Carbon Dioxide and Climate', Woods Hole, Massachusetts, 23–27 July, 1979.
45 Zeke Hausfather, 'Explainer: How Scientists Estimate "Climate Sensitivity"', *Carbon Brief*, 19 June 2018.
46 James Hansen et al., 'Climate Sensitivity: Analysis of Feedback Mechanisms', *Climate Processes and Climate Sensitivity, Geophysical Monograph Series*, vol. 29, 1984, pp. 130–63.
47 IPCC, 'Fourth Assessment Report', 2007, p. 32, Figure 1.2.
48 Reto Knutti, Maria Rugenstein & Gabriele Hegerl, 'Beyond equilibrium climate Sensitivity', *Nature Geoscience*, vol. 10, 2017, pp. 727–36.
49 Sherwood et al., 2020.
50 'Making Sense of "Climate Sensitivity"', *NASA Climate*, 8 September 2020.
51 Kenneth Gillingham et al., 'Modeling Uncertainty in Integrated Assessment of Climate Change: A Multimodel Comparison', *Journal of the Association of Environmental and Resource Economists*, vol. 5, no. 4, 2018, pp. 791–826.
52 Moore's law is the observation that the number of transistors in a dense integrated circuit (IC) doubles about every two years. Moore's law is an observation and projection of a historical trend. Rather than a law of physics, it is an empirical relationship linked to gains from experience in production.
53 Stern, 2007, pp. 162–63.
54 Nordhaus, 2017, p. 12.
55 Nordhaus, 2017, pp. 8–9.
56 William Nordhaus, 'Projections and Uncertainties about Climate Change in an Era of Minimal Climate Policies', *American Economic Journal: Economic Policy*, vol. 10, no. 3, 2018, pp. 333–60. See in particular Table 4 on p. 353.
See also Peter Christensen, Kenneth Gillingham & William Nordhaus, 'Uncertainty in Forecasts of Long-run Economic Growth', *Proceedings of the National Academy of Sciences of the United States of America*, vol. 115, no. 21, 2018, pp. 5409–414.
57 Chris Hope, 'The $10 Trillion Value of Better Information about the Transient Climate Response', *The Royal Society Publishing*, 13 November 2015.
58 United Nations Department of Economic and Social Affairs, 'World Population Prospects 2017', New York, 2017.
59 Jorgen Randers, 'We Won't Be Nine Billion', *Tedx Talks*, TEDX Maastricht, 11 May 2014; 'Don't Panic', *The Economist*, 24 September 2014; Darrell Bricker & John Ibbitson, *Empty Planet: The Shock of Global Population Decline*, Crown, New York, 2020, pp. 42–47; Sanjeev Sanyal, 'The Wide Angle: The End of Population Growth', *Deutsche Bank Periodical*, May 2011.
60 '10 Million Newborns Registered in China in 2020, Falling Below Warning Levels, Experts Warn', *Global Times*, 9 February 2021; 'China's Fertility Rate Falls Below Warning Line, Population May Decline', *Global Times*, 12 February 2020.
61 These figures are based on unpublished data that was provided by the authors of the below article. It was produced by research supported by the Institute for Health Metrics and Evaluation at the University of Washington. See Stein Emil Vollset

et al., 'Fertility, Mortality, Migration, and Population Scenarios for 195 Countries and Territories From 2017 to 2100: A Forecasting Analysis for the Global Burden of Disease Study', *The Lancet*, vol. 396, no. 10258, 2020, pp. 1285–306.

8. WHY REFORM IS IMPORTANT

1 For a prominent reference, see Nicholas Kaldor, 'A Model of Economic Growth', *Economic Journal*, vol. 67, no. 268, 1957, pp. 591–624. The assertion that the labour and capital shares are broadly constant over time is presented as a stylised fact in many undergraduate macroeconomic textbooks. It is part of the rationale behind the fact that the workhorse macroeconomic growth model, the Solow Model, uses the 'Cobb-Douglas' production function.

2 Piketty, 2014, pp. 199–203.

3 Gianni La Cava, 'The Labour and Capital Shares of Income in Australia', Reserve Bank of Australia, Bulletin, March 2019.

4 For overarching stats, see Piketty, 2014 and 2020, and 'Growing Unequal? Income Distribution and Poverty in OECD Countries', OECD, 2008.

5 For the US, see Claudia Goldin & Robert Margo, 'The Great Compression: The Wage Structure in the United States at Mid-Century', *Quarterly Journal of Economics*, vol. 107, no. 1, 1992, pp. 1–34. For Australia (and similar results in a separate study for NZ), see Andrew Leigh, *Battlers and Billionaires,* Black Inc., Melbourne, 2013, Figure 4 and pp. 33–39.

6 In Australia, those on an income of over $80,000 have lost, on average, three teeth to tooth decay, compared to ten for those on incomes below $20,000. Those on high incomes are also happier and experience pain less frequently than those on low incomes. See Introduction and Chapter 5 of Leigh, 2013. But Andrew Leigh points out that care should be taken with the data in drawing conclusions about the impact of growing inequality. In the technical note to Chapter 5, he notes that 'while a person's own income is a powerful predictor of health outcomes, there's little evidence that the poor get sicker when the rich get richer'. For a discussion of the relationship between income and life expectancy in Australia, see also Philip Clarke & Andrew Leigh, 'Death, Dollars and Degrees: Socio-economic Status and Longevity in Australia', *Economic Papers*, 2011, vol. 30, no. 3, pp. 348--55. See also Anne Case & Angus Deaton, *Deaths of Despair and the Future of Capitalism*, Princeton University Press, New Jersey, 2020.

7 'Wall Street Gets the Flak, But the Tech CEOs Get Paid All the Money', *Bloomberg*, 10 July 2020.

8 Jane G. Gravelle, 'Wage Inequality and the Stagnation of Earnings of Low-Wage Workers: Contributing Factors and Policy Options', *Congressional Research Service*, R46212, 5 February 2020.

9 'Wall Street Gets the Flak but the Tech CEOs Get Paid All the Money', 10 July 2020. See also Lawrence Mishel and Jori Kandra, 'CEO Pay has Skyrocketed 1,322% Since 1978', Economic Policy Institute, 10 August 2021.

10 According to Autor, Dorn and Hanson, around a quarter of the decline in manufacturing output in the US can be attributed to trade with China: see David Autor, David Dorn & Gordon Hanson, 'The China Syndrome: Local Labor Market Effects of Import Competition in the United States', NBER Working Papers No. 18054, May 2012. See also: David Autor, David Dorn & Gordon

Hanson, 'Untangling Trade and Technology Evidence: Evidence from Local Labour Markets', *The Economic Journal*, vol. 125, May 2015, pp. 612–47.

11 In the US, a study found that those in commuting zones most affected by trade with China experienced income falls per adult of US$549. In contrast, in these communities, welfare payments went up by only $58 per adult. Moreover, of the $58 in additional transfers, only 23 cents came from TAA. See Autor, Dorn and Hanson, 'The China Syndrome'.

12 David Autor, Lawrence F. Katz & Melissa S. Kearney, 'Trends in U.S. Wage Inequality: Revising the Revisionists', *The Review of Economics and Statistics*, vol. 90, no. 1, May 2008, pp. 300–23.

13 Claudia Goldin & Lawrence Katz, *The Race Between Education and Technology*, Harvard University Press, Cambridge, Massachusetts, 2008.

14 ABS 6345.0, 'Wage Price Index', Australian Bureau of Statistics, 17 November 2021. See also Jim Stanford, 'Historical Data on the Decline in Australian Industrial Disputes', The Australia Institute, 30 January 2018, pp. 1, 6–7; Shane Wright, 'Wages Growth Slumps to Worst on Record as Industries Suffer Pay Cuts', *Sydney Morning Herald*, 12 August 2020.

15 ABS 6345.0, 'Wage Price Index', 17 November 2021. See also Geoff Gilfillan, 'The Extent and Causes of Wage Growth Slowdown in Australia', *Analysis & Policy Observatory*, 9 April 2019.

16 Jeff Rubin, *The Expendables: How the Middle Class Got Screwed by Globalisation*, Scribe, Melbourne, 2020, p. 215.

17 Amy Bernstein & Anand Raman, 'The Great Decoupling: An Interview with Erik Brynjolfsson and Andrew McAfee', *Harvard Business Review*, June 2015.

18 Jacob S. Hacker, *The Great Risk Shift: The New Economic Insecurity and the Decline in the American Dream*, Oxford University Press, Oxford, 2019, pp. 15, 17.

19 Arne Kallegberg, 'Job Insecurity and Well-Being in Rich Democracies', *The Economic and Social Review*, vol. 49, no. 3, 2018, pp. 241–58. See also Arne Kalleberg, *Precarious Lives: Job Insecurity and Well-Being in Rich Democracies*, Polity Press, Cambridge, 2018; Jan Breman & Marcel van der Linden, 'Informalizing the Economy: The Return of the Social Question at a Global Level', *Development and Change*, vol. 45, no. 4, 2014, pp. 920–40.

20 Guy Standing, 'Meet the Precariat, the New Global Class Fuelling the Rise of Populism', *World Economic Forum*, 9 November 2016.

21 David Autor, 'Why Are There Still So Many Jobs? The History and Future of Workplace Automation', *Journal of Economic Perspectives*, vol. 29, no. 3, Summer 2015. For Australia for the period 1966–2016, see Figure 3 of Jeff Borland & Michael Coelli, 'Are Robots Taking Our Jobs?', *The Australian Economic Review*, 30 November 2017, pp. 377–97.

22 Borland & Coelli, 'Are Robots Taking Our Jobs?'. See Section 6 in particular.

23 Lillian Alexander, 'Understanding Insecure Work in Australia', Discussion Paper, The McKell Institute, January 2019; Edward Cavanough, 'Why is Job Insecurity so Prevalent in Australia?', The McKell Institute, January 2019.

24 Rebecca Cassells, 'Future of Work in Australia', Bankwest Curtin Economic Centre Report, April 2018, p. ix.

25 'Despite the Popular Wisdom, Job Insecurity Is Not Growing in Australia', *The Conversation*, 17 July 2018.

26 Uber drivers received compensation of US$11.77 per hour after netting off Uber fees. In order to calculate a 'wage' equivalent of $9.21, the following was deducted in order, from passenger payments: all Uber fees, such as booking fees

and commissions; vehicle expenses; and the cost of a modest benefits package, including mandatory employer-side payroll taxes. Lawrence's estimate also takes into account expense and benefit interactions with the federal tax code. The 'wage' equivalent of $9.21 is at the 10th percentile of earnings (i.e. the bottom 10 per cent). See Lawrence Mishel, 'Uber and the Labor Market: Uber Drivers' Compensation, Wages, and the Scale of Uber and the Gig Economy', Economic Policy Institute, 15 May 2018.

27 Erin Currier et al., 'The Precarious State of Family Balance Sheets', The Pew Charitable Trusts, January 2015, pp. 10–12. See also Hacker, *The Great Risk Shift*, pp. 85–86.

28 Autor, 2015, pp. 3–30.

29 Autor, 2015, p. 15.

30 Lawrence Katz & Robert Margo, 'Technical Change and the Relative Demand for Skilled Labor: The United States in Historical Perspective', NBER Working Papers No. 18752, February 2013.

31 Robert Shiller, *The New Financial Order: Risk in the 21st Century*, Princeton University Press, Princeton, 2003.

32 See Collier, 2019, p. 125.

33 David Autor, 'Work of the Past, Work of the Future', *AEA Papers and Proceedings*, vol. 109, May 2019, pp. 1–32. See pp. 15-20 and in particular, Figures 12–14.

34 Autor, 2015. See Figure 3, p. 15.

35 Reserve Bank of Australia, 'Chart Pack: Factors of Production and Labour Market, Labour Underutilisation Rates', data accessed 2 February 2022.

36 Based on unpublished measures of underemployment of men and women by ANZCO Skill Level captured by the quarterly Australian Bureau of Statistics *Labour Force Survey* and obtained and verified by the Australian Parliamentary Library.

37 Chambers et al., 'Underemployment in the Australian Labour Market', in *Reserve Bank of Australia Bulletin,* Reserve Bank of Australia, June 2021; Nicolas Buffie, 'Underemployment versus Unemployment', Centre for Economic and Policy Research, Washington DC, 1 September 2016.

38 National Bureau of Economic Research, 'The Effect of Default Options on Retirement Savings', *Bulletin on Aging and Health*, No. 3, September 2006.

39 'Older "Left-behind" Voters Turned against a Political Class with Values Opposed to Theirs', *The Guardian*, 25 June 2016.

40 Victoria Bateman, 'Brexit: Two Centuries in the Making', *UK in a Changing Europe*, 23 November 2016.

41 Matthew J. Goodwin & Oliver Heath, 'The 2016 Referendum, Brexit and the Left Behind: An Aggregate-level Analysis of the Result', *The Political Quarterly*, vol. 87, no. 3, 2016, pp. 323–32.

42 David Autor et al., 'Importing Political Polarization? The Electoral Consequences of Rising Trade Exposure', *American Economic Review*, vol. 110, no. 10, October 2020, pp. 3139–83.

43 Thomas Frank, *What's the Matter with Kansas?*, Metropolitan Books, New York, 2004, pp. 67–68.

44 Lilliana Mason, *Uncivil Agreement: How Politics Became Our Identity*, University of Chicago Press, Chicago, 2018, p. 14.

45 Diana C. Mutz, 'Status Threat, Not Economic Hardship, Explains the 2016 Presidential Vote', *Proceedings of the National Academy of Sciences of the United States of America*, vol. 115, no. 19, May 2018, pp. E4330–E4339. See also 'It Was

Cultural Anxiety that Drove White, Working-Class Voters to Trump', *The Atlantic*, 9 May 2017.

46 John Sides, Michael Tesler & Lynn Vavreck, *Identity Crisis: The 2016 Presidential Campaign and the Battle for the Meaning of America*, Princeton University Press, Princeton, 2018.
See also the discussion of this issue in Klein, 2020, pp. 119–22.

47 Roberto Stefan Foa and Yascha Mounk, 'The Democratic Disconnect', *Journal of Democracy*, vol. 27, no. 3, July 2016, pp. 7–9.

48 Rubin, *The Expendables: How the Middle Class Got Screwed by Globalisation*, p. 216.

49 Joseph Bamat, 'Melenchon and Le Pen Win Over Youth in French Vote', *France24*, 24 April 2017.

50 'Youthful Nationalists: The East is Pink', *The Economist*, 13 August 2016.

51 'Migrants bucking the Stereotype and Ditching the Major Parties in Favour of Pauline Hanson's One Nation', *ABC News*, October 27, 2019; 'Warning on Millions of Australians Who Struggle to Work More Hours', *Sydney Morning Herald*, 8 December 2019.

52 Australia, Austria, Belgium, Canada, Denmark, France, Germany, Greece, Ireland, Italy, Japan, Netherlands, New Zealand, Norway, Portugal, Spain, Sweden, Switzerland, UK and the US.

53 Peter Lindert, 'Are Government Social Programs Bad for Economic Growth?', in Jon Bakija (eds.) Lane Kenworthy, Peter Lindert and Jeff Madrick, *How Big Should Government Be?*, University of California, Davis, 2016, pp. 34–66.

54 See a review of the literature by Jon Bakija in '*How Big Should Government Be?*'. See in particular, pp. 98–106.

55 International Monetary Fund, Government Finance Statistics Yearbook and data files, and World Bank and OECD GDP estimates.

56 Ibid.

10. WHAT POTENTIAL LOSSES SHOULD BE COVERED?

1 Autor, 2015, pp. 3–30.

2 Autor, 2019, p. 23.

3 As many as 47 per cent of jobs in the US are at high risk (70 per cent) of being automated within the next few decades. See Carl Benedikt Frey & Michael Osborne, 'The Future of Employment: How Susceptible Are Jobs to Computerisation?', *Oxford Martin*, September 2013, p. 38; 57 per cent of jobs in the OECD at risk from automation, see: Carl Benedikt Frey, Michael Osborne & Craig Holmes, 'Technology at Work v2.0: The Future Is Not What It Used to Be', Oxford Martin School and Citi, January 2016, p. 7; approximately 40 per cent of jobs in Australia at high-risk from automation in next ten to fifteen years, see Hugh Durrant-Whyte et al., 'Australia's Future Workforce? The Impact of Computerisation and Automation on Future Employment', Committee for Economic Development of Australia, June 2015, p. 60; 44 per cent of current jobs in Australia will be negatively affected by computerisation and technology in the next twenty years: see Mark Reading, Jeremy Thorpe & Tony Peake, 'A Smart Move: Future-proofing Australia's Workforce by Growing Skills in Science, Technology, Engineering and Maths (STEM)', PWC, April 2015, p. 10.

4 Arntz finds that 9 per cent of jobs are automatable in the US in a study across the OECD focusing on tasks rather than occupations. See Melanie Arntz, Terry Gregory & Ulrich Zierahn, 'The Risk of Automation for Jobs in OECD Countries: A Comparative Analysis', OECD Social, Employment and Migration Working Papers Working Papers No. 189, OECD, 2016, p. 14.
5 James Manyika et al., 'Jobs Lost, Jobs Gained: What the Future of Work Will Mean for Jobs, Skills and Wages', McKinsey Global Institute, November 2017.
6 Jim Chalmers & Mike Quigley, *Changing Jobs: A Fair Go in the New Machine Age*, Black Inc., Melbourne, 2017, see Chapter 5.
7 Frank Levy & Richard Murnane, 'Dancing with Robots: Human Skills for Computerized Work', Third Way, NEXT Research Papers, Massachusetts Institute of Technology, 2013.
8 AlphaBeta, 'Future Skills: To Adapt to the Future of Work, Australians Will Undertake a Third More Education and Training and Change What, When and How we Learn', Report for Google, 2018.
9 Cavendish, 2020, p. 31.
10 'How Retirement Was Invented', *The Atlantic*, 24 October 2014.
11 Karen Eggleston & Victor Fuchs, 'The New Demographic Transition: Most Gains in Life Expectancy Now Realized Late in Life', *Journal of Economic Perspectives*, vol. 26, no. 3, Summer 2012, pp. 139–42.
12 Shlomo Benartzi, Alessandro Previtero & Richard Thaler, 'Annuitization Puzzles', *Journal of Economic Perspectives*, vol. 25, no. 4, Fall 2011, pp. 143–64. See also Richard Thaler, 'The Annuity Puzzle', *The New York Times*, 4 June 2011.
13 See Recommendations 21 and 22 of 'Australia's Future Tax System: Report to the Treasurer', *Henry Tax Review*, December 2009, p. 84. See also the discussion on pp. 34–36.
14 Rhema Vaithianathan, 'Using Income Contingent Loans to Pay for Health Care', in *Income Contingent Loans*, International Economic Association Series, Palgrave Macmillan, London, 2014, p. 165.
15 Joshua Gans & Stephen King, 'The Housing Lifeline: A Housing Affordability Policy', *Agenda*, vol. 11, no. 2, 2004, pp. 143–55.
16 Kenneth Baldwin, Bruce Chapman & Umbu Raya, 'Using Income Contingent Loans for the Financing of the Next Million Australian Solar Rooftops', ANU Centre for Climate Economics and Policy Working Papers No. 249513, August 2015.
17 Timothy Higgins, 'Essays in the Development and Costing of Income Contingent Loans', ANU, October 2010; Bruce Chapman & Timothy Higgins, 'An Income Contingent Loan for Extending Paid Parental Leave', *Australian Journal of Labour Economics*, vol. 12, no. 2, August 2009, pp. 197–216.
18 Joshua Gans & Andrew Leigh, 'Innovation + Equality: How to Create a Future that Is More Star Trek than Terminator', MIT Press, Massachusetts, 2019, see Chapter 6.
19 'The Israeli Technological Eco-system: A Powerhouse of Innovation', *Deloitte*, 2021.
20 Mark Minevich, 'How the US Can Learn About Successful Innovation Strategies From Israel, The Startup Nation', *Forbes*, 29 May 2020.
21 Bruce Chapman, Timothy Higgins & Joseph Stiglitz, *Income Contingent Loans: Theory, Practice and Prospects*, International Economics Association Series, Palgrave Macmillan, New York, 2014, p. 26.
22 Bruce Chapman, *Government Managing Risk: Income Contingent Loans for Social and Economic Progress*, Routledge, London, 2006.

23 Milton Friedman, 'The Role of Government in Education', in Robert Solow (ed.), *Economics and the Public Interest*, Rutgers University Press, New Brunswick, New Jersey, 1955, pp. 123–44.
24 Chapman, Higgins, & Stiglitz, 2014, pp. 17–18.
25 Social impact bonds can also be referred to as a 'impact bonds', 'social benefit bonds' (Australia); 'social impact partnerships' (Europe) and 'pay-for-success financing' (the US).
26 Emily Gustafsson-Wright, Sophie Gardiner & Vidya Putcha, 'The Potential and Limitations of Impact Bonds: Lessons From the First Five Years of Experience Worldwide', Brookings Institution, July 2015, p. 48.
27 Stefanie Tan et al., 'Widening Perspectives on Social Impact Bonds', *Journal of Economic Policy Reform*, vol. 24, no. 1, 2021, pp. 1–10.
28 Ryan Bain, 'A Critique of the UK Government's Innovation Fund Pilot to Reduce Youth Unemployment – Learning Lessons for Social Impact Bonds', 22 December 2019, pp. 12–13.
29 Gustafsson-Wright, Gardiner & Putcha, 2015, p. 49.
30 Ibid.
31 Timothy Aeppel, 'How the On-demand/Gig Economy Is Redefining Work', MIT IDE Research, June 2016.
32 Lawrence Katz & Alan Krueger, 'The Rise and Nature of Alternative Work Arrangements in the United States, 1995–2015,' *ILR Review*, vol. 72, no. 2, 2019, pp. 382–416.
33 Mastercard and Kaiser Associates, 'The Global Gig Economy: Capitalizing on a ~$500B Opportunity', Mastercard Gig Economy Industry Outlook and Needs Assessment, May 2019.
34 'Fifth Food Delivery Driver Dies Following Truck Crash in Central Sydney', *The Sydney Morning Herald*, 23 November 2020.
35 Shiller, 2003. See chapters 8–13 for an outline of the ideas described in the text.
36 As one example, see the discussion of the impact of labour mobility on overall productivity in Australia: Dan Andrews & David Hansell, 'Productivity-Enhancing Labour Reallocation in Australia', Treasury Working Paper, December 2019.

11. WHAT MECHANISM IS BEST TO MANAGE RISK?

1 Peter Diamond, 'A Framework for Social Security Analysis', *Journal of Public Economics*, vol. 8, no. 3, 1977, pp. 275–98.
2 Chetty & Finkelstein, 2012, pp. 8–9.
3 George Akerlof, 1970, pp. 488–500.
4 See a useful discussion in Moss, 2002, pp. 17–20.

12. WHO SHOULD PAY?

1 Joint Parliamentary Committee on Social Security, 'Second Interim Report of the Joint Parliamentary Committee on Social Security', Parliament of Australia, October 1941, p. 3. See also Watts, 1980, p. 193.
2 Feldstein, 2005, p. 4.
3 To fully calculate the cross-subsidy, it would be necessary to take account of the fact that many people on higher incomes have a very low likelihood of losing

their jobs. Tenured university professors are an extreme example! See Martin Feldstein, 2005, p. 5.

4 Mark McLennan & Jonathan Skinner, 'The Incidence of Medicare', *Journal of Public Economics*, vol. 90, no. 1–2, January 2006, pp. 257–76. See Table 2 on p. 267 and Table 3 on p. 269, which set out the regressive nature of intra-cohort transfers.

5 Jonathan Skinner & Weiping Zhou, 'The Measurement and Evolution of Health Inequality: Evidence from the U.S. Medicare Population', NBER Working Papers No. 10842, October 2004.

6 McLennan & Skinner, 2006, pp. 8–12, 35.

13. HOW SHOULD LOSS BE COMPENSATED?

1 Barr, 2001, p. 29.

2 Barr, 2001, pp. 25–29.

3 Milton Friedman, *Capitalism and Freedom*, University of Chicago Press, Chicago, 1962. See also Milton Friedman & Rose Friedman, *Free to Choose*, Avon Books, New York, 1980.

4 Dean Plueger, 'Earned Income Tax Credit Participation Rate for the Tax Year 2005', *IRS Research Bulletin*, 2009, pp. 151–95. See Table 8 on p. 179.

5 European Commission, 'The Social Situation in the European Union 2008,' Directorate-General for Employment, Social Affairs and Equal Opportunity, Brussels, 2009, p. 45.

6 Hans Dubois & Anna Ludwinek, 'Access to Social Benefits: Reducing Non-take-up', Eurofound, Publications Office of the European Union, Luxembourg, 2015. See in particular Table 1, pp. 12–13.

Similar findings can be found at: Manos Matsaganis, Alari Paulus & Holly Sutherland, 'The Take-Uu of Social Benefits', Research Note, European Observatory on the Social Situation, 2008, pp. 1–17. See pp. 3–4 in particular.

7 Esther Duflo, 'The Economist as Plumber', *American Economic Review*, vol. 107, no. 5, 2017, pp. 1–26.

8 Amy Finkelstein and Matthew Notowidigdo, 'Take-up and Targeting: Experimental Evidence from SNAP', NBER Working Papers No. 24652, 2018.

9 Juliet Rhys-Williams, 'Something to Look Forward to. A Suggestion for a New Social Contract', in John Cunliffe & Guido Erreygers (eds), *The Origins of Universal Grants*, Palgrave Macmillan, London, 1943, pp. 161–69.

10 Friedman, 1962. See also Friedman & Friedman, 1980.

11 'Australians Support Universal Health Care, so Why Not a Universal Basic Income', *The Conversation,* 13 February 2018.

12 Peter Dawkins, 'The Five Economists' Plan: The Original Idea and Subsequent Developments', Centre for Economic Policy Research Discussion Paper No. 450, November 2002.

13 Ross Garnaut, 'Investing in Full Employment', in *Social Democracy in Australia's Asian Future*, Asia Pacific Press, Canberra, 2002.

14 Ingles & Plunkett, 'Effective Marginal Tax Rates'. See in particular, graphs on pp. 2, 3, 9, 11, 14–15, 17.

15 Office for Budget Responsibility, 'Welfare Trends Report', UK Government, London, January 2018, see pp. 104, 107.

16 This 'back of the envelope' estimate is similar to Robert Reich's estimate of a cost of US$3.9 trillion for a UBI providing $1000 per month. He provided

this estimate in his review of two books arguing the case for a UBI: Annie Lowrey, *Give People Money: How a Universal Basic Income Would End Poverty, Revolutionize Work, and Remake the World*, Crown Publishing, New York, 2018; Andrew Yang, *The War on Normal People: The Truth about America's Disappearing Jobs and Why Universal Basic Income Is Our Future*, Hachette Books, New York, 2018.

17 Garnaut estimates A$40 billion per year, at least initially. This estimate would be highly sensitive to a range of assumptions and is worth examining through more detailed modelling. See Ross Garnaut, 'The Case for a Basic Income', in *Reset: Restoring Australia After the Pandemic Recession*, La Trobe University Press, Melbourne, 2021.

18 Abhijit Banerjee, and Esther Duflo, *Good Economics for Hard Times: Better Answers to Our Biggest Problem*, Allen Lane, London, 2019, pp. 289–92. For the US, see evidence from the New Jersey Income Maintenance Experiment (and subsequent experiments) that tested the impact of a negative income tax (NIT). The NIT reduced labour supply, but only marginally. Similar conclusions were drawn in relation to unconditional transfer programs such as the Alaska Permanent Fund (US$2000 per year) and the casino dividend in Cherokee lands (US$8000 per year) – see pp. 291–92.

19 A universal benefit for children was a recommendation in 'Inequality' by Anthony Atkinson. See Anthony Atkinson, *Inequality: What Can be Done?*, Harvard University Press, Cambridge, 2015.

20 Finkelstein & Notowidigdo, 2018.

14. HOW CAN OUTCOMES BEST BE ACHIEVED?

1 Productivity Commission, 'Shifting the Dial: 5 Year Productivity Review', 3 August 2017, p. 46.

See also Robin Osborn et al., 'Primary Care Physicians in Ten Countries Report Challenges Caring for Patients with Complex Health Needs', *Health Affairs*, vol. 34, no. 12, 2015, pp. 2104–12.

2 Cavendish, 2020, pp. 172–73.

3 See discussion in Barr, 2001, re the challenges of defining healthcare outcomes, other than at a very high level.

4 See Productivity Commission, 2017, pp. 7–11.

5 See a useful discussion in Productivity Commission, 2017, *Supporting Paper No. 2: Non-Market Sector Productivity*, Canberra, 3 August 2017, pp. 3–4. See also Box 1 from this paper for a discussion in relation to the relationship between market prices and a multi-faceted product like a car.

6 Jason Annabel, 'Enhancing Measures of Non-market Output in Economic Statistics: A Roadmap', Australian Bureau of Statistics, September 2019.

7 See a useful discussion and additional sources in: Productivity Commission, 2017, *Supporting Paper No. 2: Non-Market Sector Productivity*, 3 August 2017, p. 16.

8 Productivity Commission, Productivity Commission, 2017, *Supporting Paper No. 2: Non-Market Sector Productivity*, pp. 22–23.

9 Jerry Muller, *The Tyranny of Metrics*, Princeton University Press, Princeton, 2018, p. 18.

10 For a comprehensive examination of the risks when designing metrics and publicly reported KPIs, see Muller, 2018. See in particular the discussion of

key risks in using publicly reported KPIs on pp. 22–28 and the case studies in chapters 7–13.

11 NDIS, 'Consultation Paper: Supporting You to Make Your Own Decisions', June 2021, p. 6.

12 Alan Milburn, 'Diversity and Choice within the NHS', Speech to the NHS Confederation, 24 May 2002.

13 Productivity Commission, 'A Better Way to Support Veterans', No. 93, 27 June 2019, p. 26.

14 Paul Rosen, 'The Patient as Consumer and the Measurement of Bedside Manner', *The New England Journal of Medicine Catalyst*, March 2017, p. 1.

15 Productivity Commission, 2017, p. 66. See also Productivity Commission, 2017, *Supporting Paper No. 5: Integrated Care*, 3 August 2017, pp. 26–29.

16 OECD, 'Recommendations to OECD Ministers of Health from the High-level Reflection Group on the Future of Health Statistics: Strengthening the International Comparison of Health System Performance Through Patient-reported Indicators', OECD, Paris, 2017.

17 Kate Breckenridge et al., 'How to Routinely Collect Data on Patient-reported Outcome and Experience Measures in Renal Registries in Europe; an Expert Consensus Meeting', *Nephrology Dialysis Transplantation*, vol. 30, no. 10, 2015, pp. 1605–14; Jack Chen, 'Integrated Care Patient Reported Outcome Measures and Patient Reported Experience Measures – A Rapid Scoping Review', NSW Agency for Clinical Innovation, 2016; Stephen Duckett, Maree Cuddihy & Harvey Newnham, 'Targeting Zero: Supporting the Victorian Hospital System to Eliminate Avoidable Harm and Strengthen Quality of Care', Report of the Review of Hospital Safety and Quality Assurance in Victoria, Department of Health and Human Services, October 2016.

18 See the Health Net case in Gawande, 2014, p. 176.

19 Gawande, 2014, pp. 170–76.

20 Gawande, 2014, p. 176.

21 Gawande, 2014, pp. 176–77; Jennifer Temel et al., 'Early Palliative Care for Patients with Metastatic Non-Small Cell Cancer', *New England Journal of Medicine*, August 2010, pp. 733–42; Joseph Greer et al., 'Effect of Early Palliative Care on Chemotherapy Use and End-of-Life Care in Patients with Metastatic Non-Small Cell Lung Cancer', *Journal of Clinical Oncology*, vol. 30, no. 4, 2012, pp. 394–400.

22 Gawande, 2014, pp. 87–92.

23 Linda McSweeny, 'Cutting the Commute for Students with a Disability', *Pursuit*, University of Melbourne, 4 June, 2020.

24 Indeed, they argue further that healthcare should move beyond integrated care to 'population health systems', which would reflect lifestyle, the environment and other determinants of health. Hugh Alderwick, Chris Ham & David Buck, 'Population Health Systems Going Beyond Integrated Care', The King's Fund, London, 2015, p. 12.

25 Bill English, 'Speech to the Treasury: Guest Lecture Series on Social Investment', New Zealand Treasury, 18 September 2015.

26 See Davidson, Hampson & Connolly, 2020, pp. 2–5.

27 Productivity Commission, 2017, pp. 144–45. See also G. Ross Baker et al., *High Performing Healthcare Systems: Delivering Quality by Design*, Longwoods Publishing Corporation, Toronto, 2008.

28 Brent James & Gregory Poulsen, 'The Case for Capitation', *Harvard Business Review*, July–August 2016.

29 G. Ross Baker et al., 2018, p. 153.
30 Productivity Commission, 2017, pp. 145–46.
31 Natasha Curry & Chris Ham, 'Clinical and Service Integration: The Route to Improved Outcomes', The King's Fund, London, 2010.
32 Alderwick et al, 2015, p. 12.
33 Douglas McCarthy, Kimberley Mueller & Jennifer Wrenn, 'Kaiser Permanente: Bridging the Quality Divide with Integrated Practice, Group Accountability, and Health Information Technology', Case Study: Organised Health Care Delivery System, Commonwealth Fund, New York, June 2009.
34 Jed Emerson, Jay Wachowicz & Suzi Chun, 'Social Return on Investment: Exploring Aspects of Value Creation in the Nonprofit Sector', REDF, 2000, p. 135.
35 Jayne Jönsson, 'Social Return on Investment: Rooms for Improvement and Research – A Background Study on SROI to Identify Research Gaps', Forum for Social Innovation Sweden, 2013.
36 See Taylor Fry, 'Submission to the Australian Government Inquiry on Intergenerational Welfare Benefit Receipt, 20 December 2018.
37 Jonathan Boston & Derek Gill, *Social Investment: A New Zealand Policy Experiment*, Bridget Williams Books, Wellington, 2017, p. 11. See also Michael Mintrom, 'Broader Perspectives', in Jonathan Boston & Derek Gill (eds), 2017, pp. 74–90; Killian Destremau & Peter Wilson, 'Defining Social Investment, Kiwi-Style', in Jonathan Boston & Derek Gill (eds), 2017, pp. 34–73.
38 Taylor Fry, 'Annual Report on the Benefit System for Working-Age Adults: As at 30 June 2017', prepared for the Ministry of Social Development, Wellington, 30 June 2018.
39 Taylor Fry, 'Submission to the Australian Government Inquiry on Intergenerational Welfare Benefit Receipt', submission to the Select Committee on Intergenerational Welfare Dependence, 20 December 2018, p. 3.
40 English, 'Speech to the Treasury: Guest Lecture Series on Social Investment'.
41 Taylor Fry, 'Submission to the Australian Government Inquiry on Intergenerational Welfare Benefit Receipt', 20 December 2018, p. 7.
42 Boston & Gill, 2017, p. 11. See Michael Mintrom (pp. 74–90) for the view that the approach represents a paradigm shift and Sir Michael Cullen for the critical view.
43 David Donaldson, 'The NZ Investment Approach: Boon or Bane?', *The Mandarin*, 2 August 2016. See in particular comments from Don Arthur of the Australian Parliamentary Library: 'There is some risk that an investment model could have perverse effects if implemented in Australia. For example, some highly successful interventions could be ruled out by the investment approach because the benefits they provide flow to program participants and the broader community rather than to the Treasury.'
44 Productivity Commission, 'A Better Way to Support Veterans', p. 26.
45 Examples include the Carolina Abecedarian Project and the Perry Preschool Study. See Clare O'Neil & Tim Watts, *Two Futures: Australia at a Critical Moment*, The Text Publishing Company, Melbourne, 2015, p. 58.
46 Sharon Begley, 'Think Preventative Medicine Will Save Money? Think Again', *Reuters*, 29 January 2013.
47 Michael Maciosek et al., 'Greater Use of Preventative Services in U.S. Health Care Could Save Lives at Little or No Cost', *Health Affairs*, vol. 29, no. 9, September 2010, pp. 1656–60.
48 Gerald Riley & James Lubitz, 'Long-Term Trends in Medicare Payments in the Last Year of Life', *Health Services Research*, vol. 45, no. 2, 2010, pp. 565-76.

49 Ryan Nunn, Jana Parsons & Jay Shambaugh, 'A Dozen Facts about the Economics of the U.S. Health-Care System', The Hamilton Project/Brookings, March 2020, p. 10.
50 Congressional Budget Office, 'How CBO Analyzes Approaches to Improved Health through Disease Prevention', June 2020, pp. 15–16.
51 English, 2015.

15. SYSTEMATIC RISKS

1 Michael Osterholm, 'Preparing for the Next Pandemic', *The New England Journal of Medicine*, vol. 352, no. 18, May 2005, p. 1839.
2 Osterholm, 2005, p. 1842.

16. THE SHORT-TERM RESPONSE: MITIGATION, RISK SHARING AND PREPARATION

1 Productivity Commission, 'Natural Disaster Funding Arrangements', Productivity Commission Inquiry Report, vol. 1, no. 74, December, Canberra, 2014.
2 Productivity Commission, 2014, p. 7.
3 Productivity Commission, 2014, p. 39.
4 Productivity Commission, 2014, p. 40.
5 Shiller, 1993; Jonathan Ostry & Jun Kim, 'Boosting Fiscal Space: The Roles of GDP-Linked Debt and Longer Maturities', IMF Departmental Paper No.18/04, March 2018; Robert Shiller et al., 'Sovereign GDP-linked Bonds: Rationale and Design', Centre for Economic Policy Research, 16 March 2018.
6 Ostry & Kim, 2018.
7 Shiller et al., 2018.
8 Longer-maturity debt is another risk sharing mechanism in that it reduces the likelihood of default and reduces the default premium.
9 Ostry & Kim, 'Boosting Fiscal Space', pp. v-vi.
10 Shiller et al. 2018.
11 Shiller et al., 2018, p. 102.
12 Osterholm, 2015, p. 1842.
13 Michael Osterholm & Mark Olshaker, 'Chronicle of a Pandemic Foretold: Learning From the Covid-19 Failure – Before the Next Outbreak Arrives', in 'The Next Pandemic: Why the World Was Not Prepared for Covid-19', *Foreign Affairs*, vol. 99, no. 4, July/August 2020, pp. 7–8.
14 Osterholm & Olshaker, 2020, p. 9.
15 Dwight Eisenhower to Hamilton Fish Armstrong, 31 December 1950, in Louis Galambos et al. (eds), *The Papers of Dwight David Eisenhower, Volume XI: Columbia University*, Johns Hopkins University Press, Baltimore, 1984, p. 1516.
16 Laurie Garrett, 'The Return of Infectious Disease', *Foreign Affairs*, 2020 (originally published Jan/Feb 1996), p. 25.
17 Garrett, 2020, p. 26.
18 Garrett, 2020, p. 38.
19 Adam Forrest, 'Matt Hancock Admits Hollywood film Contagion Helped Shape His Vaccine Response', *Independent*, 4 February 2021.
20 'US Never Spent Enough on Emergency Stockpile, Former Managers Say', *USA Today*, 16 April 2020.

21 Hansard, 'Public Hearings of the Senate Select Committee into Covid', Parliament of Australia, 23 April 2020, p. 4.
22 Lance Williams, 'California Once Had Mobile Hospitals and a Ventilator Stockpile. But It Dismantled Them', *Los Angeles Times*, 27 March 2020.
23 '$400 Million Boost for Hospitals Set', *Los Angeles Daily News*, 24 June 2006.
24 Max Fisher, 'Coronavirus "Hits All the Hot Buttons" for How We Misjudge Risk', *New York Times*, 13 February 2020.
25 William D. Nordhaus, 'The Challenge of Global Warming: Economic Models and Environmental Policy in the DICE-2007 Model', May 2007.
26 William Nordhaus, 'Climate-Change Projections with Minimal Policies', *American Economic Journal: Economic Policy*, vol. 10, no. 3, 2018, pp. 333–60. See Table 2.

17. THE LONG-TERM SOLUTION: BALANCING THE INTERESTS OF GENERATIONS

1 Walter Mischel, Yuichi Shoda & Monica Rodriguzez, 'Delay of Gratification in Children', *Science*, vol. 244, no. 4907, 1989, pp. 933-38.
2 Walter Mischel et al., 'Cognitive and Attentional Mechanisms in Delay of Gratification', *Journal of Personality and Social Psychology*, vol. 21, no. 2, 1972, pp. 217.
3 George Szpiro, *Risk, Choice, and Uncertainty: Three Centuries of Economic Decision-Making*, Columbia University Press, New York, 2020, p. 7.
4 Emil Kauder, *A History of Marginal Utility Theory*, Princeton University Press, Princeton NJ, 1965, p. 16.
5 Kauder, 1965, pp. 17–18.
6 Daniel Bernoulli, '*Specimen Theoriae Novae de Mensura Sortis* (Exposition of a New Theory on the Measurement of Risk)', *Econometrica*, vol. 22, no. 1, January 1954, pp. 23–36.
7 Hermann Heinrich Gossen, *The Laws of Human Relations and the Rules of Human Action Derived Therefrom*, MIT Press, Cambridge, 1854.
8 Emil Kauder, 'Chapter VI. The Achievements: A Comparison of Menger, Jevons, and Walras', in *A History of Marginal Utility Theory*, Princeton University Press, Princeton, 1965.
9 Szpiro, 2020, pp. 103–04.
10 Using data from diaries in which people record satisfaction from activities throughout the day in the US and UK, the author finds similar diminishing marginal utility from activities across both countries: Jonathan Gershuny, 'Activities, Durations, and the Empirical Estimation of Utility', *European Sociological Review*, vol. 29, no. 5, October 2013, pp. 996-1009; Centre for Time Use Research, Department of Sociology, University of Oxford, Paper No. 2009-07, Sept 2009; Ed Diener, Weiting Ng & Wlliam Tov, 'Balance in Life and Declining Marginal Utility of Diverse Resources', *Applied Research in Quality of Life*, vol. 3, no. 4, 2008, pp. 277–91.
11 As before, if a person's utility function, or preferences, evolve over time but exhibit diminishing marginal utility in each period, maximising lifetime utility will be achieved by equalising *marginal* utility across all time periods.
12 Stern, 2006; John Quiggin, 'Stern and his Critics on Discounting and Climate Change: An Editorial Essay', *Climatic Change*, vol. 89, 2008, pp. 195–205.

13 In support of his approach, Stern cited support from very prominent economists including Robert Solow, John Maynard Keynes, Amartya Sen and Frank Ramsey. John Quiggin, Joseph Stiglitz and Jeffrey Sachs were also supportive of the review. William Nordhaus was critical of the discount rate, preferring a market discount rate for intergenerational. Other economists such as Mendelsohn, Weitzman, Dasgupta and others have also raised questions about the choice of discounting parameters.
14 Brad DeLong, 'Partha Dasgupta Makes a Mistake in His Critique of the Stern Review', *Grasping Reality,* 30 November 2006; see also the works of Frank Ramsay, Keynes, Solow, Tjalling Koopmans, Geoffrey Heal, Thomas Sterner and William Cline. There is a useful discussion of the implications of discounting over the long term in Chapter 2 of Nigel Lake, *The Long Term Starts Tomorrow*, Frog Publishing, Sydney, 2018.
15 Blomberg is a prominent advocate of this position.
16 Rates of 4–7 per cent are sometimes used. See the government benefit-cCost analysis guides for the US, Australia and the UK as examples.
17 Department of the Treasury, '2021 Intergenerational Report', Canberra, 2021.

18. CONCLUSION

1 OECD, 'Health Care Systems: Getting More Value for Money', Economic Policy Department Policy Notes No. 2, Paris, 2010.

APPENDICES

1 This data is based on an average of Germany, France, the UK and Sweden.
2 Thomas Piketty, *Capital and Ideology*, Harvard University Press, Cambridge, 2020, p. 459.
3 Congressional Budget Office, 'The 2019 Long-Term Budget Outlook', 2019.
4 Christopher Chantrill, 2019. The historical statistics are from the St Louis Federal Reserve, which is an official Census bureau publication. This has been supplemented by CBO projections of major federal social insurance programs to 2050. This graph is likely to understate the overall increase in government spending as the projections 2020–2050 only factor the likely increase in federal government spending.

Index

Printed in the USA
CPSIA information can be obtained
at www.ICGtesting.com
LVHW042133181024
794197LV00004B/823